ARTfolio 2021

A Curated Collection of the World's Most Exciting Artists

Edited by
Douglas King

Juror
Beatriz Esguerra

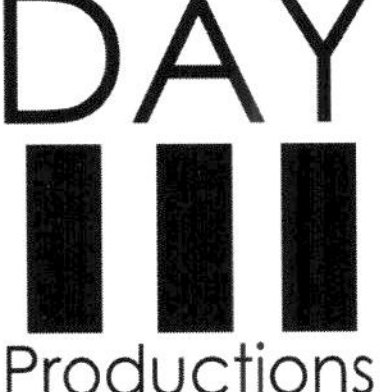

DAY
Productions

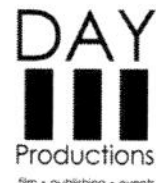

CONTENTS

Introduction

What a year it has been since launching this venture.

The first edition, *Art Folio 2020*, went to print just as news of COVID-19 was released. Because many printers are located in China, this was distressing news and caused a long delay in the printing of that book. Little did we know at that time just how much we would all be affected. Galleries have closed, some permanently, exhibits and shows were canceled, the entire world retreated into their homes.

2020 was a difficult year to enjoy art, let alone produce it, even though many artists had the time and solitude to create. But, if you've ever tried to be creative during times of stress, you know that even though you have the time, sometimes the will is simply not willing. Compounding the problem is the systemic race problem in society, which resulted in civil unrest and unhappiness for a great many people. This past year has been one of the hardest, so this is the time we need art in our lives more than ever.

I'm excited to present to you the second annual *Art Folio*. It has been challenging to get to this place, but the journey, as difficult as it was, has been worth it. To be able to bring to you nearly 200 amazing and exciting artists who were selected for this edition is one of the great joys for me.

What makes an artist one of the "world's most exciting"? Granted, that is an awfully bold statement on our part, but I stand by it. Even though some of these artists are self-taught or may have never exhibited in a gallery or art fair before, that does not make them any less of an artist or any less exciting in the art world.

I think we must first separate the illusion that the commerce of art is the same as the quality of art. Just because Jeff Koons or Damien Hirst sell work for millions does not make them any more of an exciting artist than those in the pages of this book. It does make them incredible marketeers.

What *does* make the artists exhibited here exciting, at least to me, is their passion to create beauty despite what is taking place in the world and despite being told by many that their work is not art or not good enough. The artists in this book are exciting because they have each produced a body of work with bold intention, strong will, and a creative spirit that is unique to them and them alone. They are exciting because where once was blankness, they had the vision to fill that void with color, motion, and texture; they had the confidence to make a mark and then display it for the world to see and critique.

That is exciting.

The artists in this book created not one singular work, but, in some cases, a lifetime of work. They have explored a theme or motif extensively, thus creating a body of work that illustrates the evolution of an idea as well as their own evolution as artists.

During the call for entries and the subsequent jury process, we review hundreds of works of art (each artist was allowed to submit up to five pieces). We became lost in the depths of oil, acrylic, fabric, metal, wood, and so much more. With each new artist, we found ourselves enveloped into a unique world not of our own creating, but one that has escaped (or, been set free) from the mind of an individual with a passion to express themselves.

That is exciting.

I want to add that, as with any juried exhibit, not every artist that submitted work is published in these pages. This is not a judgment on whether or not their work is good or right, it is simply a matter of taste, logistics, and an artist's ability to follow instructions. I want to encourage all artists, those published and unpublished, those who exhibit and those still waiting: Don't ever let anyone tell you your work is "wrong" or "not good enough." Not even us. Someone can tell you they do not like your art, but it does not make it wrong, it does not make it bad. Your art is your art. Keep painting. Keep creating.

Only another artist can understand the need, not desire, an artist has to create. We are driven, not led. To create is as important as breathing, so even though a work is not selected, it is still art. It still has value. Keep painting. Keep creating.

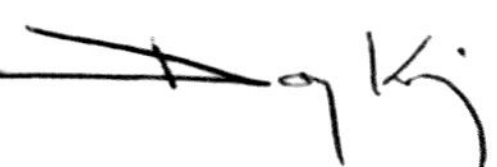

This year we are thrilled to announce that we opened the submissions up to more figurative contemporary art. *Art Folio 2020* was dedicated to the abstract art form, but we realized that there is incredible work being made that is figurative but not traditional. We could label the work Pop-Art, Low Art, Modern Art. However you wish to label it at the end of the day, it is art.

We hope you will be as excited to explore the work of the artists in these pages as we have been publishing this book. It is with great joy, and excitement, that we offer to you *Art Folio 2021*.

The *Art Folio 2021* curation took place during July 2020.

The first step in the weeks-long process was compiling all the artists' submissions and the hundreds of images into the individual categories. Next, our curator, Beatriz Esguerra, reviewed the work of all the artists. She made her selection from work that stood out to her and chose the winners of Best in Show and gold and silver titles in each category.

We greatly appreciate the time and effort that Beatriz spent helping to select the work for the second annual *Art Folio*, and, to each of the artists selected, congratulations for work that captured our imagination and attention.

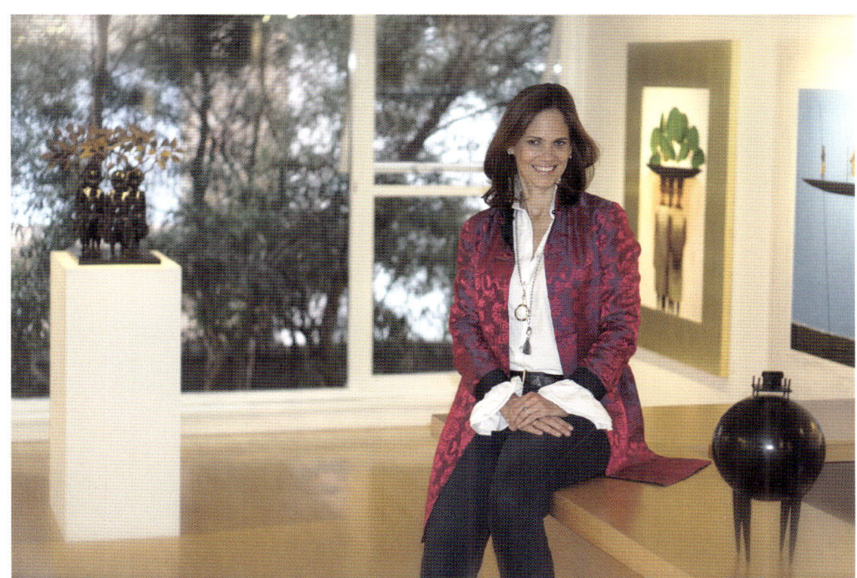

Beatriz Esguerra – Curator, 2020

"I have one mission: to enrich lives through art, with integrity and professionalism," says Beatriz Esguerra, director of Beatriz Esguerra Art.

Esguerra has been accomplishing her mission for more than thirty years. Her namesake gallery, located in Columbia and with an appointment-only space in Miami, Florida, promotes selected Columbian artists and is committed to fostering the careers of the emerging and established artists it represents.

"Permanence, transcendence, intelligence, aesthetics, harmony, and skill are the values that BEA looks for in art," Esguerra says.

Beatriz Esguerra founded her gallery, Beatriz Esguerra Arte, in Bogotá, Columbia, in 2000 after receiving academic training in art history at Middlebury College in Vermont. Following college, she worked in the museology department of the Gold Museum of Bogotá and served as the founding editor in chief of the Bogotá Museum of Modern Art's quarterly magazine, *Arte*. She then went on to enjoy a successful ten-year career as an independent art consultant and finally elected to open her eponymous gallery.

Her work with the gallery has placed her at the forefront of Latin American arts. Esguerra has been instrumental in establishing a global dialogue between famed Columbian and international mid-career to long-career artists. She has carefully curated projects, exhibitions, and publications, and participated in art fairs around the world to showcase the art of artists who may not otherwise be seen on a world stage. And, she has done it with integrity and professionalism because she believes art should be an integral part of everyone's life.

"Art should enrich both the soul and mind, in that order," Esguerra says.

We are honored to have Beatriz Esguerra as the curator for our second edition.

beatrizesguerra-art.com

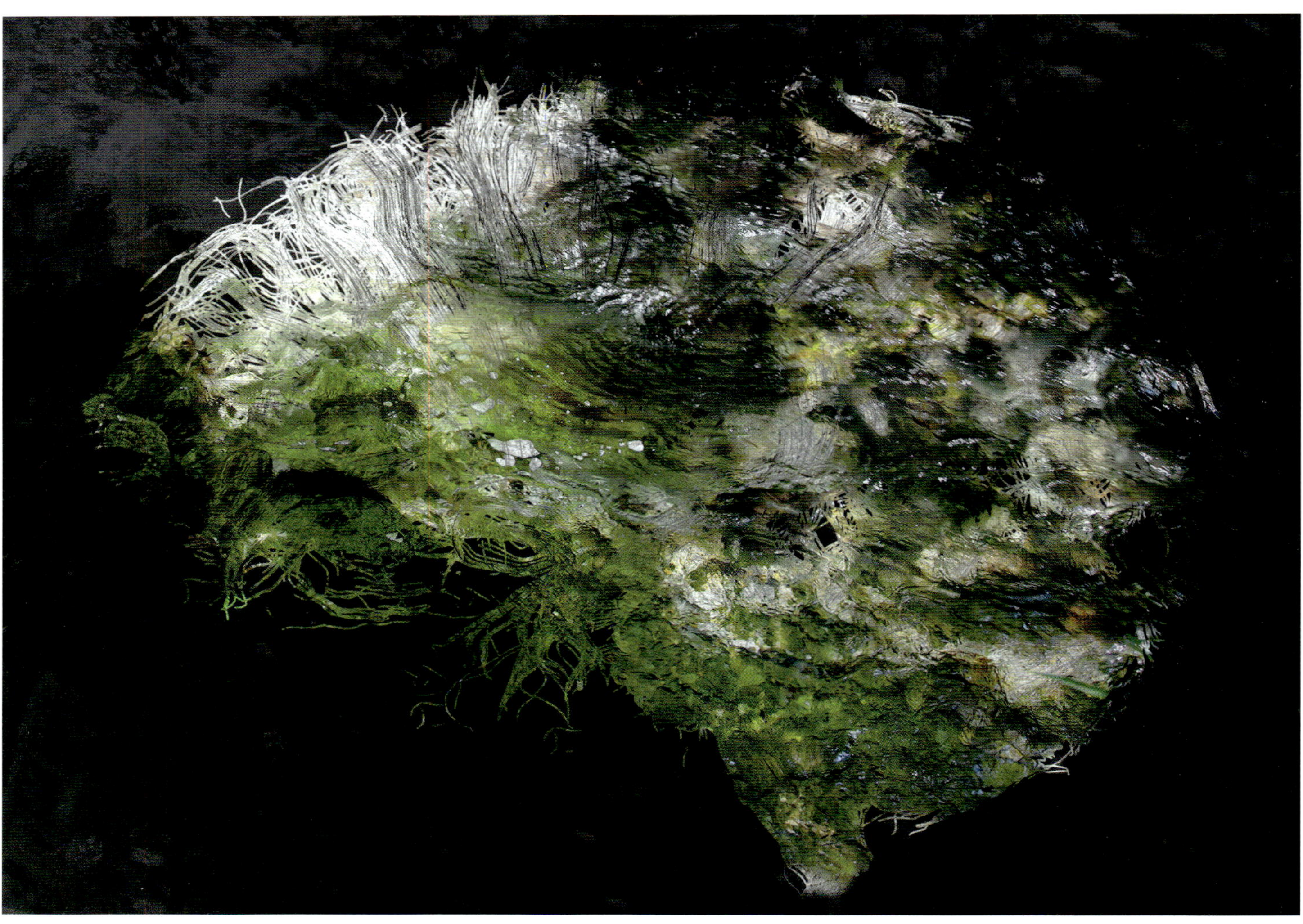

Yas Crawford

Yas Crawford was born in Wales, where both the arts and the geological landscape have, it seems, subliminally seeped into his being and heavily influence his work.

The mapped landscape revealed in his images often acts as a vessel to transport the story in a certain time, creating a safe place for the viewer to absorb the information. It acts as a background, positioning the micro and the macro of the internal and external human landscape. His sets of images are produced often as a photographic scientific experiment cataloged for success or failure and reflected in their numbering. The abstraction recognizes areas of ambiguity often explored through topography and geometrical shape, removing the onerous requirement of controls and variables and leaving space for subjective expression.

"Through an exploration of perspective, complexities, and scientific multidisciplinary collaborations, I create imagery that explains, reveals, and connects us consciously to the ambiguous and unknown," Crawford says.

Cognition VII
Digital Photography
1414 x 2000 px.

OPPOSITE
Torn
Digital Photography
1481 x 2000 px.

yc@yascrawford.co.uk
yascrawford.com
@yascrawfordphotography

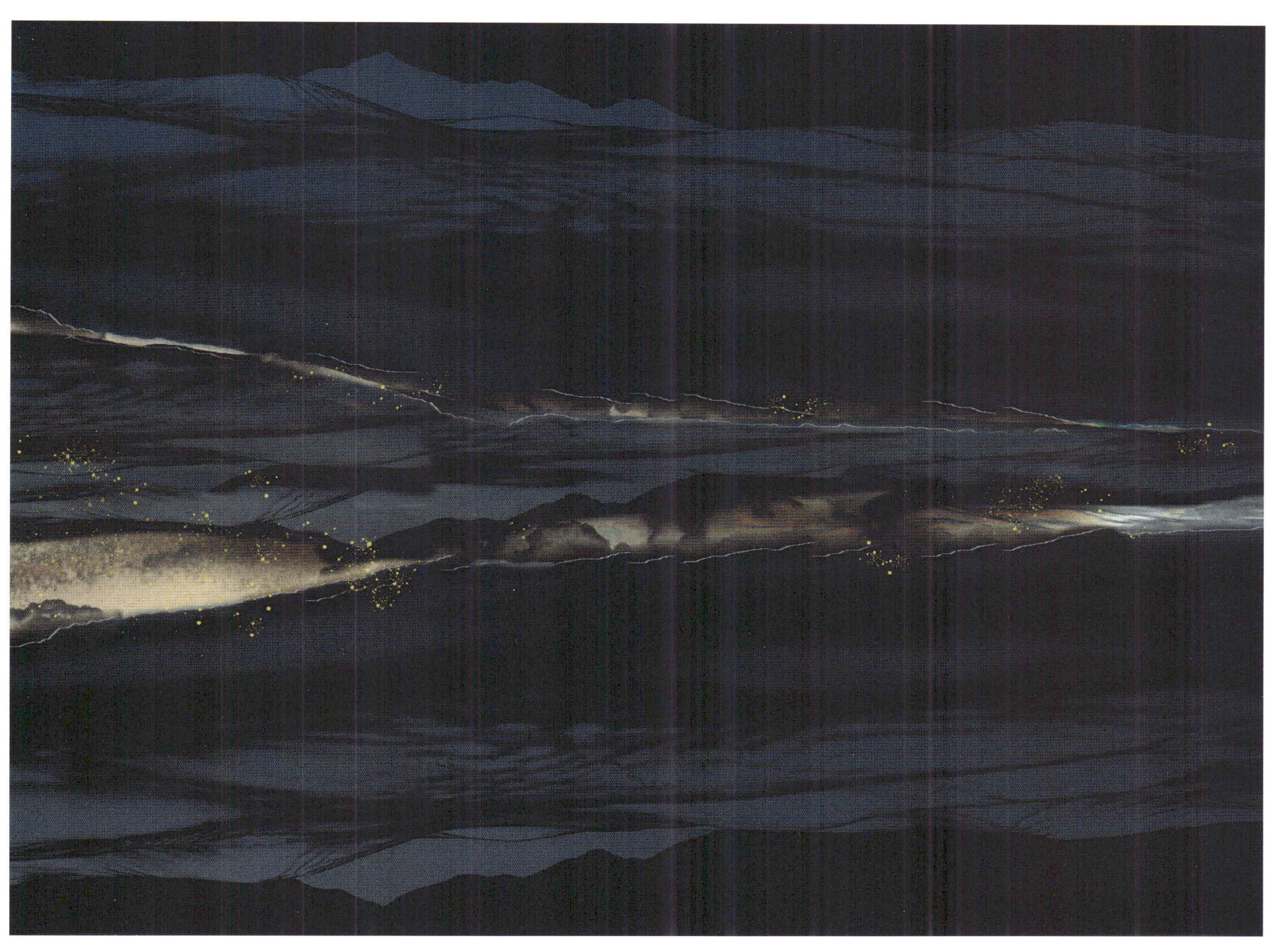

ABSTRACT PHOTOGRAPHY – GOLD

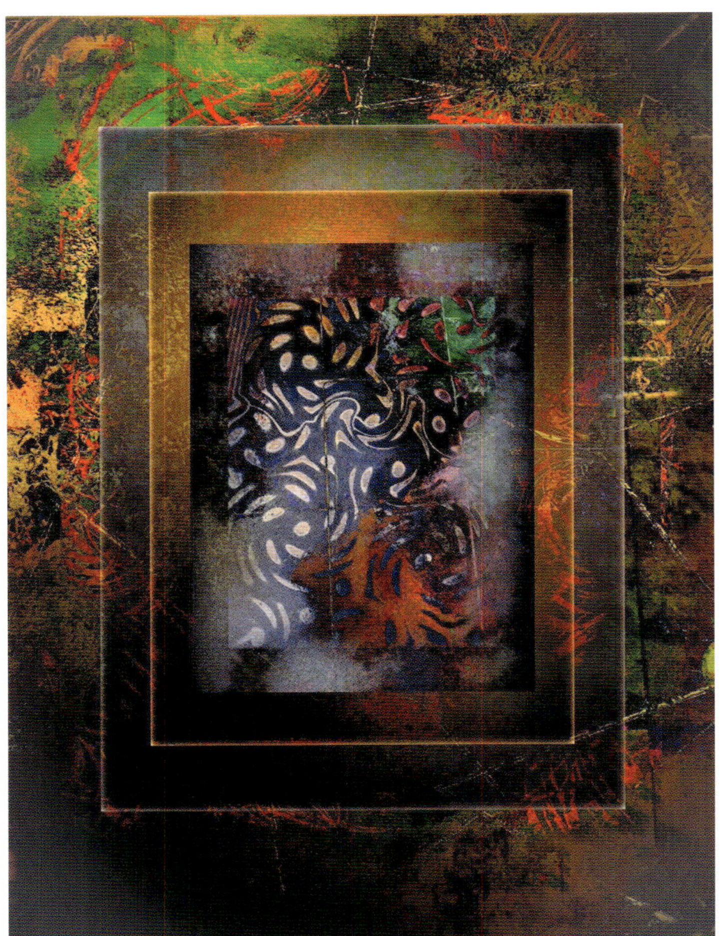

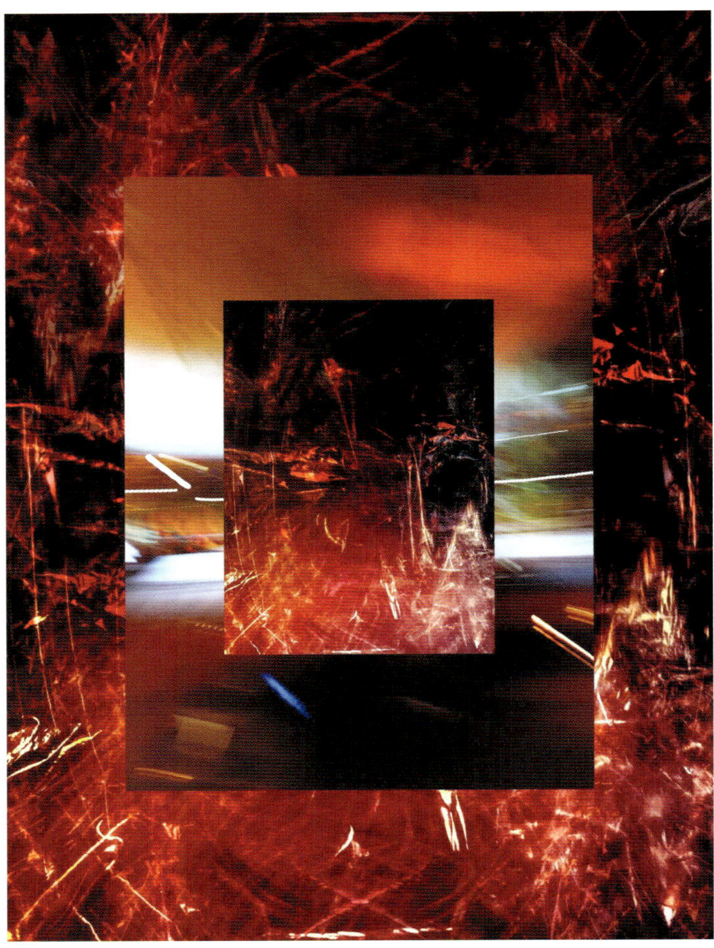

Muge Bayraktar

For Muge Bayraktar art is all about emotions and human behavior. By awakening similar emotions in the viewer through her art, Bayraktar's aim is to remind the audience that no matter what our differences are, we are all human and we all feel the same. Considering the fact that humans are complex beings and not all of our emotions are positive, nor are all of our behaviors good, she believes that the explanation lies in the enigmatic side of human psychology. Abstract photography to Bayraktar is the perfect medium to express her views. Driven by an impetuous desire to reveal the sublime concealed within the ordinary, the artist initiates the editing process through which she utilizes geometry, repetition, color, perspective, and texture. By combining the final image with concepts, Bayraktar creates her own language to state her worries and concerns about the future of humanity from the perspective of present-day values.

LEFT: *Nostalgia*
Digital Photography
1494 X 2000 px.

RIGHT: *Passion*
Digital Photography
1500 x 2000 px.

OPPOSITE
From Organic to Digital
Digital Photography
1500 x 2000 px.

mugebayraktar34@
gmail.com
mugebayraktar.com
@mugebay

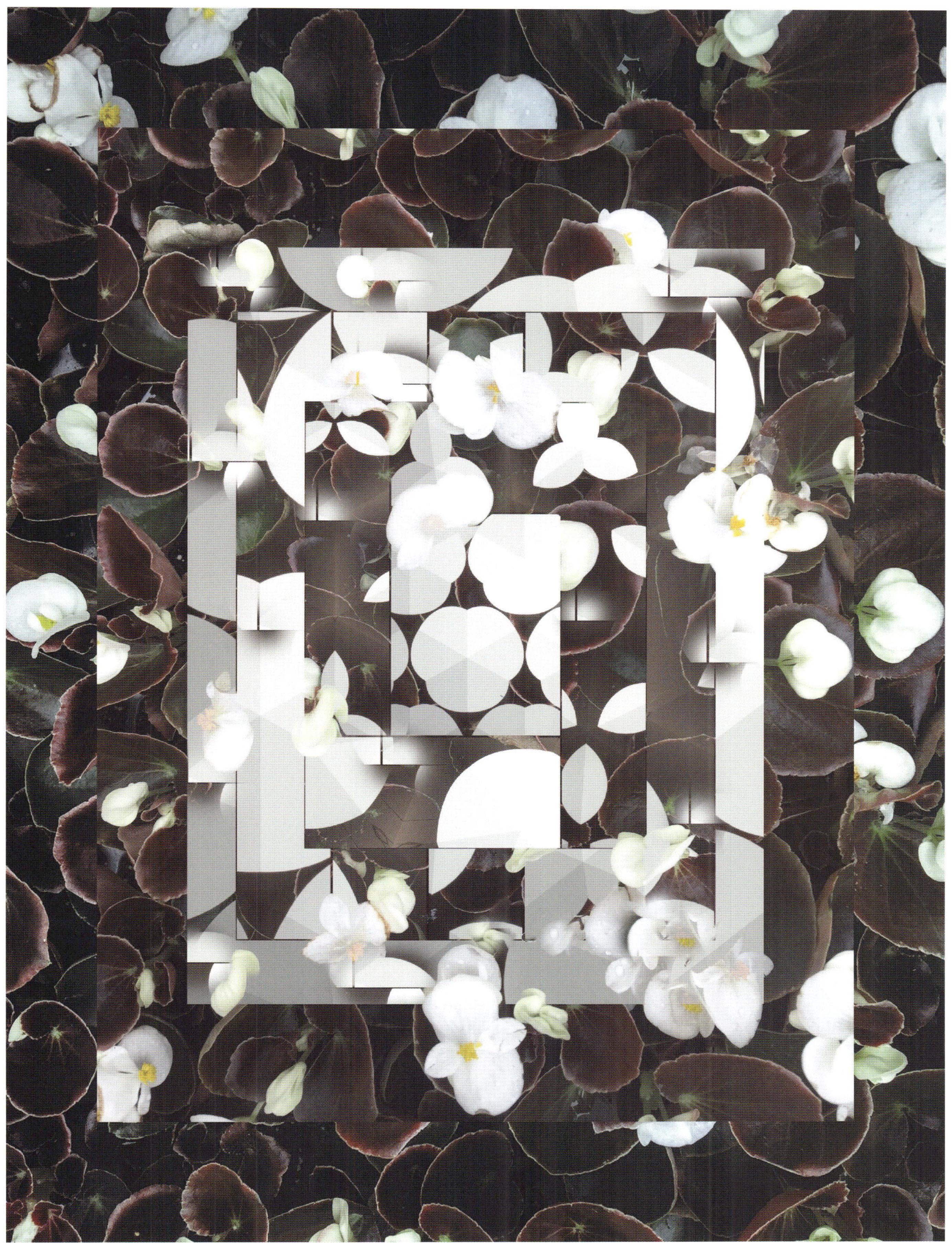

ABSTRACT PHOTOGRAPHY – SILVER

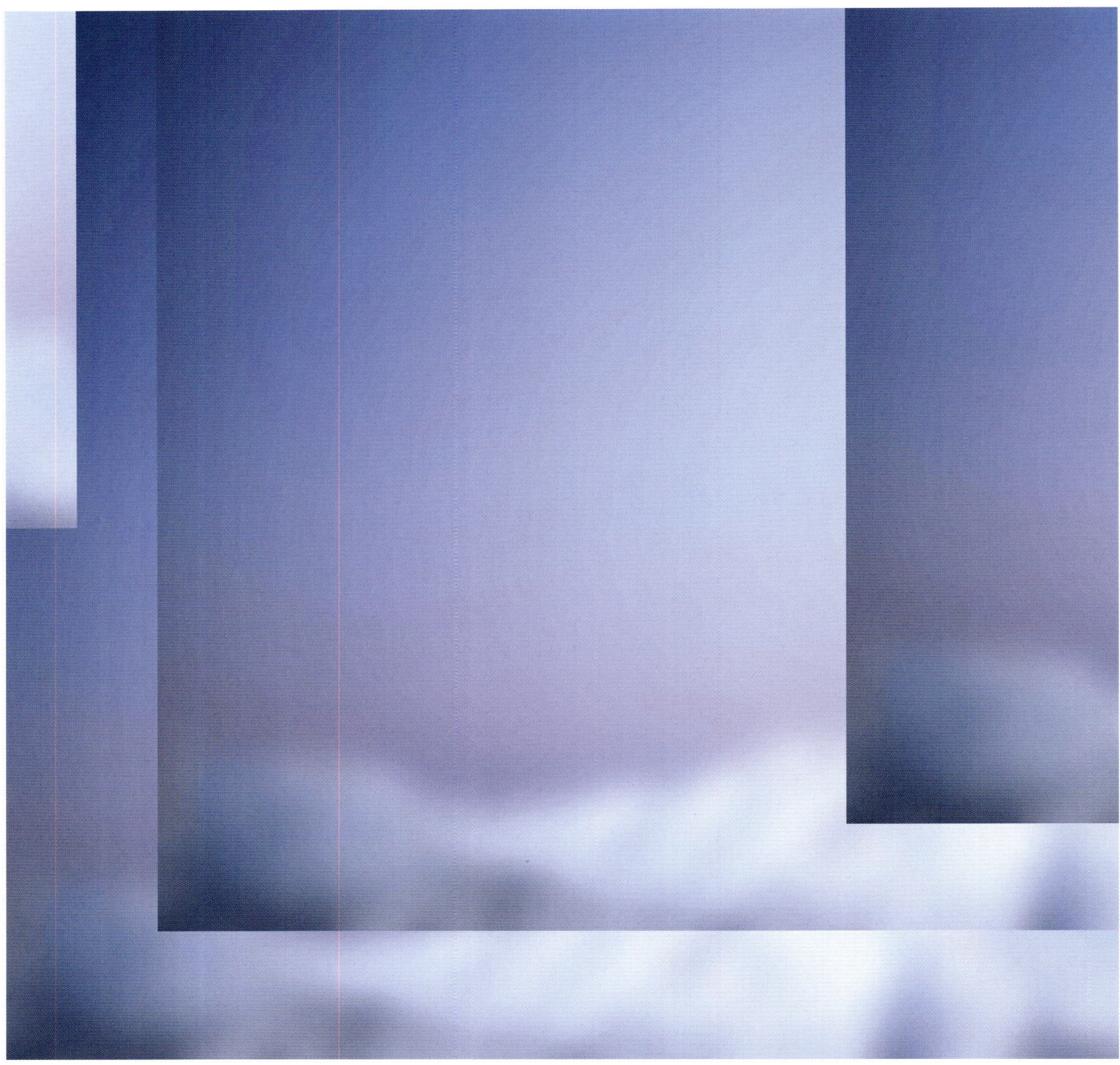

Ana Leal
Drawing from minimalist traditions, Ana Leal's work renders landscapes and architectural structures into new visual compositions, distorting reality through repetition and abstraction. Recognizable elements, from landscapes to everyday objects, are magnified, multiplied, and fragmented, inviting viewers to create free associations and question their own perception.

Skyscraper windows, high-rise balconies, mountains, or lakes become elaborate patterns.

Leal uses geometry and abstraction as a visual language of form and color to create photographic compositions that can exist independently of our visual references in the real world. Repetition and fragmentation are recurrent elements of those series. In addition to being simply photographs, they

are also pure paintings, brushstrokes made through a lens, dubious colors and abstract shapes, vestiges of landscapes that invite us to dive into their inner labyrinths.

Her abstract series are usually presented in multiples. Each piece has two or three variations that build upon each other, exposing the evolution and complexity of the image.

Blurry Pure 1
Photography on canvas
30 x 30 in.

OPPOSITE
Blurry Blues 1
Photography on canvas
30 x 30 in.

anacpsleal@gmail.com
analealphotography.com
@analealphoto

ABSTRACT PHOTOGRAPHY

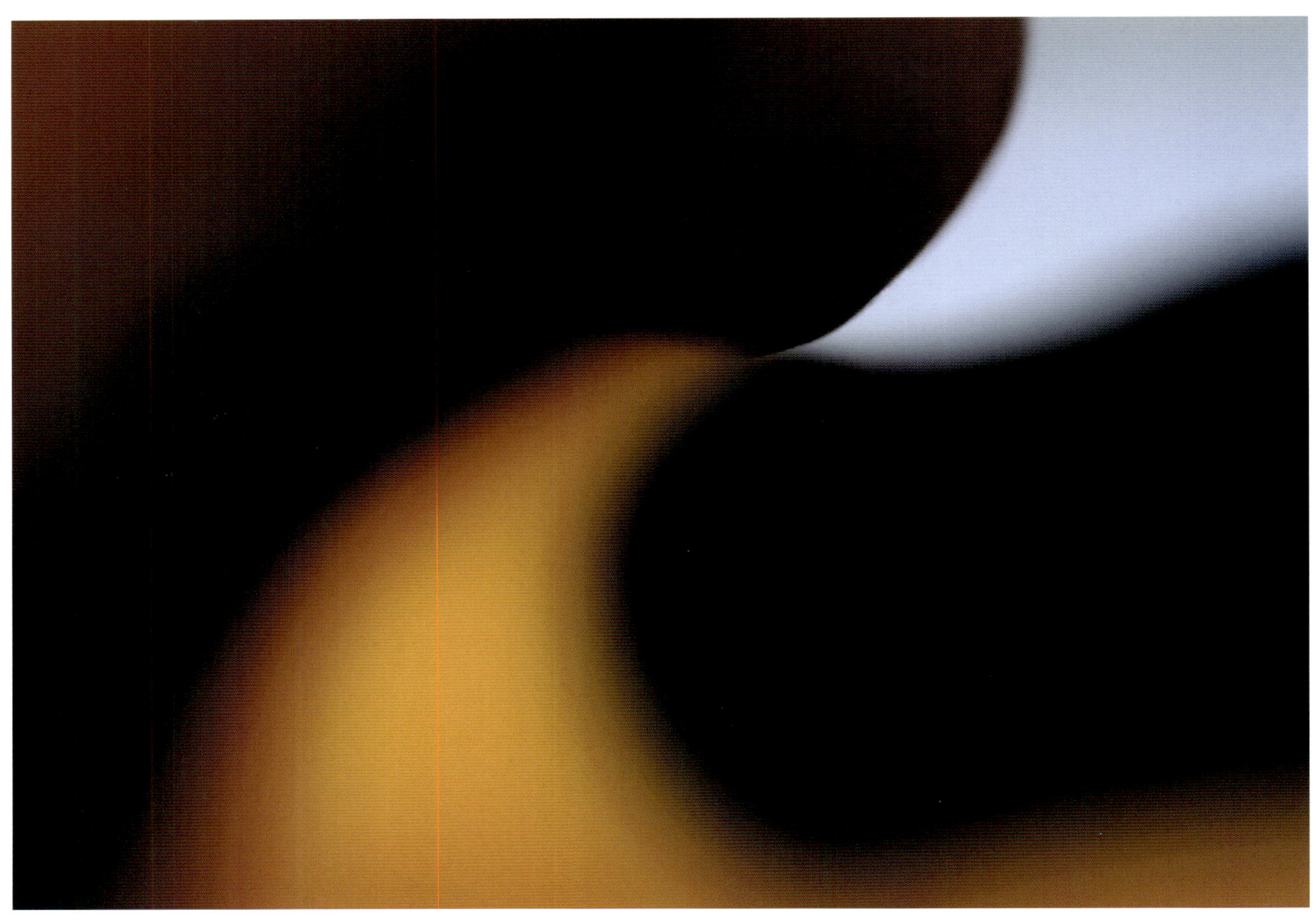

Yelda Akıllıgöz
Yelda Akilligöz has been interested in photography for many years. Her interest in abstract photography began after she studied macro and contemplative photography. The idea that the artist feels most intricately connects with her work is phenomenology, which the artist says is about looking inside. It is the direction of consciousness to phenomena by reflection. To connect with the phenomenon, we use our immanent perception and capture it with categorical relativity.

Akilligöz takes advantage of the images and descriptions that she has reduced to eidos in her mind while photographing existents and experiences. She makes sense of the ambiguities and the unseen. She travels deeply, using the phenomenological reduction in the abstract world by moving away from prejudices, renouncing her admissions, avoiding nature and the sciences of mind, avoiding philosophical dogmas, and being independent of space and time. With pure reflection and immanent perception, Akilligöz depicts the abstract visuals as described in her consciousness.

Union
Photography
1333 x 2000 px.

yelosca@gmail.com
@soyut.
photophylosophyart

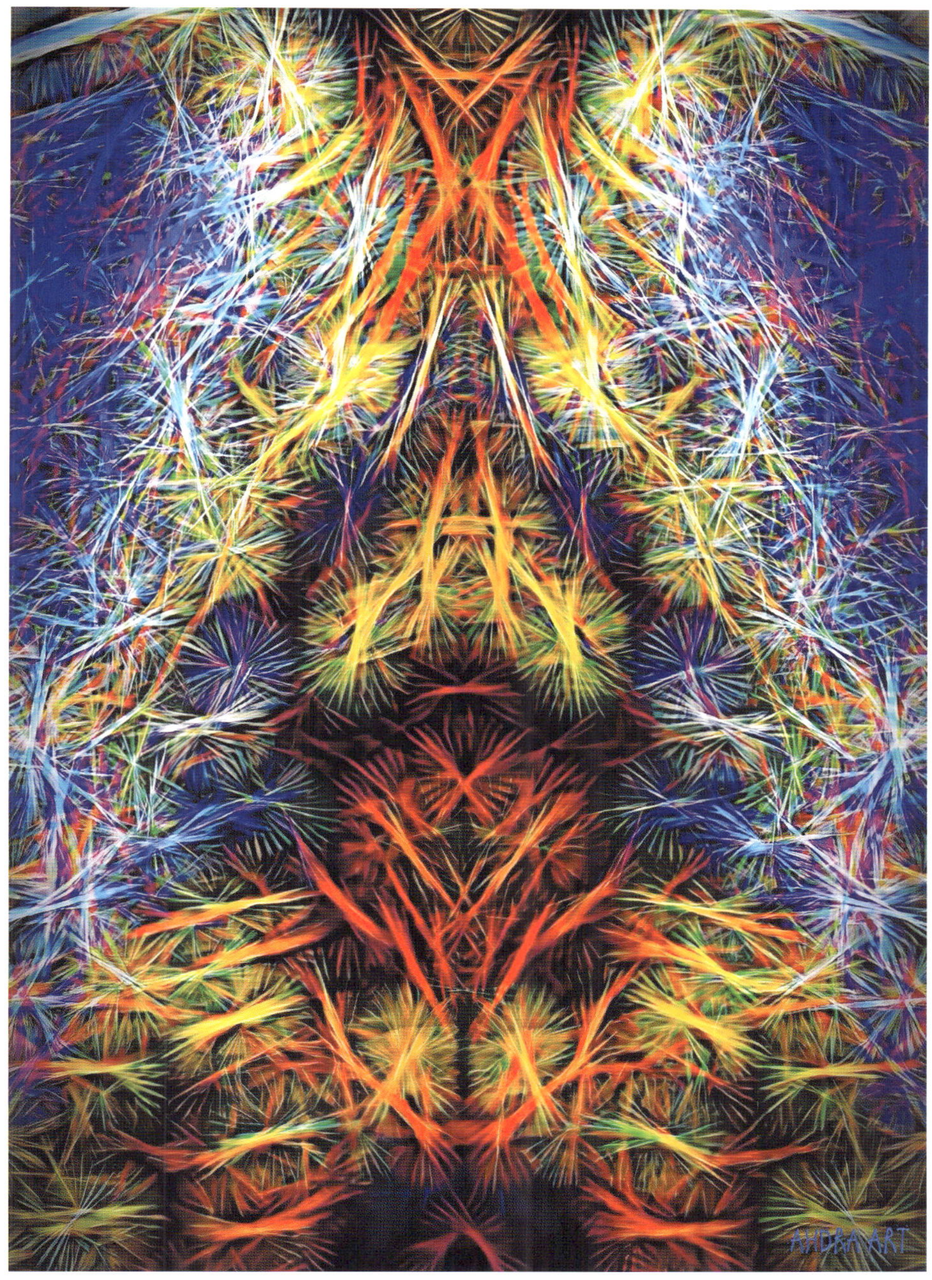

Deborah Anderson

Deborah Anderson's photographic creations are visual projections of moments in life based in subjective experience as well as objective fact. They have become a narrative reminder of where she has been, where she is, and where she's going.

Photography has taught Anderson how to "see" not just look at subject matter. It has become an entire new way of looking at the world, which then becomes much more interesting and complex. Always drawn to the provocative, edgy, controversial, and moved by the political environment and issues that impact our daily lives and the larger world, her photos are derivations from a place of unsettlement with a constant yearning to make things right.

Digital photography has opened Anderson's world by allowing her to create images in weird and wonderful ways, to convey a creative perspective on any subject from mundane to fantastical. The artist believes we are all here to help one another create meaning in our lives. And her work seeks to do the same.

To The Within
Photography
14 x 10 in.

blanche6028@aol.com
ahdraart.com
@blanche6028

ABSTRACT PHOTOGRAPHY

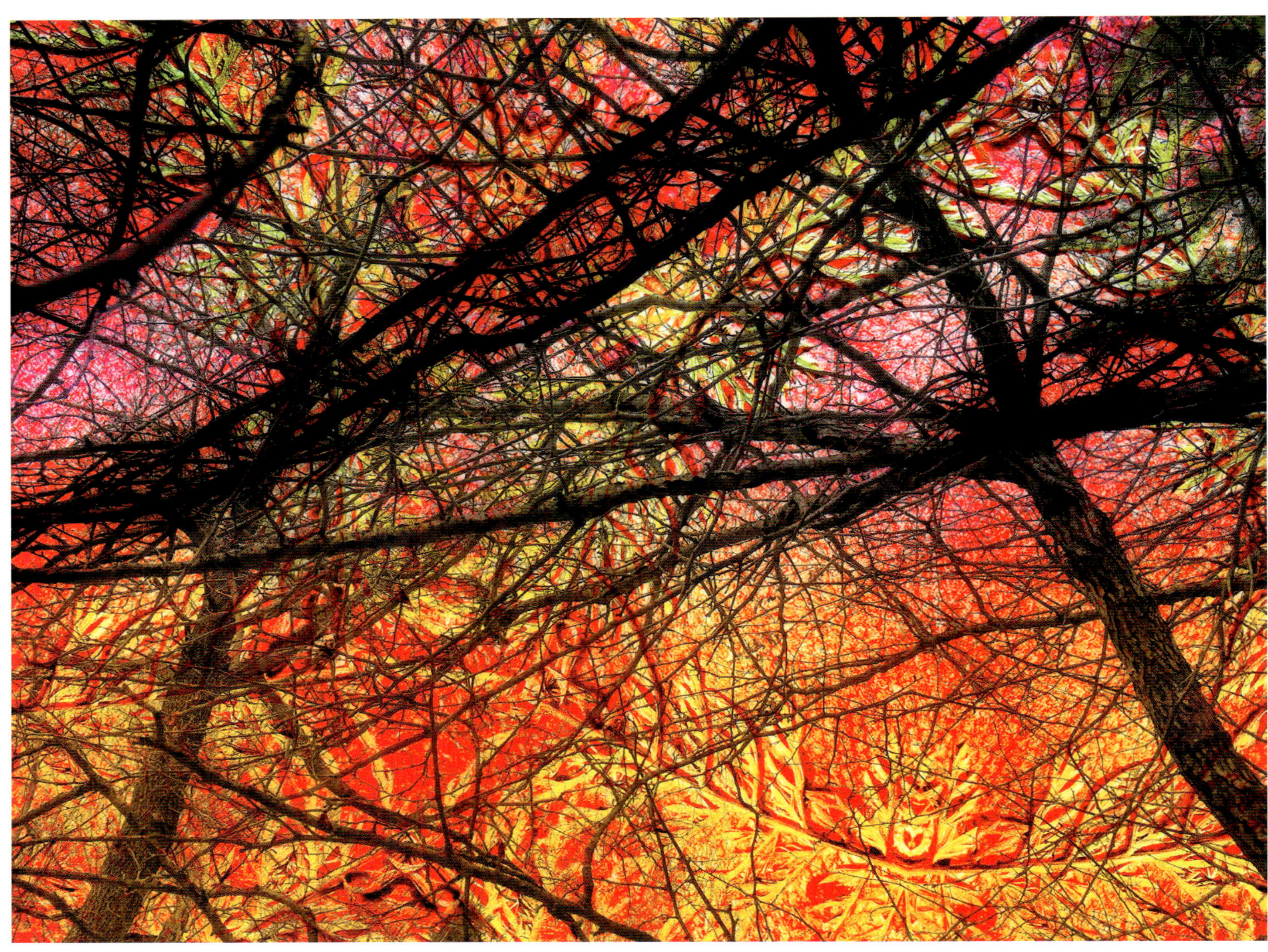

Jocelyne Béïque
Jocelyne Béïque is a kind of UFO in the art world. Twenty years ago, she began to explore a new kind of expression by including real plants and fresh flowers in abstract paintings. She then her work has evolved with botanic discoveries that continuously transform her link with nature. The artist has collected plants and flowers from North America during long road trips she has taken and when she lived in a van for two years to collect specimens. She works exclusively using an iPad Pro, and her work is completely digital. Her botanical skills and interest expand daily and have brought her to call her work, Botanical Choreography. Through her work, Béïque celebrates the infinite beauty of nature and puts plants into a creative dance to nourish the viewer's fascination.

Reddish
Mixed media, digital graphic
9 x 12 in.

jobeique@gmail.com
@eny_lecoj

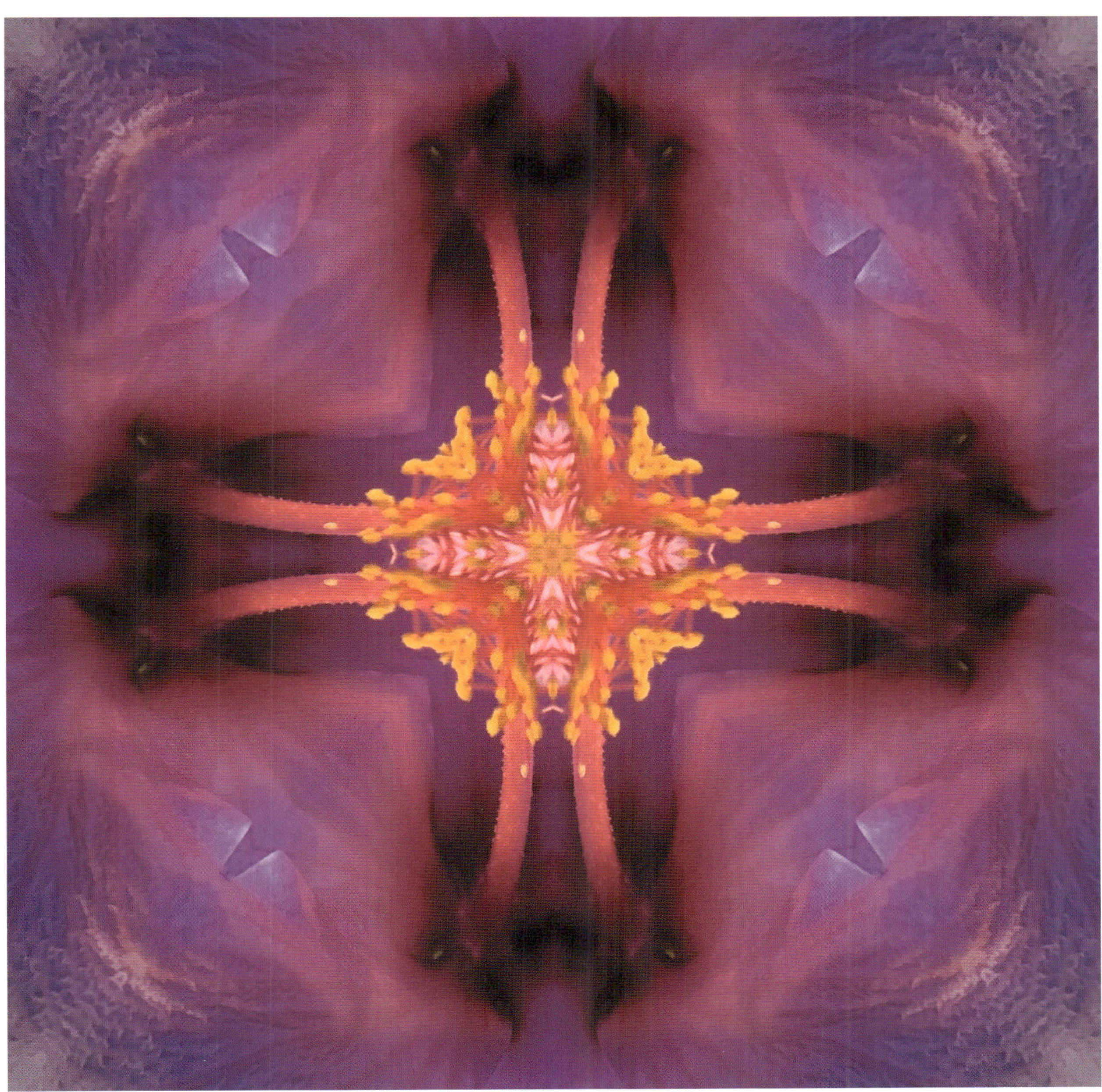

Petra Bernstein

Petra Bernstein's work is influenced by her history and revolves around her thoughts and emotions. Her artwork is a visual interpretation of all that inspires her. Bernstein's diverse ideas originate in the complexity of her mind, where she is able to create something that is unique to her and free from boundaries. Reality, imagination, and abstraction all coexist with no explanation required.

Bernstein uses both photography and painting to express her deep connection with nature. Her artwork ranges from close-up photographs and paintings of botanicals and water surfaces to abstract interpretations of nature's mysteries. The artist's abstract works are inspired by forms, shapes, colors, and lines that she finds in nature. Sometimes, Bernstein uses double exposure to merge her paintings with her photographs, allowing her to create something that is truly her own.

Heavenly Hibiscus
Archival photo print on aluminum Dibond
30 x 30 in.

pmbernstein@comcast.net
petrabernstein.com
@petra.bernstein

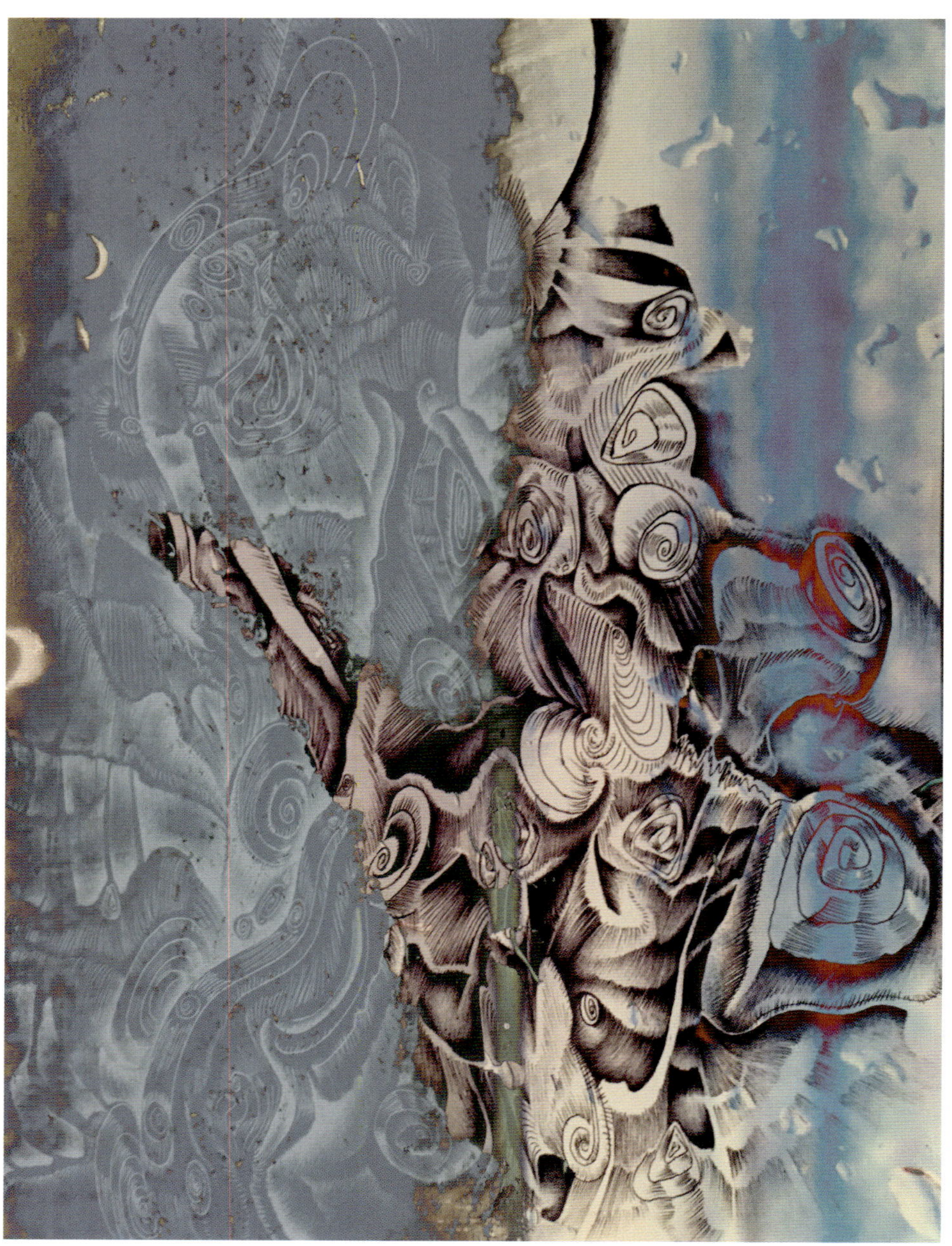

April Fretwell
April Fretwell's artwork involves objective and nonobjective themes. Her objective work focuses on her personal journey and feelings about her many roles as a female—mother, teacher, and artist. The artist uses a wood-burning tool to draw how she sees her world, and then she adds color with watercolor paint to communicate specific feelings about it. Fretwell also enjoys the freedom of Abstract Expressionism as a therapy for herself. In her "therapy drawings" and other nonobjective artwork, she follows her emotional intuitions toward line, shape, and color to communicate feelings and clear her head. She enjoys various techniques, including encaustic painting, ballpoint ink drawings, photography, and digital media. Digital media allows Fretwell to combine her drawings with personal photographs to create a strong sense of mood and feeling. Digital manipulation also allows her to play with composition by showcasing texture, heightened contrast, and the power of line.

Pour Me Out
Digital photography over ink drawing
10 x 8 in.

aprilfretwel@gmail.com

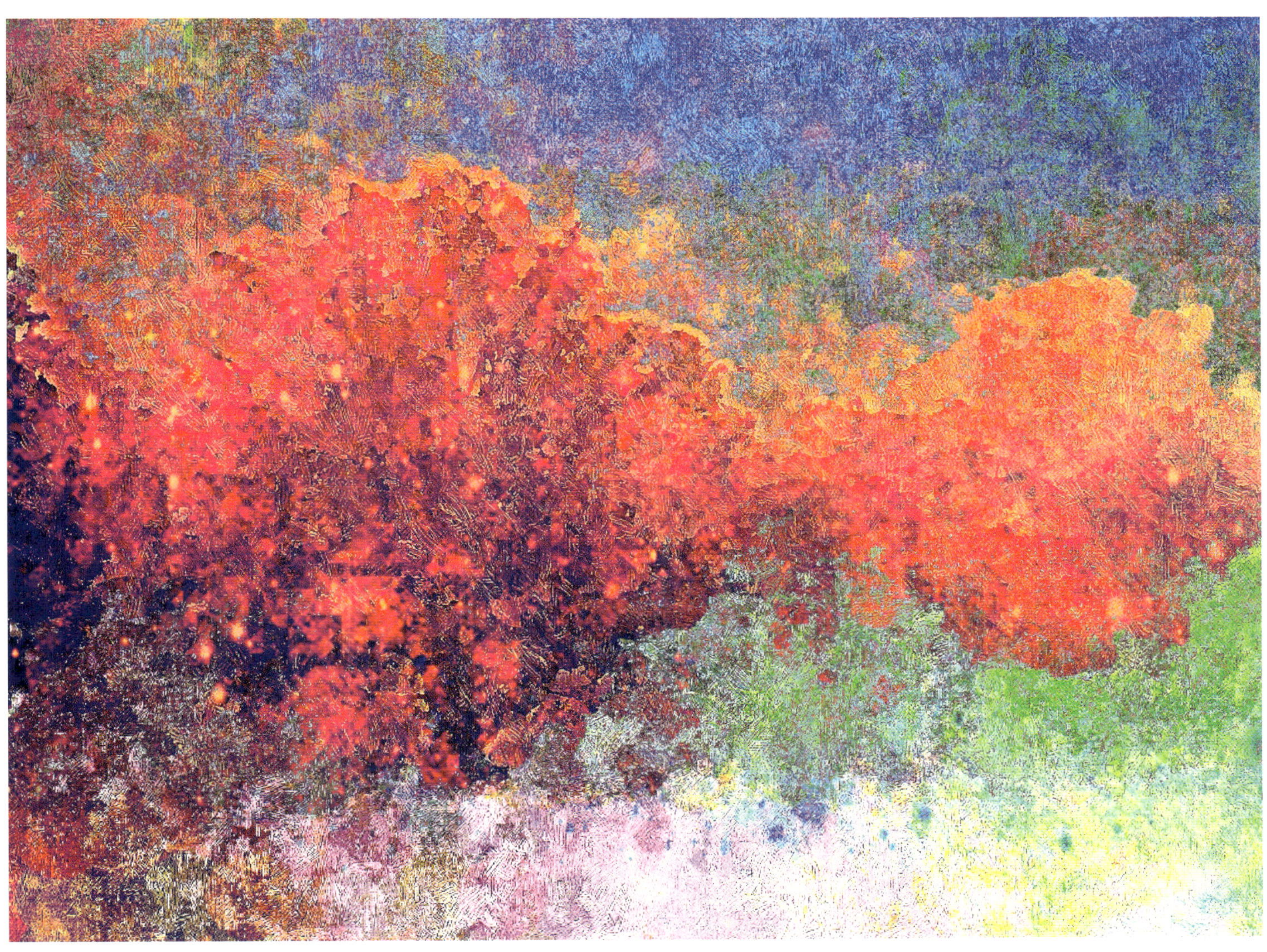

Rick Hurst

As a result of becoming profoundly deaf at the age of two, Rick Hurst's visual sense heightened to new levels. His childhood refuge was to immerse himself in the natural world around him—experiencing the beauty of nature, the vibrancy of color, and the variety of architecture. He discovered the world of digital art along with photography as a means to capture the beauty and spirit of nature and the real world. Hurst melds his photography into digital artworks using multiple layers, color transformations, and advanced art filters, thus developing images through many iterations. Each digital image is the artist's personal expression of inspiration from his surrounding environment, explored to a new level through his artistic imagination. Hurst's motivation is to energize curiosity in viewers and prompt introspection. He wishes to feed the inner being as his images resonate with viewers.

Evolution
Archival-quality digital transformation on metal panel
30 x 40 in.

RickHurstArt@gmail.com
RickHurstArt.com
@rickhurstart

ABSTRACT PHOTOGRAPHY

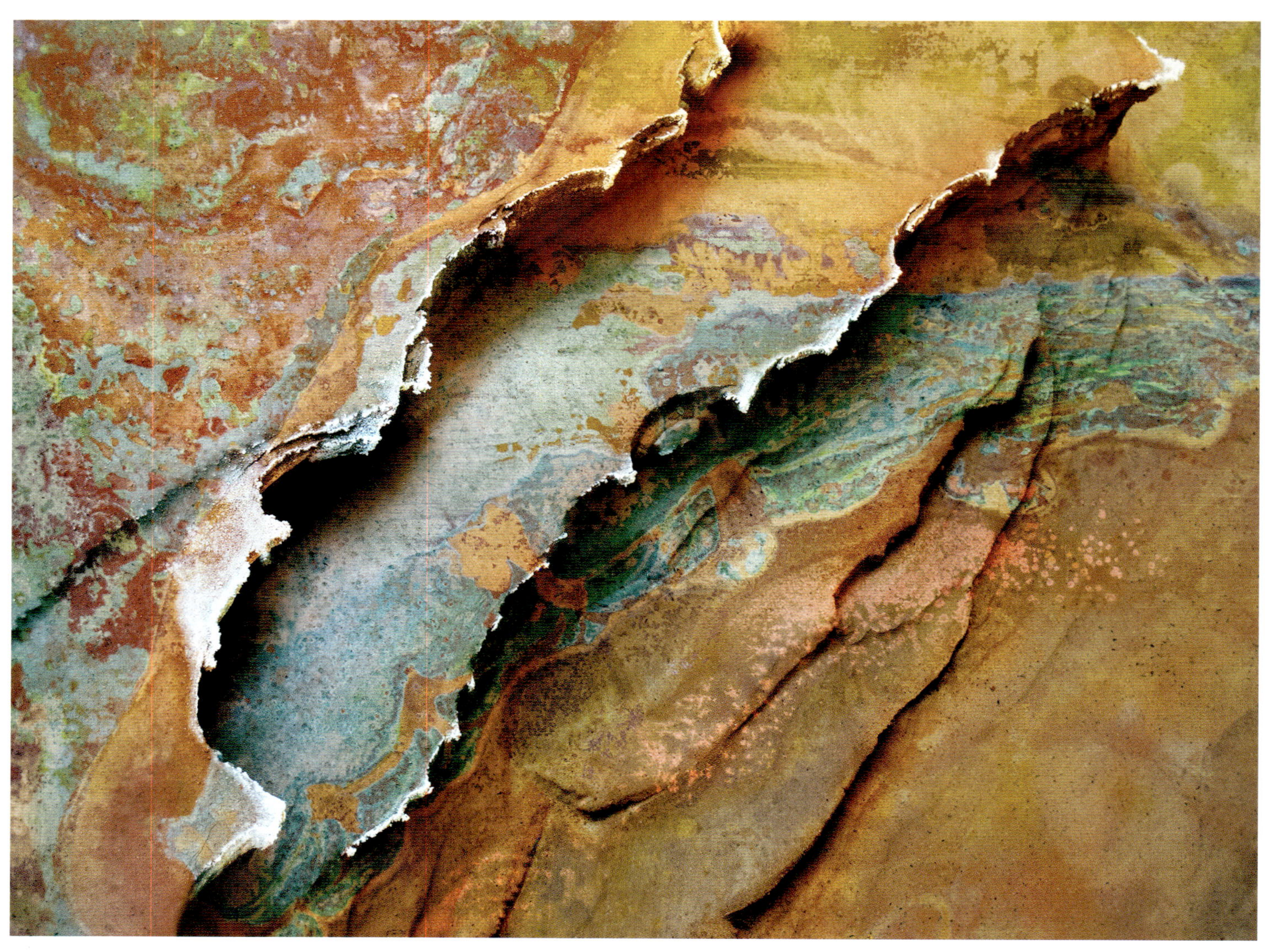

Joey Morgan

Joey Morgan is driven to bring nature inside through striking abstraction. The artist is inspired by the natural world—the hues, contours, and textures of canyon walls, sand patterns, tree bark, sandstone formations, and plant life. These intricate details, shapes, and designs are formed biologically or by wind, fire, and water over time. Chemistry also inspires Morgan. The effects of chemical reactions on copper produce an array of vivid colors and patterns. "It's when chemistry becomes 'art,'" Morgan says.

The initial step in Morgan's creative process is to create and photograph patina-style copper. He then digitally merges photos of the metal with one or more close-up photos of nature. Next, he scales, skews, or distorts to enhance the texture and depth of the composition. Nature gives us our most spectacular art forms, but Morgan adds another dimension, perspective, twist, and thought-provoking view to send the viewer on a visual journey.

Step Into It
Digital composite
16 x 20 in.

jmmorgan21@gmail.com
artmixedup.com
@artmixedup

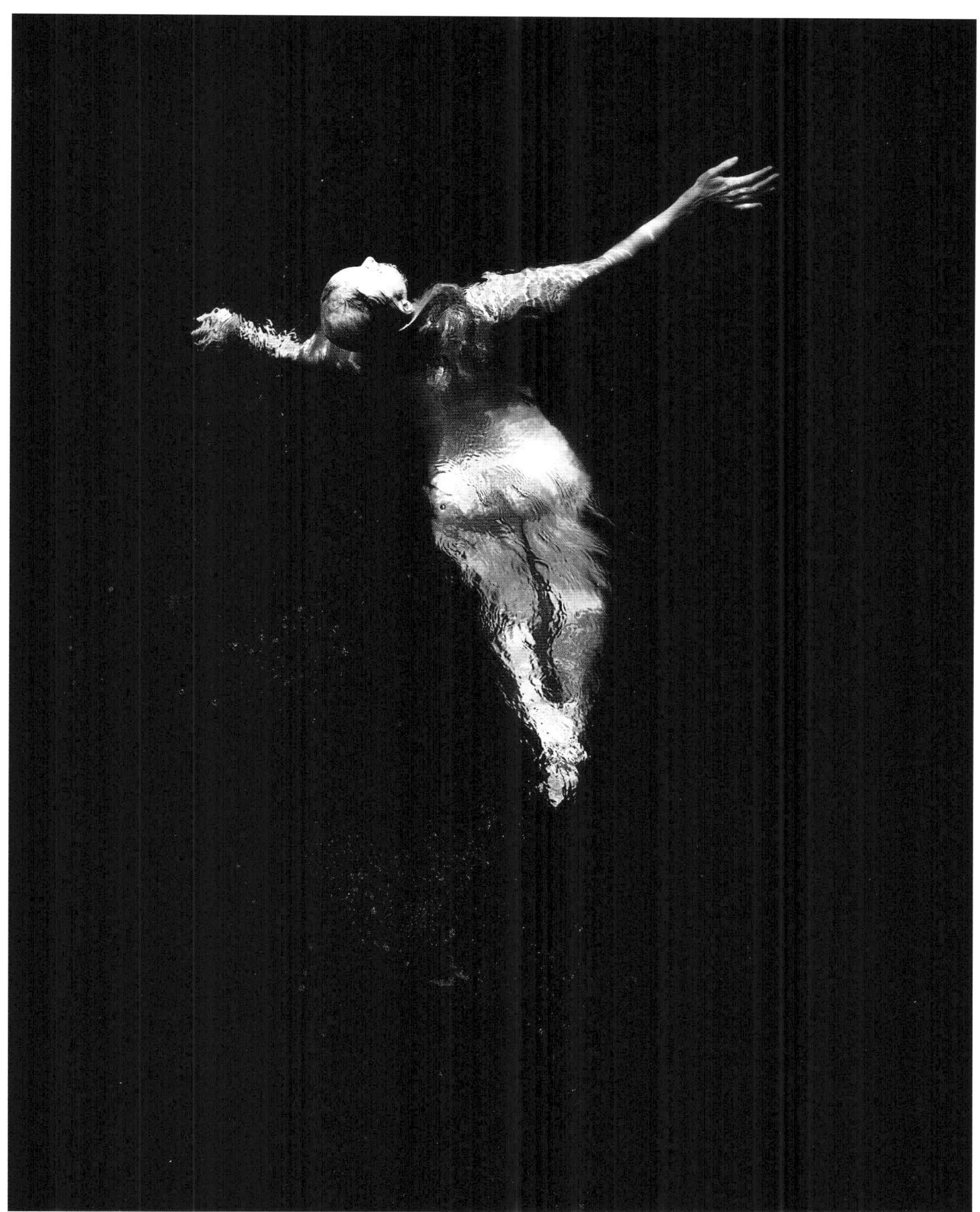

Marika Pentikainen

Marika Pentikainen feels that the important events that happen in a person's life tell her so much about how people care about each other, how they care about themselves, and what things feel like to them at any given moment. The artist is interested in all of these little moments, for example when people are face-to-face and silent, and how they present themselves to each other in different situations. She is interested in the gaze of living beings and the thoughts behind that gaze. She tries to capture those thoughts using photography, and bringing out emotions and vulnerability are important in her work. "I want to bring out things that the subject doesn't know how to dig out of themselves," she says. "I feel that there is always some kind of mentally stimulating message that subconsciously pulses out from deep inside of me in my work."

Birth
Digital photography
30 x 40 in.

marika@photosmarik
.com
marikapentikainen.com
@photosmarik

ABSTRACT PHOTOGRAPHY

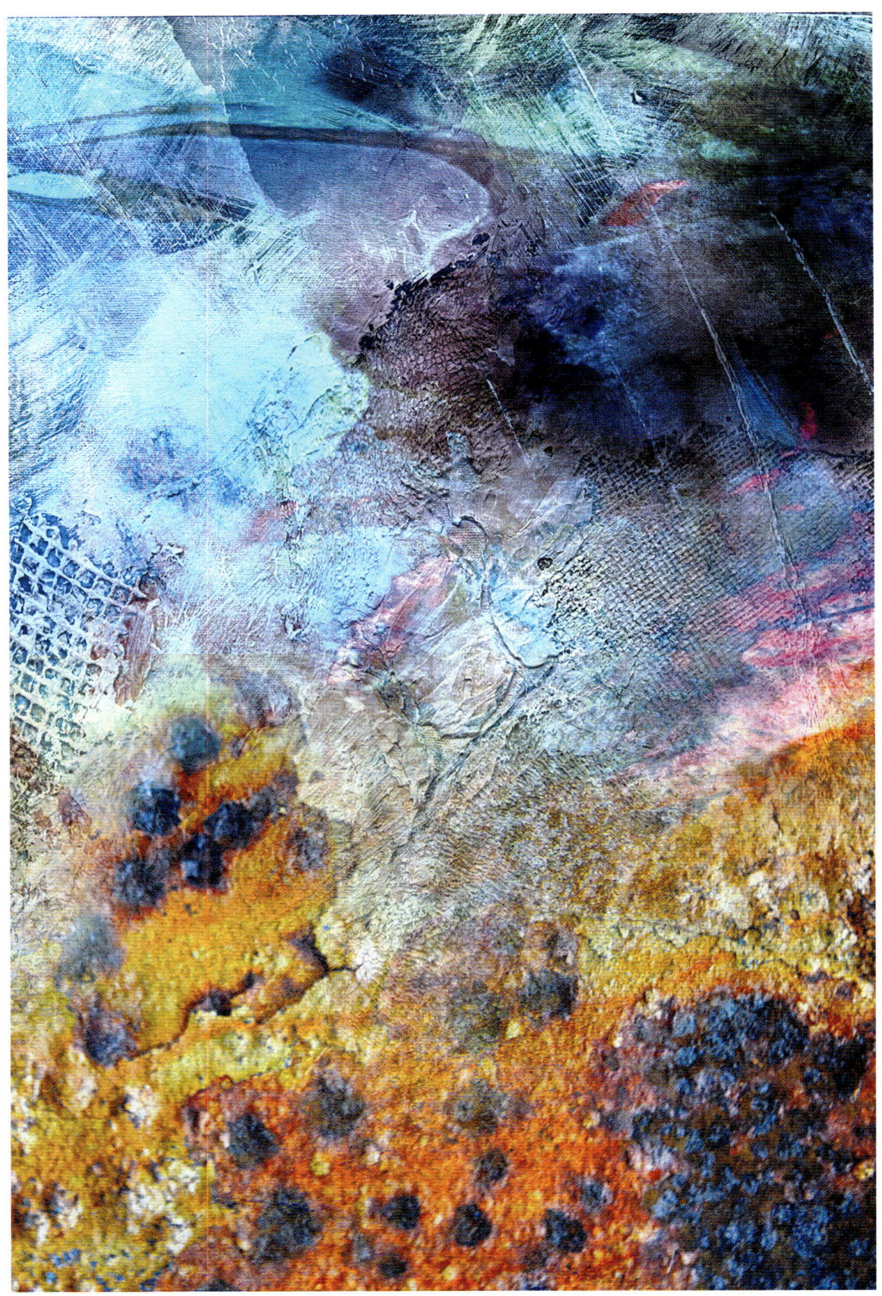

Peter Toth

Peter Toth is a photographer, a painter, a 3-D artist, a poet, and a photo impressionist. His digital body of work is where he can be the most bold and experimental. Photographs, textures, and mixed-media paintings get photographed and re-photographed and layered into an image. It's an evolutionary process through the addition of different textural layers, often driven by places Toth has traveled and the natural world he has observed. Toth has a library of hundreds of textures from all over the world, and they all lend themselves in unique ways to making an image. These layers and textures are manipulated over and over until they feel right to him. Toth's approach is to find a balance between composition and color that begins to resonate with what he wants to accomplish in a certain piece. Some pieces have a story, while others are just a pure and joyful expression of textures, shapes, and color.

Songs of the Surf
Print on aluminum
24 x 36 in.

peter@
peterTphotography.com
peterTphotography.com
@peterTfineart

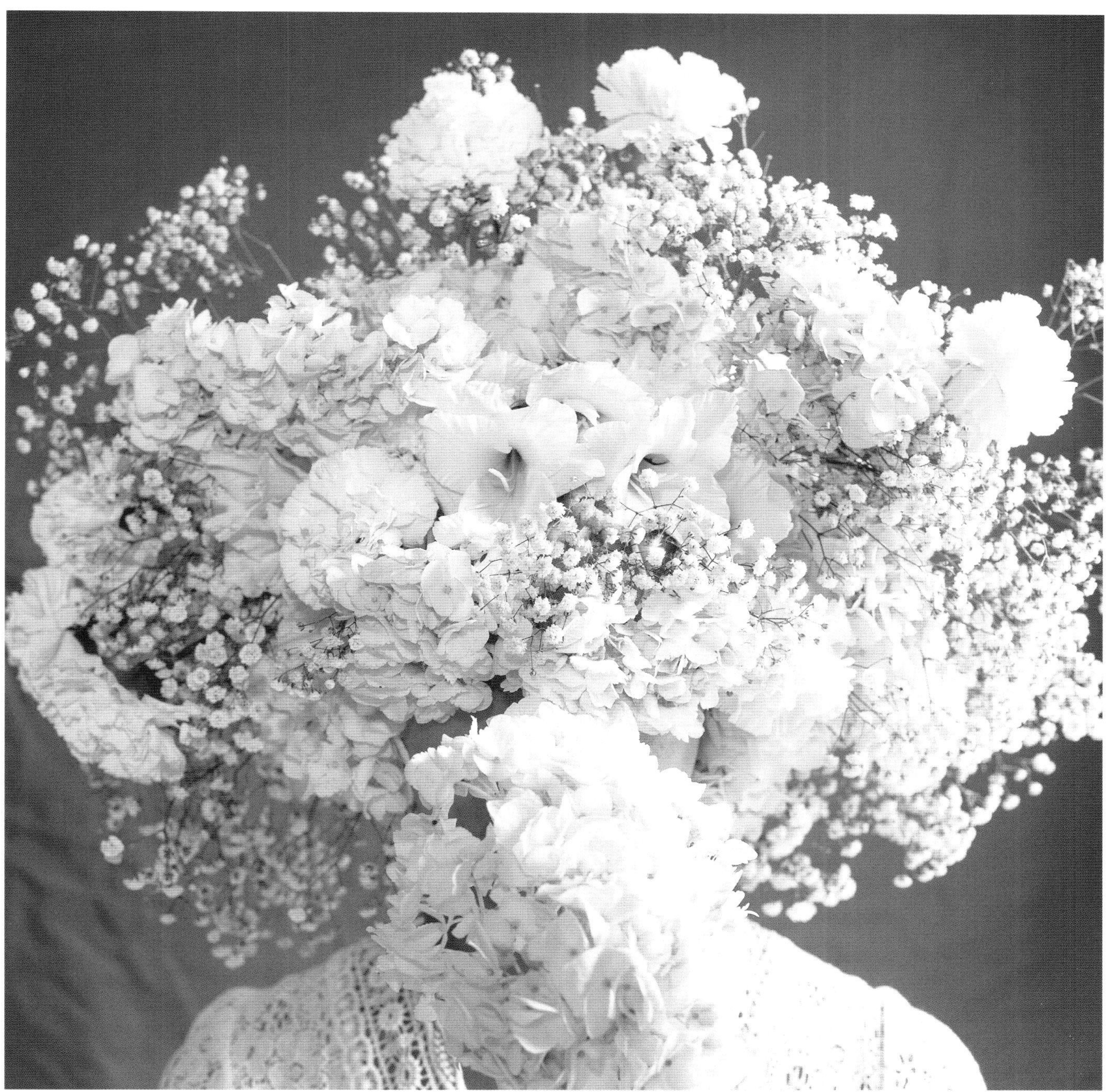

Ziesook You

Broqpa is the name of a small village in Nepal. Ziesook You first learned of it from the TV documentary *The Last Empire*. Every day the women work to grow flowers in their gardens. Because they live surrounded by mountains of stone, they call flowers "love." Their love is the power for them to survive in this sterile environment. The artist's work starts from sharing their attitude toward life and the people around her. The artist wishes to share it with the hope of showing the scent of Broqpa, in which a tiny thing called a flower is a trigger for finding happiness. The artist processes her work to feel the spiritual joy called happiness as in the spirit of Broqpa. *The Scent of Broqpa* has been an ongoing series created by working with twins, single mothers, seniors, and multicultural and various age groups since 2016.

Scent of Broq-pa
03012020
Photography
36 x 36 in.

Ziesookyou@gmail.com
ziesookyou.com
@ziesook

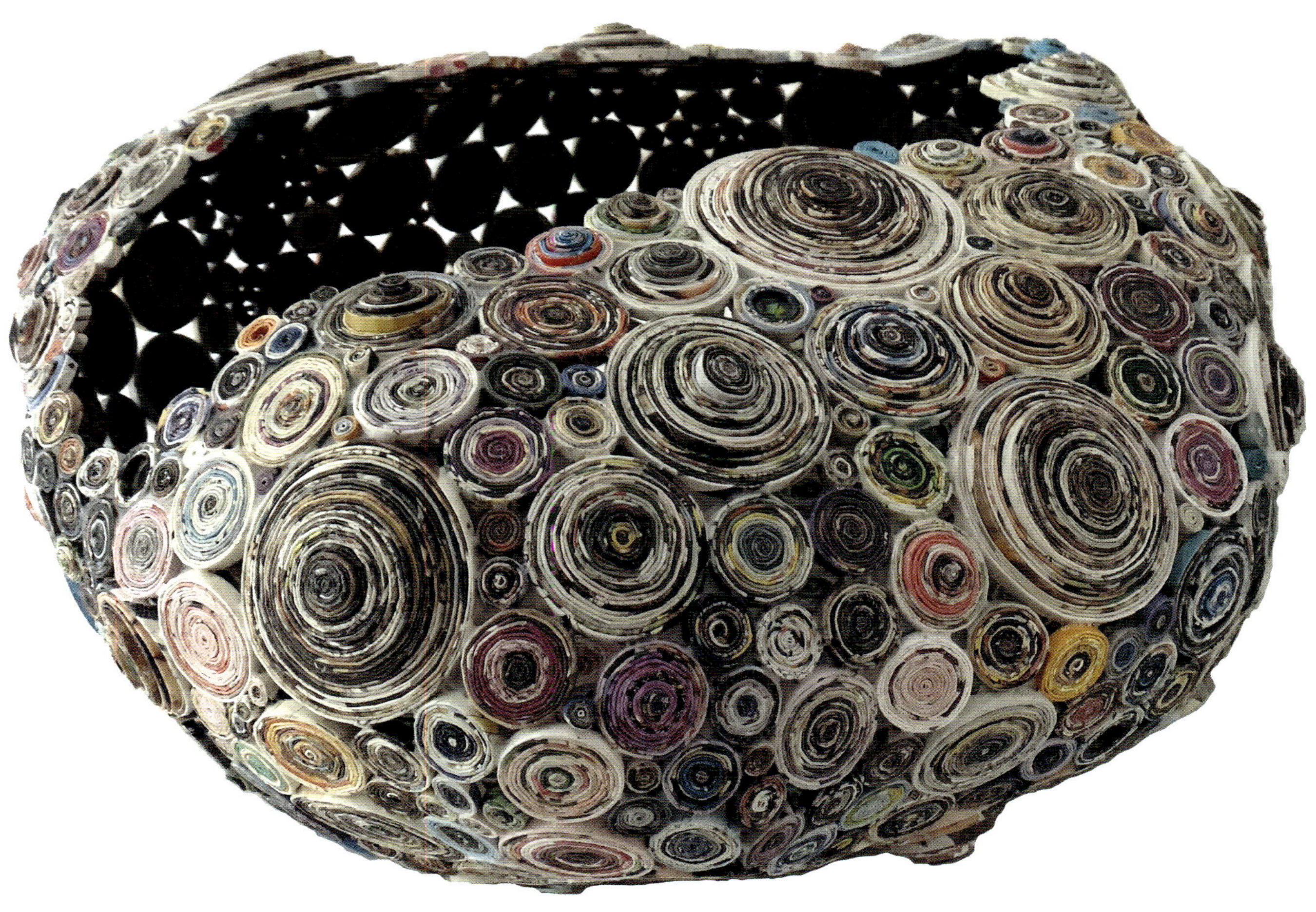

Flavia Lovatelli

"Art is the unspoken language, that which moves us, connects us, breaks the borders and unites us," Flavia Lovatelli says. To illustrate this, she tries to create work that evokes emotions at the sensory level—fascination, perplexity, confusion, doubt—and produces an intense desire to touch the work, feel the textures and densities.

Lovatelli was born a creative soul; a natural "repurposer," she salvages and recycles what she can and loves to reinvent what she finds. She is a tactile artist who has always been driven to create dimensional work. She is fascinated by art that includes random found objects injected into it with care. Her work is spontaneous, dictated by materials that find their way to her. Being a sustainable artist, Lovatelli realizes that she is drawn to specific textures, shapes, and colors, all verging on earthy tones, soft and inconspicuous.

Womb
Recycled paper
12 x 24 x 21 in.

OPPOSITE
Bibika
Recycled paper resin & found objects
19 x 17 x 16 in.

flovatelli@yahoo.com
flavia-lovatelli.com
@flovatelli

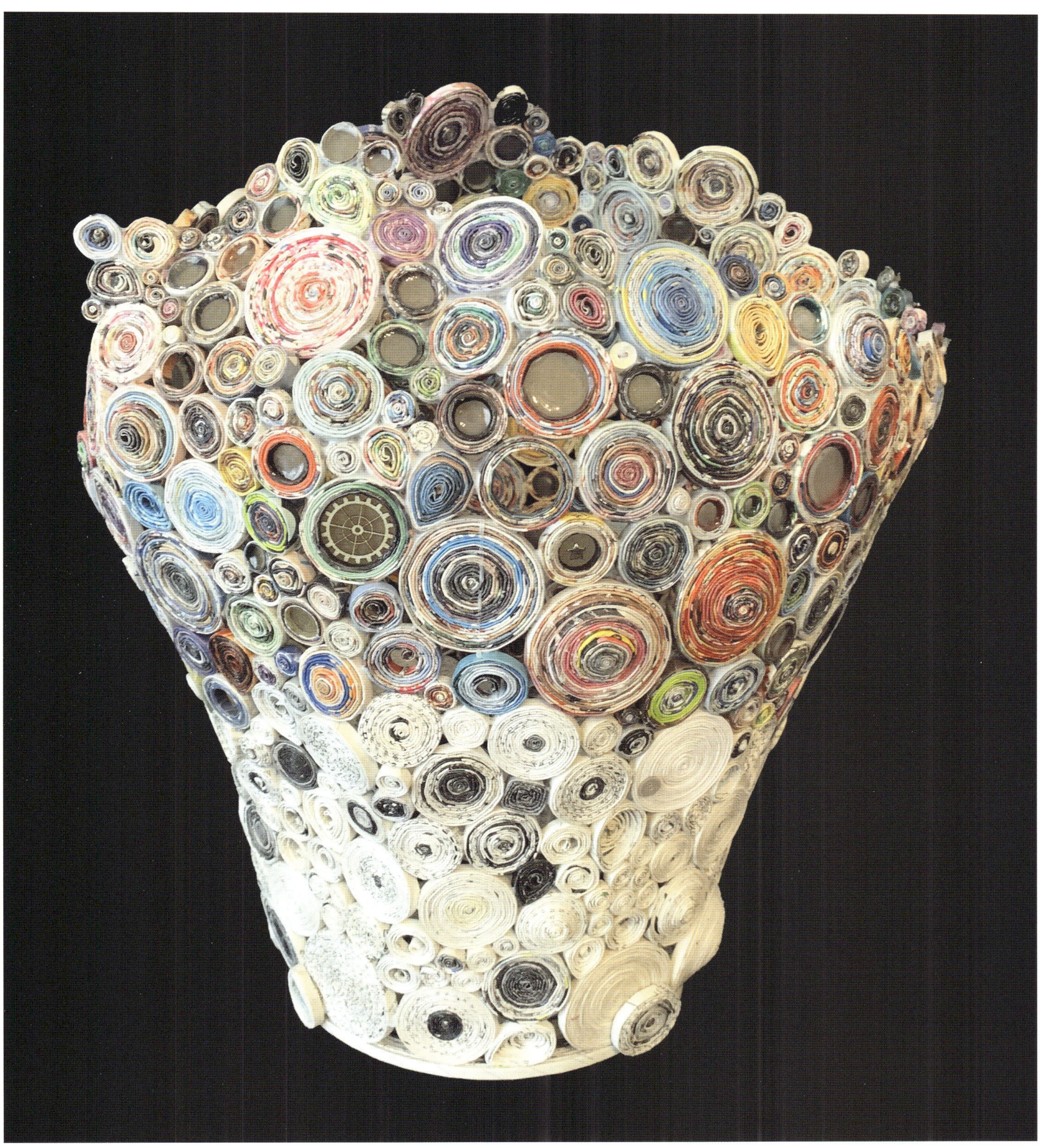

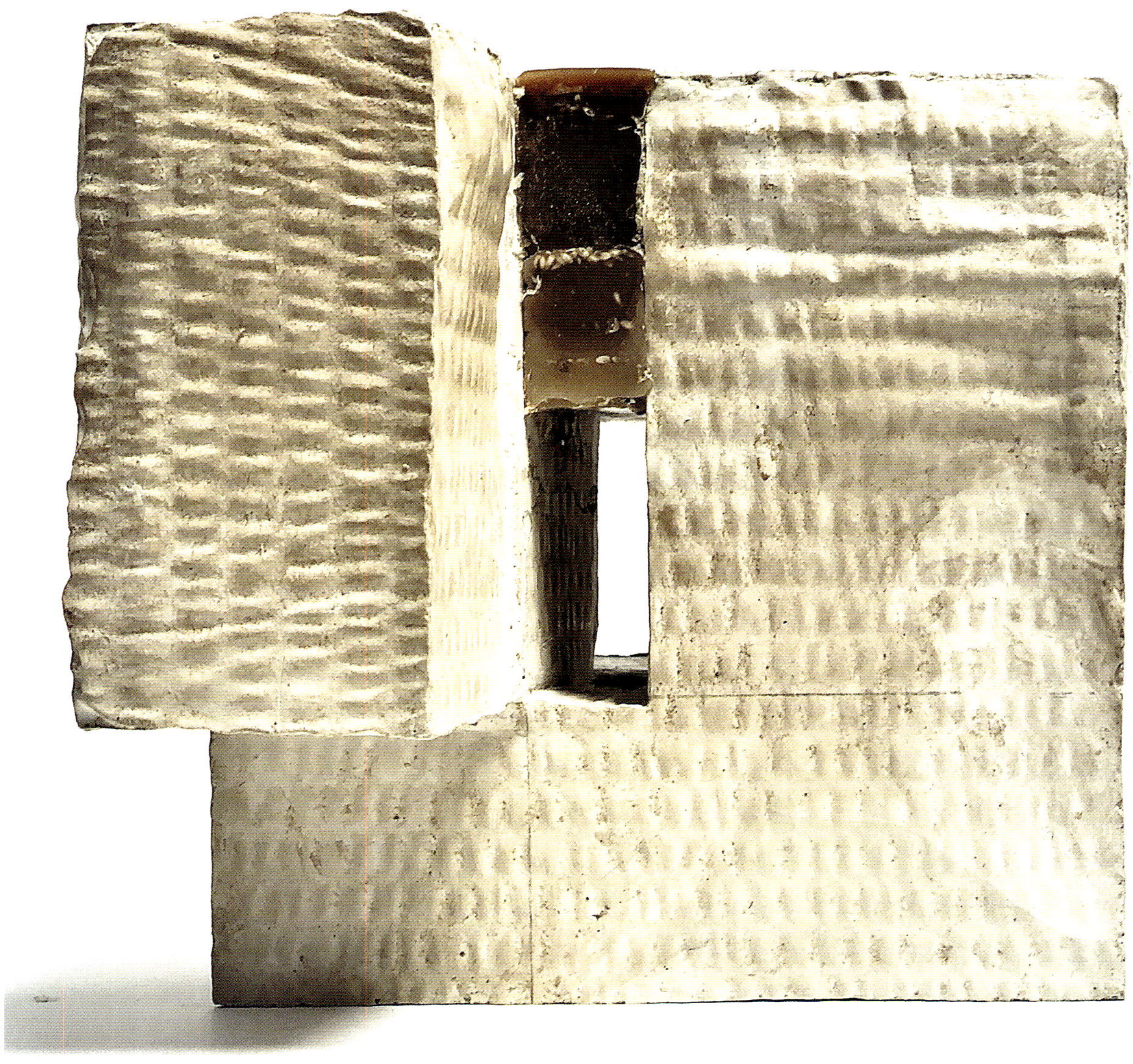

Pia Simmendinger
Spatial thinking is an integral part of Pia Simmendinger's work. The artist immerses herself in the most diverse spaces: the examination of positive and negative spaces, light and shadow, colors, and surfaces. She works predominately with plaster and wax. These materials inspire her because of their naturalness, their difference, and their wonderful haptics.

Precision combines with the imprecision, and it is exactly these contrasts that interest her. Simmendinger examines the heaviness and lightness of the volumes in relation to one another—as they almost touch, but not quite, as they almost tilt over, yet stay upright. The surfaces and their structures are important. In the end, it is the clear forms and breaks that unite. It takes many steps until a sculpture

is finished. The creation process with all the waiting and processing phases creates an indescribable closeness between the artist and the art. In the end, it is there, the sculpture, and it simply wants to be touched.

Balance #2
Plaster and wax
7 x 7 x 4 in.

OPPOSITE
Touch #2
Plaster and wax
6 x 4.7 x 4 in.

psimmendinger@
me.com
pia-simmendinger.ch
@PiaSimAtelier

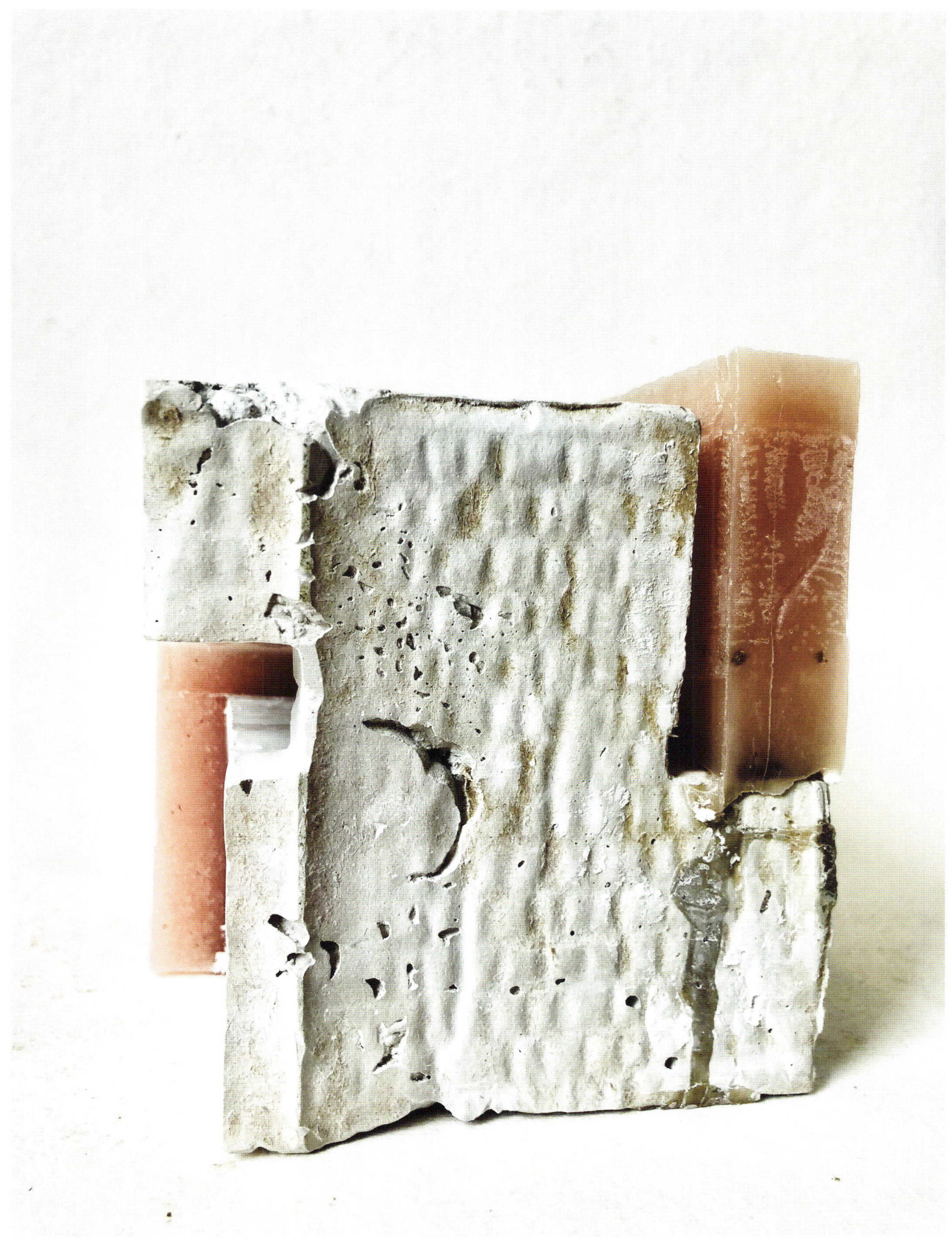

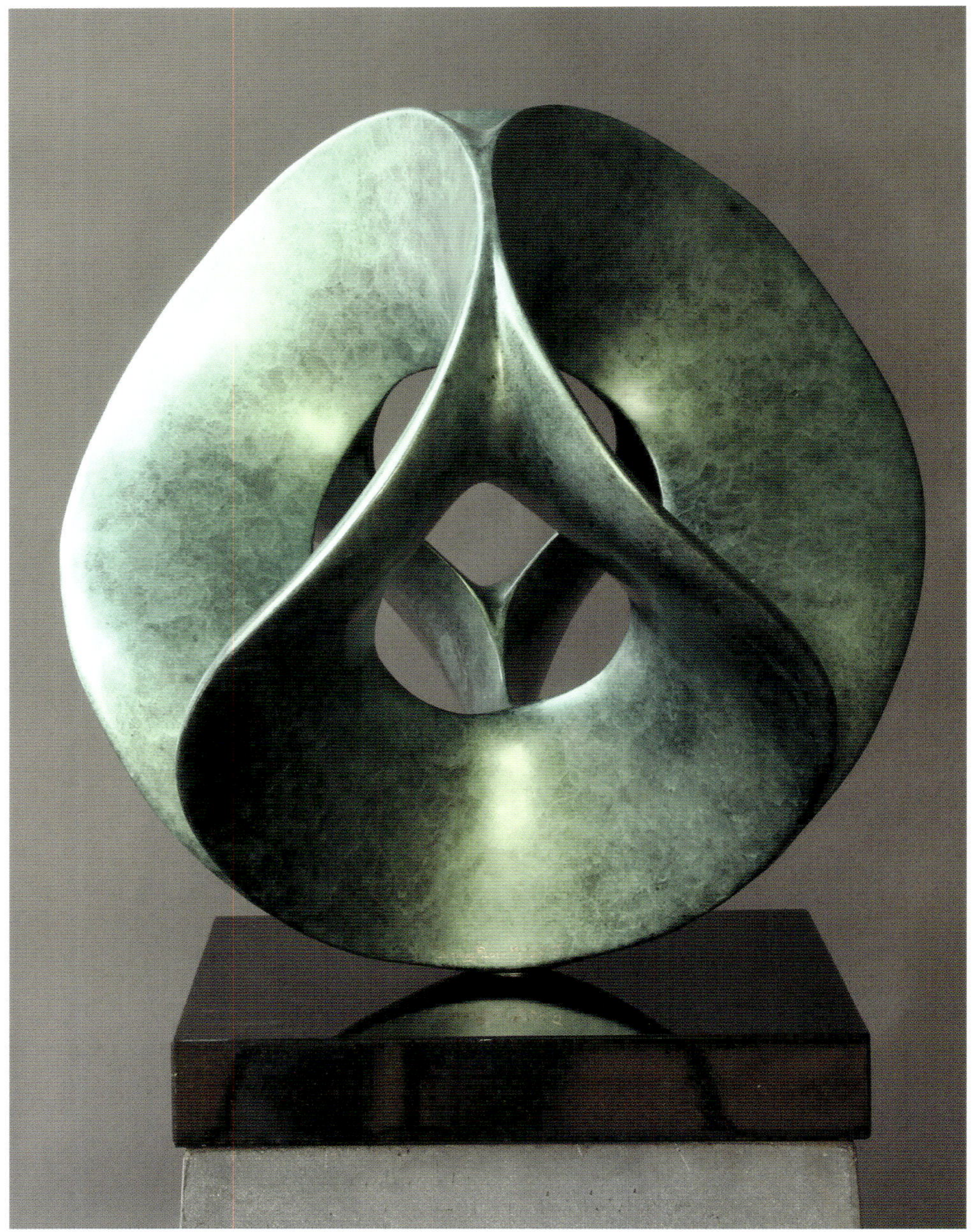

T Barny

A native of California with a BFA from the Rhode Island School of Design, T Barny has been creating sculpture professionally for four decades. It is his great love of stone as a medium that allows him to create serene and evocative works. The artist personally imports selected stone from quarries around the world, carving his pieces from massive blocks of granite, alabaster, calcite, and, his favorite, marble. Barny allows the natural rhythms of the materials to guide him to a final product. He makes use of negative space as much as the positive body in order to establish an affinity with the stone, evoking a feeling as sublime as the pieces themselves. Barny works hard so that his sculptures generate the kinetic illusion of movement and fluidity, especially in his Möbius strip-like works, with a single, traceable, looping edge.

CARDIA B - Heart
Bronze, Jade patina
Editon of 225
23 x 22 x 22 in.

sculpture@tbarny.com
tbarny.com
@tbarnysculpture

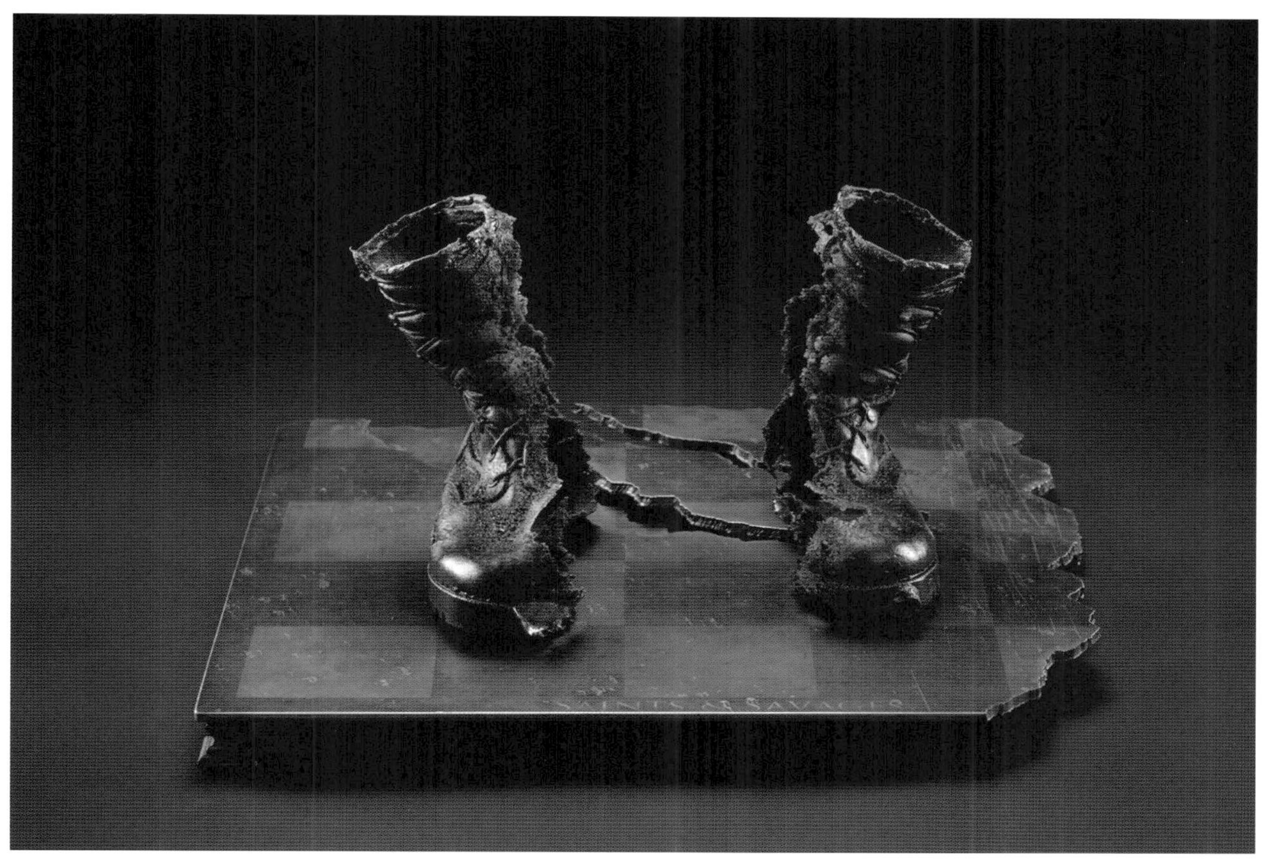

Geoffrey Bowton

The battlefield introduces unimaginable conflicts that bleed over into the lives of military veterans. With art, the intangible wounds veterans carry may become tangible, instigating conversation and support. Glass is a material that can embody these intangible things. Glass is fragile, opalescent, or translucent—it can hold form, shatter, break, and be mended, formed, packed, and shaped. It is a material that transforms under high temperature and pressure, much like the environment of deployment and war.

When trekking through Afghanistan during combat operations, American *Saints* wear boots like these, propelling them toward the imminent threat of death. Geoffrey Bowton connected with an old pair of boots and converted them to glass—reminding him of a time and place that he traveled through serving as an infantryman.

After spending time handling and converting the original service boots into glass, the mental and physical consequences from deployments became even more apparent post service—helping Bowton understand, heal, and grow.

Saints & Savages
Mixed Media
26 x 26 x 15 in.

geoffreybowton.com
@geoffreybowton

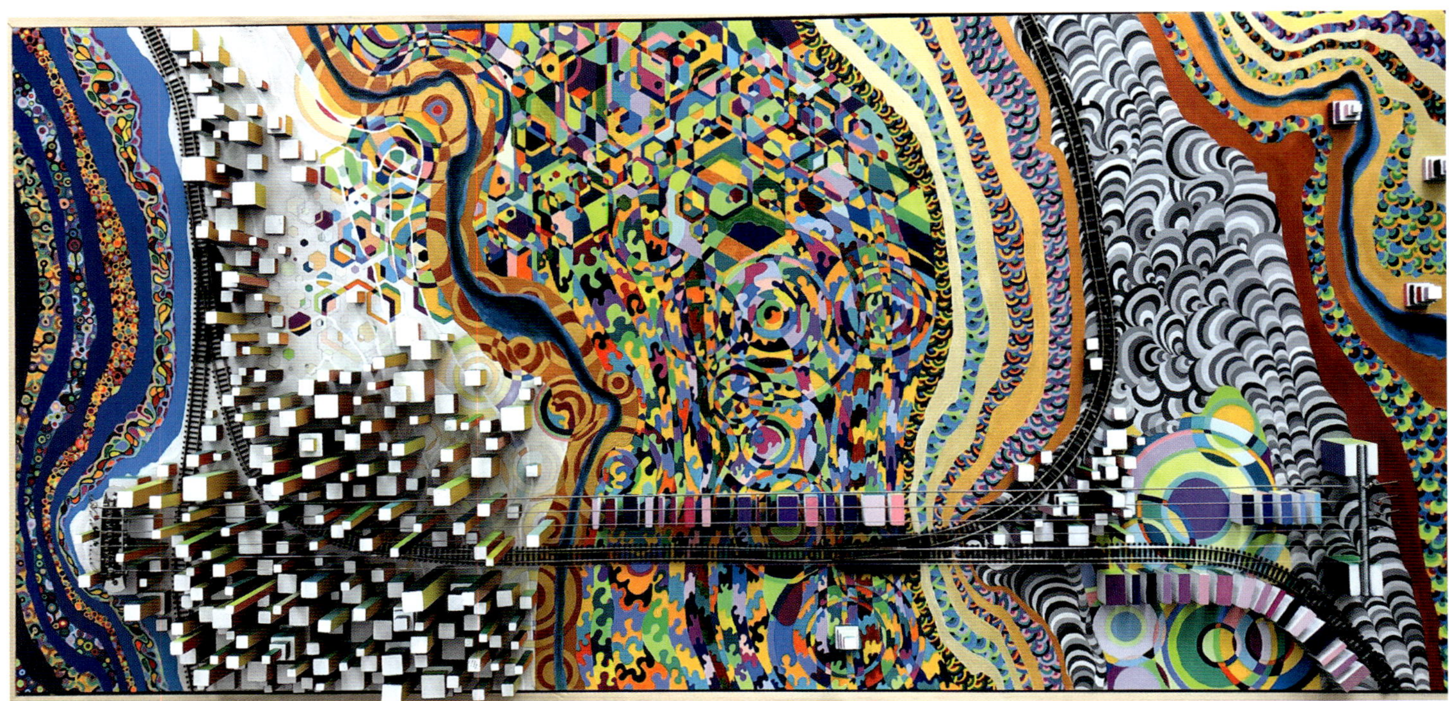

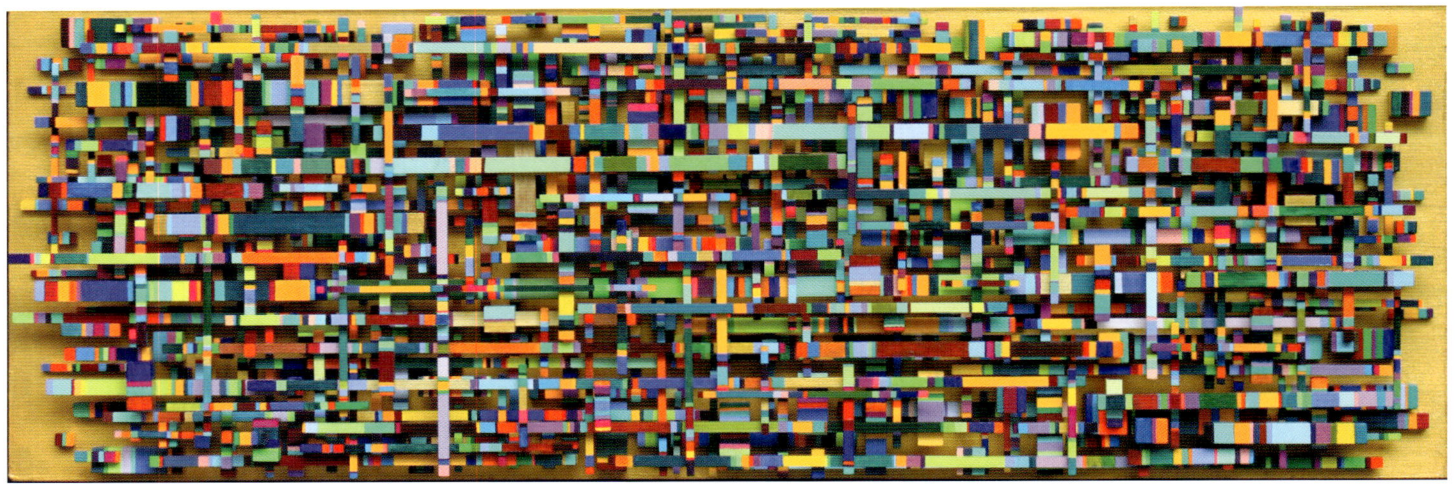

Andrew Chalfen

The ripples, radiance, fractal blooms, and clustered shapes of Andrew Chalfen's paintings, drawings, and mixed-media pieces reference aerial views, cartography, architectural renderings, musical notation, urban-like densities, and other natural and man-made patterns, many spilling out over edges, suggesting unseen continuations. His process mirrors that of his songwriting and music arranging, involving the repetition of a small selection of formal elements, subtle variation, the timbre of color palette, rhythm, and randomization strategies.

Chalfen's work shows a sheer joy in precise, dense patternmaking. The viewer may not know what to focus on first and become overwhelmed and subsequently absorbed in the details, which is akin to the experience of mediation or a divine/psychedelic experience. More recent abstract geometric pieces, including painted sculptures, explore themes of nostalgia, anxiety, climate change, play, allusions to scientific data and musical expression and notation, and deconstructions reflective of, and perhaps counter to, accelerating social and psychic instability in the world.

TOP: *Vibration Lands*
Mixed media on panel
23.5 x 49.5 in.

BOTTOM: *Problem Solved*
Acrylic and wood on panel
14.5 x 38 in.

andrewdchalfen@gmail.com
andrewchalfen.com
@i.think.like.midnight

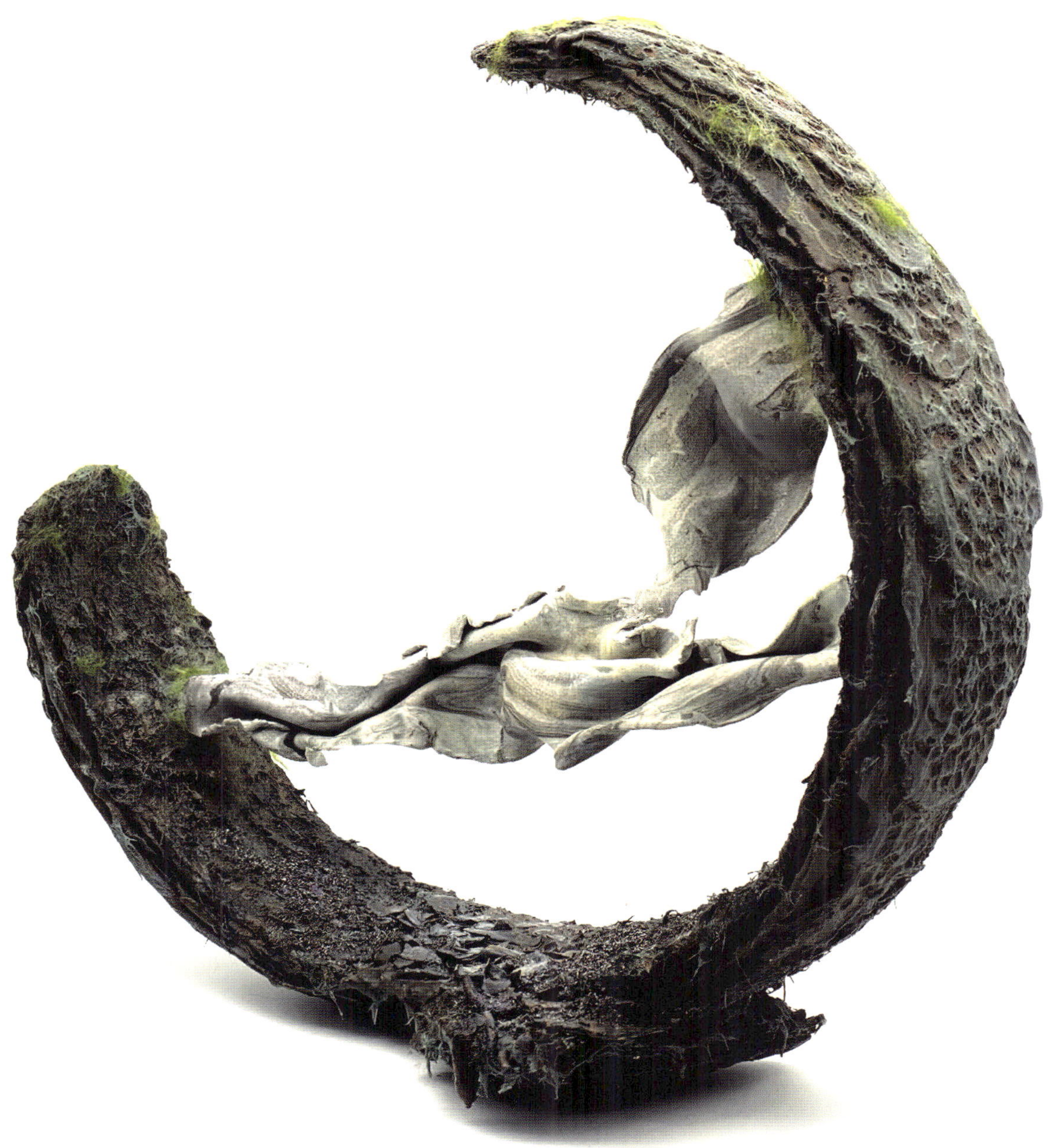

Christy Chor

Christy Chor cares about the future of the natural world amidst disastrous interventions by humans. Chor's work reflects on the causes and consequences of our ecological crisis, triggers the alarm bells of disaster, and galvanizes the audience into action to save nature for generations to come. Her body of work emphasizes the contrast between poetic moments and chaotic happenings in nature. With a combination of raw clays and nonbiodegradable particles, Chor has sculpted a landscape, combining representations of natural elements such as clouds, waves, stones, sand, and fossils with elements of human industrial waste. She uses contrasting elements to underline the importance of balance and coexistence.

The Broken Circle
Cone 6 stoneware with mixed media
23 in. dia. x 9 in. depth

christyymchor@gmail
.com
christychor.com
@christychor.ceramics

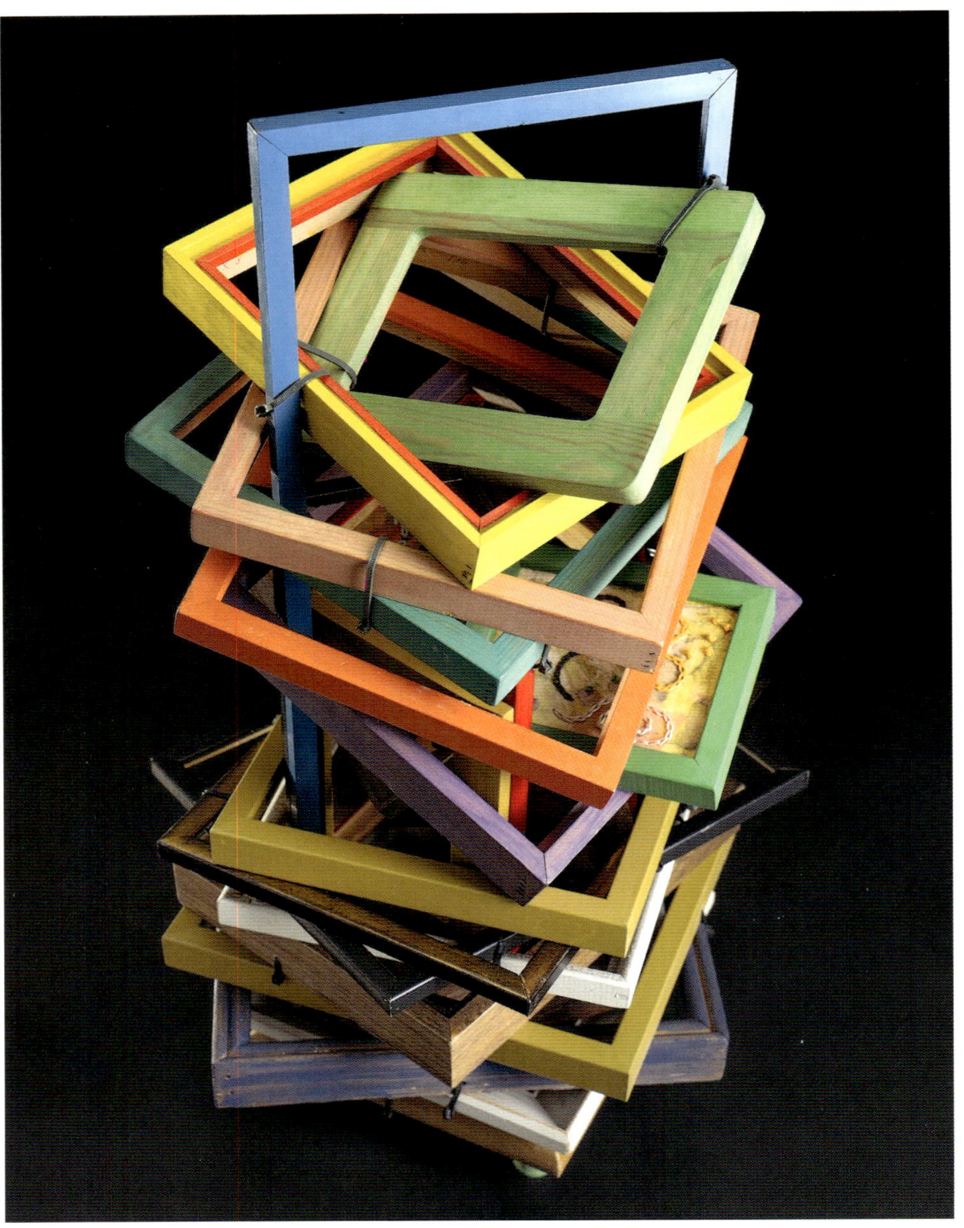

Emily Dorvin

Emily Dorvin calls herself a sculptural basketmaker. She is known for her innovative, "transordinary" vessels. Challenging the original definition of basketry, Dorvin explores contemporary interpretations of this traditional craft utilizing nontraditional materials. She transforms the ordinary through the processes of manipulation, construction, alteration, patterning, layering, repetition of singular elements, coiling, weaving, and assembling to create dense arrangements of common urban objects. She sculpts with fiber and interacts with the material, pattern, color, design, shape, and texture.

Dorvin's use of repurposed, recontextualized materials is a commentary on the overconsumption of commercial goods, societal excess, and throwaway consumerism. Her work references everyday life and our relationship with our urban environment. The artist uses the vessel form with an emotional and personal vocabulary to speak about life's issues. Her process is intuitive, and the ideas evolve as she creates, building and growing as layers present themselves.

Reframed
Wood frames, painted paper, embroidery floss, cable ties
25 x 14 x 14 in.

emily@emilydvorin.com
emilydvorin.com
@emilydvorin

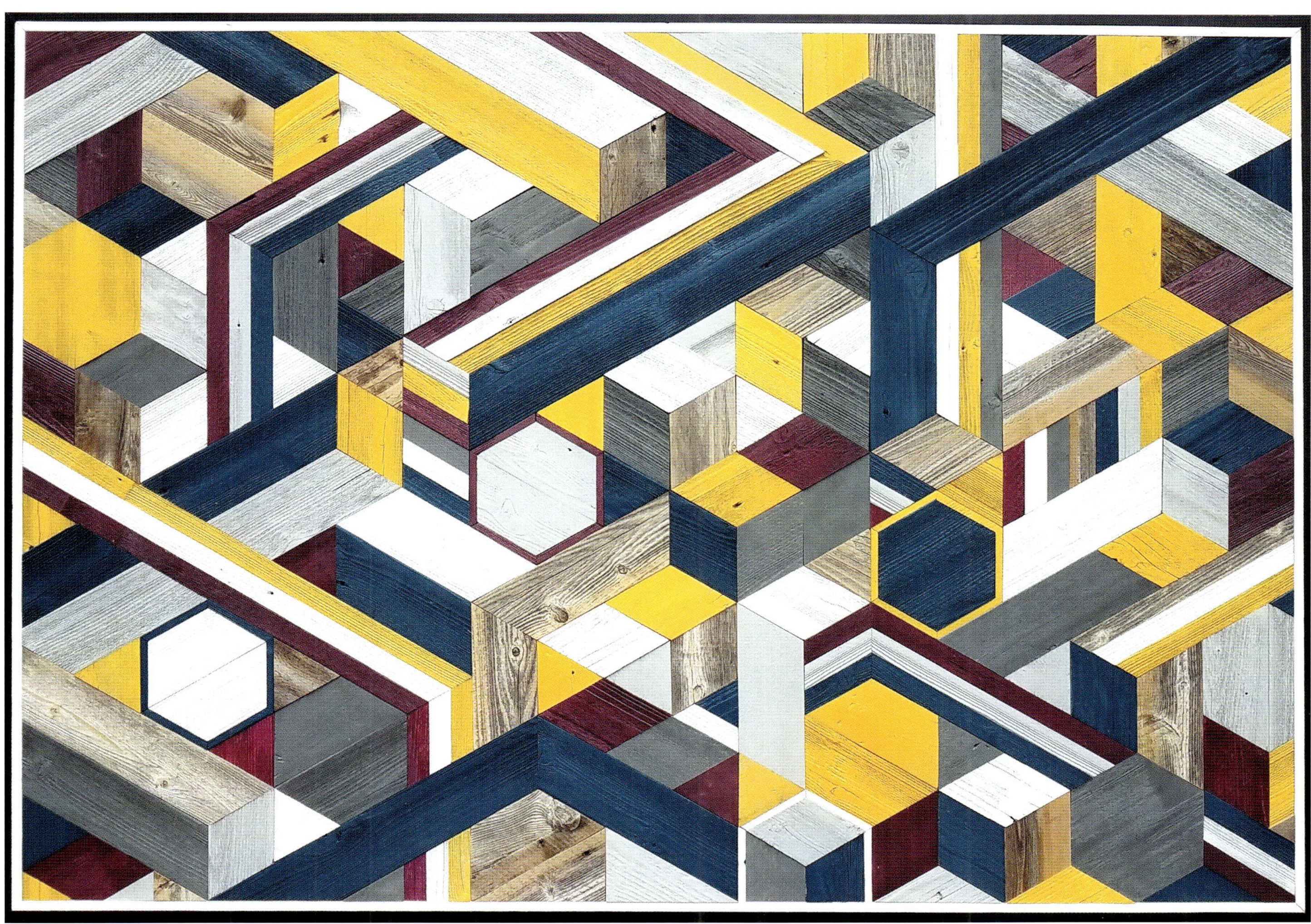

Ryan Ekmark

After walking away from art for nearly two decades for a career in healthcare, Ryan Ekmark inadvertently found his way back in 2017. The source of his unconventional return: sobriety. With plenty of time on his hands while putting his life back together, Ekmark renewed his old passion while experimenting in a medium he'd never used before, wood. He found inspiration through geometric patterns and reclaimed lumber. Self-taught, his transition to creating large, colorful pieces of wooden wall art was challenging but extremely rewarding. No two pieces of his art are the same. Ekmark frequently explores depth and optical illusions through his version of op art and kumiko, a traditional Japanese technique that uses many wooden bars crossed and laid to form various designs and expressions. Ekmark is constantly challenging himself to take bigger risks and design artwork that makes the viewer question if the piece was created with a paintbrush and not a miter saw.

Harry
Wood
50 x 70 in.

recoveredcalling@
yahoo.com
@recoveredcalling

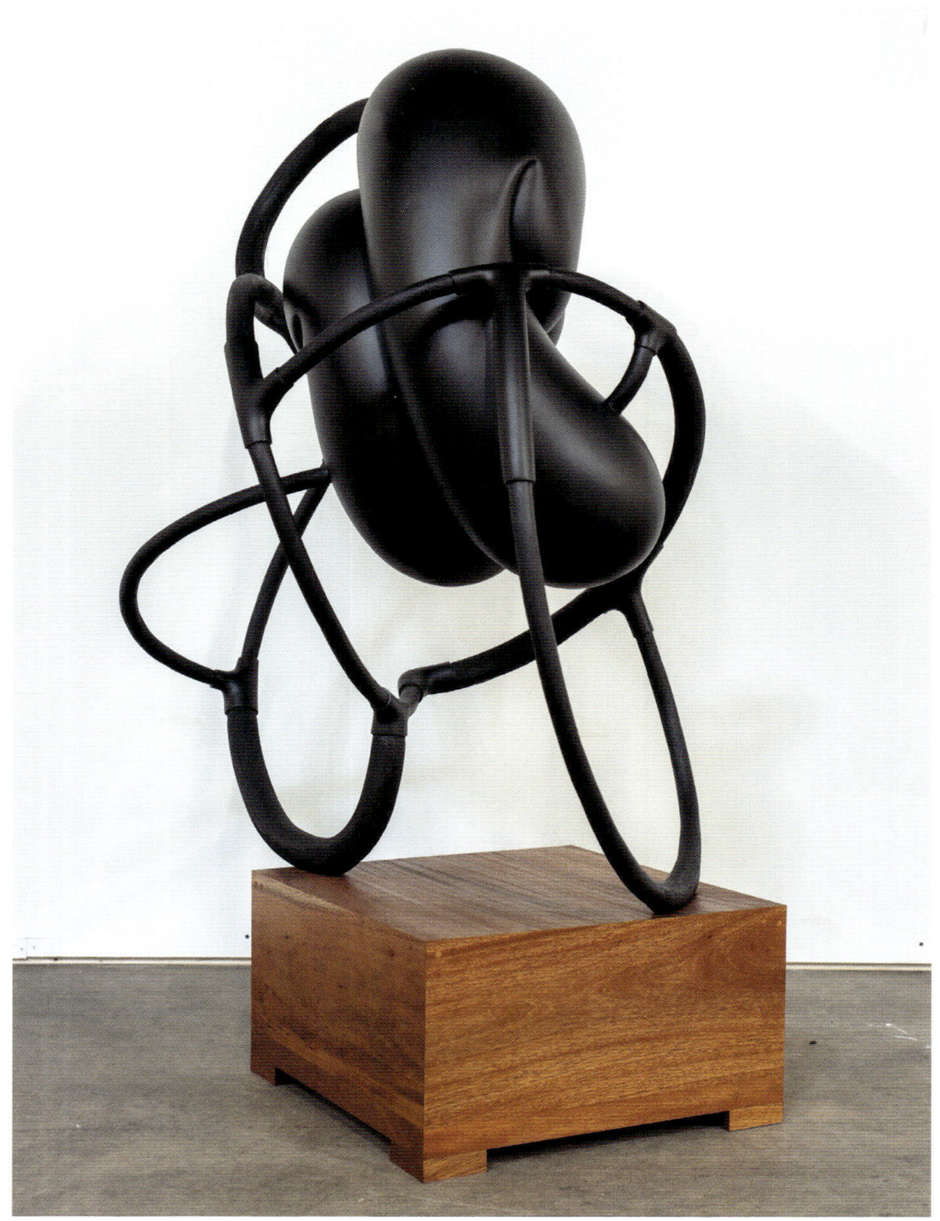

Ralph Pàquin

Ralph Pàquin's inspiration often has no concrete origin but arrives through the mass of information absorbed over years of observation and artistic creation. An exploration of the human condition is at the core of his work, in which he scrutinizes what it means to exist and attempts to capture the essence of the human experience. Pàquin's artworks seek to consider the interiority of the human form and its links to primordial life.

In his work, "organomorphic" shapes play on ideas of genetics and the structure of the human body, while another series makes a seamless transition into the macroscopic world of aesthetics and form in relation to time and space from the microscopic world of genes and chromosomes. Some of his work subconsciously channels celestial origins of existence through modern astronomical and archaeological findings of our primordial history. Other concepts behind the works explore notions of faith, philosophy, and biotechnology filtered through the artist's own quirks and dreams.

Boötes Voids
Hand-cast industrial grade organopolymer, enamel paint and steel on handcrafted Honduran mahogany base
62 x 40 x 30 in.

rpaquinart@gmail.com
ralphpaquin.com
@rpaquinart

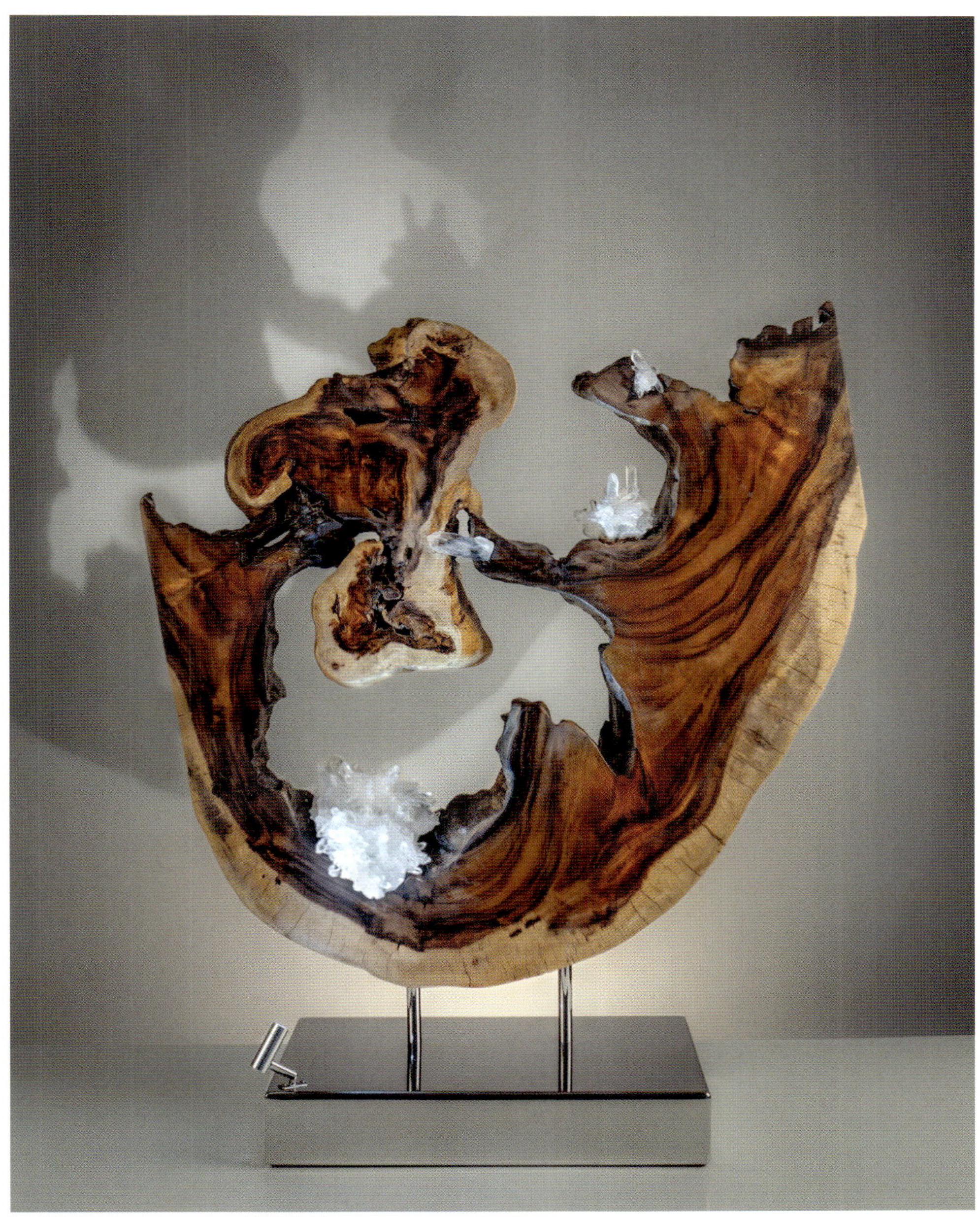

Dorit Schwartz

Art is a bridge to the human spirit. Dorit Schwartz's sculptural work exists to stir feelings that others may experience, to dive into the depths of human strength and fragility. Schwartz's creative process represents her uncommon appreciation for the organic beauty found in nature. Her works of art create expressive forms that explore sensuality, inviting people in, magnetically drawing them to touch the sculptures.

Schwartz revels in working with such rare mediums as cork, raw stone, driftwood, and crystals. Not only does she showcase the materials' natural value, but she also creates new forms of art by fusing parts that enhance each other's beauty. The finished works then inspire the observer to journey from element to element, eventually taking in the entire piece as a whole—interpreting and deciphering their own meanings as their personal reactions and feelings combine with the art.

Facets of Love
Quartz crystal, acacia wood, stainless steel base
36 x 31 x 12 in.

doritfineart@gmail.com
doritschwartzsculptor
.com
@doritschwartzsculptor

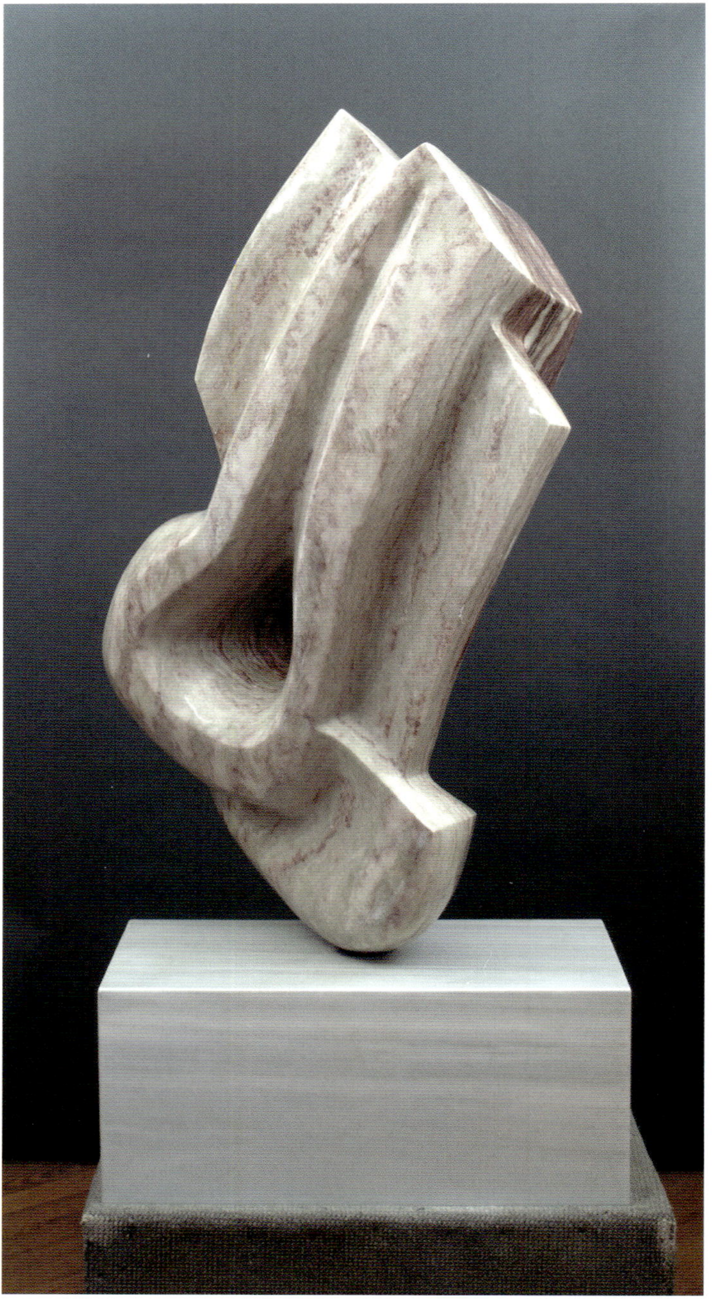

Joel Shapses

As a sculptor, Joel Shapses' inspiration comes from a variety of areas, including the various material he uses. He doesn't like to limit his creativity to one material or style. If he is working on an abstract piece, often the media itself helps to guide him to the finished creation. Representational works have a special inspiration, which comes from the human or animal form. When working in stone, the grain of the stone may not let Shapses choose the final form, so he has to allow nature to help him achieve the final result.

Other materials help Shapses in the creative process. In addition to stone, the artist works in aluminum, bronze, resins, clay, and fused glass. The use of fused glass, neon, and LED lights has led to new avenues of creative possibilities. Combining materials also creates new vistas of inspiration and creativity.

Spirit of 83
Raspberry alabaster
60 x 36 x 15 in.

joelshapsesstudio@
gmail.com
@joelshapsesartist

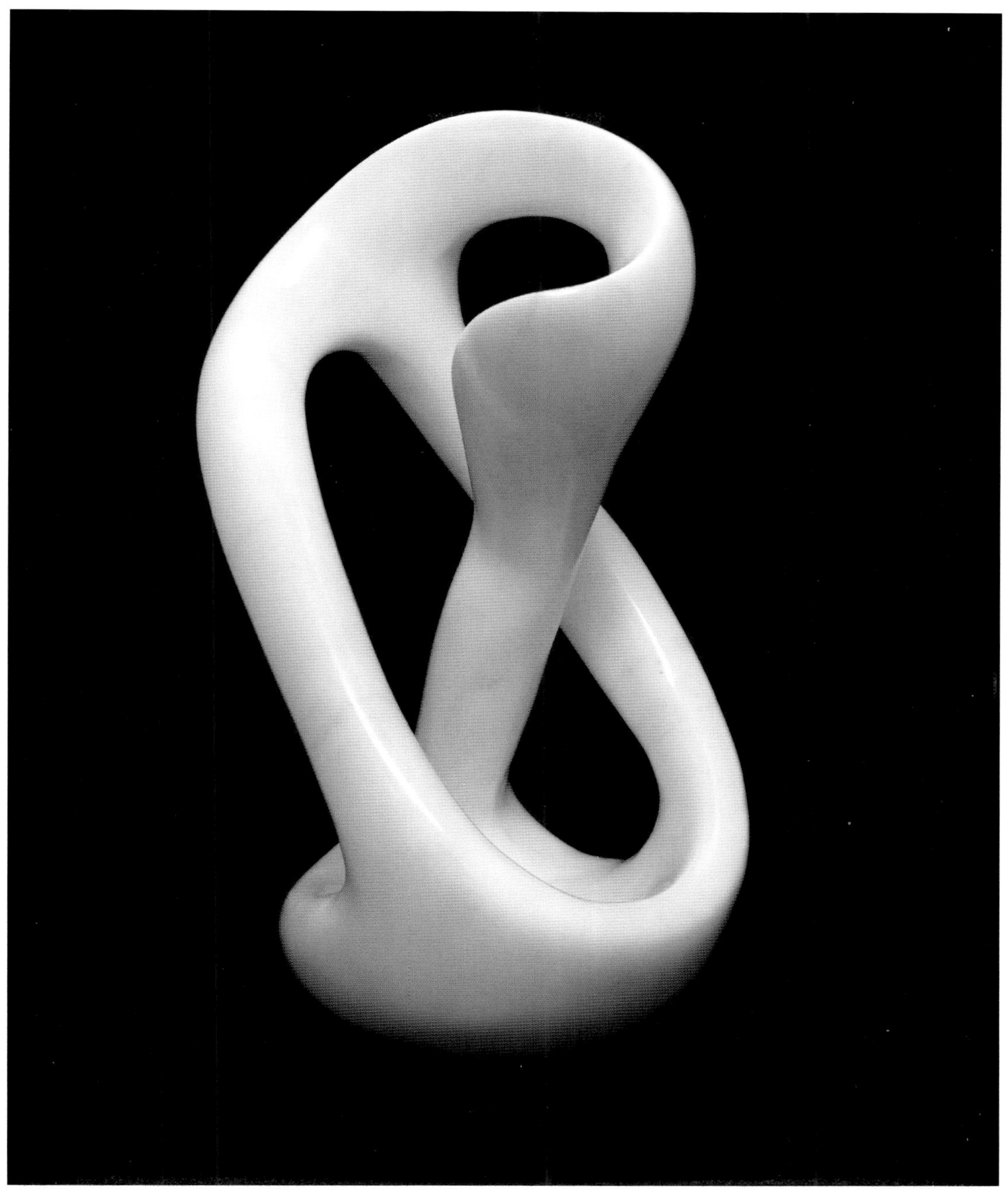

Todd Sorrin

Todd Sorrin became captivated by the concept that he was not really creating anything, but instead simply revealing something magical, already hidden within the stone. He often works with massive blocks of Italian Carrara marble. Sorrin notes that working with stone is not easy. "If you chisel away too much material, you can't repair it. Stone has faults, grain, weaknesses, and imperfections that can cause you to alter your plan," he says. But the artist also notes that when he metaphorically gets inside the stone, it begins to "talk" to him and dictate the direction he needs to go. Sorrin's works often take months or years to complete, and he never quite knows if the result of all his work will be a perfectly good stone reduced to nothing.

Infinity
Italian carrara marble
14 x 7 x 6 in.

todd@sorrin.com

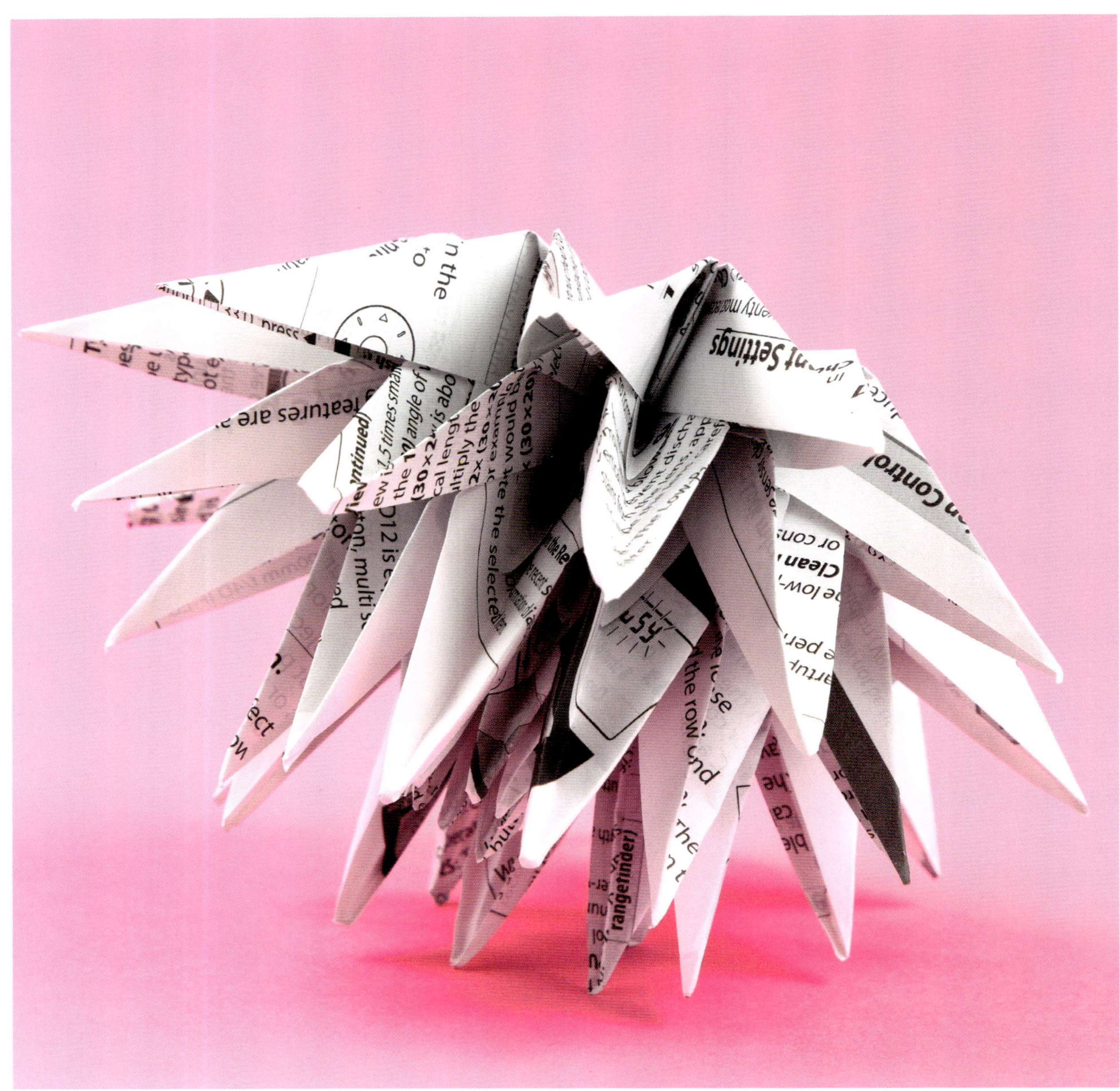

Chan Suk On

Chan Suk On is inspired by everyday life experiences. Her artistic journey has taken her from documentary photography to conceptual art. Creation is a process that starts from zero to transform ideas into works of art.

One day, the artist picked up an expired camera manual. The manual was made of white paper, and Chan Suk On began to fold different sculptural forms. In her work, she deconstructs the language of the alphabet so that it becomes a spontaneous moment. The texts are about photography randomly distributed. It is a poetic process. Chan Suk On plays with the positive and negative space of the forms. The paper sculptures are light in weight and dance in space.

Art Manual
Paper
19.5 x 19.5 in.

chansukon@gmail.com
chansukon.com
@sukon.chan

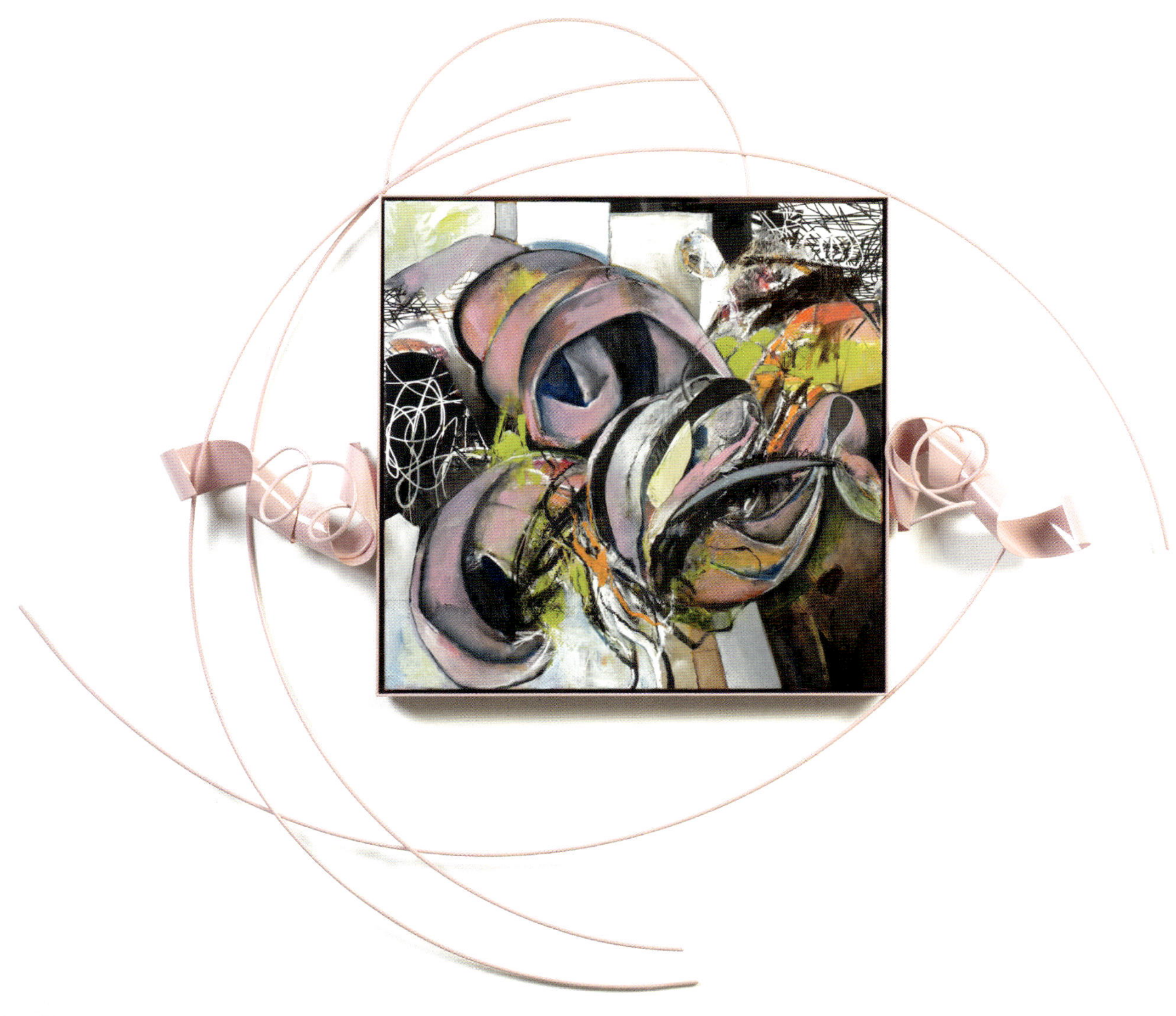

Kim Thoman

Kim Thoman's art is based on a personal philosophical belief that duality exists in everything. Incorporating levels of symbolism and various materials, Thoman is fascinated with opposites. She is aware of opposing forces in the world around her, such as intellect and intuition, male and female, stillness and movement, body and soul, light and dark, and, of course, life and death. In this space of opposing forces, Thoman aims to bring her sense of duality into balance in hopes of finding real truths. Her desire is to present opposite sides of any truth in order to see the real picture. In addition to the philosophical concerns in her work, natural elements emerge that are symbols for her own growth. At the same time, she is also drawn to the world of technology and the mechanics of the external world. Once again, duality feeds her creativity.

Entanglement 8
Powder coated welded
steel & oil paint
72 x 80 x 14 in.

kim@kimthoman.com
kimthoman.com
@kim.thoman

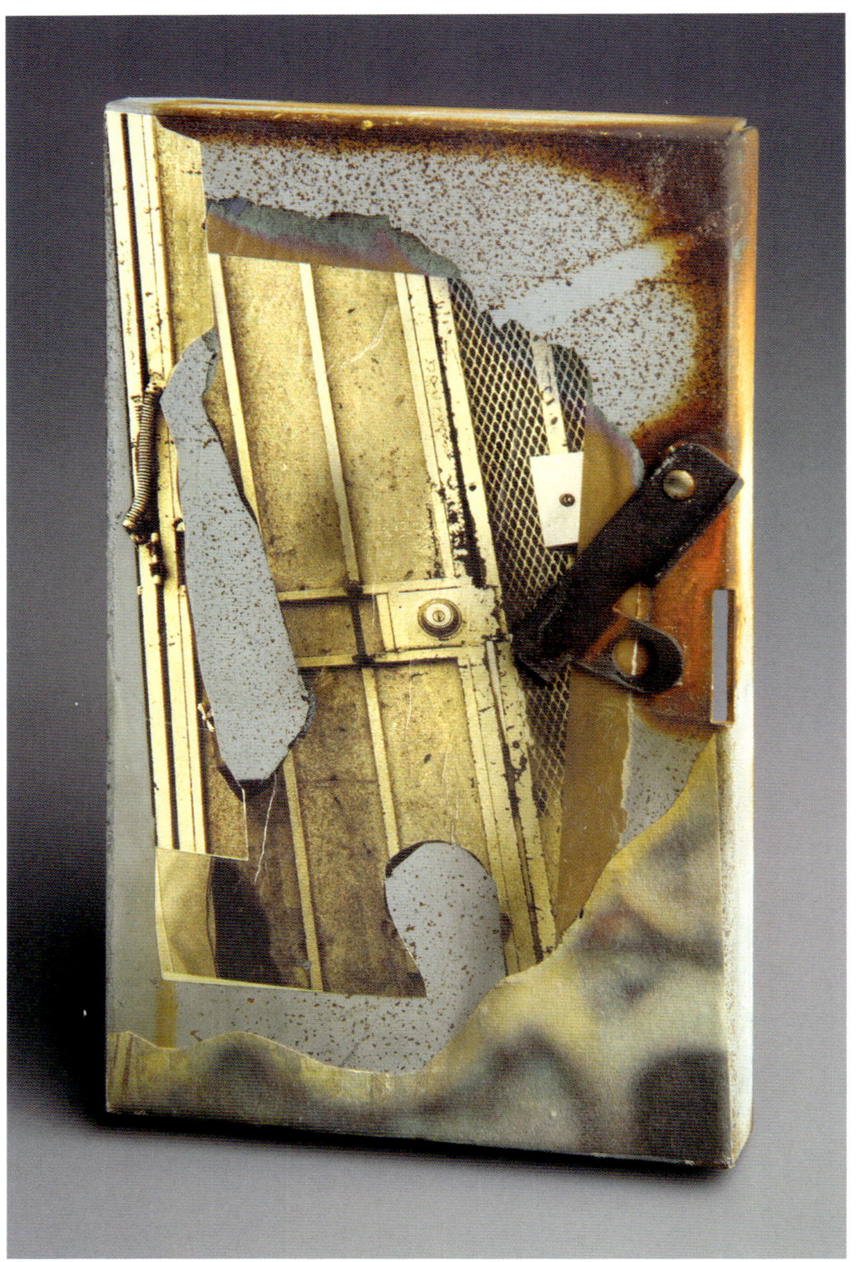

Will Ursprung

Will Urspung's oeuvre is primarily concerned with a reverence for the found object, and the intuitive and often random properties of collage elements. By combining disparate parts and textures, both visual and tactile, one can create an interesting and exciting composition that evokes an emotional response. The collage idiom can be likened to the improvisation of jazz and may make a statement about our disposable society. Sources of inspiration for the artist, besides the object itself, are primitive art, as well as Celtic, Norse, and Native American myth. Modern aphorisms and metaphors are additional grist for the creative mill.

Diaspora de la Penitentaire
Found steel object with collage
10 x 8 in.

holcombe.photo
.service@gmail.com

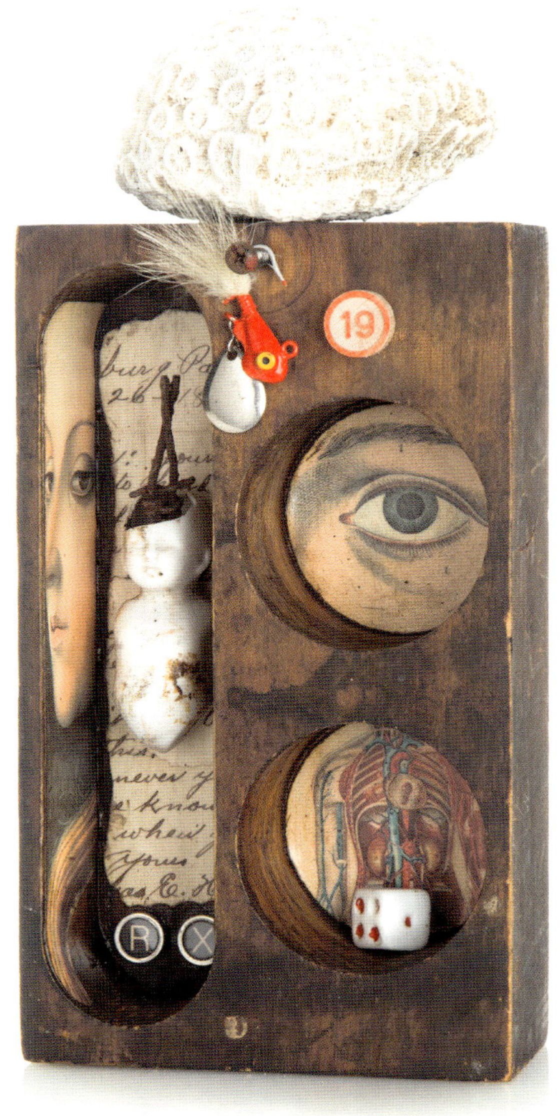

Jody West

There is always an inspiration to breathe new life into found objects from the past. Regardless of the age or value of an object, creating a piece of assemblage art has the potential to ignite a new appreciation for it. Jody West's inspiration started from a treasure trove of photographs, ephemera, and antiques inherited from her family. Now, virtually anything that crosses her path during a visit to an antiques store, a stroll through the woods, or looking through an old box that holds the possibility of a forgotten piece of history can inspire a piece.

West brings a passion for design, collage, and assemblage to her work. Many pieces are inspired by one component and the rest comes together as she adds additional objects. Some pieces have a more personal meaning, and some are just whimsical and inspired by joining random salvaged items together in a new and interesting way.

Fishing for a Cure
Mixed Media
11.25 x 5.25 x 2.5 in.

jwest140@shentel.net
jwestfoundart.com
@jodywestfoundart

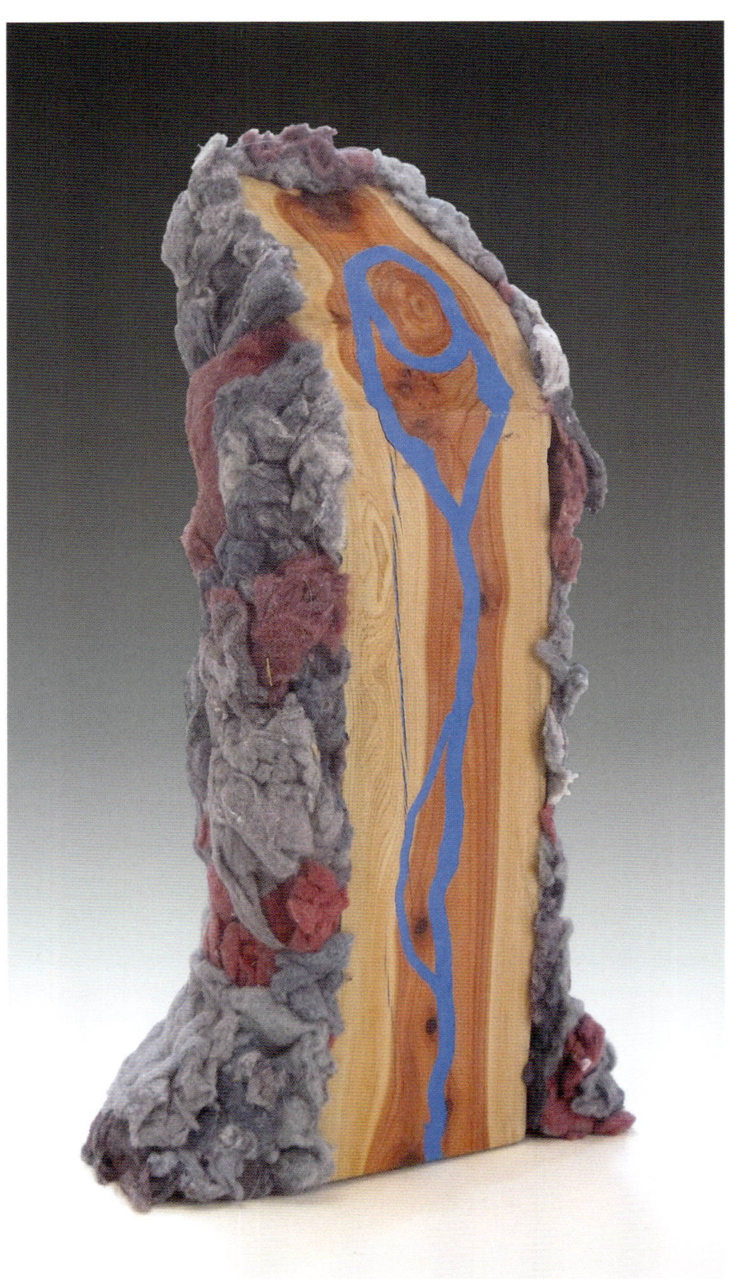

Dan Woodard
Dan Woodard's work, which has frequently been described as elegant yet also earthy and powerful, is primarily informed by the artist's own subconscious and a spontaneous interaction with a variety of materials. He has always been fascinated and mystified by the construct of time; in much of his abstract work, his goal is to capture the transformation, entropy, and/or degradation that occur with the passage of time. Woodard's most recent series showcases sculptures that have a direct connection to a specific period of time in his life. He creates these pieces in order to fix various spans of time, from a moment to a year, into a tangible form.

Many of these works also incorporate actual materials from his daily life. Through these sculptures, the artist is both exploring his incomprehension of time and attempting to provide an iconic image that will anchor him to a given time frame.

It Will All Come Out in the Wash
Wood, pigmented epoxy, dryer lint
14 x 8 x 6 in.

danwoodard@sbcglobal
.net
danwoodard.com
@dansculptor

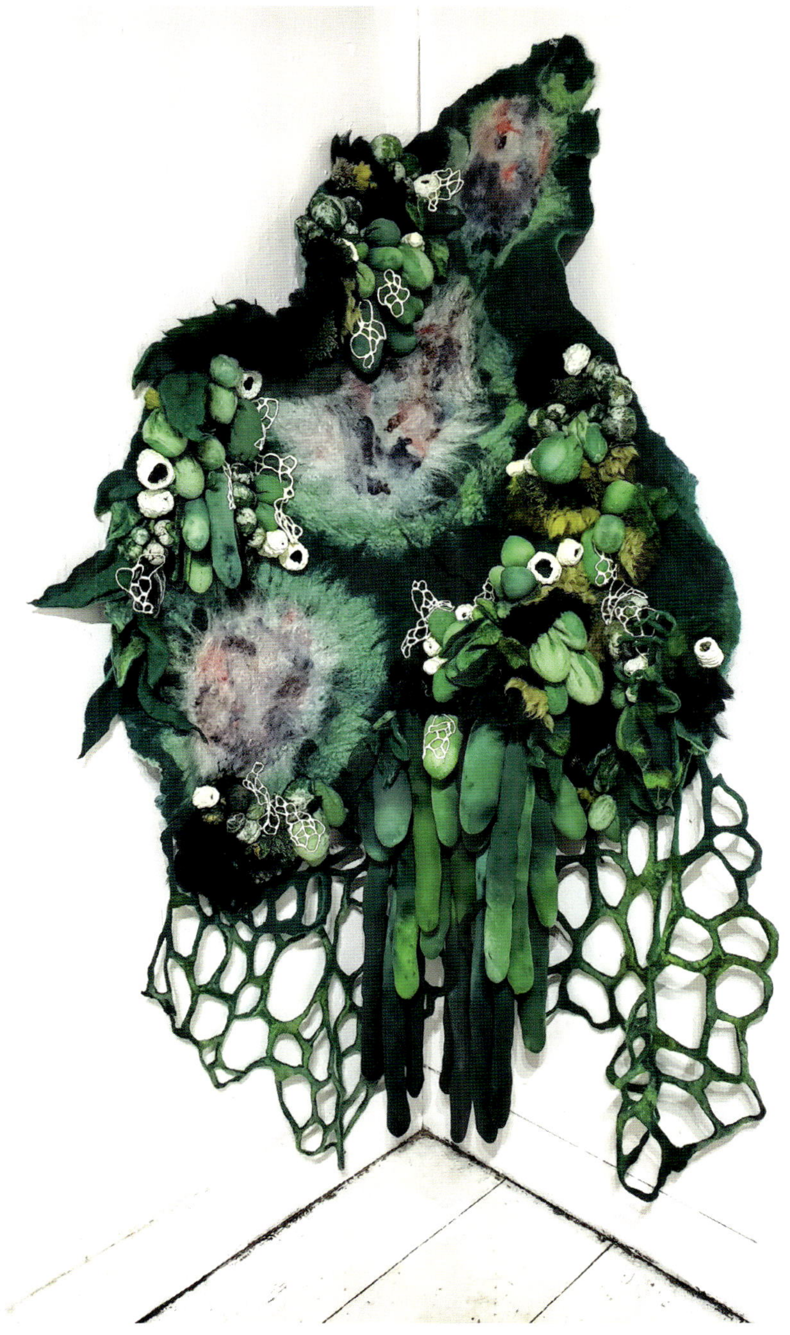

Mallory Zondag

Mallory Zondag creates fiber art to address our relationship to the natural world. We find comfort in nature, but more often than not, it's nature that we have shaped and sculpted into an ideal under our control. We are a part of the natural world's cycles of balance—growth and decay, creation, and entropy—yet decay makes us uncomfortable. Zondag's work examines these forms of entropy in our world and in ourselves, as well as our human impact on this planet. Using wool, wax, fibers, paint, and found objects, she creates forms and textures that explore the visual and emotional impact of growth and decay. The artist finds a strange beauty in the uncomfortable certainty that we are not permanent. Her use of textile and sculptural techniques confronts our relationship with nature, our adoration and destruction of the natural world, and conveys the message that we are made of earth and one day we all return.

Friend
Felted wool, mixed fiber embellishments
60 x 36 in.

mkzondag@gmail.com
mallorymakes.com
@badwolf124

DIGITAL – GOLD

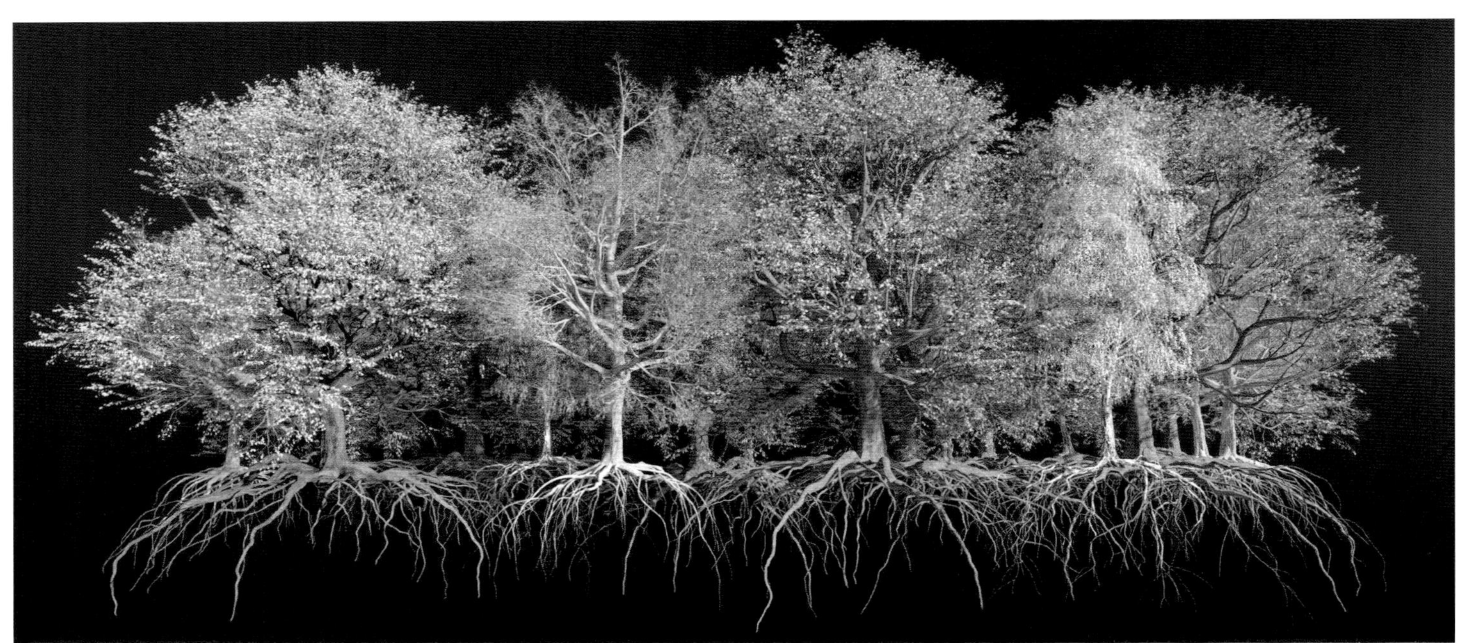

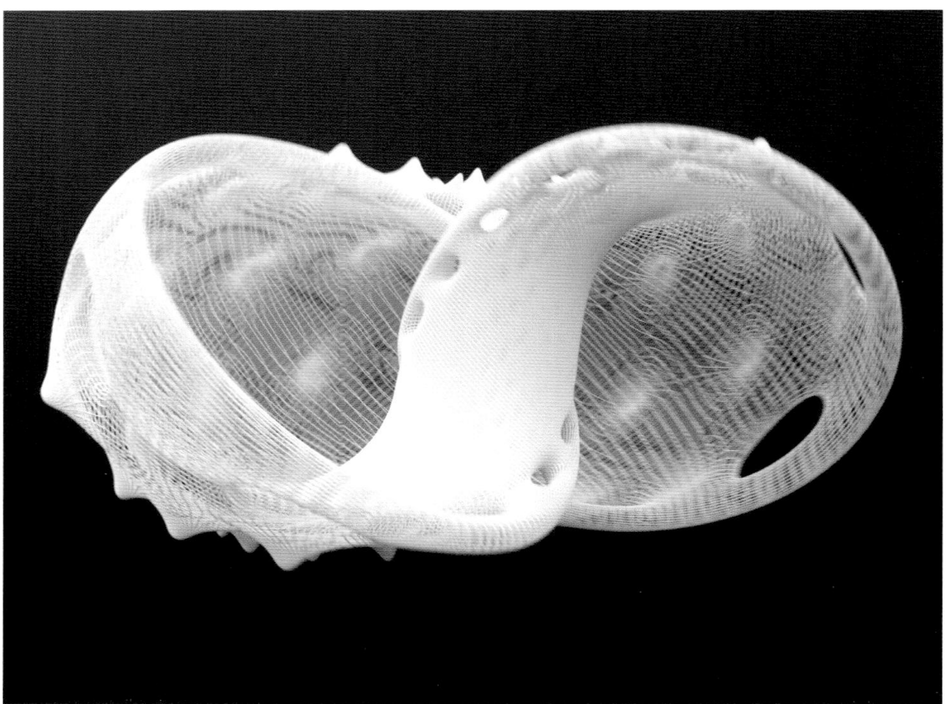

Richard Devonshire
UK-based artist Richard Devonshire utilizes cutting-edge technology to give a modern interpretation of fine art photography, painting, sculpture, and drawing. He is creating a body of work that focuses on the deeper meaning of the amazing shapes, patterns, and principles that exist in nature and the relationship with mathematics that informs us of our view of the world around us. Devonshire's creative process involves creating textured 3-D models, virtual cameras, and lighting systems that mimic real-world settings and characteristics. While the works suggest a form of photo-realism, their visual qualities also radically differ from that of photography and lend to a heightened level of detail, implying unlimited possibilities.

TOP: *Separation*
3D rendering
12.5 x 27.5 in.

Richard.Devonshire@
yahoo.com
richard-devonshire.com
@richard_devonshire_art

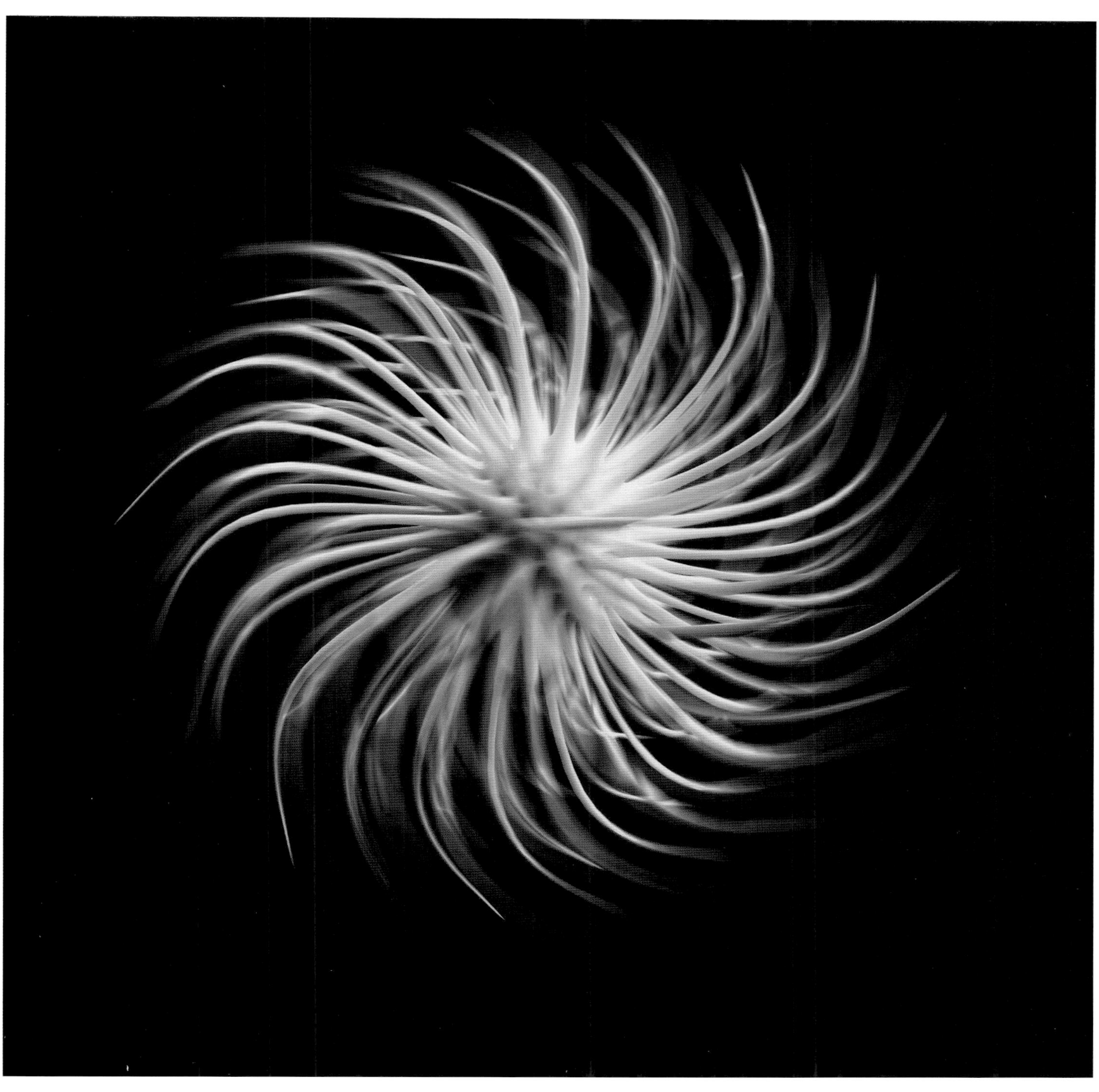

OPPSITE BOTTOM
Rules of Menory
Rewritten
3D rendering
10 x 13.7 in.

Chronoclasm
3D rendering
17.7 x 17.7 in.

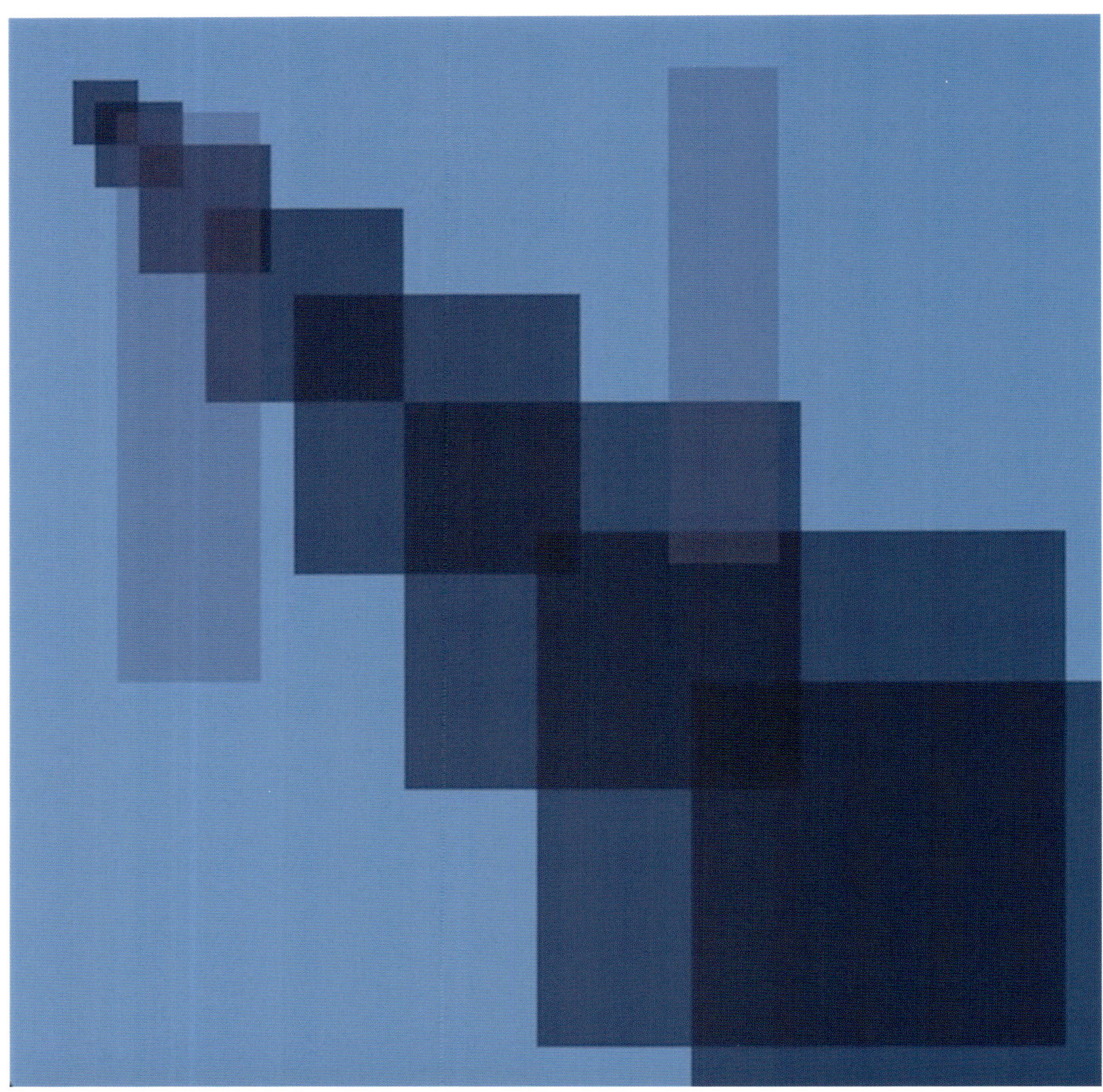

Tyler N. Horton
Tyler N. Horton's art explores the themes of purpose and meaning and whether these things even exist in what we see, hear, and feel. His work is meant to reflect on whether anything has meaning, whether there is reason behind any given occurrence, and whether life and its many events are all just unavoidable happenstance. The main aspect of life on which his art intends to focus is the interactions with others. Horton's art is based on asking questions such as what is our relation to other beings and why is it significant? Was the interaction meant to happen or is it a product of sheer coincidence? What is next for this interaction? What other interactions will occur? His art does not reveal any answers to said inquiries, but it instead offers the idea that there may not be any attainable answers, and to continue searching for them would prove futile.

Quadrilateral Gathering 004
Digital processing
2000 x 2000 px.

OPPOSITE
Eisbrecher 02
Digital Processing
2000 x 2000 px.

tnhforum@gmail.com
@tnhortonart

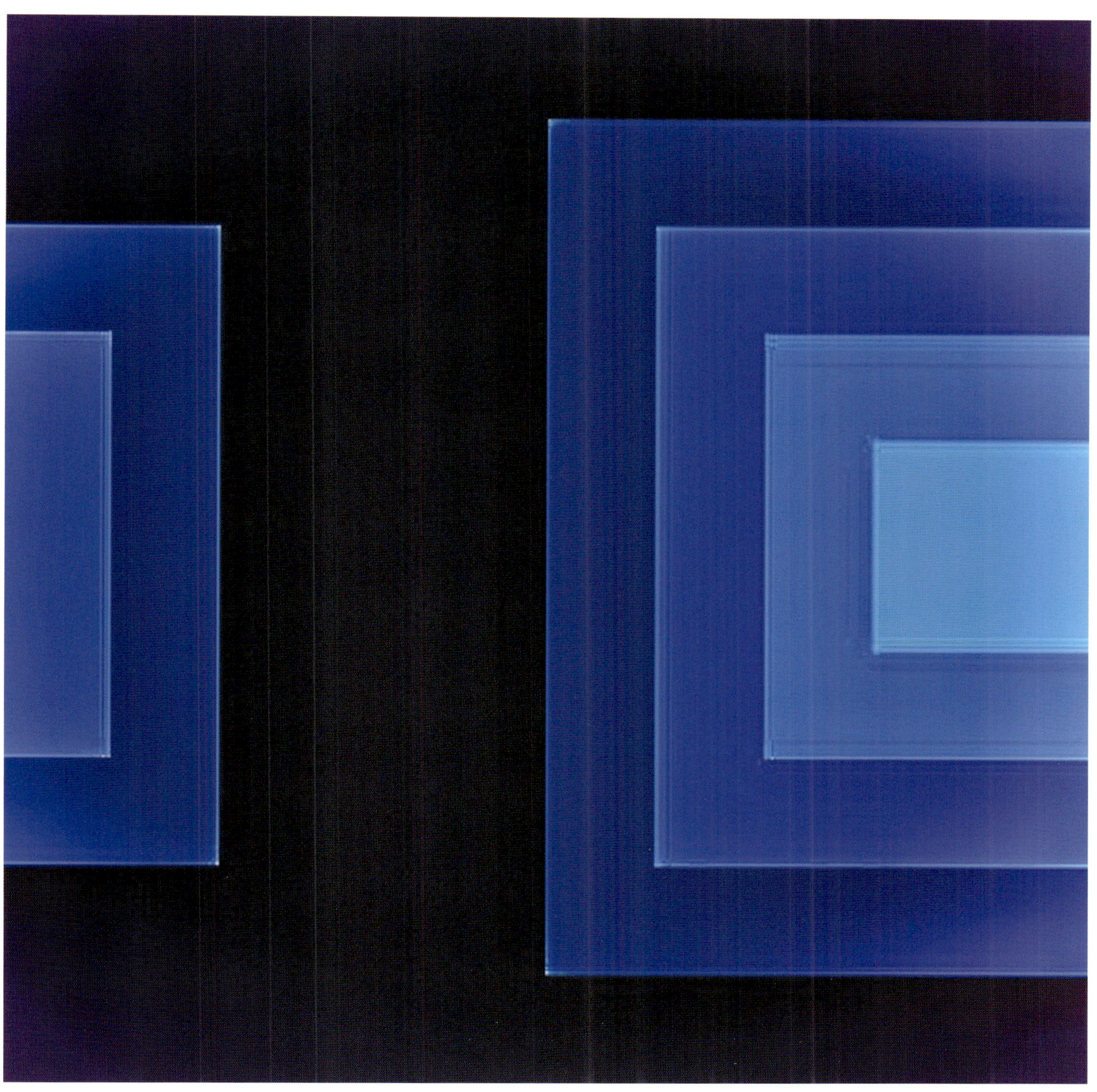

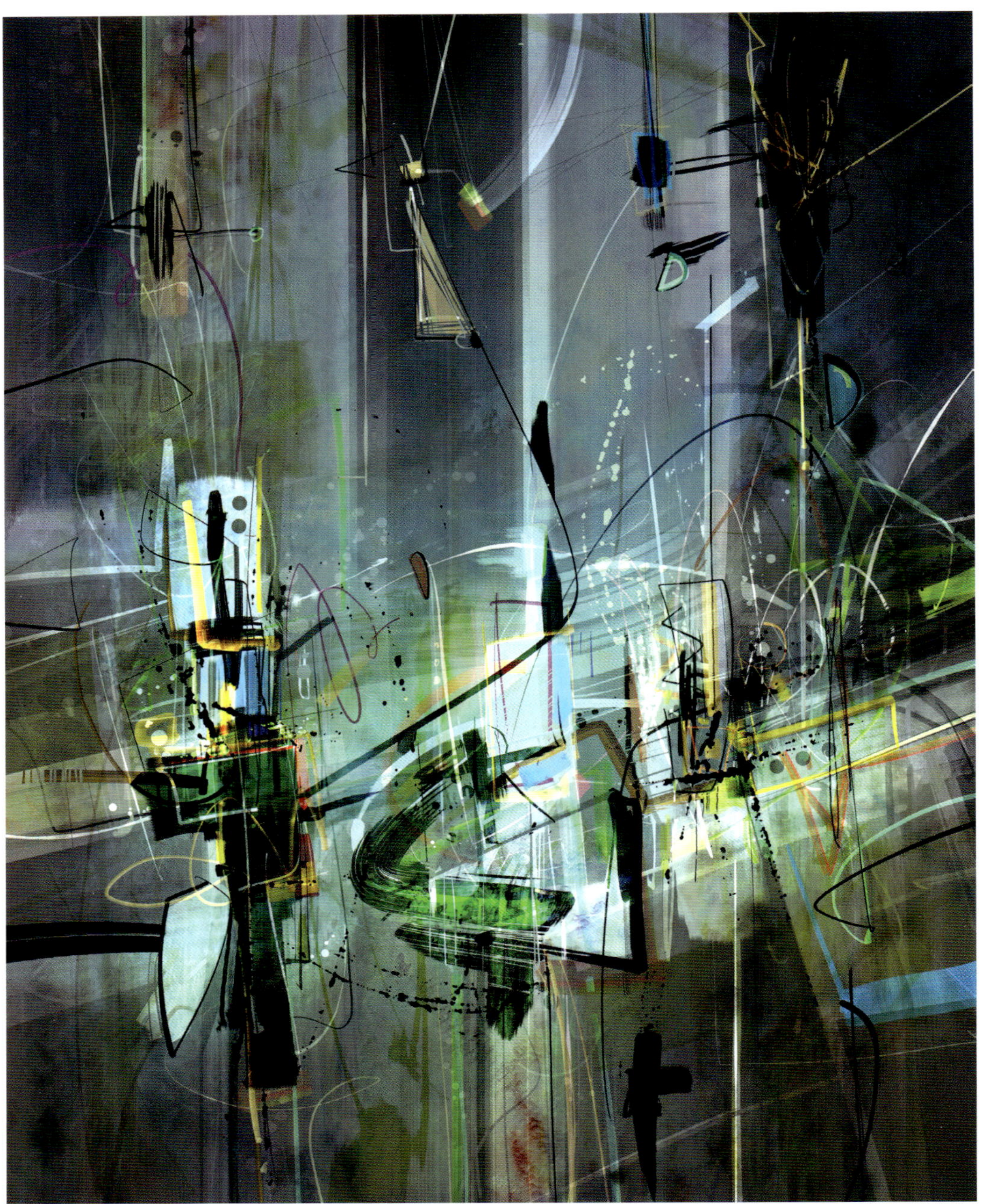

Guillermo Arismendi

Guillermo Arismendi's work is the result of years of searching for his own personal expression. The working process is a permanent dialog with the artwork, allowing them to appear as freely as possible. This process gives Arismendi the opportunity to rescue old memories, hopes and fears, as well as unexpected parts of himself. The artist owes the inspiration for the colors and movements he depicts in his paintings to music and dance. The choreography of colors and lines, the spontaneity in gestures and palettes, all are guided by a nonverbal state of mind. The beauty of mathematics also inspires Arismendi—a sense of accuracy and discipline, acting as a counterpoint to the wildest instincts in the act of creation. No restrictions are in place, only a synergy between chaos and order.

060520 II
Digital
7200 x 9000 px.

artearismendi@gmail
.com
guillermoarismendi.com
@guillermo_arismendi

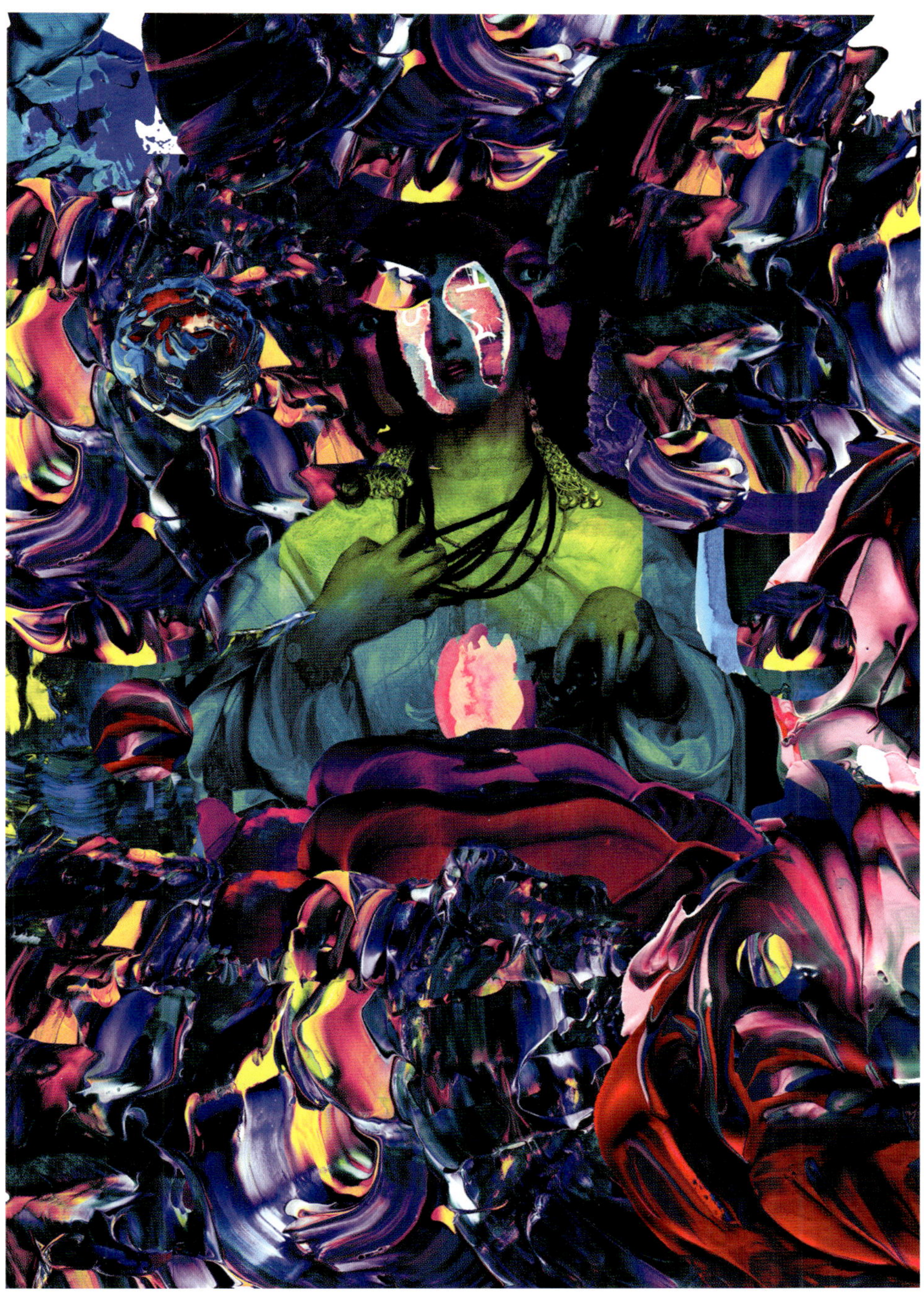

Matt Evans, aka SnowSkull

London-based visual artist SnowSkull is a multifaceted creative who draws inspiration from the mechanism of thought, memories, and the immersion of dreams. His portfolio boasts an array of different mediums, including and spanning contemporary abstract paintings, digital manipulations, music, and video collaborations. SnowSkull creates rich, textured tapestries, brought to life by bold colors and fluid forms and contrasted against stark, atmospheric backgrounds.

Navigating through a technological world, his work pushes the envelope of traditional abstract painting—utilizing a digital medium, employing ambitions, transcending the limits of his imaginative capacities, and investigating the beauty within the sublime. The digital manipulations represent and celebrate a cynosure with a nod to the awareness of the male gaze and to feminine aesthetics.

Oneironaut (2020)
Digital manipulation
23.4 x 16.5 in.

contact@snowskullart
.com
snowskullart.com
@snowskull

DIGITAL

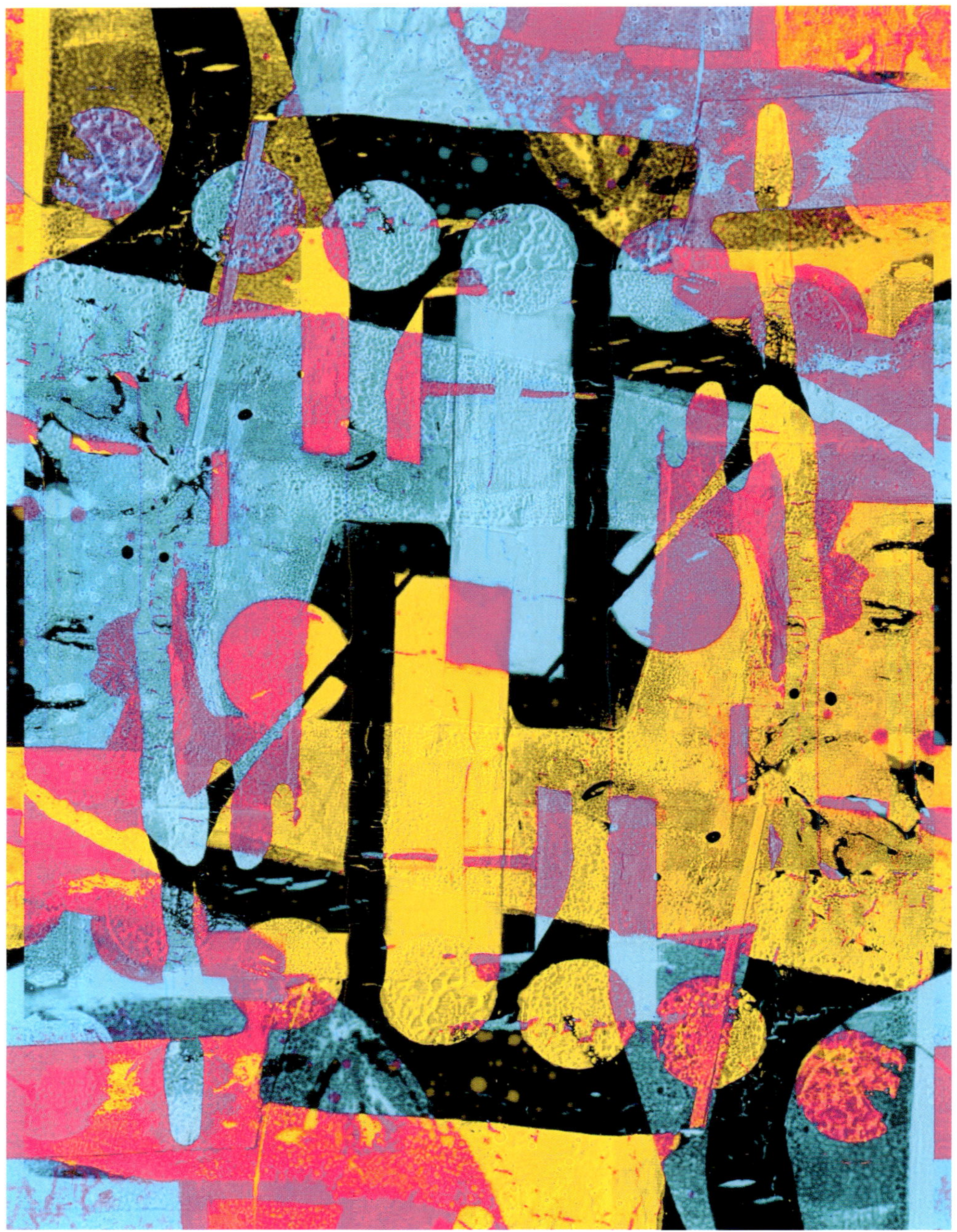

Kat Evans

Kat Evans is an Abstract Pop Expressionist based in the U.K. Her work is subject to the relevance of her surroundings. With a strong passion for art history, Evans is proud of her extensive vintage art book collection, which she dips in and out of for her collages. Evans combines popular culture and art history, using her trademark intuitive mark making and the more exact placement of collage. Evans' art is both balanced and mindful.

Although Evans is educated to a degree level, she feels strongly about how art shapes societies, and she helps bring people from all over the world together for art collaborations.

1983
Digital and mixed media
20 x 16 in.

ktheo2010@gmail.com
katevans.art
@katevansartist19

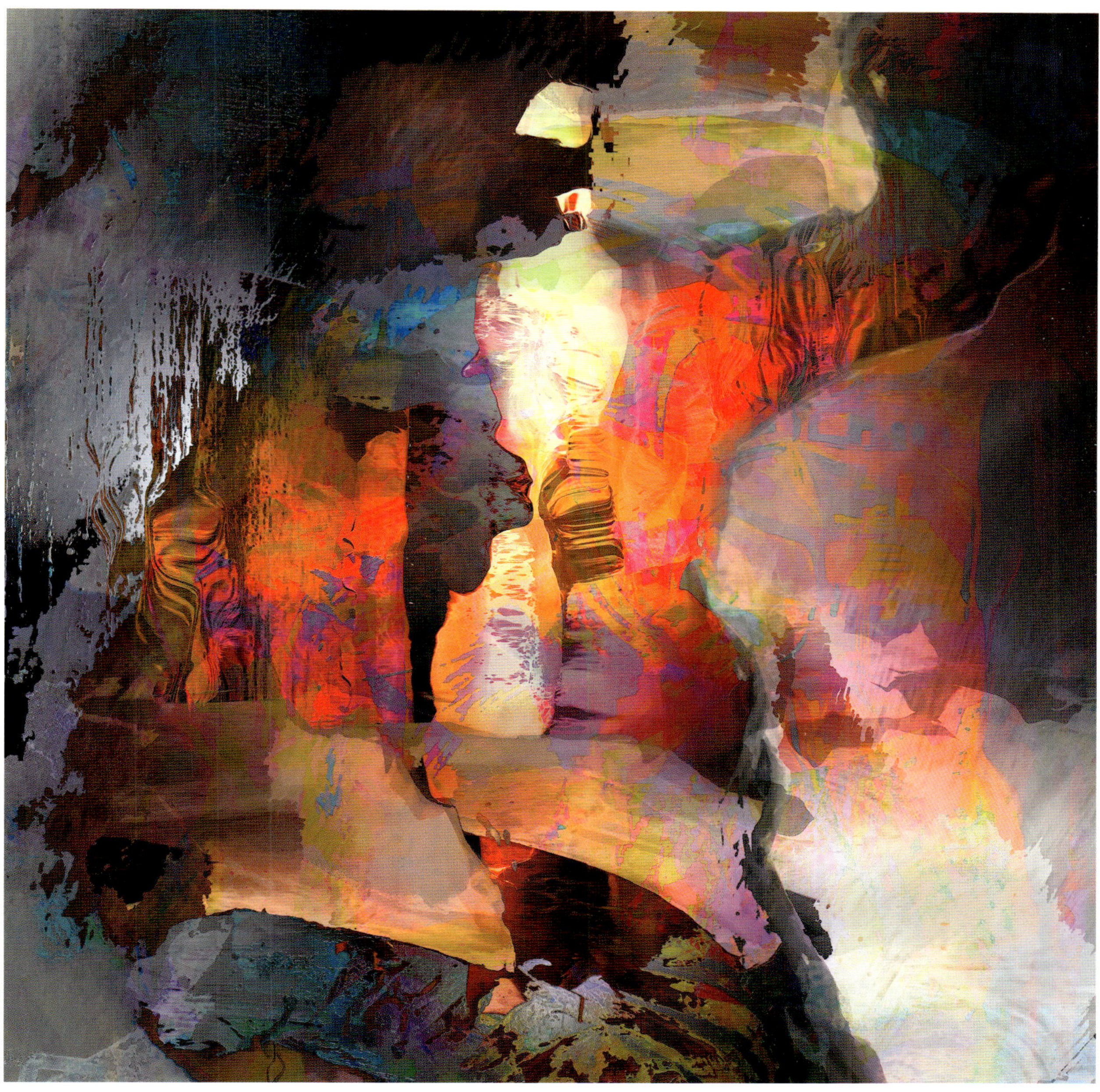

Pierre-Hugues Hétu, aka Puguess

It is impossible to remain indifferent to the art of Pierre-Hugues Hétu, better known as Puguess. He exploits digital art as others exploit painting or wood, but the artist pushes this art to surpass itself, to reach a certain complexity while playing with colors like a conductor his music. The result are works of great abstract maturity, elaborate depth, and complex and detailed ensembles.

Puguess' techniques are unique, both for his creations and for the way he presents his works. The artist constantly evolves, making it his obligation to change his voice, to move in other directions, always questioning his art. This is what allows his work to be expressive and hectic. Puguess' work takes us through several worlds, so different from each other. The artist advocates the abstract for its infinite possibilities to always reinvent itself.

Les lumières de Saint-Génie
Photoshop
39 x 39 in.

puguess@gmail.com
puguess.com
@puguess

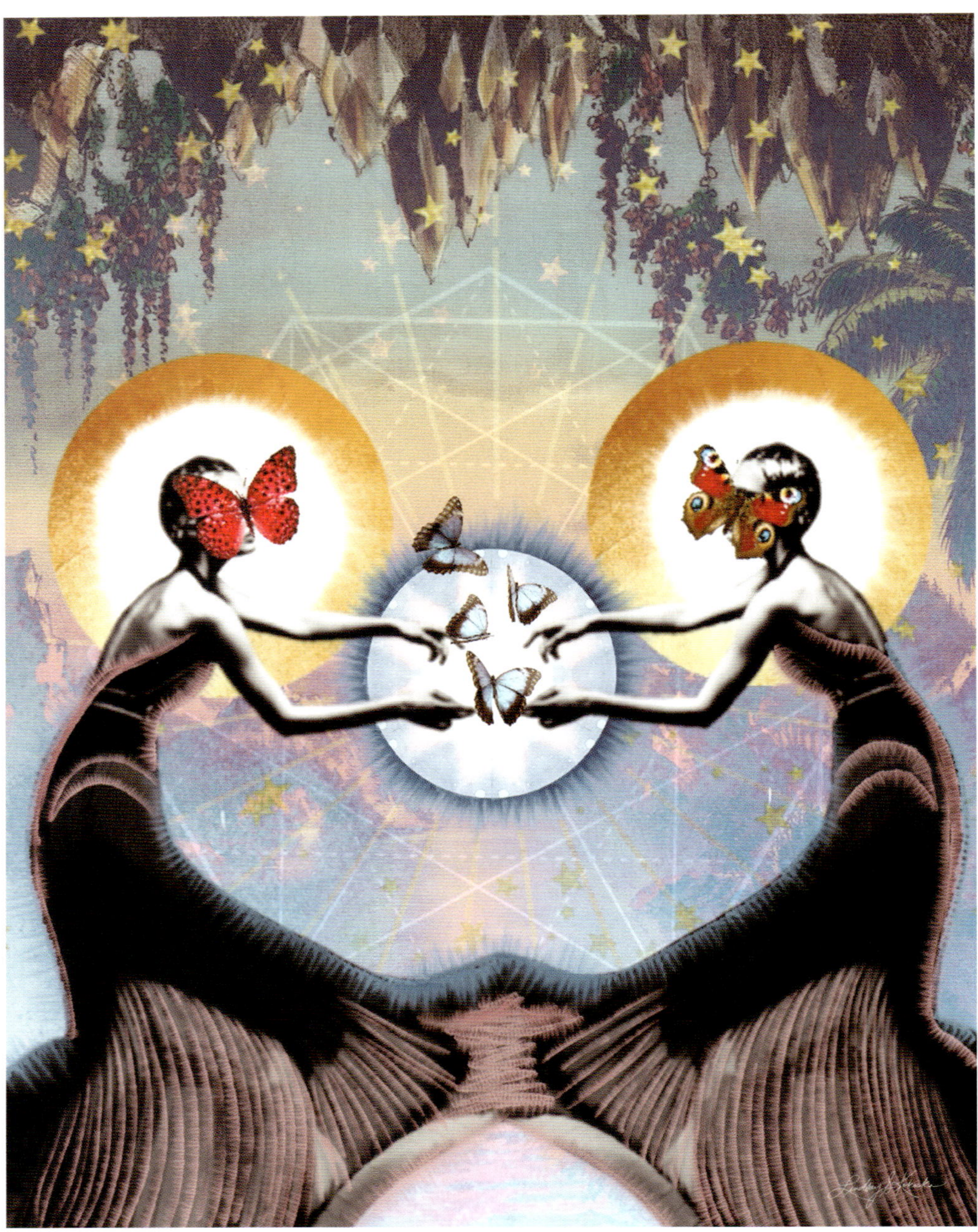

Lindsay Kokoska

As an artist, Lindsay Kokoska draws inspiration from all aspects of her life. Her exploration and development in her yoga practice, which seeks to link the worldly and the transcendent, and her love of travel and culture have allowed her to further her skills and passion in the world of art. Kokoska's art lies between the figurative and surreal worlds and always holds a dreamlike quality to it, with heavy influences of esoteric, spiritual, and mystical connections. When she creates art, she is channeling an energy that guides her, like a clairvoyant receiving a message. The artist loves utilizing sacred geometry, astronomy, nature, patterns, and shapes to create thought-provoking compositions. She feels that her art manifests the power of intuition. Kokoska hopes that her work inspires people to go inward, so they can access a deeper vision and be reminded of the connections between material and spiritual experiences, and see the magic in their lives.

Duality
Mixed media collage, digital painting
30 x 20 in.

linzy.kokoska@gmail.com
@infinite_mantra

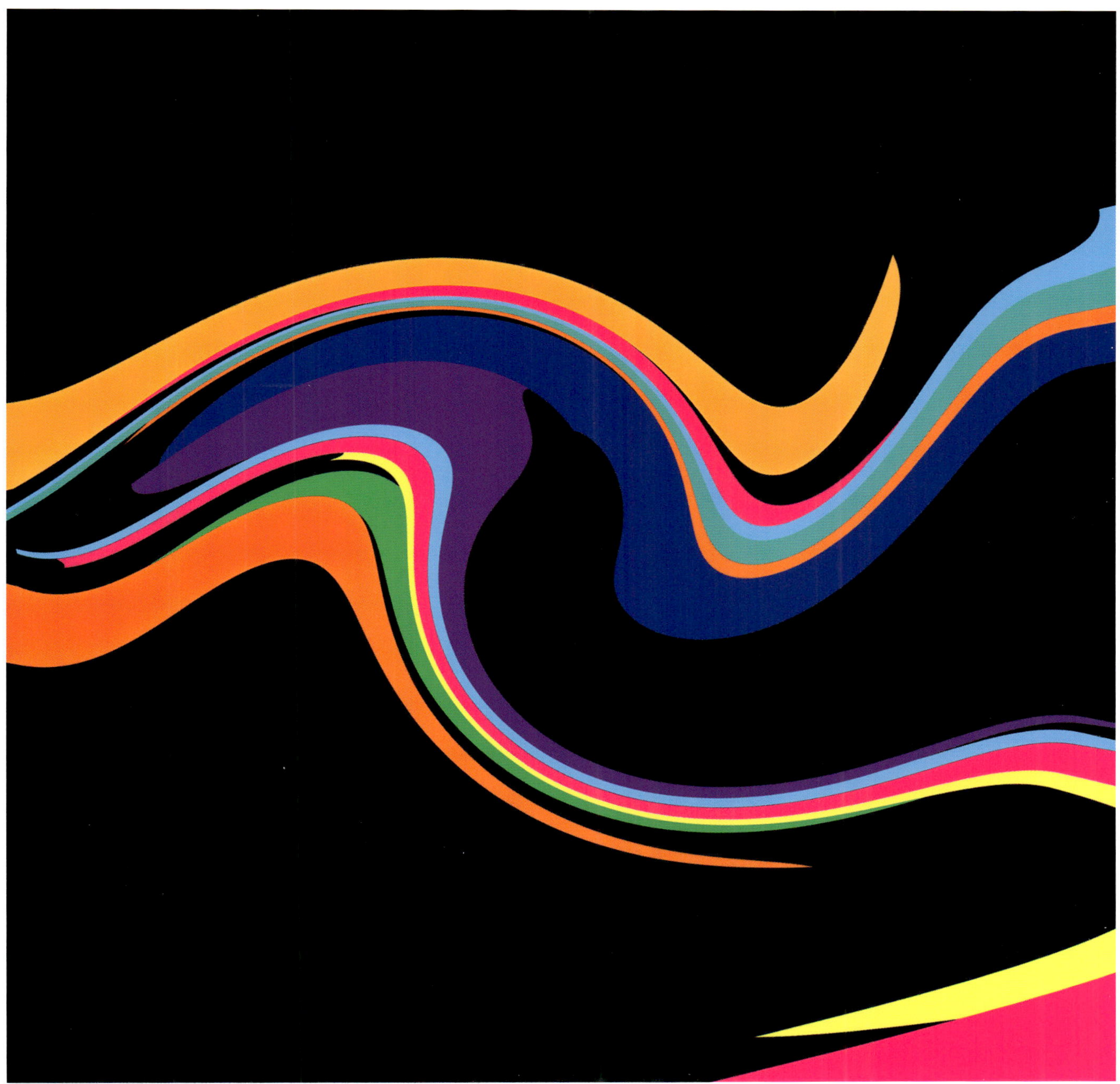

John Charles Maloney
As a digital artist predominantly working with Photoshop and Illustrator, John Charles Maloney's artistic philosophy is about creating happy aesthetics via vibrant colors and abstract shapes and forms. His artworks are about giving the viewer an aesthetically uplifting and up-tempo sensory experience. He usually creates his artwork in sets rather than individual pieces as he likes to explore the infinite possibilities of digital image manipulation software. Part of his creative methodology includes playing music when he is creating his work as this helps his concentration and artistic decision-making, which probably stems from the fact that he is also a musician. Maloney's career as a graphic designer and university lecturer has also influenced his artworks and allowed him to be extremely focused. He also sees his artwork as being versatile in the sense that it can be adapted into many formats, which ultimately makes him happy!

Fluidity Bird 01
Photoshop
12 x 12 in.

johncmaloneydigitalartist
.com
@johncmaloneydigitalartist

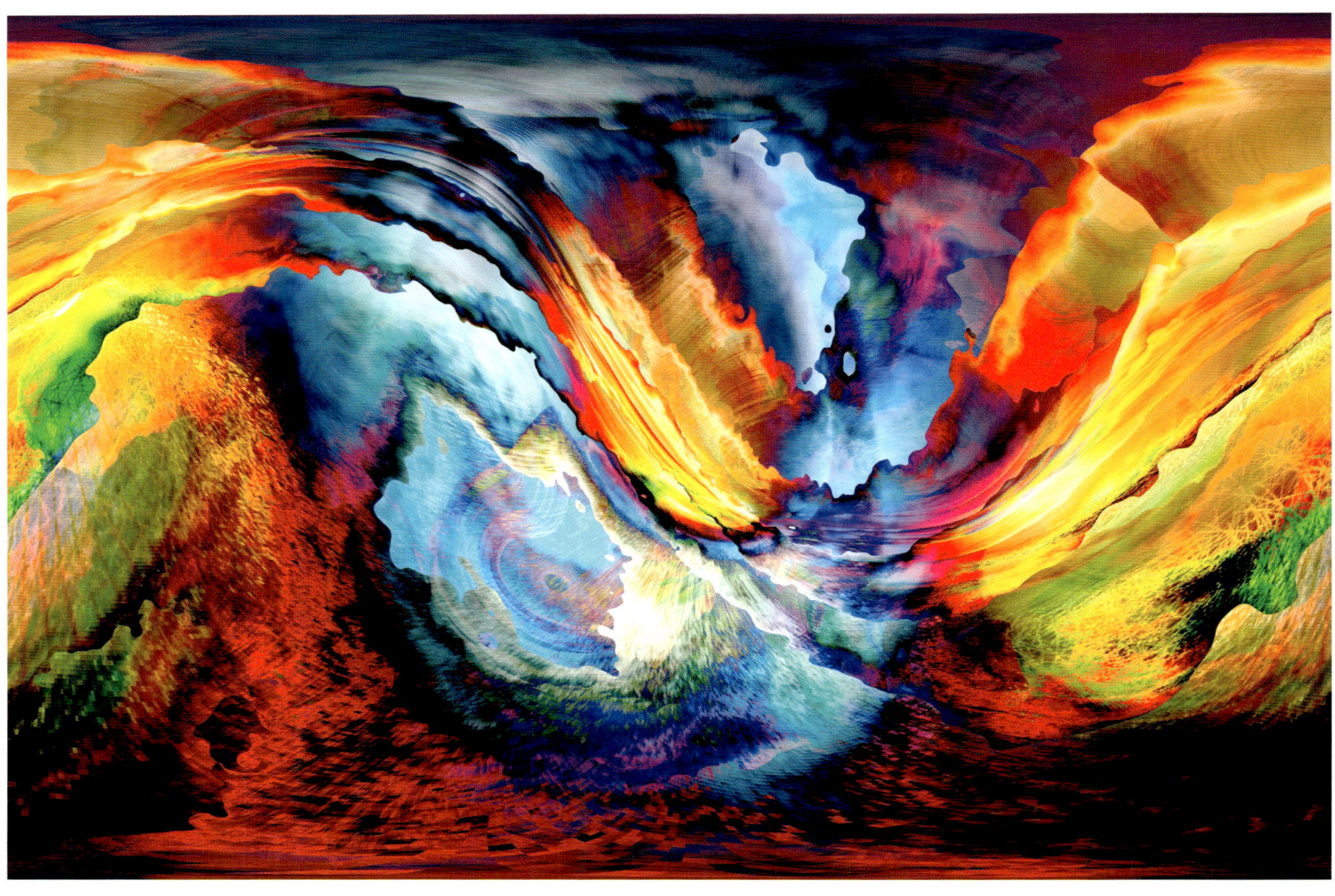

Paul Petersen

Paul Petersen is a digital artist who discovers his compositions within 3-D spherical polyhedrons that he sets up, textures, and manipulates. His creation process is improvisational. He explores the interiors of these spheres with virtual cameras, looking for visuals that resonate with him in the moment. A common theme for the artists is finding order in what first appears chaotic.

Petersen begins each work without intention and never knows in advance what subject matter will emerge. Surprise and discovery keep him enthused about finding and placing meaning in his abstractions. He thinks a part of himself comes through with the tortured geometry, in the same way that seeing something in a cloud or recognizing something in a Rorschach test inkblot reveals a part of one's psychology.

Technique aside, Petersen tries to create abstractions that have a unique kind of order, that are evocative, and that resonate with some part of him, and hopefully others as well.

Fire Playing With Fire
Digital
1200 x 1800 px.

paul@paulpetersen.net
sphericalart.com
@sphericalart

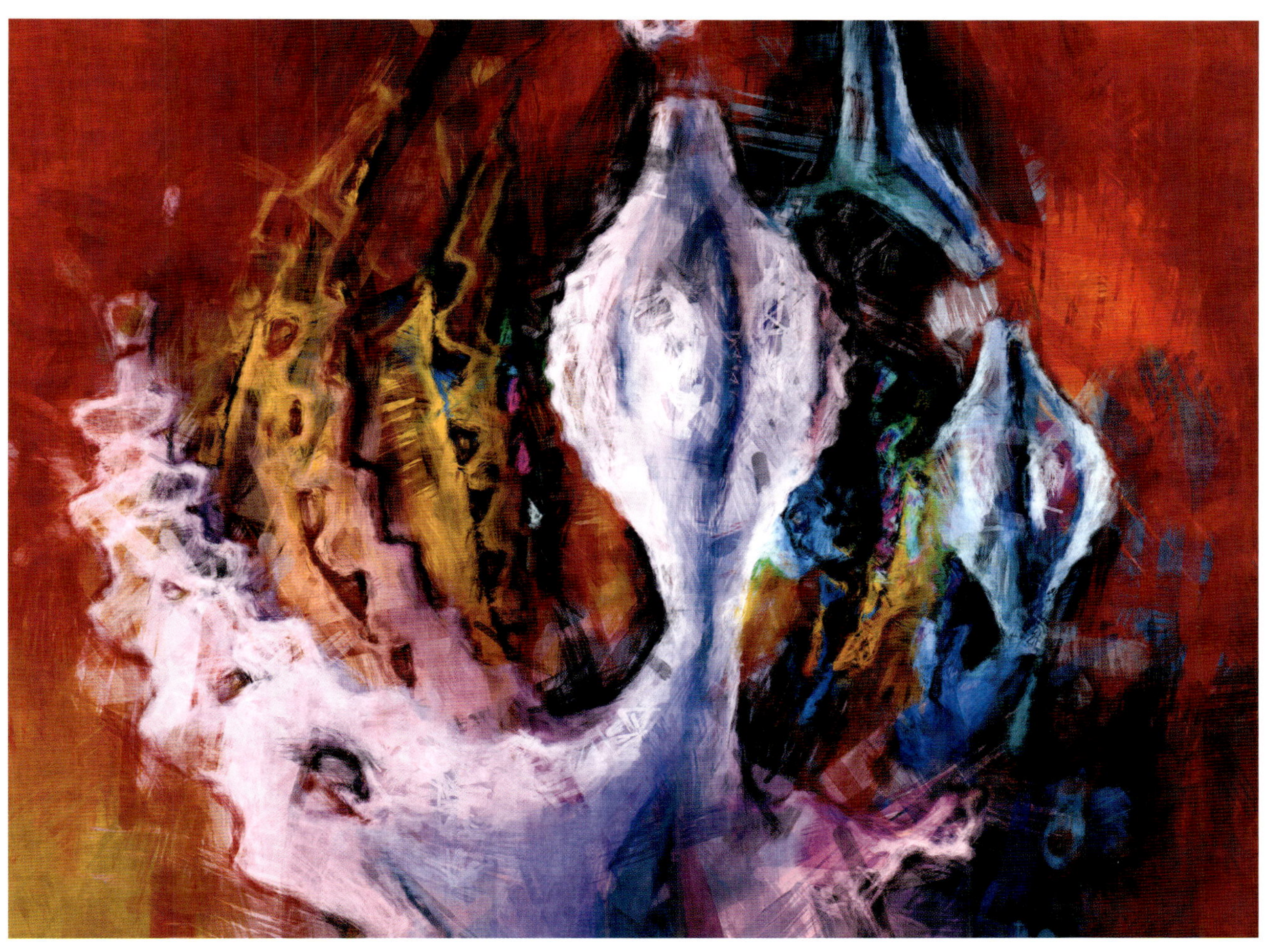

Michael Pierre Price

Michael Pierre Price's creativity has always been an internal partnership between the artist's mind, heart, and spirit. His educational background is in math, physics, and astronomy. Mathematics and physics are both the language and framework of creation, and as an artist, Price has the unique perspective of being able to speak and understand that language, which is reflected in his work. It is the primary reason he chose to become a digital artist— to create virtually and then make the imaginary real. Price also has a keen interest in neuroscience, dreams, and Buddhist teachings. His artwork is a fusion of all these things, which he continually refines. It is an expression of the sacred beauty he sees in the fractal qualities of the universe, reflected in everything from quantum mechanics to cosmology, from chaos theory to the very life that exists all around us and within us.

Taking Flight
Digital archival pigment print
18 x 24 in.

michael@
michaelpierreprice.com
michaelpierreprice.com
@mpp_digital_art

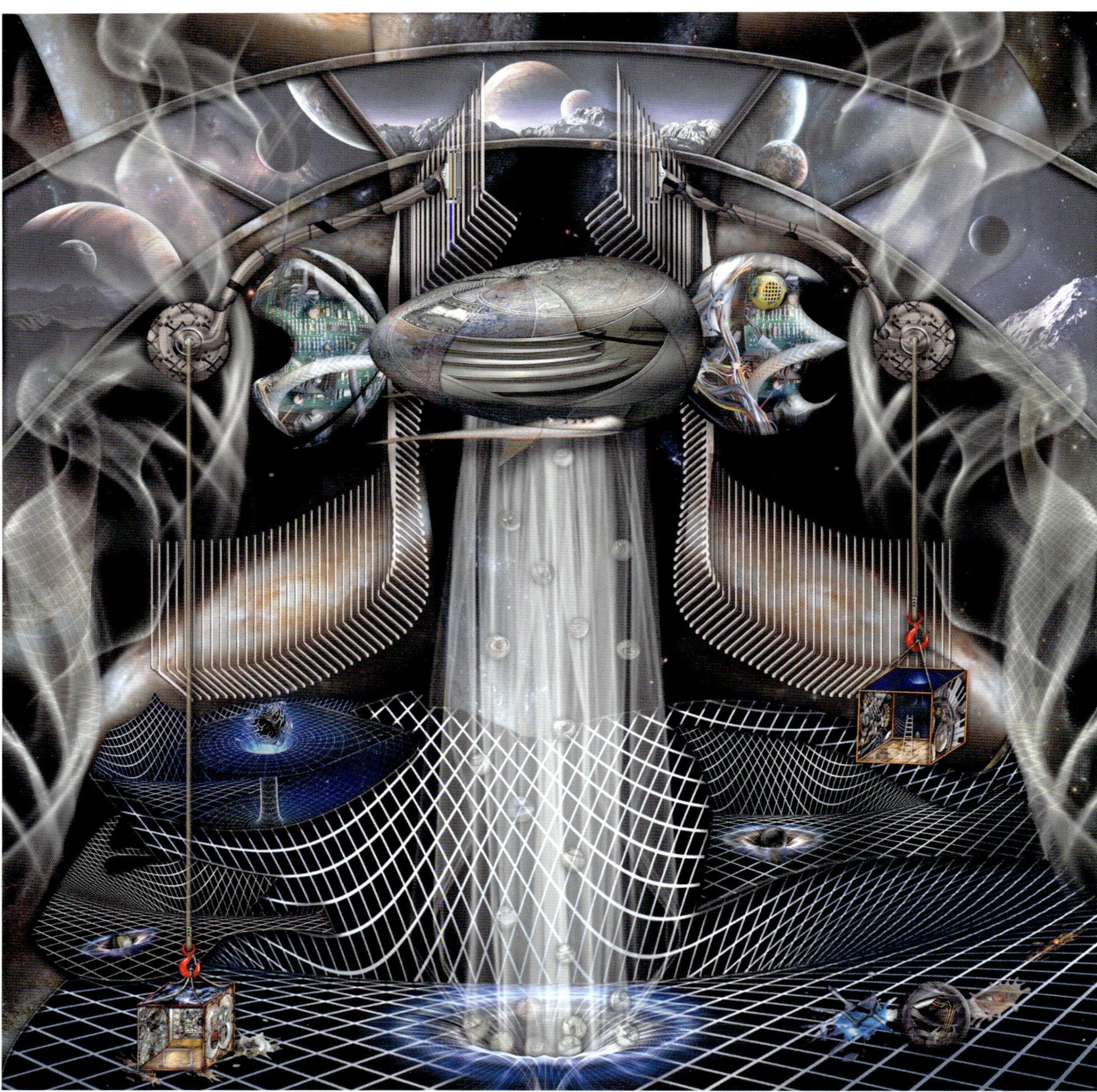

Ramon Rivas

To define the art of Ramon Rivas one has to incorporate his family, profession, experiences, and as he states: "the figure of the invisible, nonhuman witness, who receives information through multiple channels. This figure retains all of this to be processed by a brain that promotes creativity, novelty, surprise, imagination, and freshness to art." Rivas' work gives freedom to material and immaterial elements so that they participate on equal terms, as if they were people. Materials and mathematical or physical expressions participate in functions and feelings typical of human relationships. A conceptual balance is established between nonhuman elements: the strong and the weak, equality, empathy, or reassignment of roles. The artist's works show a balance between the basic elements, such as composition, textures, and colors, and above all, the creation of an energetic current that circulates throughout the work, between the material, immaterial, and human elements, which are projected outwards, enveloping themselves with the energy of the observer.

Experiential Spawning in the Multiverse
Digital
2000 x 2000 px.

ramonrivas2012@yahoo.es
rivismo.com
@ramonrivas_rivismo

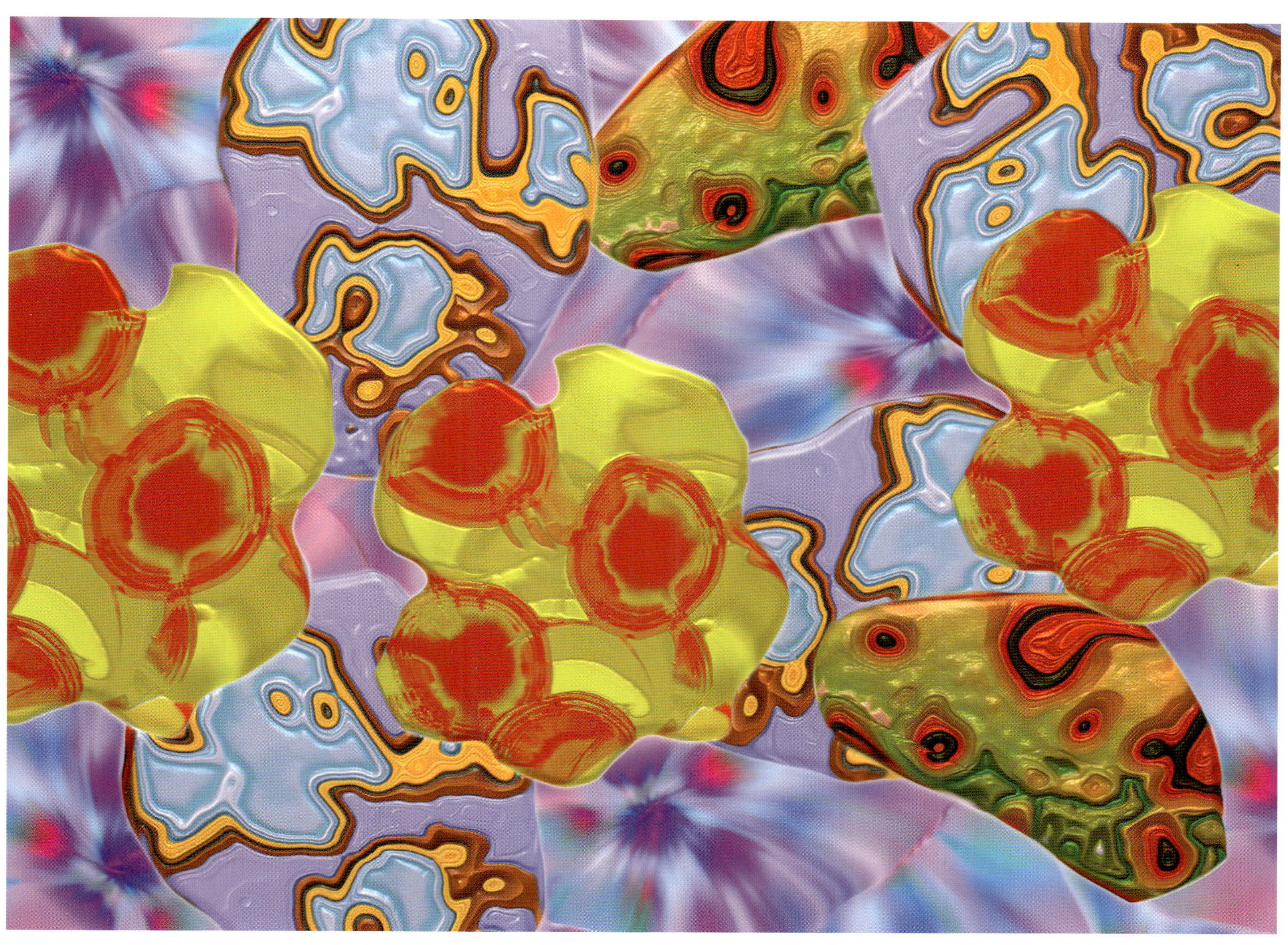

Robin Roy

Robin Roy has been a painter for forty-five years in traditional mediums. He currently works exclusively in the digital medium because he has more freedom to express himself. Roy is a romantic painter. All his work is about the single-minded pursuit of beauty. His work is seductive, sumptuous, and exotic, portraying a transcendent sense of the sublime, of joy, bliss, and ecstasy. Roy's work is the art of pure sensation. The work is abstract because it's universal, yet not self-contained or self-referential. Rather, it occupies the space between poetry and painting. Through visual and poetic metaphor, Roy considers each element in the painter's toolbox in isolation to achieve a form of compounding of painterly expression. He makes a conscious choice to emphasize the expressive power of shape and often repeats the form in a given work. He finds that repeating the same form creates a visual rhythm similar to music. It creates a harmony of elements within the work where one part is echoed in another.

Untitled
Dye Sublimation
process on ChromaLuxe
aluminum
30 x 40 in.

opinions@runbox.com
robinroyart.com
@robinroy1

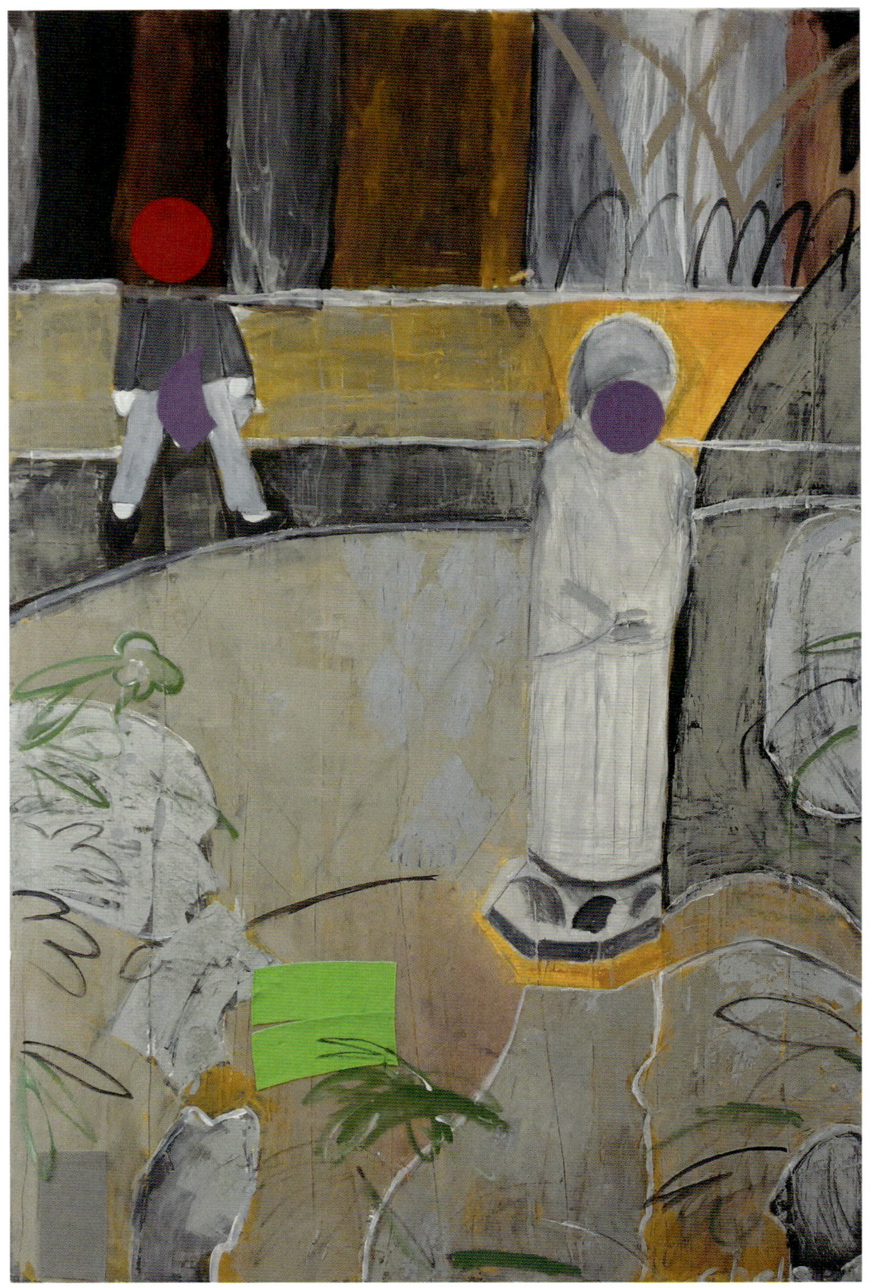

Robert Solomon

Robert Solomon's process, or technique, is successful if he follows these basic steps: First, photograph something of interest that has the potential for figure/ground relationships. Second, try to sketch the photograph as a guide for painting abstractly. Third, try to find something in the photograph that can be used as an organizing element, such as the foreground, the sky, or the shadows. Solomon then chooses a palette and balances drawing with painting. "I'm not about trying to be contemporary or relevant since I am contemporary, and I exist in society. I trust my nature to paint both masculine and feminine, so identity is not an issue for me. I have succeeded, over time, to leave the ego outside the studio, and this is the most important factor when I paint," Solomon says. Painting, like performing in front of a large audience, requires the artist to give themselves over to the act of being present and acting most intuitively.

27th St. (Chelsea, NY)
Acrylic, oil, collage
60 x 40 in.

OPPOSITE
Country Roads Full Moon
Acrylic, oil, collage
60 x 36 in.

r.rmsolo@verizon.net
robertmsolomon.com
@rmsolomon444

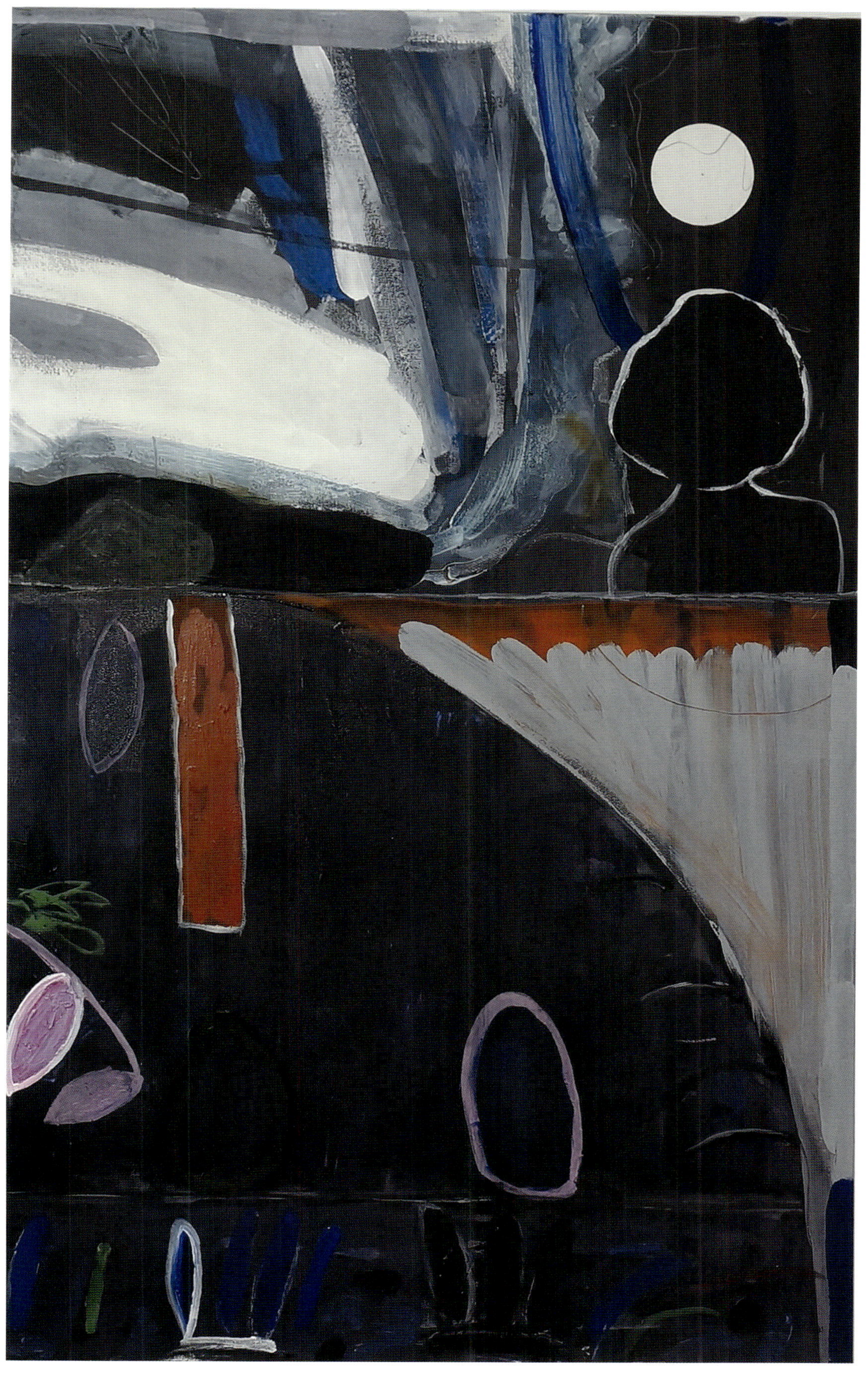

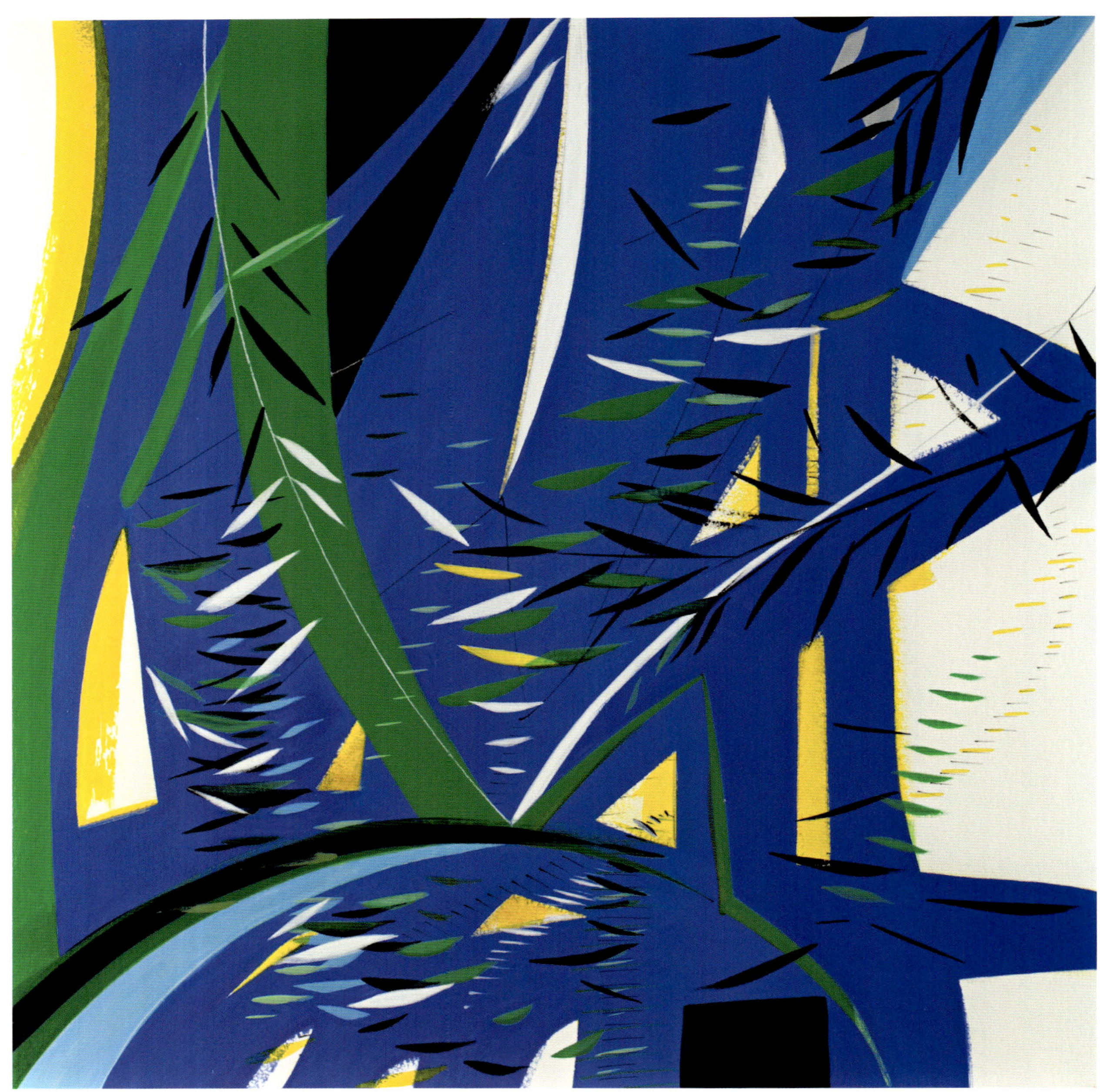

Carita Schmidt

Carita Schmidt's insights on cultural and natural landscapes have been shaped by her time living and working in Helsinki, Stockholm, Kavala, Athens, and now Berlin, where she currently resides. The diversity of structures, merging lines, and different light qualities define her work. Schmidt has developed a mark-making technique that combines drawing, painting, and playing with gesture as a way to express movement beyond borders. The question of renegotiating the notion of borders, as a choice to communicate between different areas and nations, fascinates her. "I am interested in a movement that does not stop or allow itself to be limited," Schmidt says.

The essence of her work is related to connectivity and movement. She accomplishes this sometimes with subtle abstract drawings, sometimes with energetic brushstrokes. She is always searching for a vibrant expression, making her work recognizable. nature.

Hommage to Robert Indiana with Blue
Mixed media
19.6 x 19.6 in.

OPPOSITE
Dream Builder (Garden)
Mixed media
47 x 35 in.

caritaschmidt@gmail
.com
caritaschmidt.com
@caritaschmidt_painter

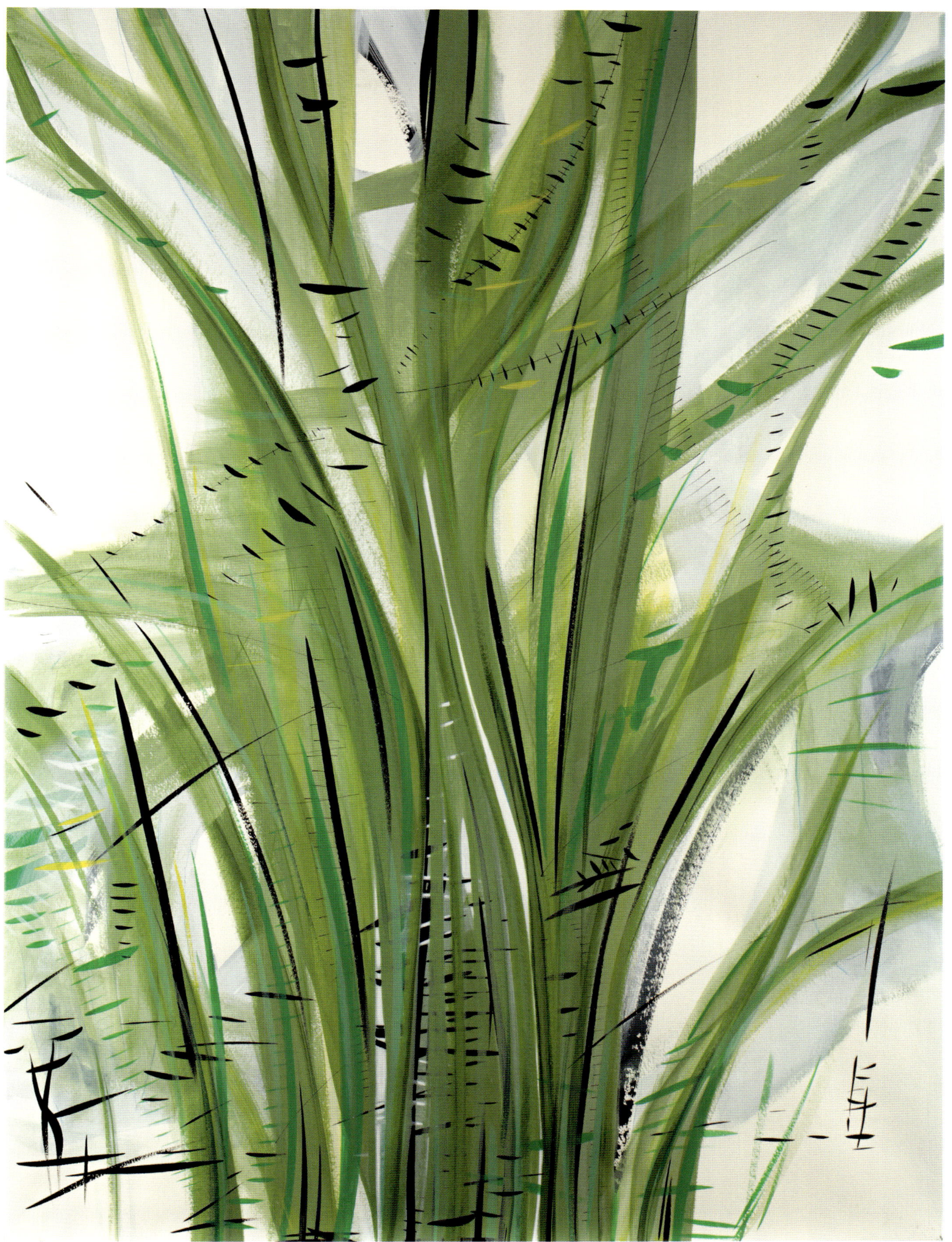

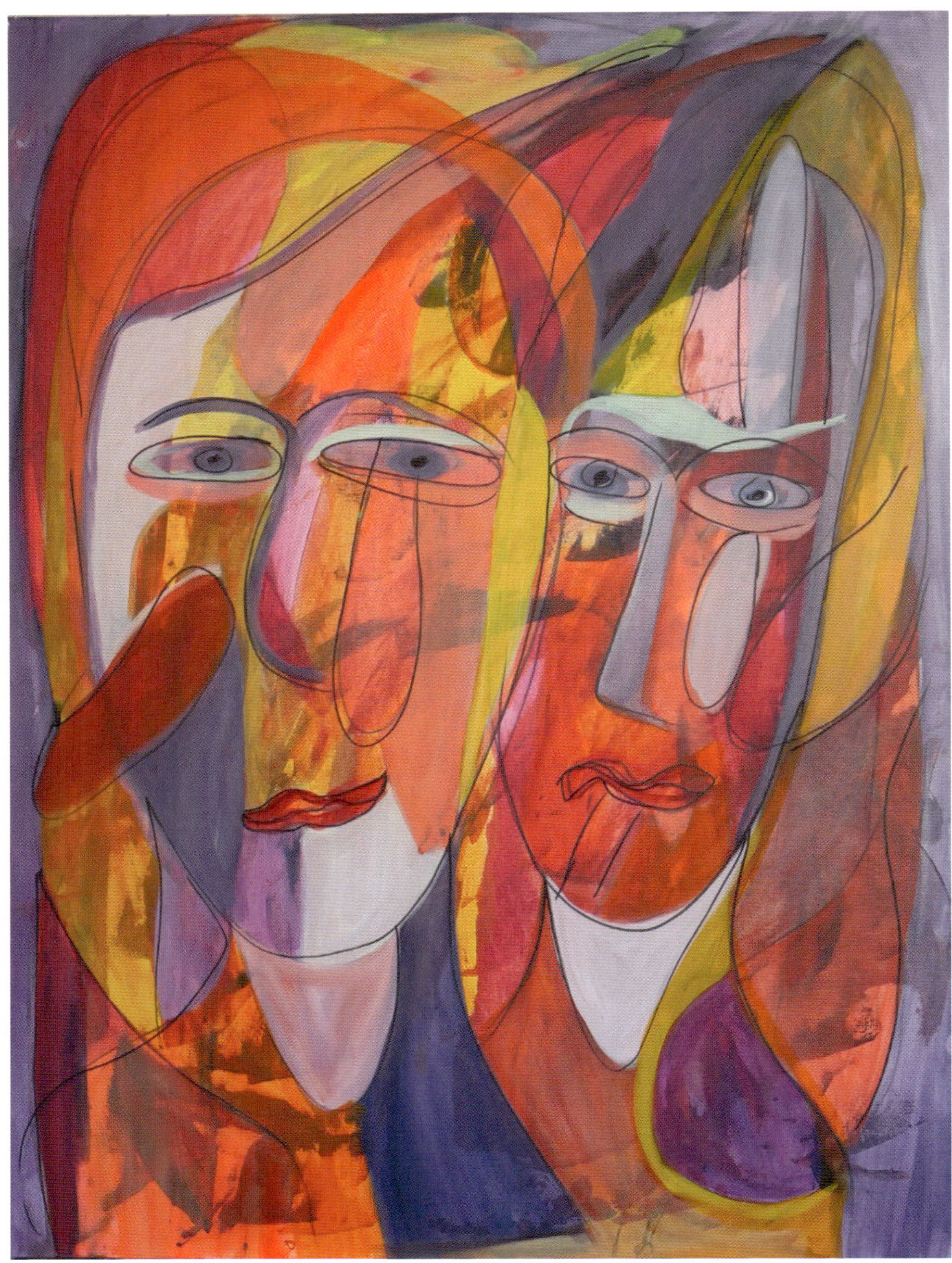

John Bacon

Being an avid collector of abstract art since the early 1990s eventually led John Bacon to create his own abstract works, which are largely nonrepresentational. His paintings are characterized by a distinctive use of color and form that make for a unique style. Always seeking to develop new techniques and colors has led to a large variety in his work. The process of creating his work is largely intuitive, without pre-determined plans. The paintings proceed from beginning to end by letting the canvas speak and show the way. This leads to a style that is totally uninhibited and presents infinite possibilities. "Art is not only visual but also emotional. It is meant to be felt as much as seen," Bacon says. "In abstract painting you see with your mind instead of your eyes. I hope to have the viewer feel first then see."

Sadness
Acrylic
48 x 36 in.

johnwb67@gmail.com
@BaconModern

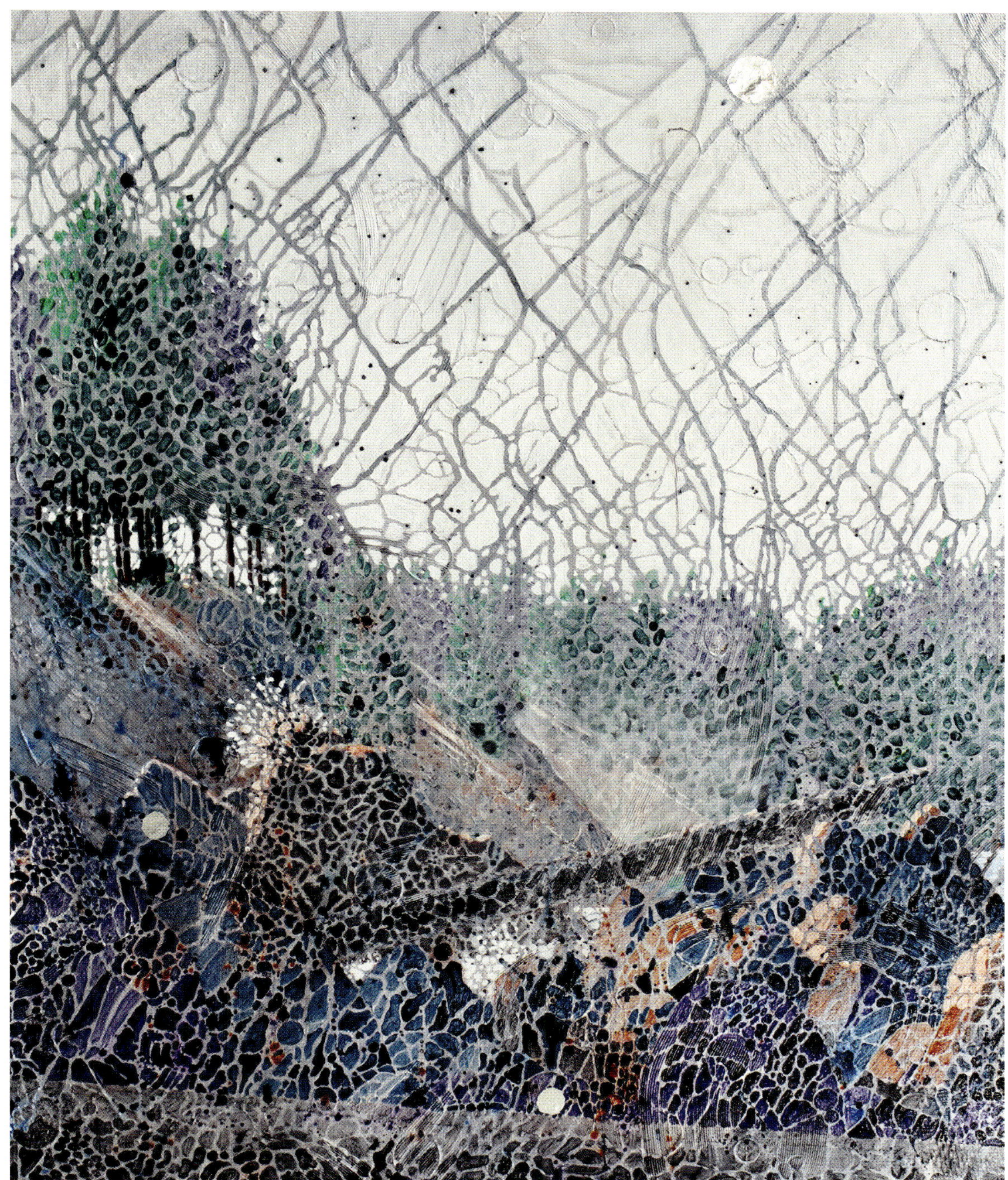

Karen Blanchet

"Occasionally we observe a certain futility in our human desire for control. Cracks in cement sporting lovely yellow blossoms indicate a natural determination to challenge the neat and tidy according to human parameters," Karen Blanchet says. The artist's work focuses on accidental organic forms as they collide with geometrical shapes. Plastic netting, metal patches, wire weaving through pollution, the work speaks to the overexploitation and the general damage humanity wreaks upon the planet. The titles of her works question the status quo and seek to inspire a desire for balance or, at the very least, a pause for reflection on where we might be headed. The work asks: Is cooperation better than control?

Evolution
Mixed media
36 x 30 in.

blanchet.fine.arts@gmail.com
karenblanchet.ca
@blanchetfinearts

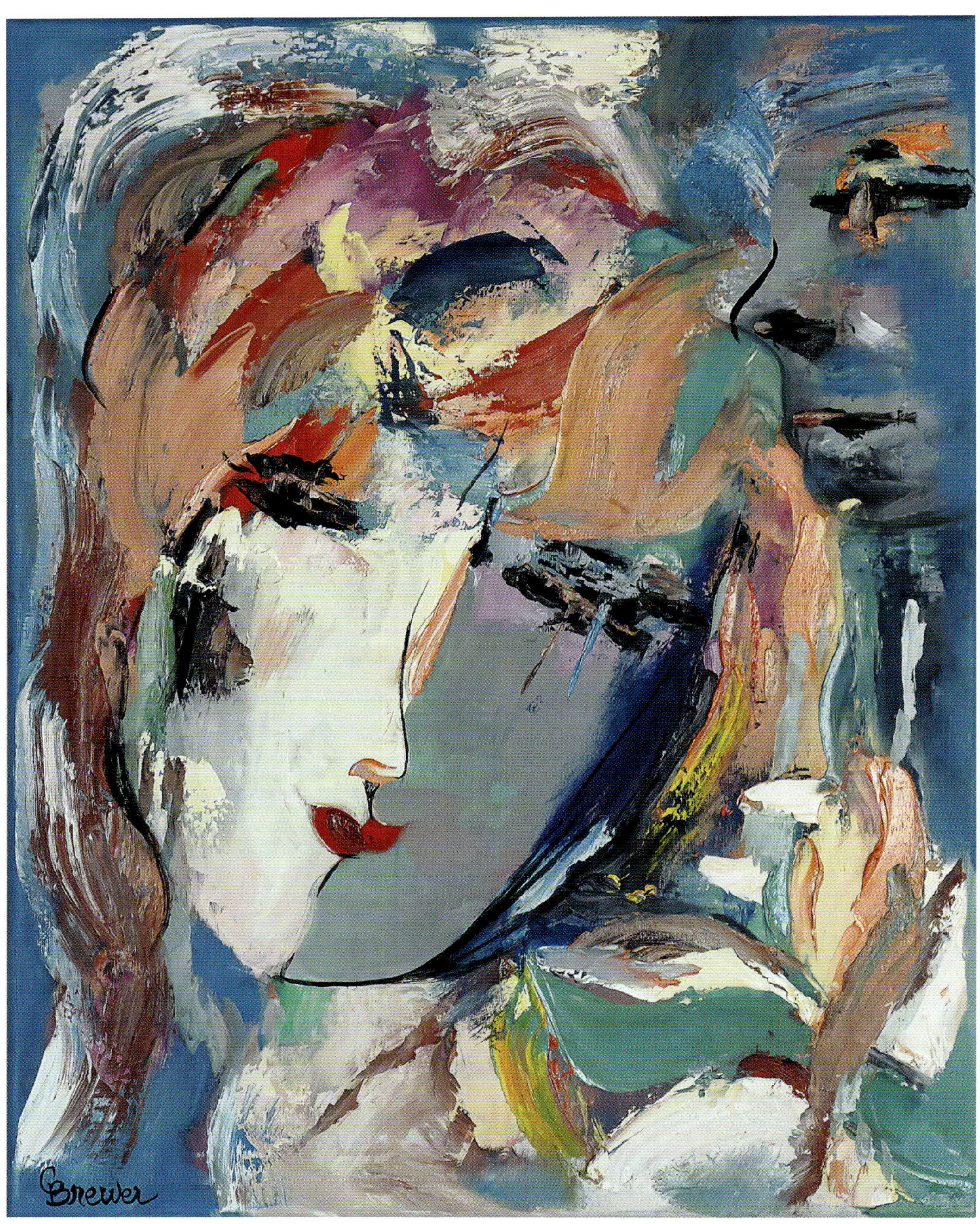

Cindy Brewer

Painting for Cindy Brewer is a joy and therapy, a creative process for expressing her inner being. Besides personal expression, evoking a feeling in others through her painting is something the artist finds tremendously rewarding. Painting abstracts offers Brewer the most freedom, whether it's nonobjective, expressionism, or representational. Her paintings evolve and emerge through many layers of paint. She achieves a three-dimensional effect by experimenting with additives, papers, and various mediums. Color, texture, the interplay with light, and the spatial relationship on the canvas create interesting work that is often unexpected and surprisingly revealing. Each painting represents one of the many cycles Brewer has experienced in the daily joys and struggles of life. Painting is a blessing and opportunity to share her inner feelings and thoughts with others.

Two Faces
Oil
20 X 16 in.

cabrewer58@yahoo.com
@cindybrewer1

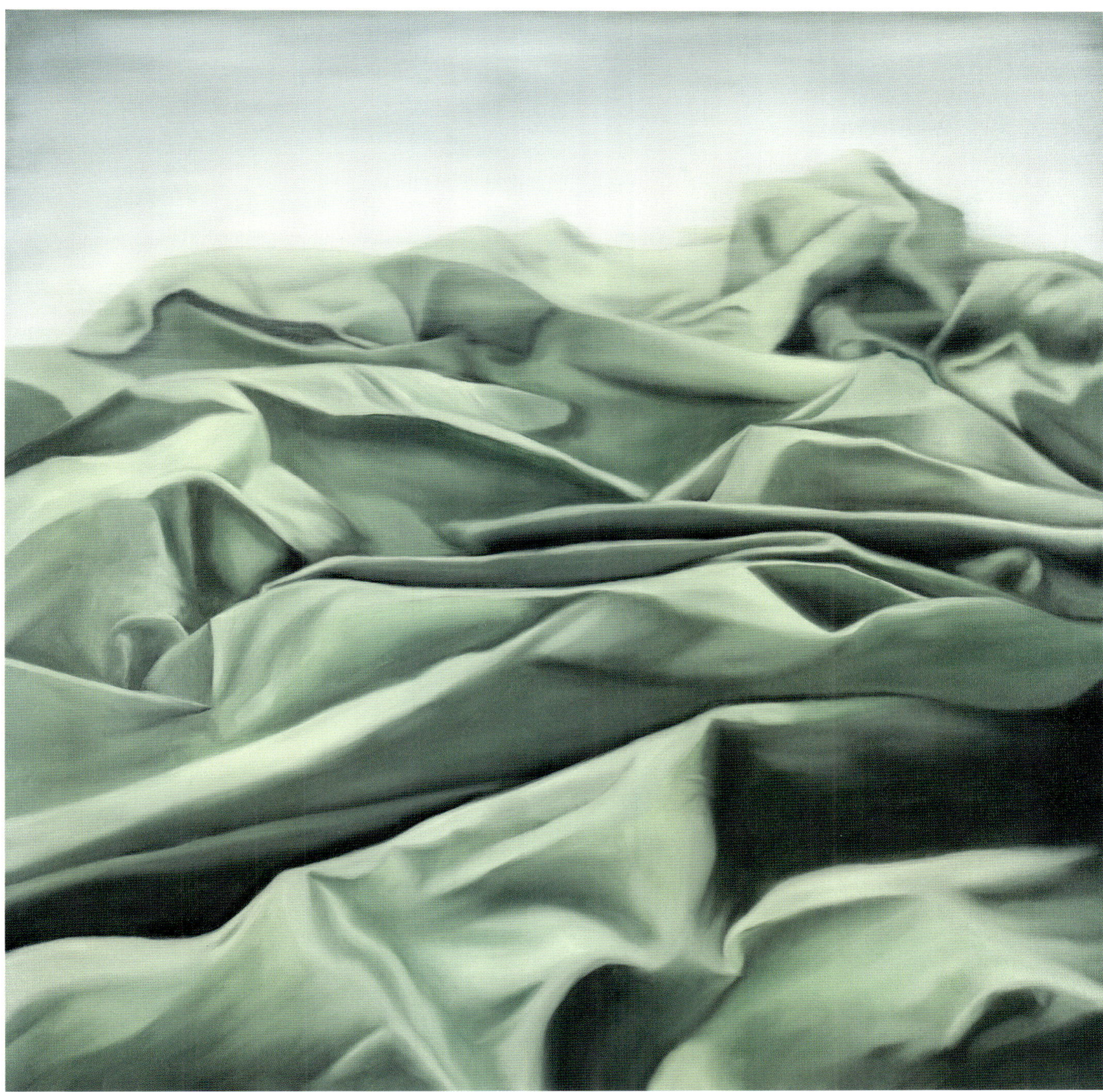

Shelly Detton

Shelly Detton's work challenges the preconceived notions of reality as it relates to time and space. What we perceive as real is limited by our perspective, our background, our beliefs. In her paintings, Detton tries to convey a sense of ambiguity to encourage the viewer to look deeper, to look beyond first impressions of what one originally labels as the subject matter. What comes to mind upon further reflection into a piece will vary with each person, as we all have different backgrounds and experiences from which to draw our conclusions. No single person's version of reality is absolute, and no view is perfectly defined in any given time frame. Even in the apparent concreteness of the present, there are folds and ridges, shadows and light, simplicity and complexity. Nothing should be taken at face value because there are infinite elements at play beyond the surface

Enigmatic Landscape
Oil
36 x 36 in.

cobalt_sm@hotmail.com
shelleydetton.com/
abstractworks
@shelleydetton

PAINTING: TRADITIONAL/CONTEMPORARY

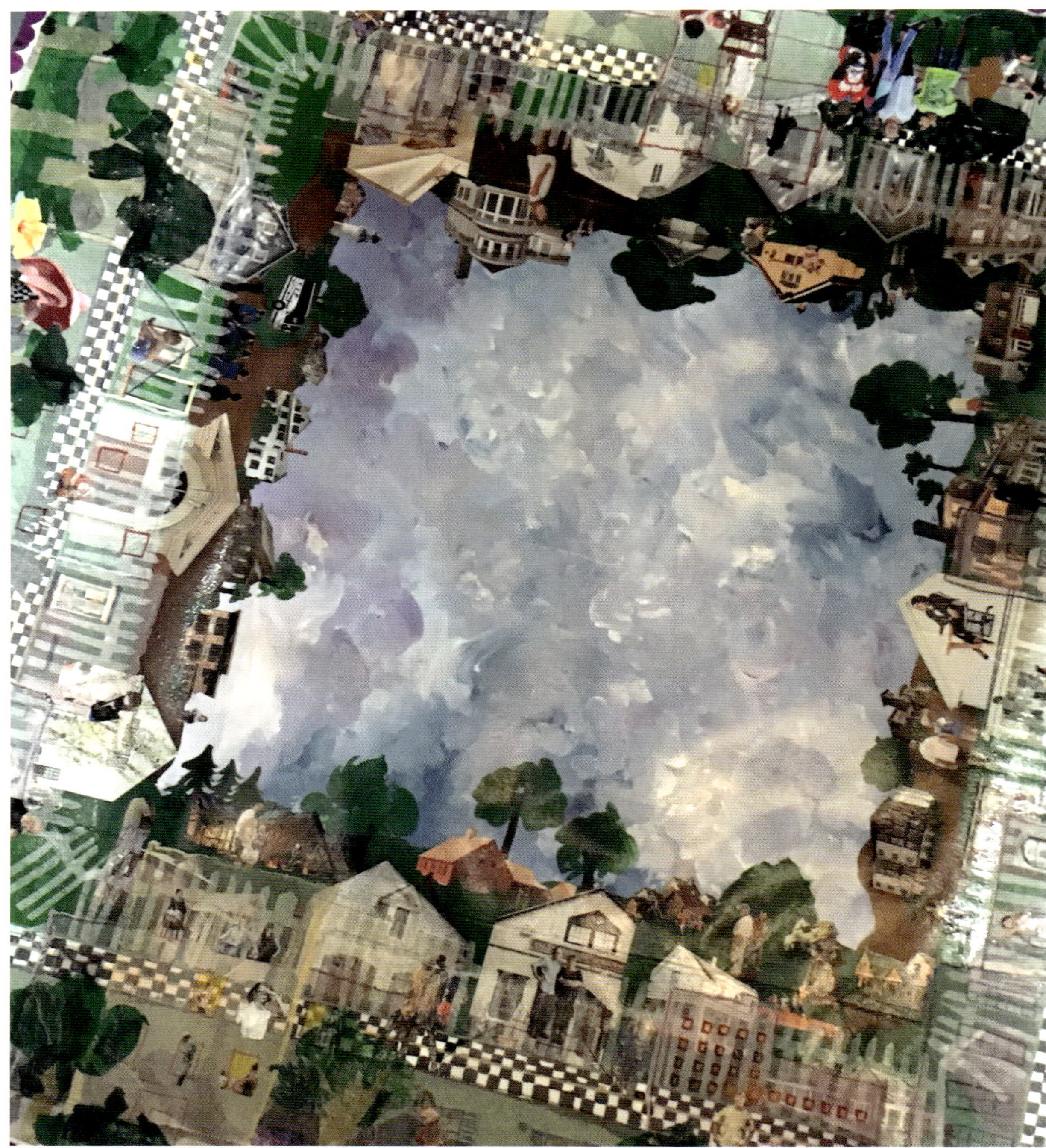

Mary Lynn Engel

Mary Lynn Engel loves to combine multiple ingredients to see what happens, whether she is baking a cake, preparing a dinner for company, or creating art. Her media of choice is the floorcloth, a canvas-backed floor covering used since Revolutionary times. Floorcloth gives Engel the opportunity to create practical custom pieces by combining paint, fabric, paper, ribbon, photographs, and even neckties. The result is a high-quality, handcrafted piece.

My Town
Mixed media
5 x 5 ft.

mld@engel.net
designbymle.com

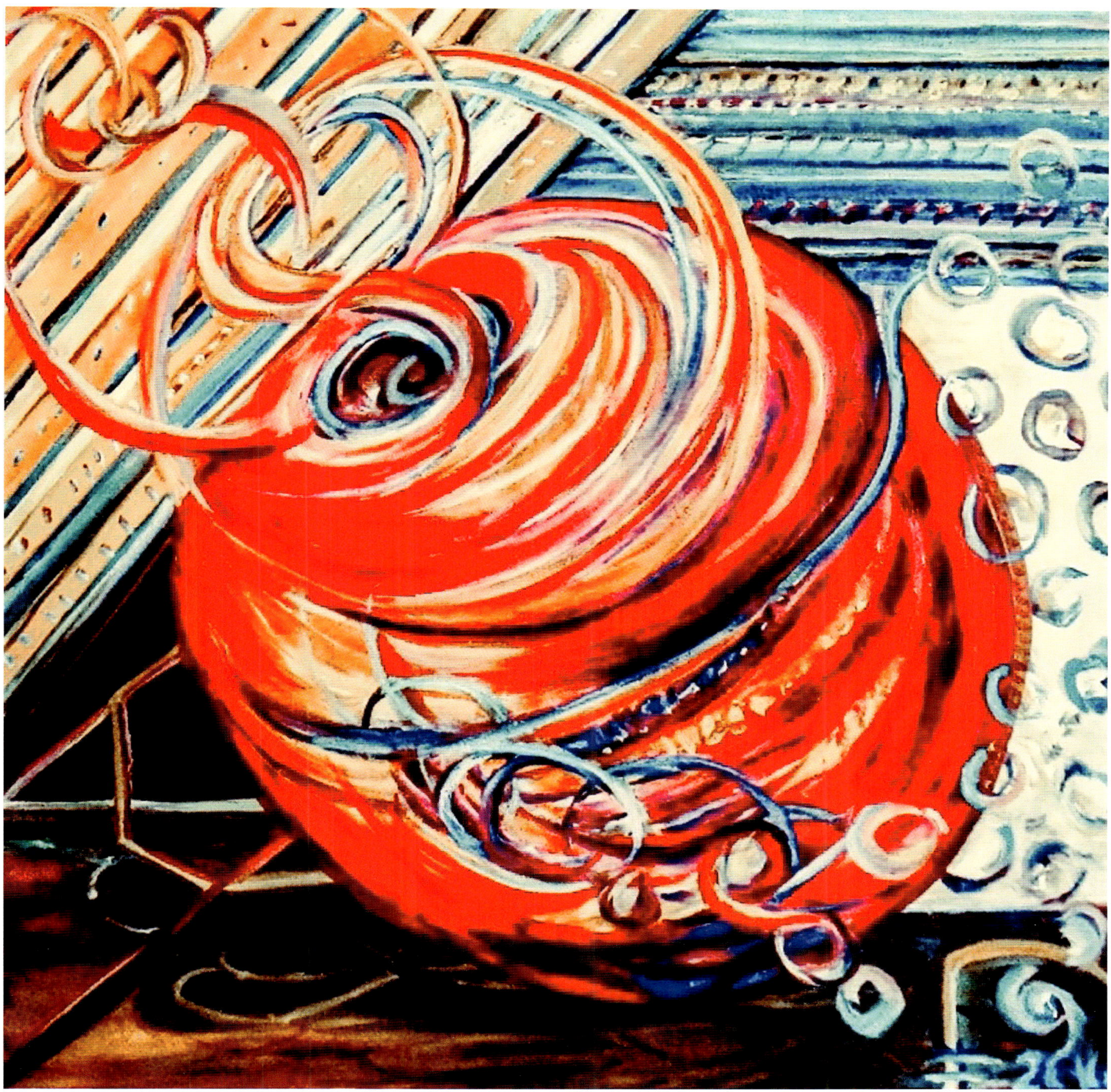

Pat Fallon

Pat Fallon conducts a great deal of research about the concepts within which she works. To keep that process simple, she has limited herself to just a few ongoing bodies of work. Apples are one; another is the nature of space itself and the particles we think belong in it. Recently, two of those bodies of work merged and became *Shedding Quarks*, where the artist imagines electrons spinning while quarks leap about in different directions simultaneously. These images are about human visualization and the mechanics of human vision that entails belief. "For us, seeing is believing," Fallon says. "And believing that what we see is real and what is not seen is not there at all. Visualization about our beliefs literally means we are having visions. Understanding this allows me to play with the content of my work."

Shedding Quarks
Acrylic
30 x 30 in.

patfallon10@gmail.com
patfallon.com

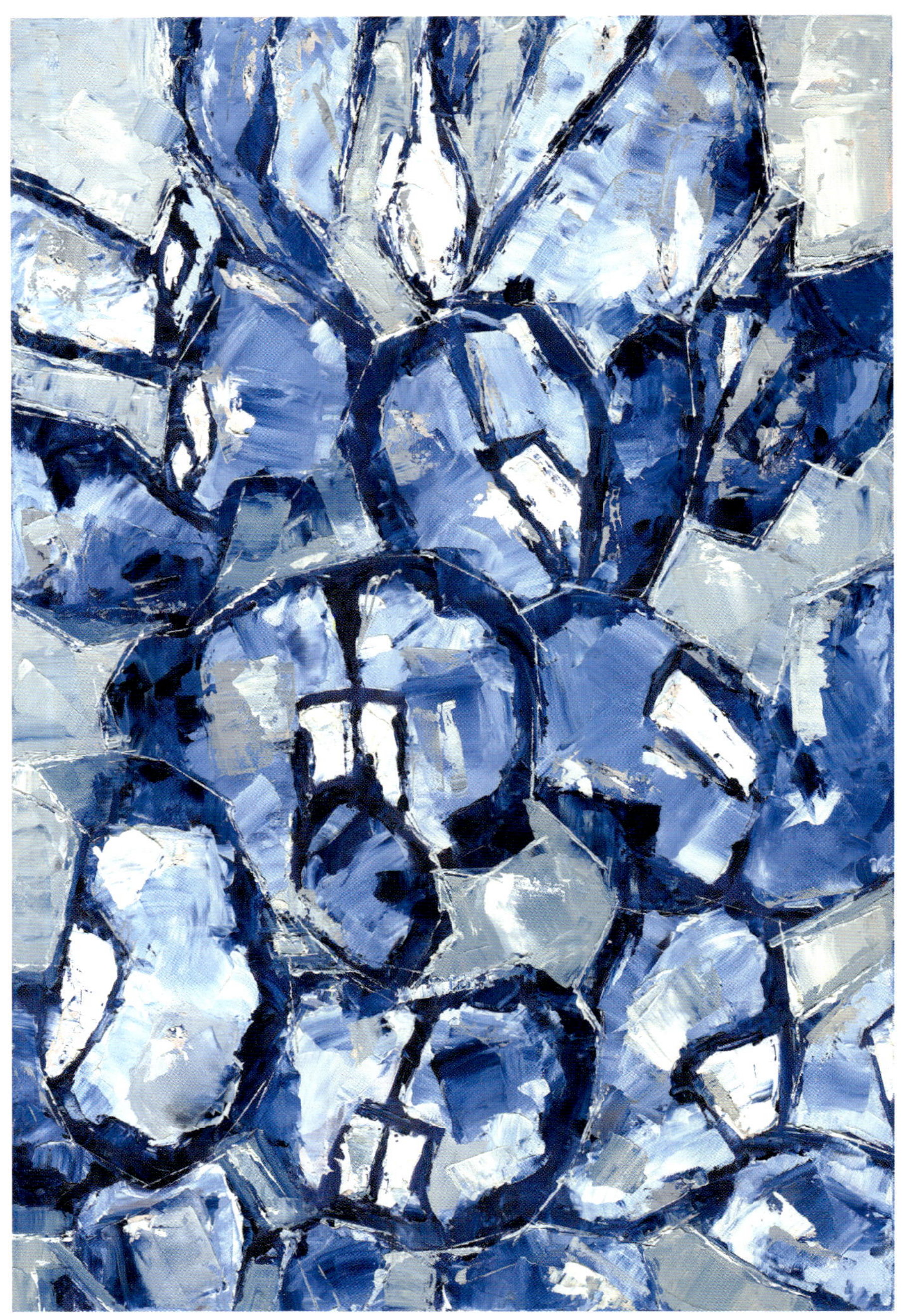

Mylinda Farr

The shapes within the form of a flower fuel Mylinda Farr's experimentation. Frequently, she relishes expanding plant delicateness into geometrical forms. With a rush of energy, when examining circles and rectangles within a blossom, the artist pushes paint with a palette knife onto canvas, as well as messy mediums of ink, charcoal, and graphite onto paper. Seizing botanical shapes requires a closeup view of plants rather than a drive-by highway wildflower splash or flush of color from a neighbor's garden. Farr's contemporary floral art prompts comments of curiosity like, "I didn't know a lupine (bluebonnet) had a square divided face." Farr has spent the last eleven years surrounded by nature, living on a small ranch and nurturing her passion for native plants, art, music, history, and family.

Into The Bluebonnet
Oil
36 x 24 in.

farrfamilytx@gmail.com
mylindafarr.com

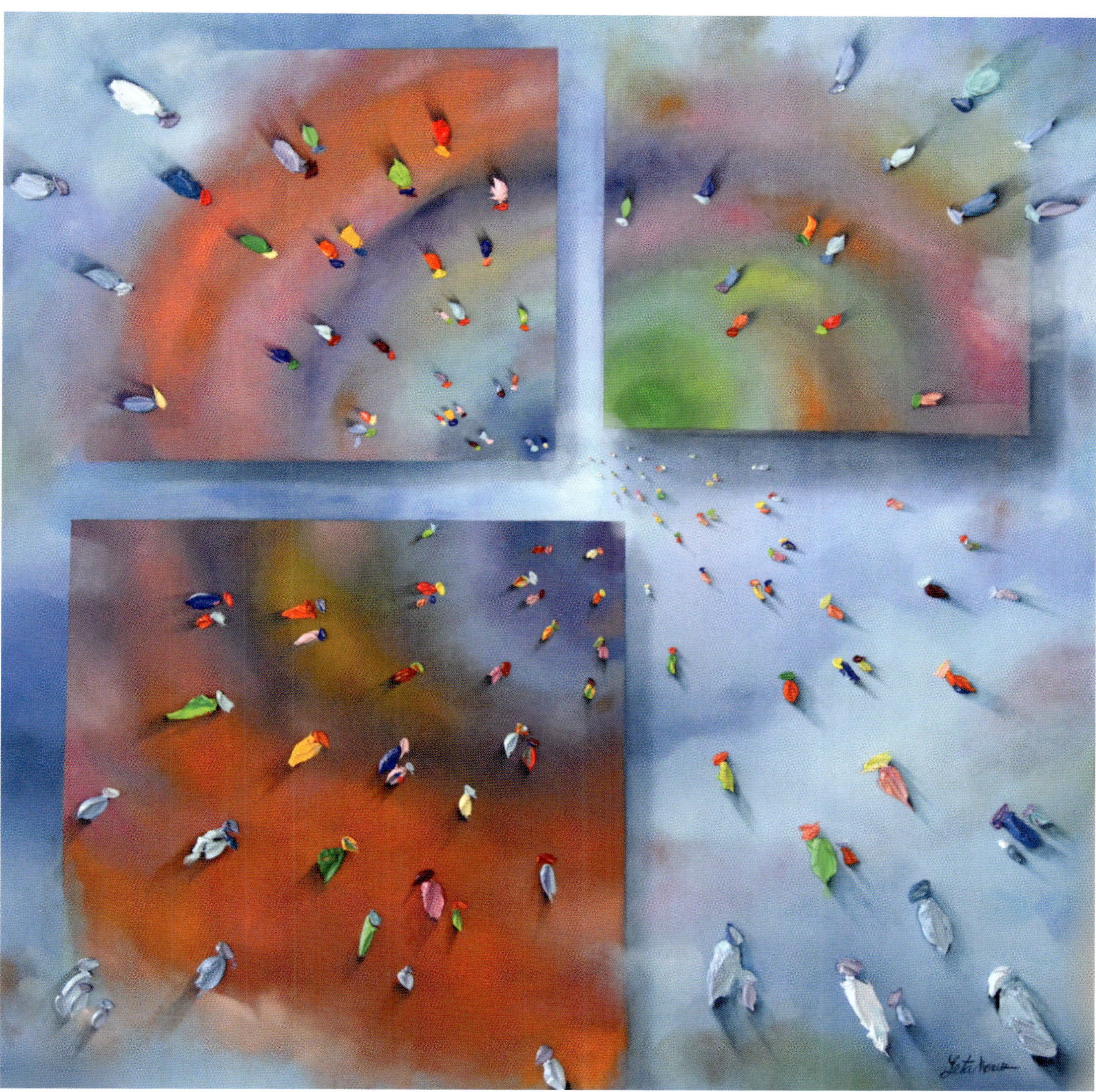

Leticia Herrera

"I believe in the kindness of humanity. I believe that our diversity is what makes this world interesting. I consider myself an expanding artist because I believe we are always transforming. My work walks with me and changes with me," says Leticia Herrera. In her art, she represents that trajectory through her *Walkers* series. The figures are searchers of beautiful emotions; they are travelers of the universe and the world. They are catchers of dreams; they are explorers of aspirations, searchers of unity and of freedom. Asking always: Who are we? Where are we going? What are we looking for? What do we want? Who do we love? In her paintings, Herrera tries to transport the viewer to those places of imagination where we are often finding ourselves. "I want to touch your soul, open your heart, and invite you to walk with me," Herrera says.

Travelers of a Colorful Mind
Oil
48 x 48 in.

leticiaherrera@
leticiaherreraart.com
leticiaherreraart.com
@leticiaherreraart

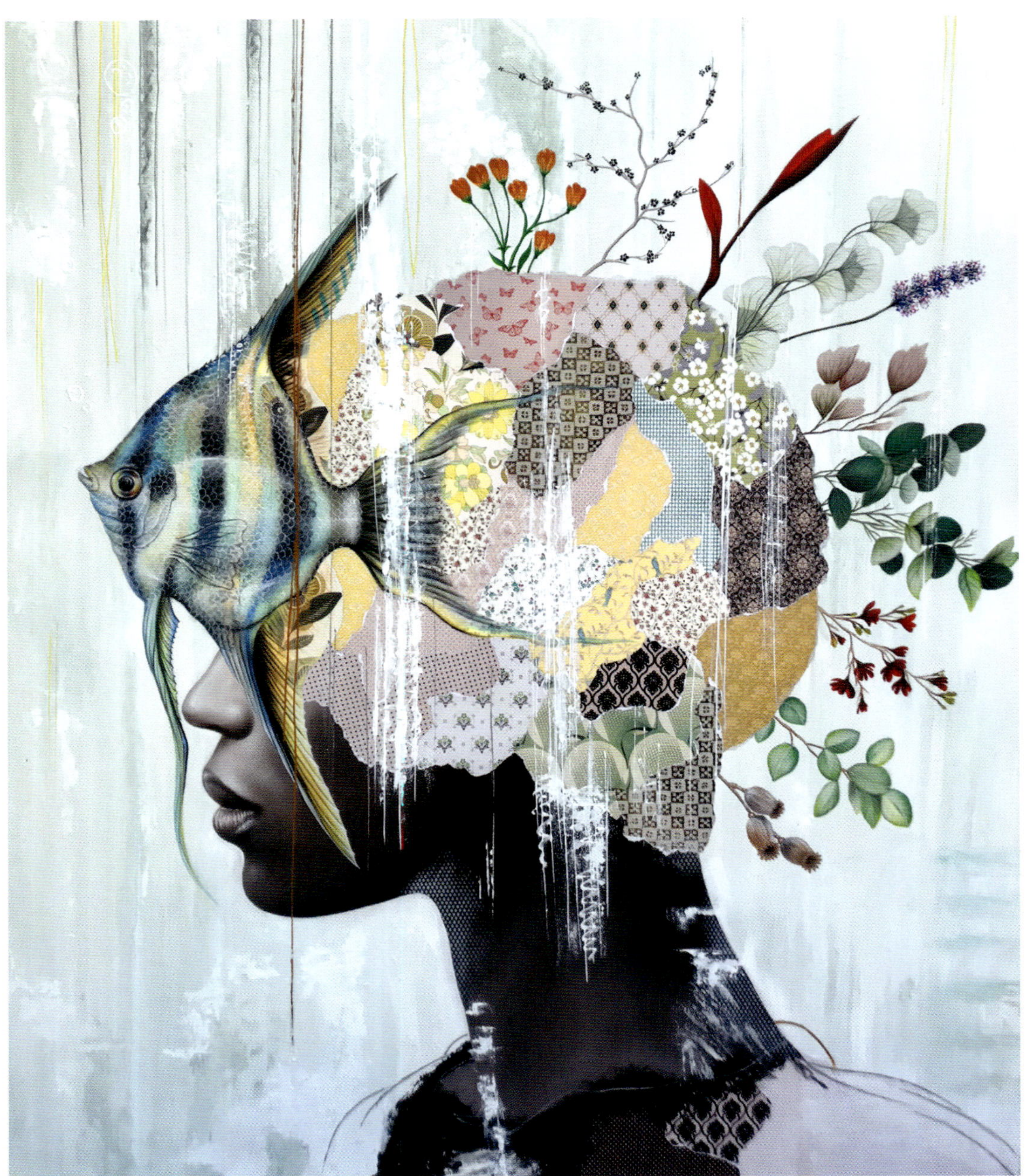

Irene Hoff

For self-taught Dutch artist Irene Hoff, the world is out of balance, which can be seen in the human and environmental challenges we are currently faced with. She craves a world where compassion, intuition, and harmony are key elements for living. Hoff's art is filled with hope and inspiration that encourages viewers to become aware of their feelings and beliefs, making space for their true selves. Unique to Hoff's art is the mixing and matching of different styles, which at first glance may seem controversial. In her paintings, she loves to modify the acrylic paint into thicker applications and to use a wide variety of hand-torn paper patterns as well as old Bali street posters.

Going with the Flow
Mixed media
51 x 47 in.

irene@irenehoff.com
irenehoff.com
@art_irenehoff

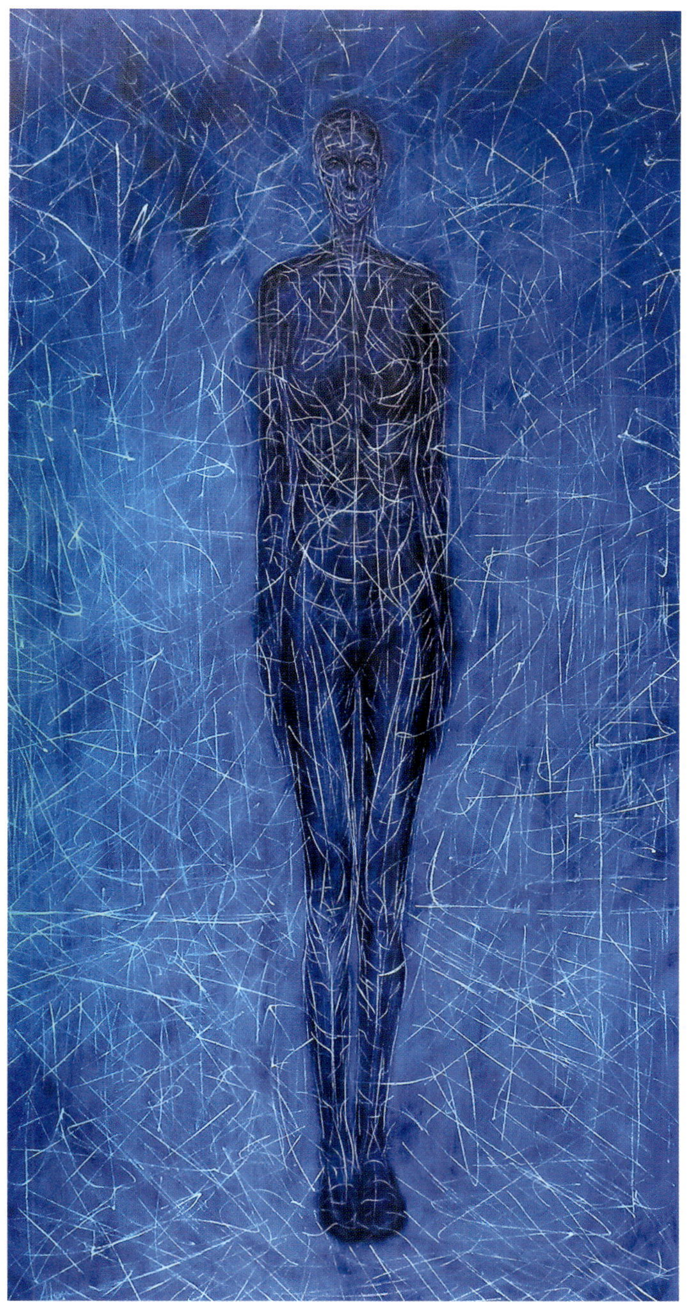

Atom Hovanesyan

Atom Hovanesyan's goal is to create a unified atmosphere and sense of luminosity in his work. Bits and pieces of forms from memory are utilized as building blocks for constructing the composition. There is no narrative or a specific reading, more of an epilogue that's open to interpretation. The artist is trying to create a space complex enough and compelling enough to act as a point of departure while retaining the often accidental mystery and painterly energy. In his latest abstract expressionist series, Hovanesyan's goal is to continue the evolution of his initial painterly approach toward a more atmospheric or surreal one. He wants to still use line and gesture as the initial scaffolding of the picture, however, in the latest series, his aim is more toward creating depth and luminosity and approaching the issue from a storytelling point of view.

*Standing Woman
(Homage to Giacometti)*
Oil on linen
81 x 40 in.

arahov63@gmail.com
artbyatom.com
@artbyatomhov

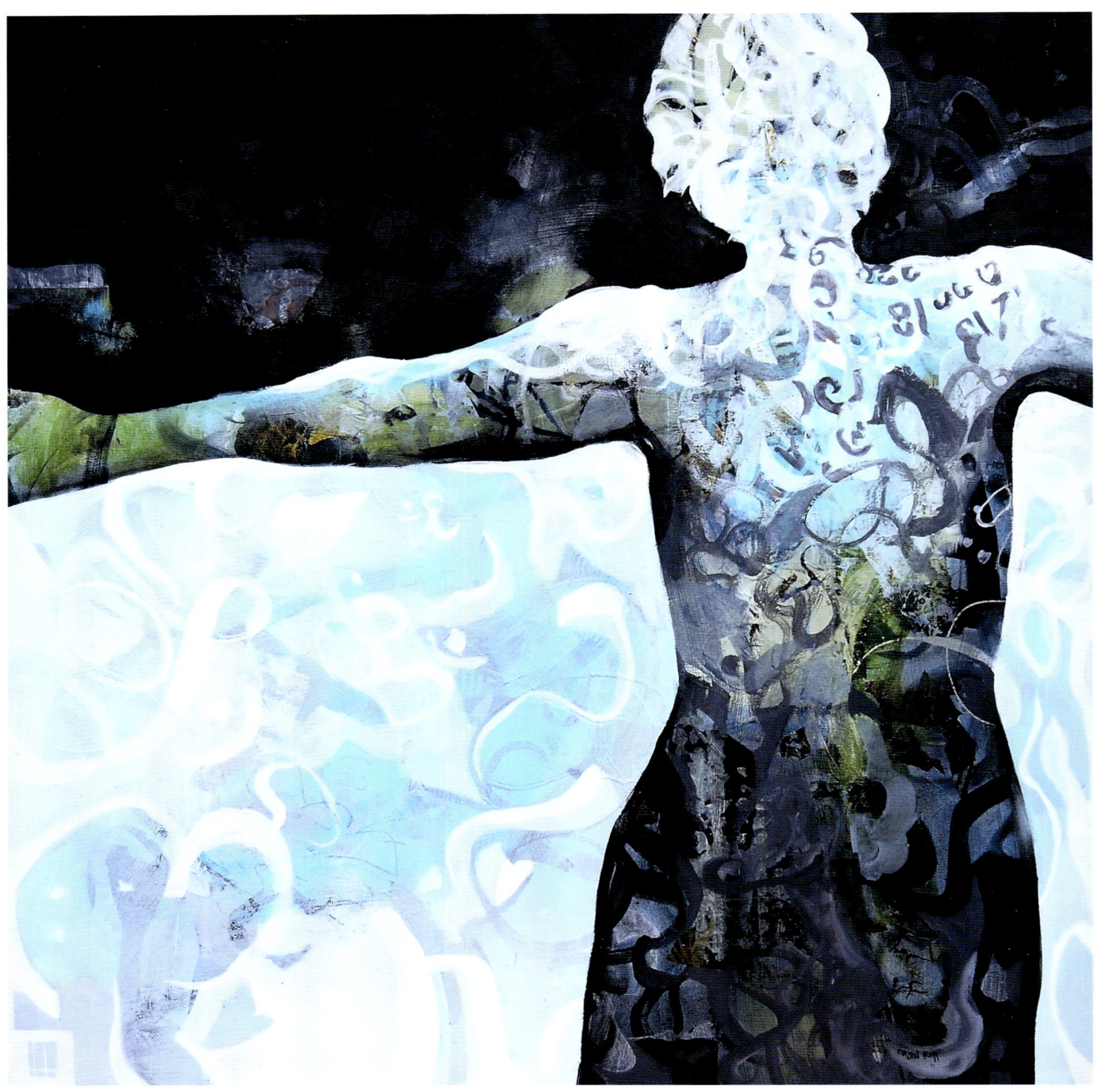

Carson Kapp

Caron Kapp was an architect. His work was commercial, massive in scale, and complex. Now, as an artist, his work is wonky, whimsical, and fearless. As an architect, he was concerned with structure, safety, and function. As an artist, he is free of those constraints, free to move into a world purely of his own creation. Persistent in his work, both in architecture and in art, is the use of line, the consistent underlying foundation. Using line as the dominant element, he has created both massive three-dimensional structures and, now as an artist, two-dimensional fantasy worlds, incorporating people, architecture, and nature. This is everything our reality offers, but these are the worlds of Kapp's imagination. Along with lines—fat, skinny, broken, any kind—the artist uses exaggerated and sensuous shapes in bright colors and energetic quick strokes. The end result is a surrealistic vision of the world.

Ocean of Love and Light
Acrylic
36 x 36 in.

carsonkapp@gmail.com
carsonkapp.weebly.com
@kappcarson

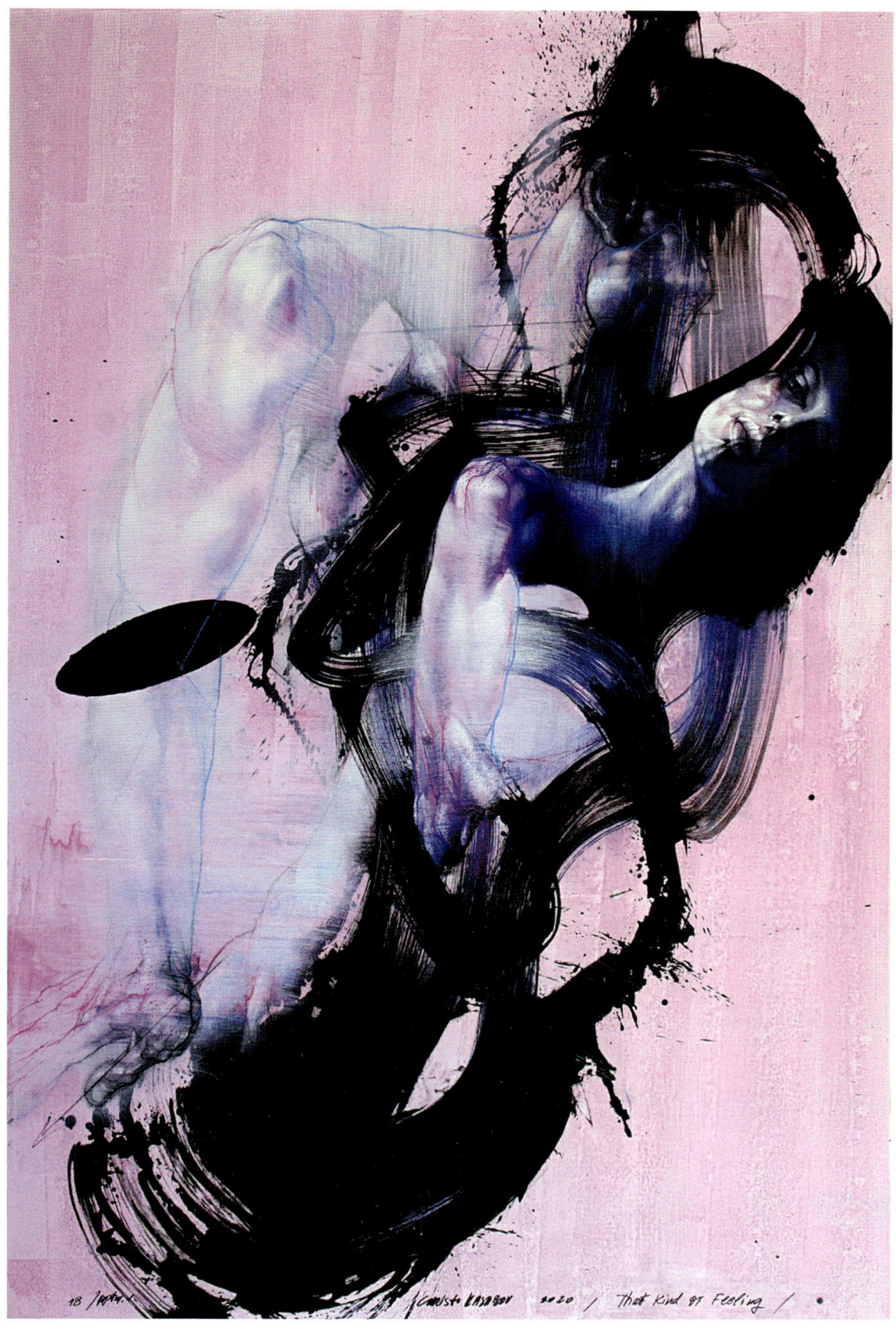

Christo Kasabov

Christo Kasabov is an artist who takes a journey to observe the relation between the conscious and the subconscious. The center of his artistic expressions is the human being between his inner world and his external world. Kasabov uses a complex alchemy of materials developed and distributed on the surface as a challenge, contradiction, and defiance of the concept of moderation, rationality, and order from the established canons of art. He explains his work as a transformation of emotions because he sees the world as a perfect and magical image of transformation, emotions, and movement that deeply touches and provokes him and reflects his artistic sensibility and imagination.

That Kind Of Feeling
Oil, acrylic and pigments
82 x 54 in.

christo.casabov@gmail
.com
christokasabo.com
@ckasabo

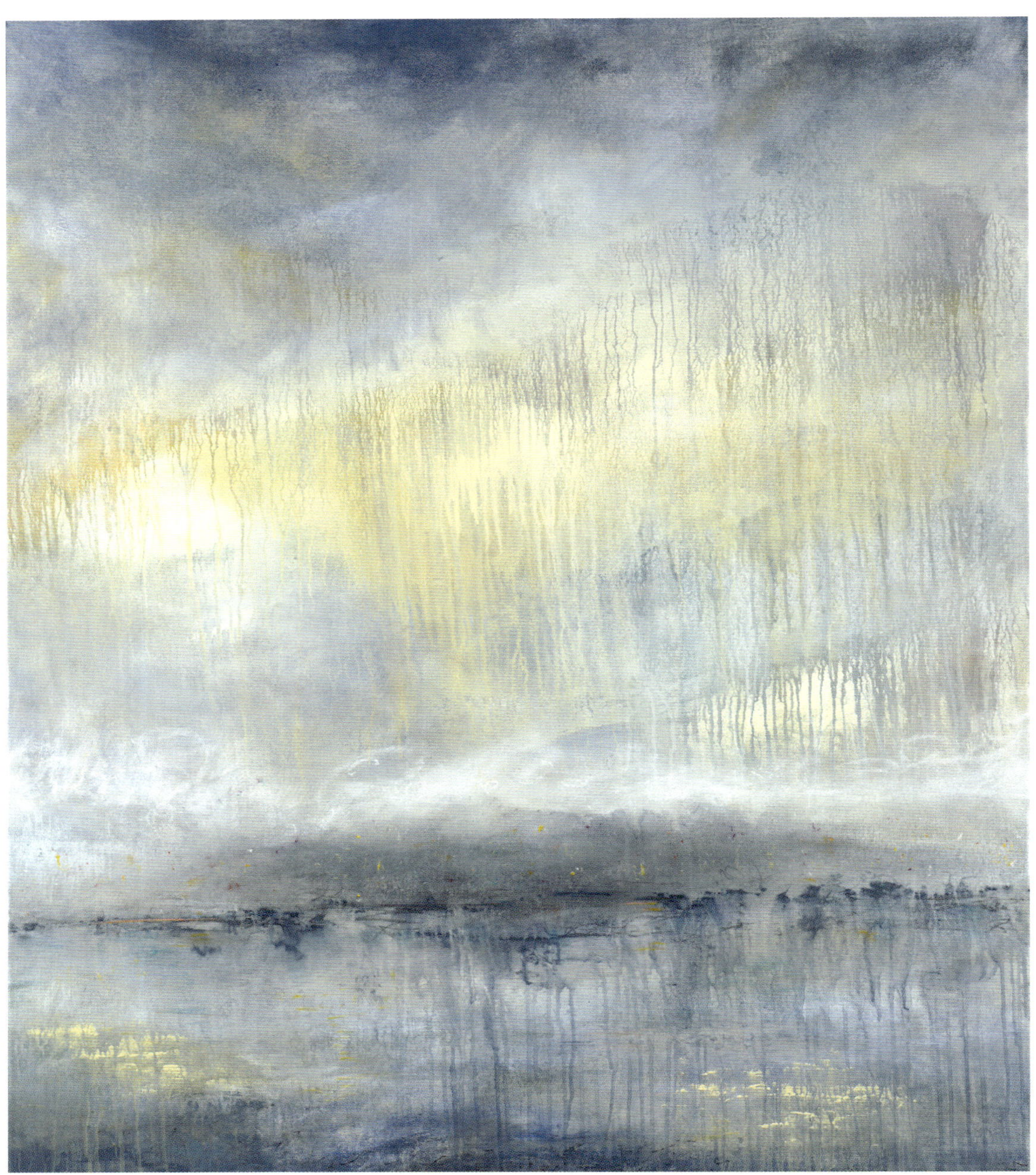

Rebecca Katz

Rebecca Katz's inspiration comes from the beauty of the atmosphere—of the sky and how it's connected with the earth. Every time she looks at what nature is presenting, the clouds, seductive with the constant movement of the atmosphere, she is reminded that life is constantly shifting and never stagnant. She gets that calm feeling when she looks at the horizon, and she resonates with translating the vast spaciousness and mystery to the canvas. Katz works in acrylic and graphite, using many layers of glazes to achieve the luminosity of the atmospheric quality in her work. She also works wet on wet and uses drips to create texture and atmosphere, which alludes to what's beneath the surface. Layers and layers of paint are applied on the canvas before she even knows how the image will present itself in its final form. Katz's paintings ask viewers to step into a world of possibility, mystery, magic, and atmosphere and to be transported through color and light and texture.

Summer Solstice
Acrylic and graphite
54 x 46 in.

rebecca@rebeccakatz
.com
rebeccakatzart.com
@rebeccakatzart

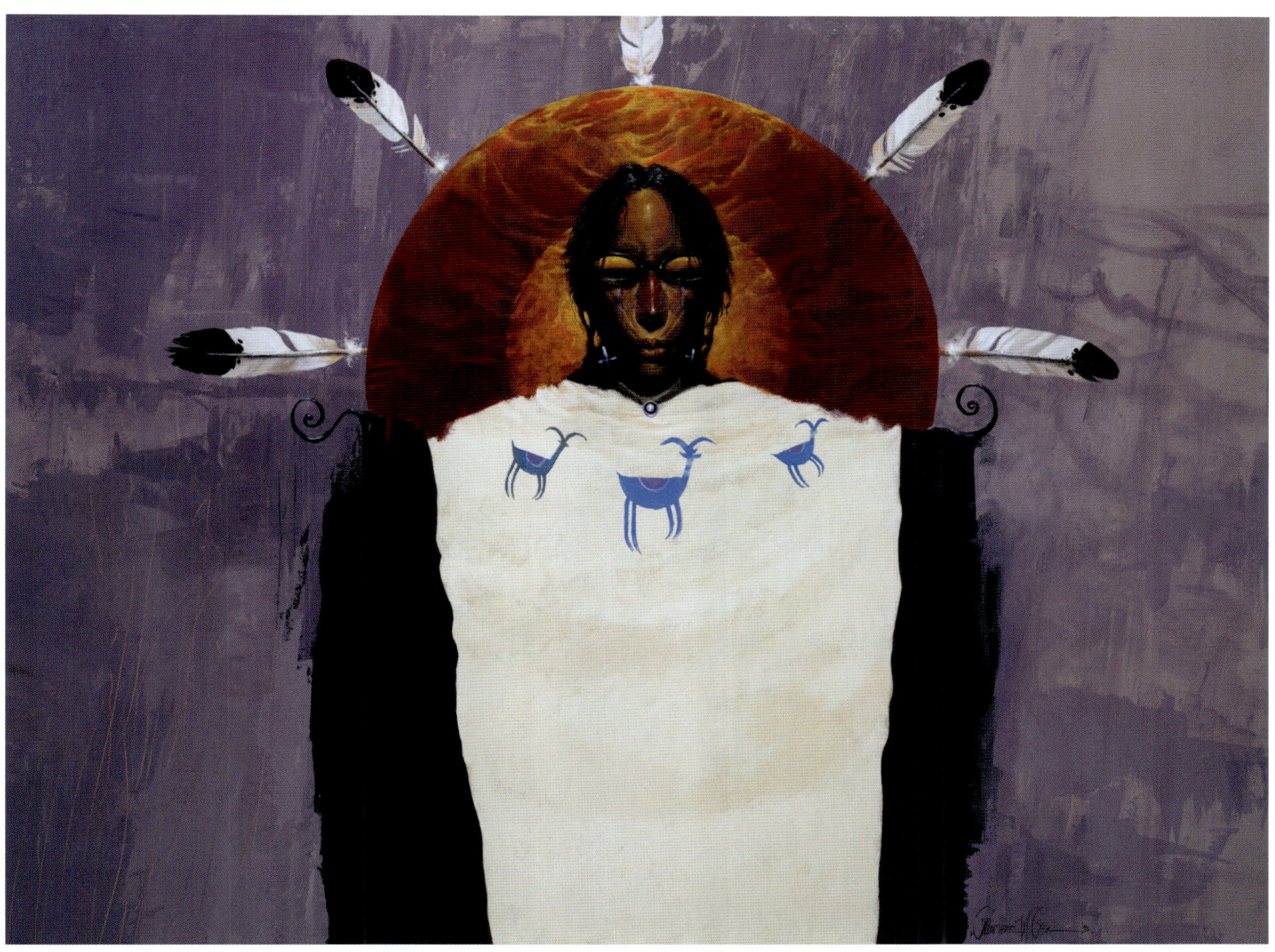

Lawrence W. Lee

It has taken fifty years for Lawrence W. Lee to finally understand one basic truth about all art: People get out of art what they bring to it. No matter what an artist is trying to communicate through a work, it will always be perceived through the life-lens of the observer. Everything they have ever seen or done has created a filter through which they now experience life—and art. Each person experiences a work of art differently, and it is as though some art can create a door where no door had been. If the art resonates through the life-lens of the viewer, that door will open, leading not out to some alien place, but inward—to self. And when a person is fortunate enough to experience a resonant piece of art and to open that amazing door, there is no end to what they can learn about themselves.

Hunter Spirit
Acrylic
36 x 48 in.

lawrence@
lawrenceleeart.com
lawrenceleeart.com
@lawrenceleeart

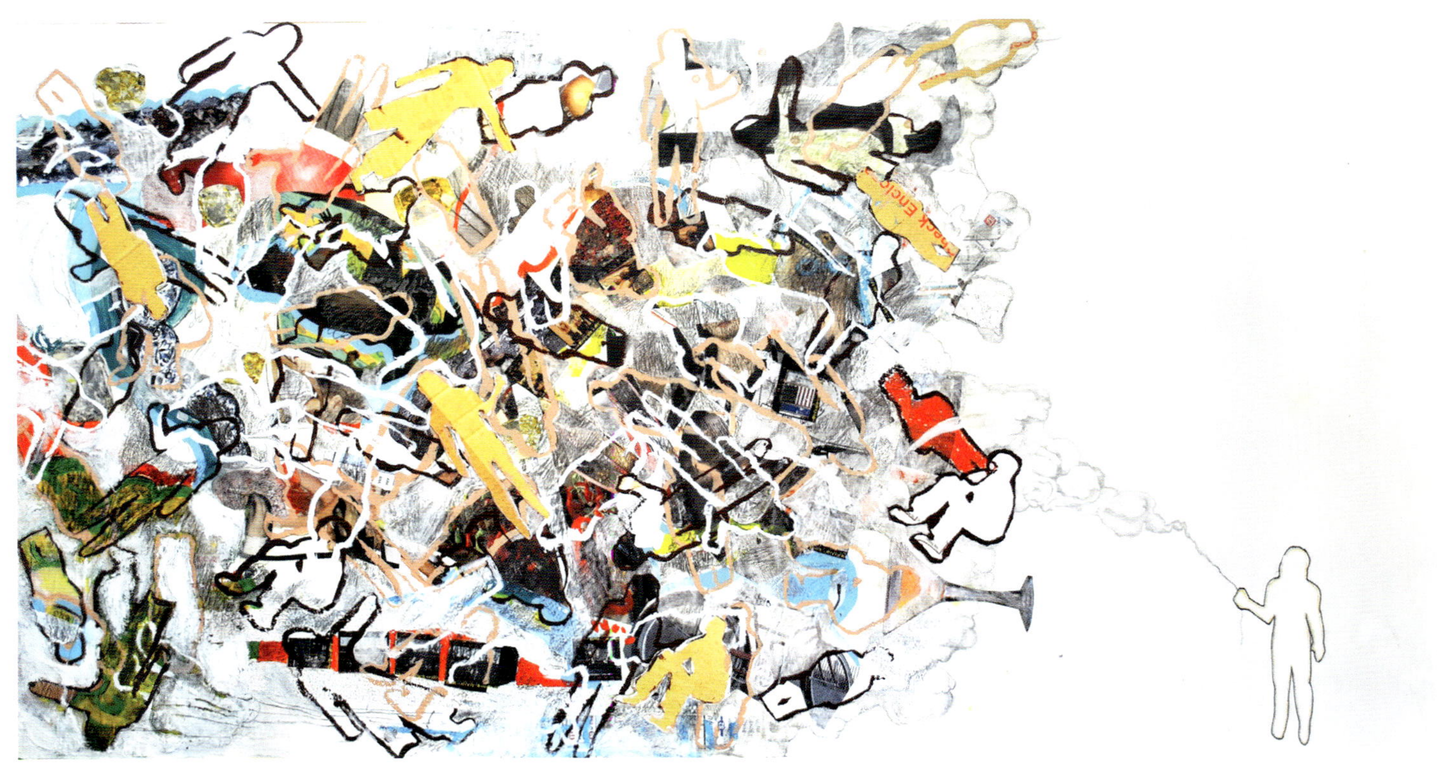

Erin Liljegren

Through paint, pencil, ink, recycled materials, and a pinch of humor, Erin Liljegren's work expresses the narrative of humans living amongst other humans and other species—in all of this man-made stuff, in this man-made landscape, in this human-designed economy. The artist focuses attention on the deprivation of natural resources, overconsumption, disposable consumer culture, and the impact of human actions in an overpopulated world. Her work can be viewed as societal portraits of the human-built landscape and a personal expression of living among this alarming, ever-changing environment.

Liljegren uses spatial composition as a metaphor for the social and physical space between people, the relationship with their acquired and discarded objects, and their environment. Bright colors and playful images cut through the din of distraction, illuminating externalities intentionally hidden beyond our view. Chaotic visual and textural mass is intentionally balanced with empty, negative space to convey the weight of the subject matter.

The Cloud I Carry
Mixed media on paper
22 x 42 in.

erinliljegren@gmail.com
erinliljegren.com
@erinliljegren

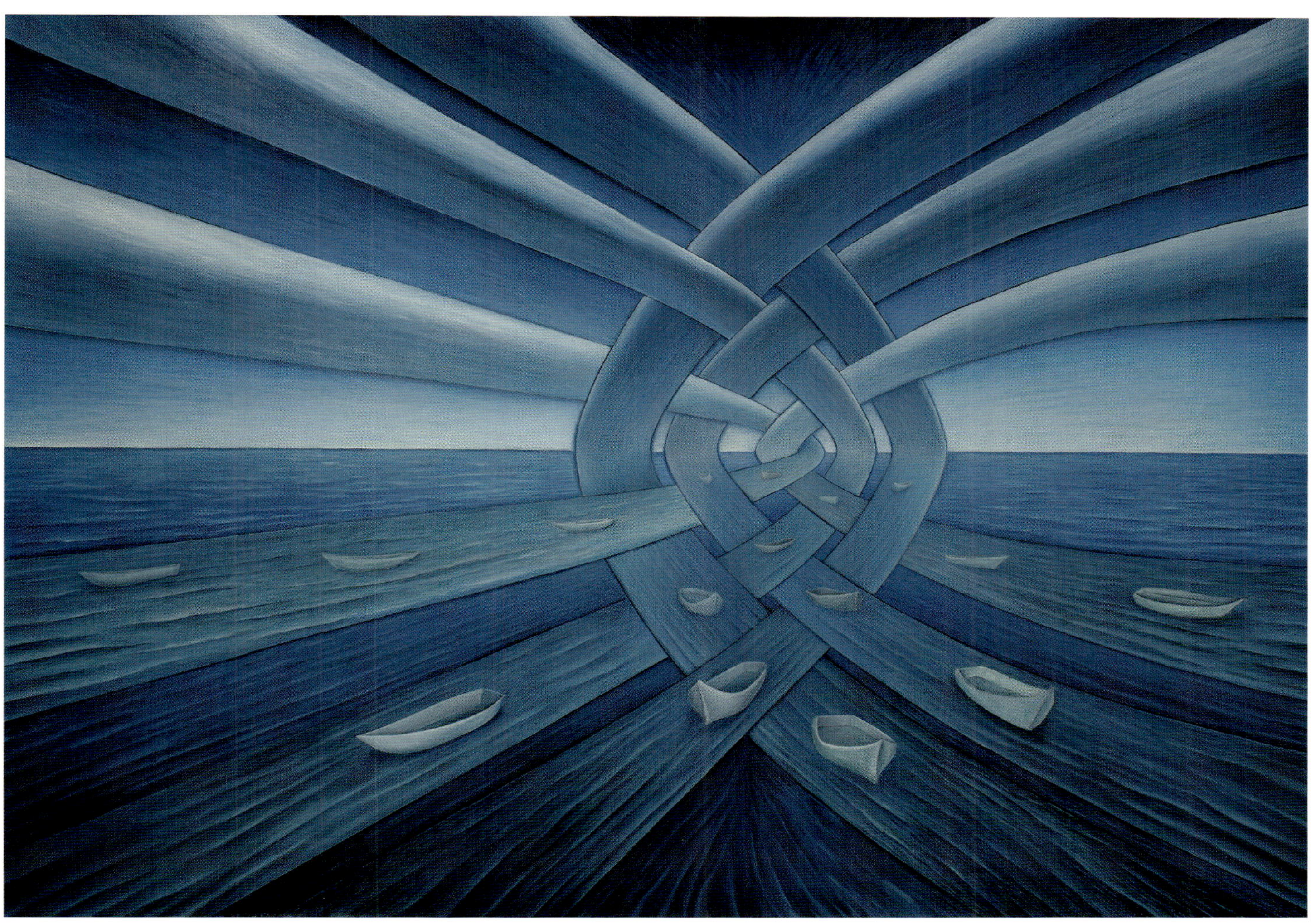

Yaroslava Liseeva

Yaroslava Liseeva's art and style grew out of her perception of reality as a versatile combination of precision and spontaneity, fluency and precipitancy, tension and harmony, conflict and balance. In her works, she appeals to emotional and spiritual dimensions. Living in chaotic times, it is important to stop and to open one's eyes and see the world around, listen to it, feel it. "When we are connected with the world through our souls, we start moving in the Flow together, with everything around, and find out our personal meanings and answers," Liseeva says.

Using traditional oil paints and focusing on classical landscape images, Liseeva tries to create a dynamic, voluminous, and flowing world. The artist feels that if we observe these phenomena with all our senses, they open for us their metaphorical essence and acquire universal, mythological characteristics.

Coming Home
Oil
27.5 x 39 in.

yaroslavaliseeva@mail
.ru
yarlis.org
@yaroslavaliseeva2019

PAINTING: TRADITIONAL/CONTEMPORARY

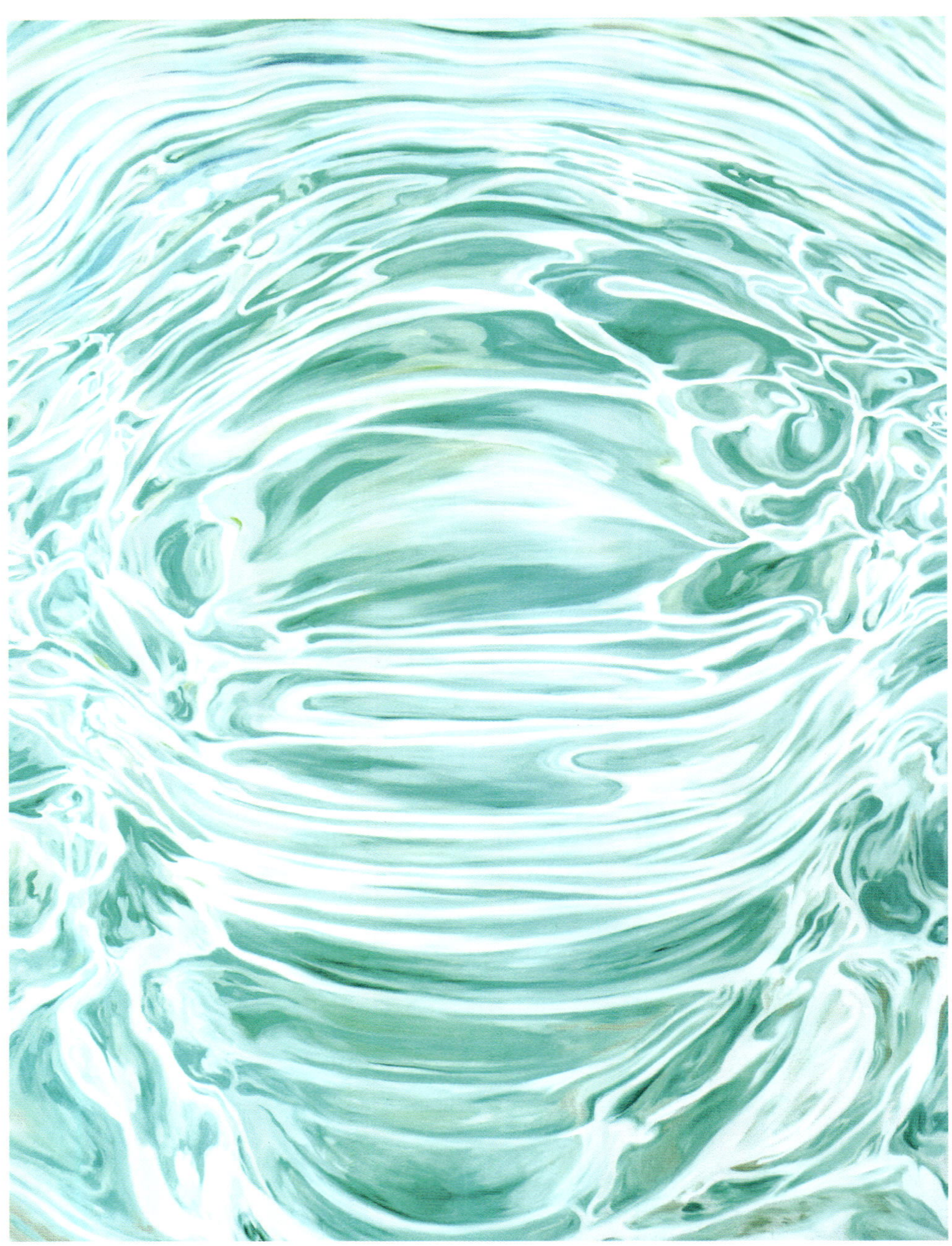

Georgia Loxton Knight
Georgia Loxton Knight's upbringing on the coast of Western Australia was filled with long summers of ocean light and sweltering afternoon mirages that permeate her work to this day. As a daughter and granddaughter of landscape painters, she suspects her early immersion in art infiltrated her view of reality in much the same way. Knight thinks of her paintings as fragments of dreams: ephemeral, illusory, and intoxicating They are waterscapes in which impossible distortions are used to playfully question our reliance on the laws of physics to accept reality. In dreams, these laws are forgotten, and we are open to wider possibilities. Water is the perfect conduit as it is known to manipulate light and is readily suggestive of a bridge between cognitive planes. The artist's abstracted compositions make use of this familiar visual material to seduce the viewer into moving into a space of transcendence, submitting to a desire for beauty over reason.

Bathysphere
Oil
78.7 x 59 in.

georgialoxtonknight@
gmail.com
georgialoxtonknight
.com
@georgialoxtonknight

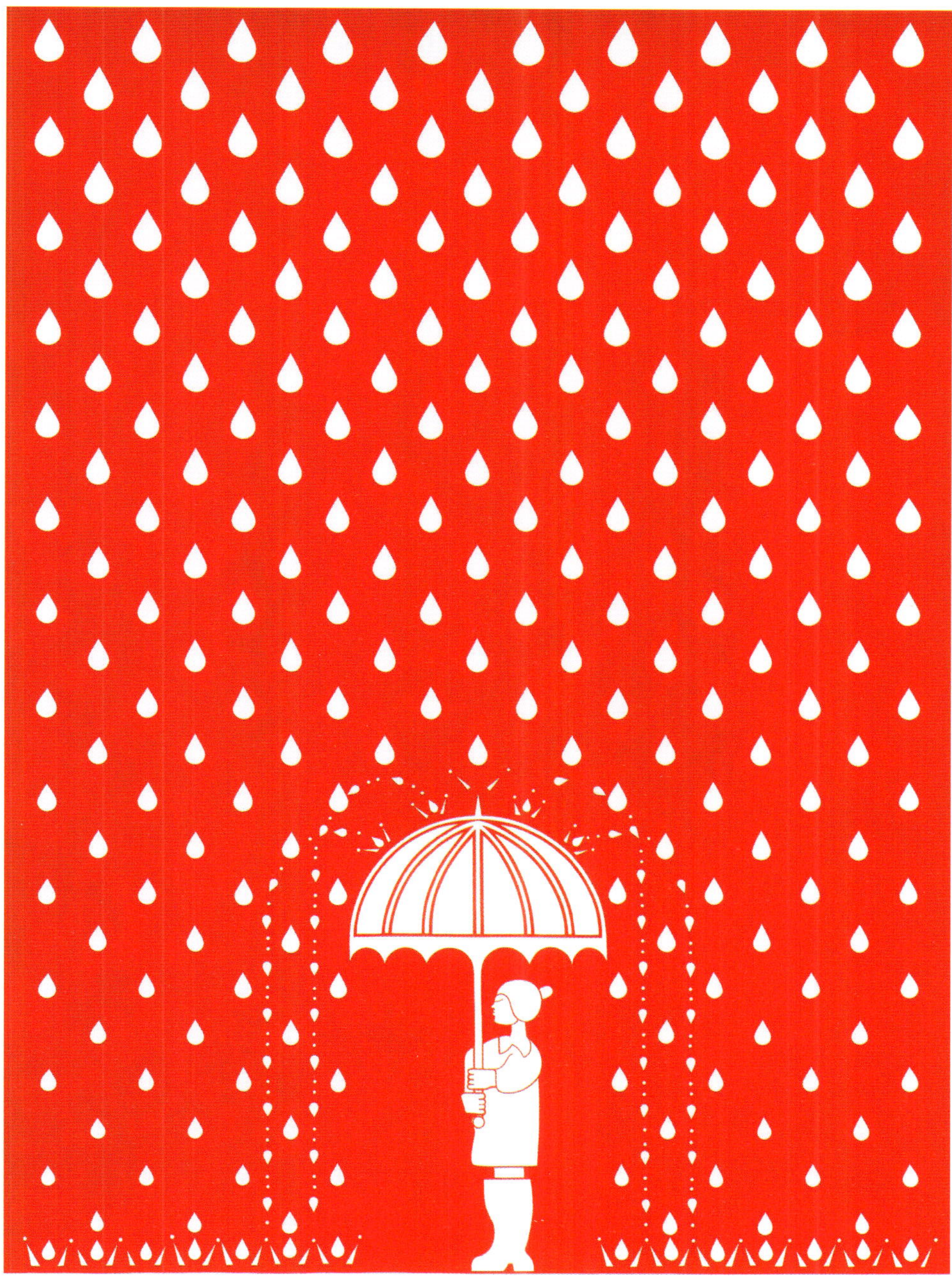

Vince MacDermot

Vince MacDermot is an artist with architectural training and background. He learned to draw and paint at a young age from Canadian painter Anne Savage. His work is geometric and mathematical. The artist's *Big Red NYC* series is a companionable twenty-five-piece batch of deliberate, large 60-by-84-inch edge-to-edge red paintings. Inside, an articulate figure, drama, or protagonist is precisely established in bright white paint. About red: It's the opposite of a complicated color strategy. "I like red," MacDermot says. "It's about impact." The artist is aware of the red plus white, one-two punch, as in the Red Cross logo and *Campbell's Soup Cans* (Warhol). For MacDermot, red is the heated springboard of a narrative relayed in white.

Rain Lover
Acrylic
84 x 60 in.

vincemacdermot@gmail
.com
vincemacdermot.com
@vincemacdermot

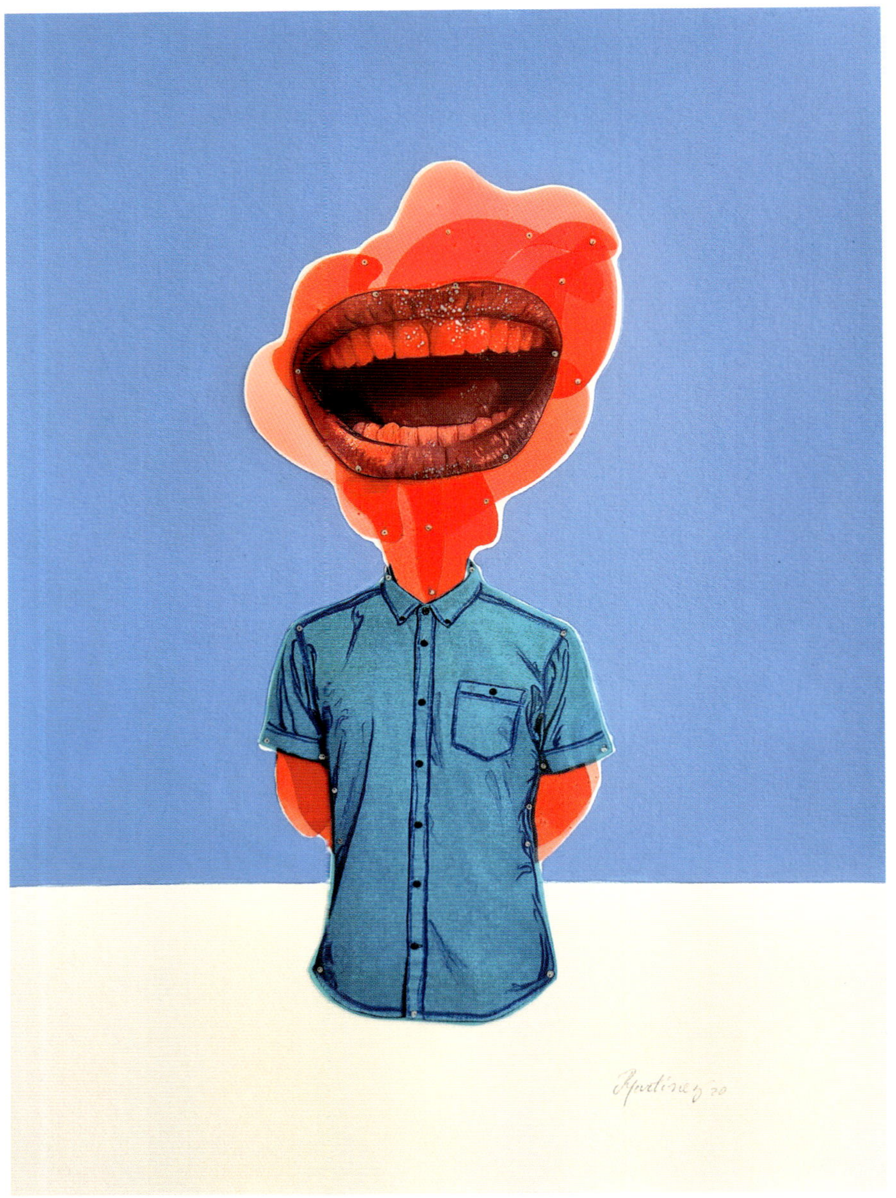

Romulo Martinez
Romulo Martinez is a faithful follower of color. His current research has led him to study the iridescent effects that show and reflect the colors of the rainbow in natural and industrial elements in our environment and societies. This aesthetic investigation began through photographic exercises to catch the color radiation inside an aqueous body after the decomposition of light. From there he investigated color through light and the materialization of this intangible phenomenon, communicating what he sees and feels from it in various techniques that evoke and reproduce colors with their shades and approximations from each other. What he discovered is a wateriness with the organicity, volume, and expansion, the light with transparency in colorless spaces to potentiate its chromatic values and sentiments housed in those colors, expressing feelings and words, all in abstract and figurative contexts, nourished by the different elements that make up the physical, geographical, and cultural space that he inhabits.

Calling to Discard
Polyethylene colored by the artist, acrylic paint and collage
15 x 11 in.

roartma@gmail.com
romulomartinez.com
@romulomartinez

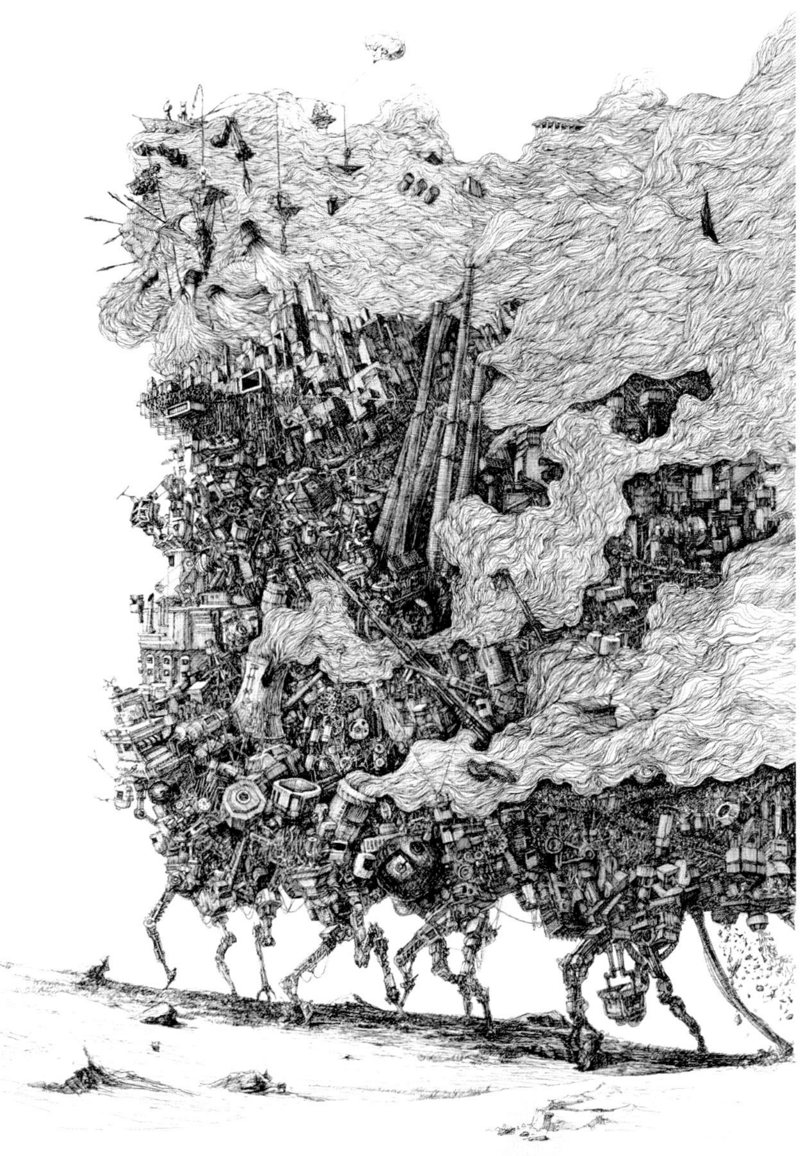

Samridh Mukhiya

In her work Samridh Mukhiya explores the human condition. Her process involves creating conceptual contents that represent and interpret experiences that shape our existence, designed to invoke awakening, healing, and manifestation through visual mantras. Mukhiya draws from within, incorporating metaphorical elements to convey ideas, experiences, and messages in her art. She spends the majority of her time conceptualizing and devising the method to convey her interpretation on matters that are psychological, sociopolitical, and spiritual, and explore consciousness and the meaning of life. A large body of her work explores mental health, communicating its importance to the public.

The majority of her art is black and white, devoid of colors so that the observer can explore thoughts preceding our uninhibited and invoked emotions. Through her art, she desires to start a dialogue with the viewer, presenting ideas that elicit curiosity and seed a perception, which grow into questions, and presenting a reexamination of ideas we have come to accept.

Symphony
Pen and ink
36 X 24 in.

mukhiyas.art@gmail
.com
mukhiyas.com
@mukhiyas.art

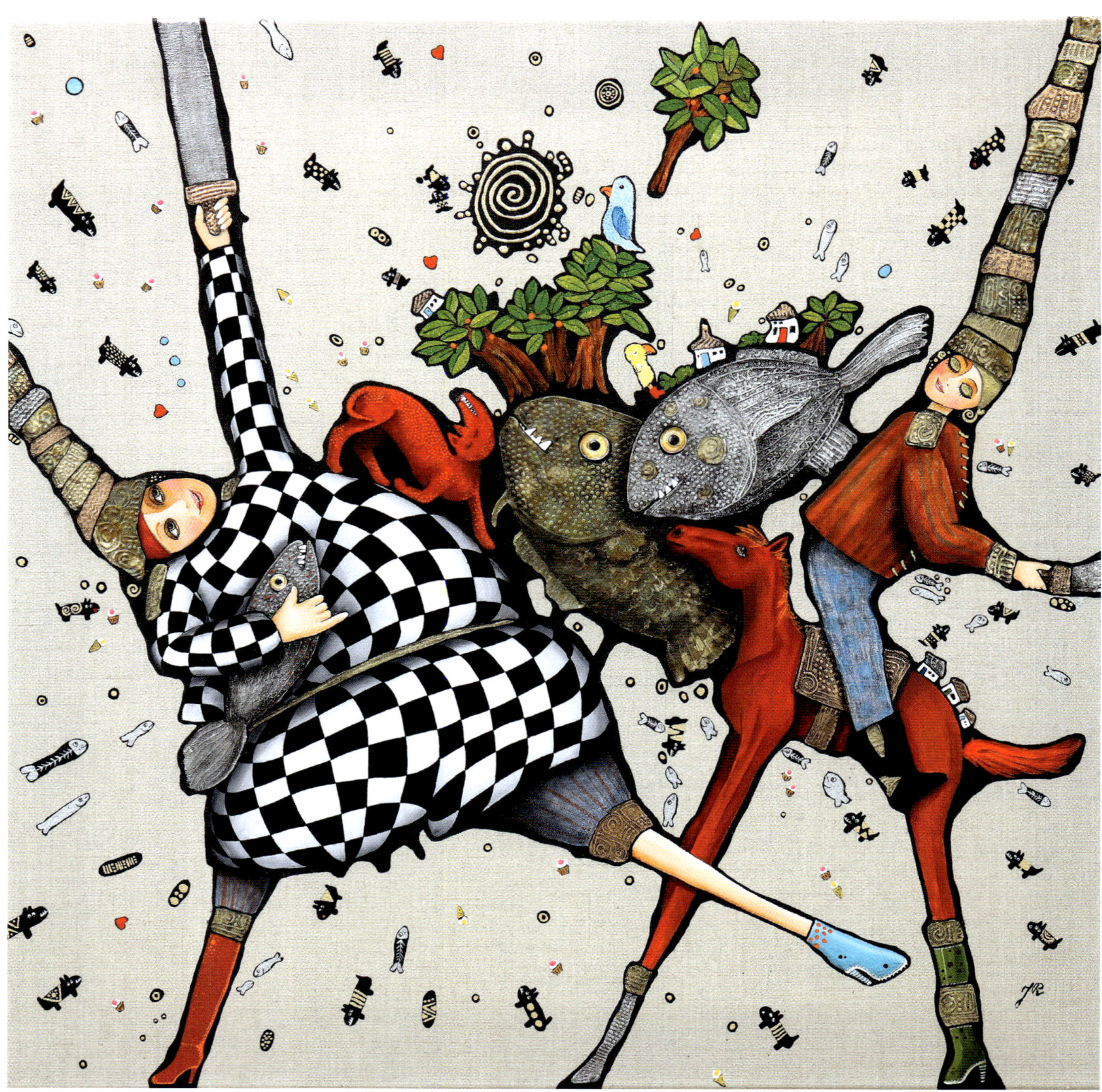

Jette Reinert

Jette Reinert wants to tell stories. Or rather, the viewers tell their own stories from her paintings. Reinert depicts the strange, the imperfect, the humorous, and the deformed with a life-affirming sense of humor and a gleam in the eye, underlined by the titles, which by now have become their own part of the artworks. "I am waging a battle against the perfectionism of our time and encourage us all to make space for the differences," she says.

The differences leap out at the viewer in an aesthetic language of form where you are drawn toward the story and the richness of detail in the painting, and you can write your own new stories, continually finding new details. "You could say, with a certain justification, that I am creating modern icons, not as religious symbols but as celebrations of humanity itself in all its diversity and beauty," Reinert says.

They Said to Me that it Would Rain with Fying Pancakes
Acrylic and metal leaf on linen
31.4 x 31.4 in.

jette@reinert.dk
reinert.dk
@jette_reinert

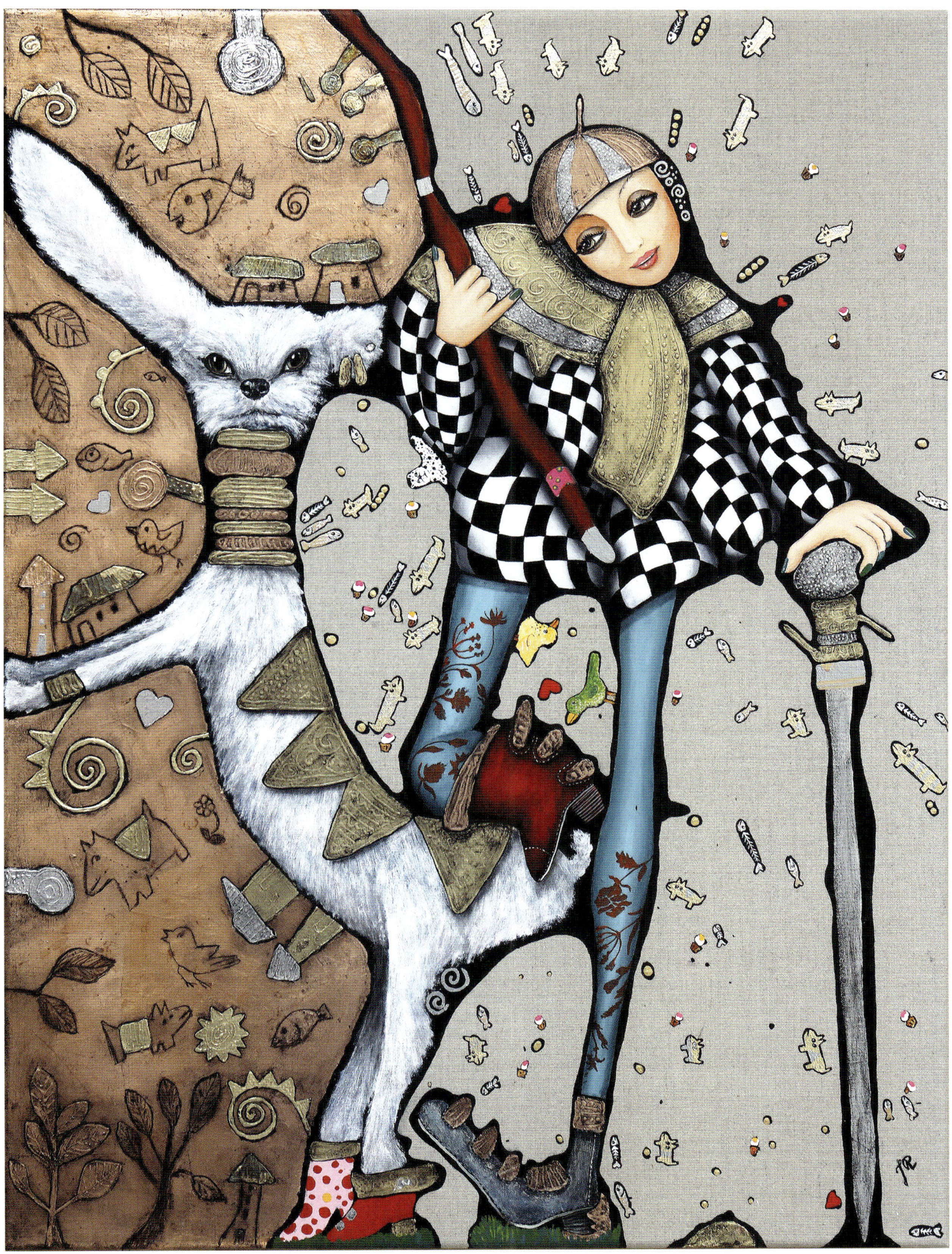

*Holger Always Wants to Dance Tango
When We Have to do the Dishes*

Acrylic and metal leaf on linen
31.4 x 25.5 in.

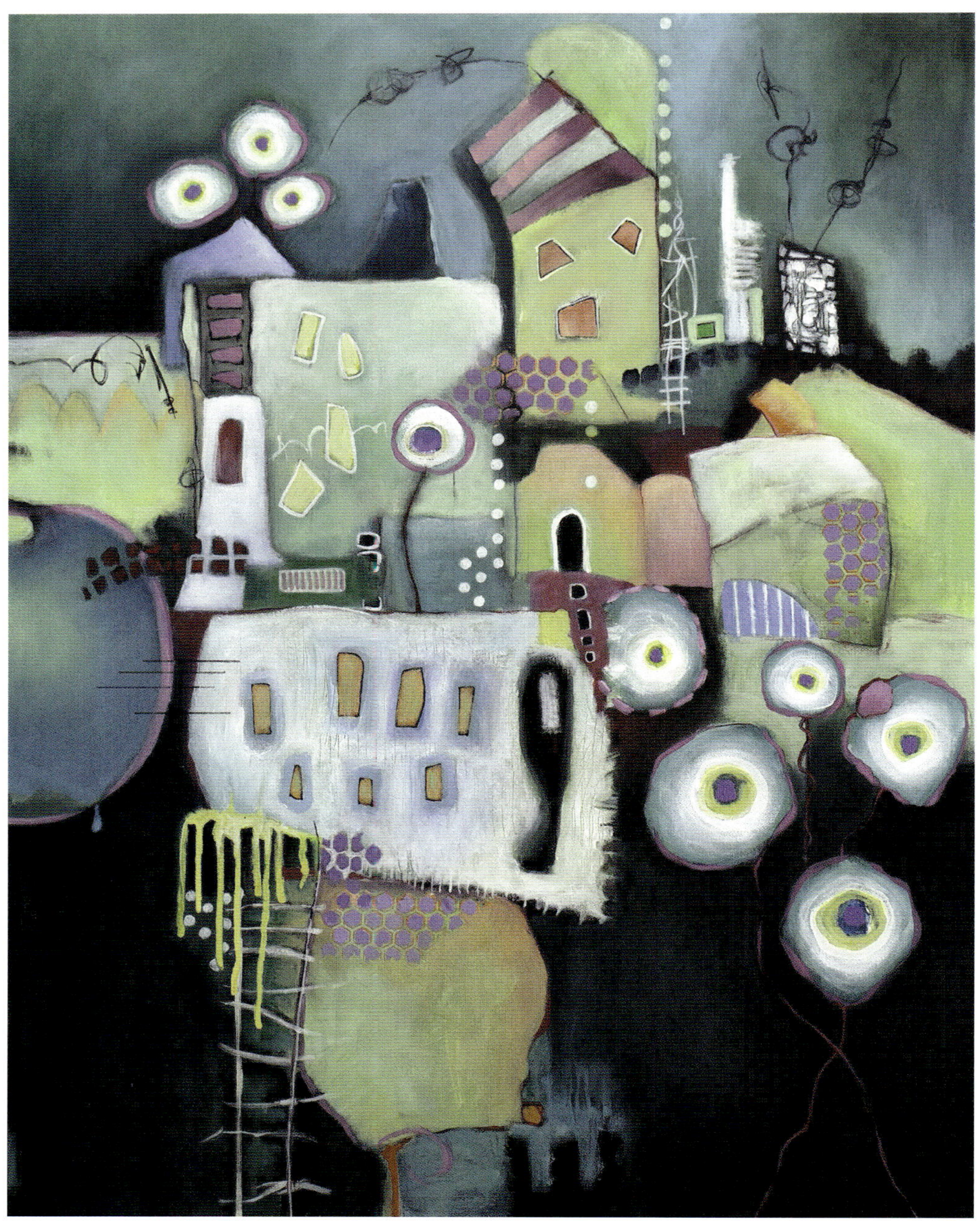

Eileen Shaloum

Eileen Shaloum is an abstract painter and mixed-media artist who uses the process of layering paint with textural components, such as collaged papers, fabric, photographs, string, and found objects. Whether on stretched canvas or unstretched canvas (wall hangings), her work has a whimsical nature. The imaginary quality of her style invites the viewer to interact with the themes of her spirited compositions. The artist's most recent body of work, *Invisible Cities*, is inspired by the book *Invisible Cities* by Italo Calvino. In this book, Marco Polo describes his journeys throughout Kubla Khan's empire in such a descriptive way that it inspired Shaloum to interpret them into fantastical landscapes and figurative compositions, which she calls "Dreamscapes." These visual journeys have become a metaphor for her life, both personal and spiritual journeys.

On Painted Stairs
Acrylic and mixed media
30 x 24 in.

eileenshaloum@gmail
.com
eileenshaloum.com
@eileenshaloum

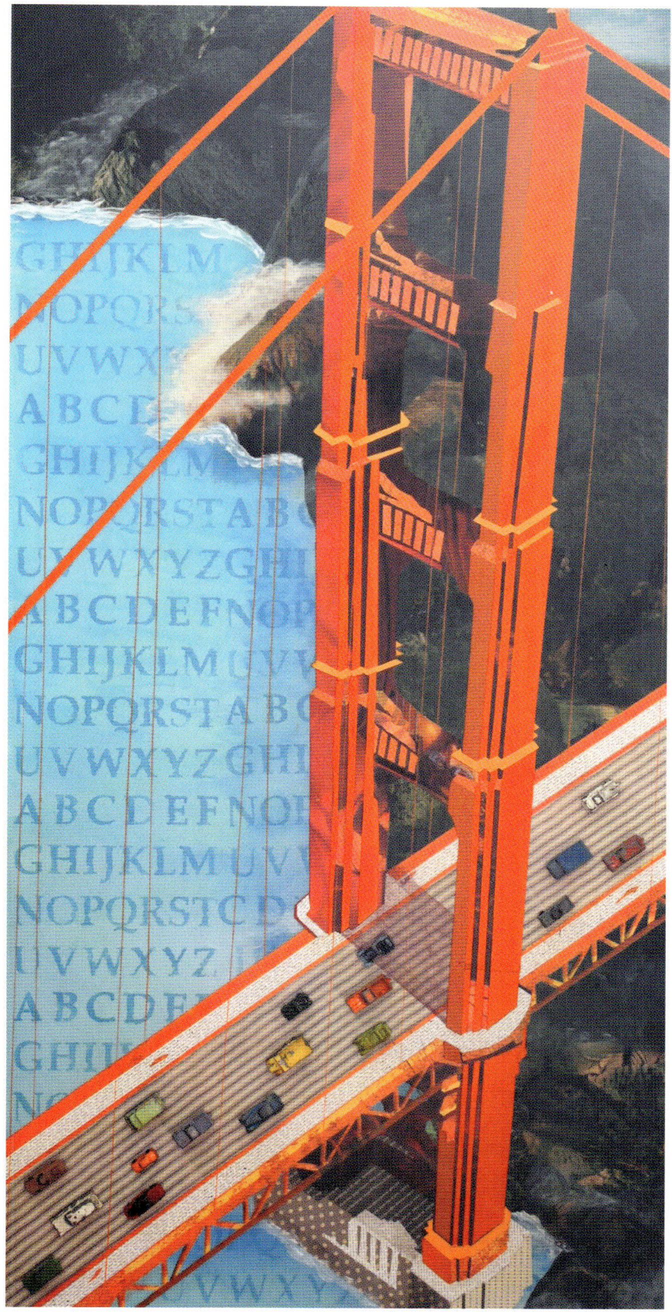

Kerri Warner

"I find art in everything, and everything finds its way into my art," says mixed-media artist Kerri Warner. The artist relishes the combination of contemporary design with the unexpected utilization of found, recycled, and/or repurposed materials. In her collages, she uses book pages, wrapping paper, found objects, and fragments of antique hardware mixed with acrylic paint over textured backgrounds to create works depicting moments in time. Warner tries to portray body language and facial expressions that might make the viewer stop and ponder the situation or stir a memory of time spent with friends or family. Adding antique elements and found objects allows the viewer to connect with the art, bringing a sense of nostalgia or sparking a memory. Each work captures daily life as subject matter in which the actual event has yet to take place or has just ended—moments frozen in time to become the memory of an event that will never take place.

Light Traffic
Mixed media collage with vintage toy cars
72 x 36 in.

kerriwarnerartist@yahoo
.com
kerriwarner.com
@kerri_artist

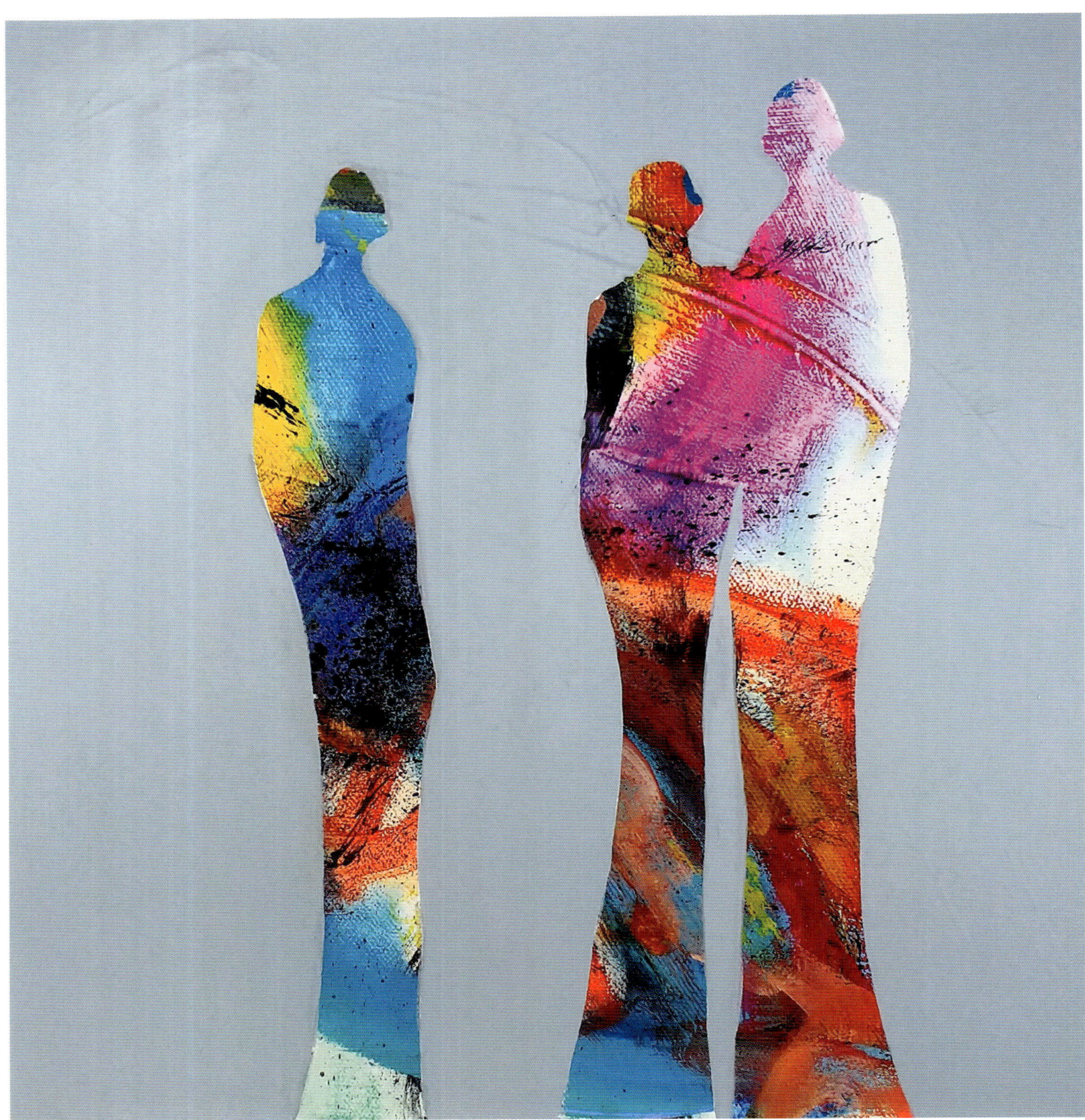

Elizabeth Wing

Elizabeth Wing is an abstract painter working mostly in acrylic and mixed media. She is interested in the human experience and how those experiences draw us together and tear us apart. She explores what's beneath the surface once barriers are removed and broken down. Her series *What's Underneath* explores people's similarities and our differences. It explores the human experience and how that connects us, unlike any other species. "When everything is stripped away, except for what's underneath, only then do we find truth," Wing says. The series speaks to community, division, and ultimately, the strength of connection—the necessity of connection.

Many layers of bold and sometimes cautious marks are symbolic of the layers upon layers that are our human existence. Some layers we cover but many move with us, informing our experiences and how we react to them.

Stillness And Movement
Acrylic
12 x 12 in.

elizabethwingemail@
gmail.com
elizabethwingart.com
@elizabethwingart

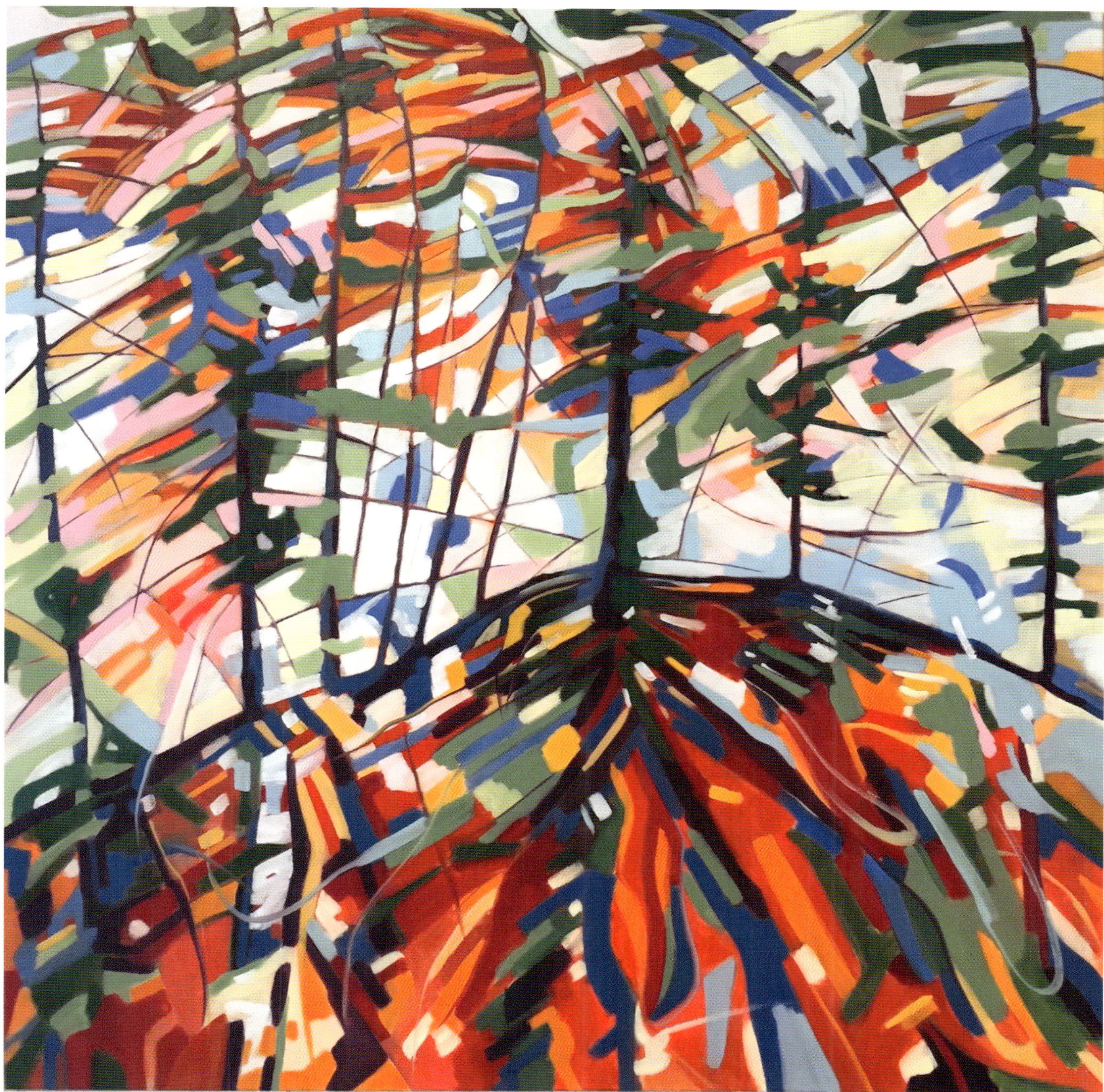

Marcia Wise

Marcia Wise's intuition and creative inspiration were both heightened while being caught in a windstorm in the woods near her home in May 2019. Wise felt it was a sort of premonition about change coming in her life, that it was personal, and she was to witness the chaos created before her as the wind grew stronger. Three months later, her husband was diagnosed with cancer. The experience of that windy storm remained with her and gave her strength. Then the coronavirus raged throughout the world and again the memory of the wind and chaos returned. Wise was inspired to paint this experience.

The artist has always been drawn to the natural world. In her youth, she was a landscape painter.
work, I express aliveness, nature and cultural issues. I use multiple layers of paint, working in both oils, acrylics and mixed media.

Ostinato
Oil
36 x 36 in.

mewise498@comcast
.net
marciarwise.com
@marciafineartist

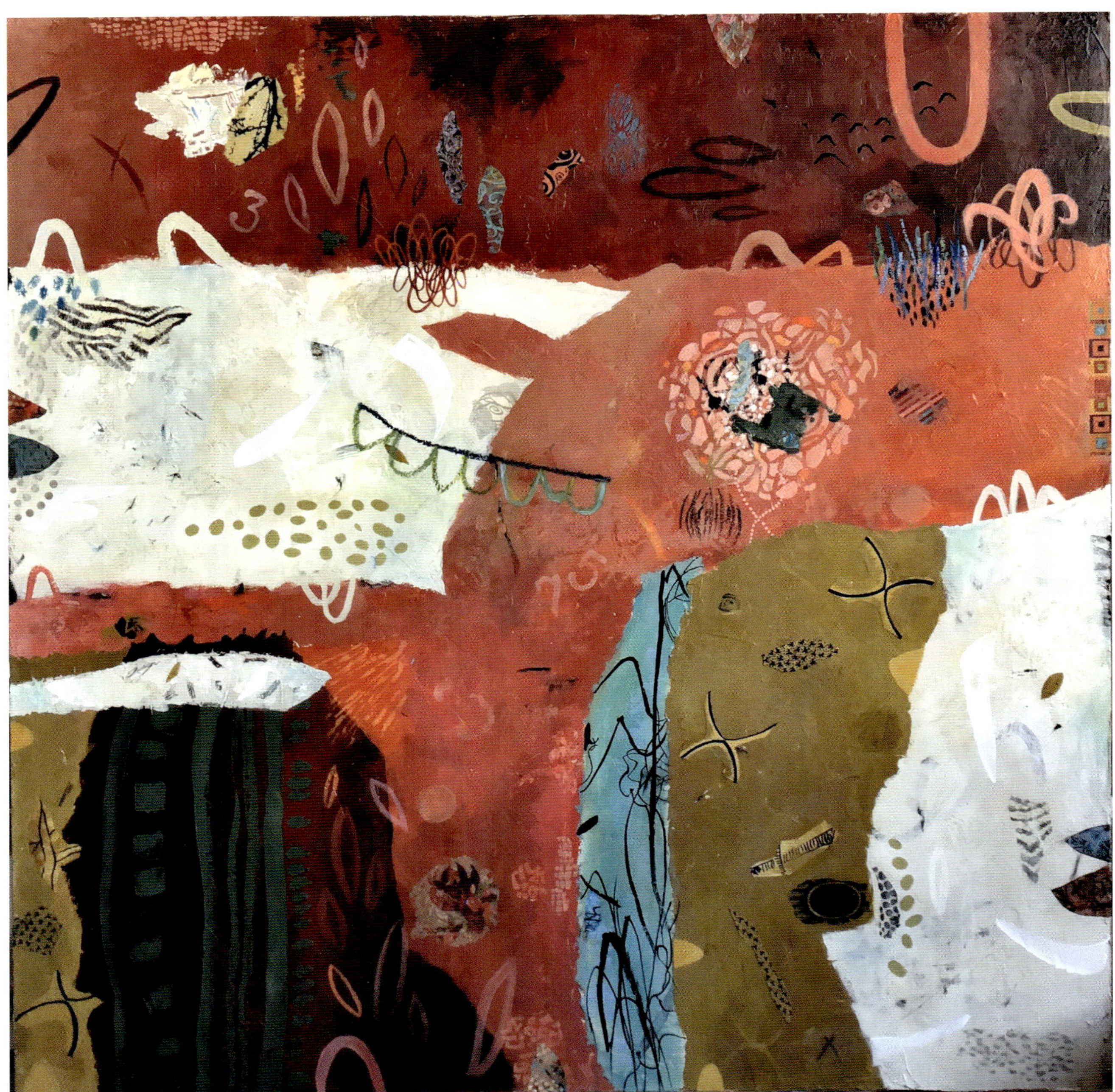

Francoise Barnes

While Francoise Barnes cares deeply about the profound issues facing our world, such as racism, violence, poverty, loneliness, etc., she does not have any specific message that she is trying to convey through her work. The first reason she goes to her studio is the almost primal need to create something that will record on paper or canvas what she has observed and loved, what has moved her. This act of creation is done first for herself. Then, it is the artist's hope that, if her work is successful at all, it will bring to others a moment of joy, beauty, and a sense of wonder or surprise. Nature, especially observed from very close, is at the basis of Barnes' inspirations, from the lacy details of a dragonfly's wing to the dots, flecks, specks, the artful unevenness of stripes and marks found in some plants, flowers, insects, or animals. She has also always had a profound love and admiration for the awesome art of indigenous cultures.

Wine and Rose
Mixed media
36 x 36 in.

OPPOSITE
Perseverance
Mixed media
36 x 36 in.

franswazz@gmail.com
franswazzart.com
@franswazzart

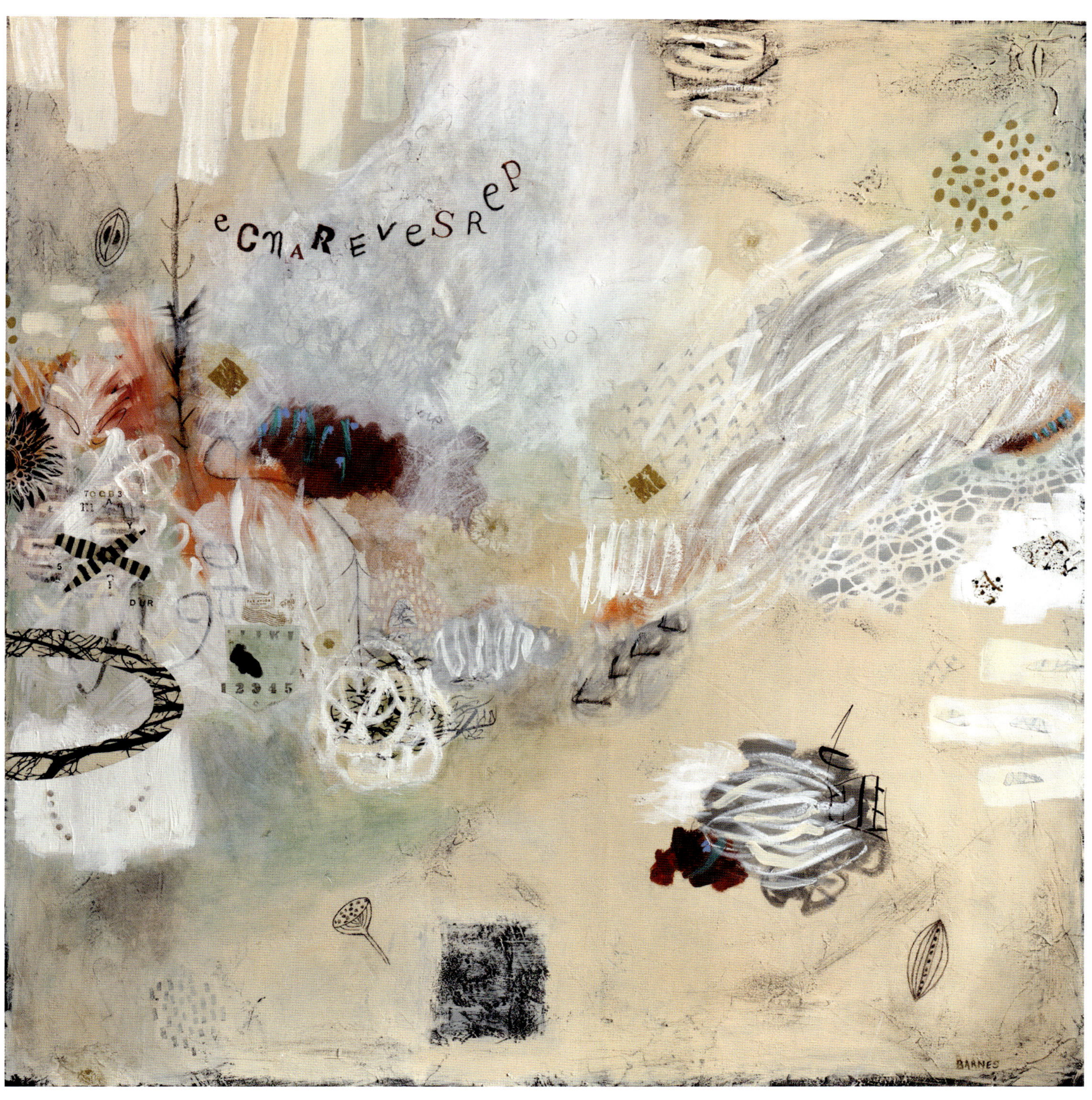
eCnAReveSReP
12345
BARNES

Machiel Roest

Machiel Roest has always had a passion for art and philosophy, particularly that of Ludwig von Wittgenstein, Friedrich Nietzsche, and Martin Heidegger. The artist started drawing and painting what their philosophy meant to him. Roest tries to find ways to bring their theories in a two-dimensional transition toward a more general understanding of what they in fact meant. Too many times philosophers are used for political or other purposes instead of just their thoughts. Roest realized that using language to read, to think, and to study the works of great philosophers is only a limited, one-sided form of philosophy. "The need arose for me to translate their beliefs into my drawn reality," the artist says. "I wanted to express my interpretation of philosophy through the universal language of art rather than through words." The titles of all Roest's paintings correspond to aphorisms or expressions made by the aforementioned philosophers.

The Belief in Truth Begins with the Doubt of all Truths in Which One has Previously Believed
Oil on paper
29.9 x 22 in.

machiel@machielr.eu
machielr.eu
@macphi

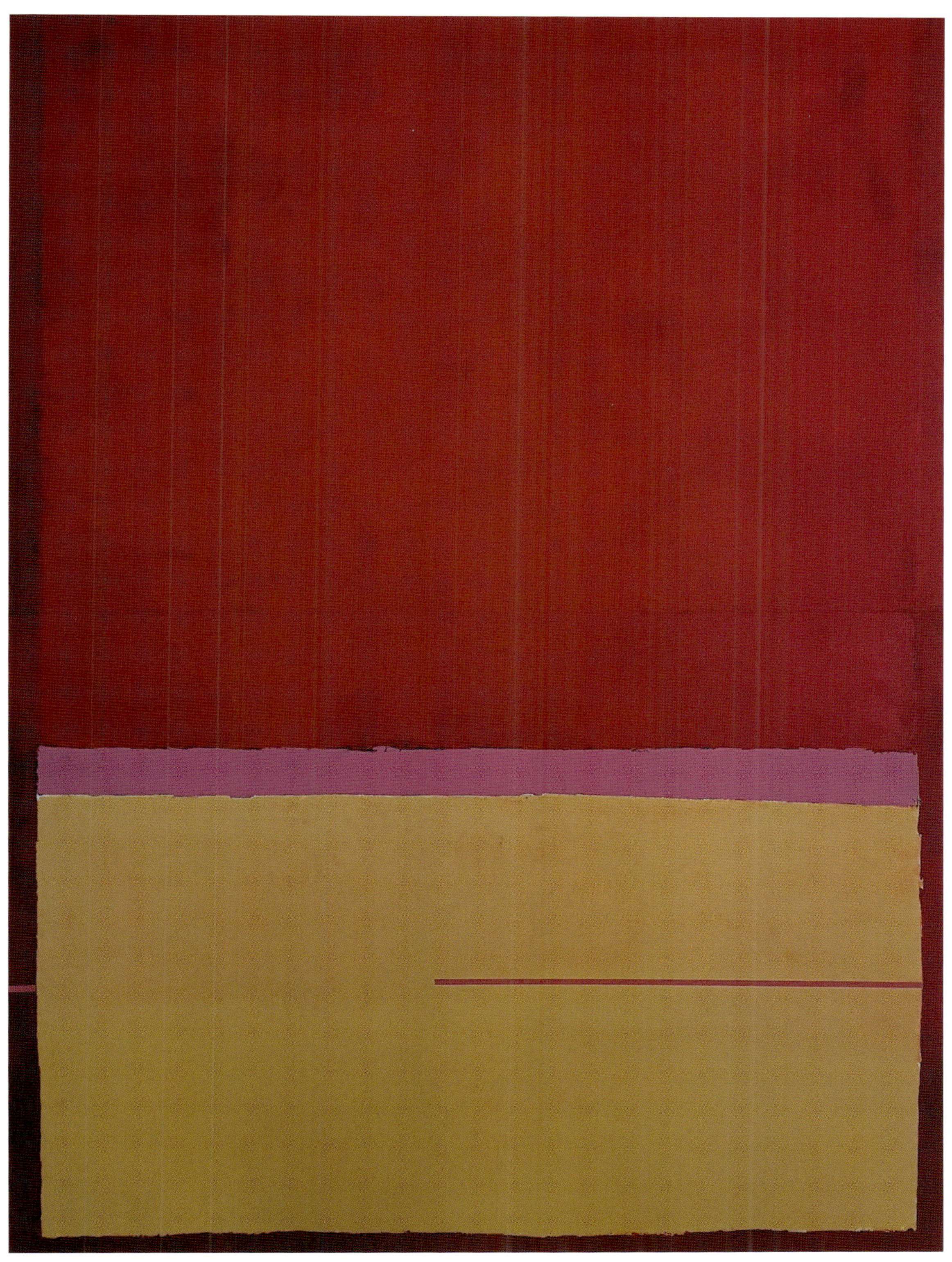

*A Politician Divides
Mankind in Two Classes:
Tools and Enemies*
Oil on paper
55 x 39 in.

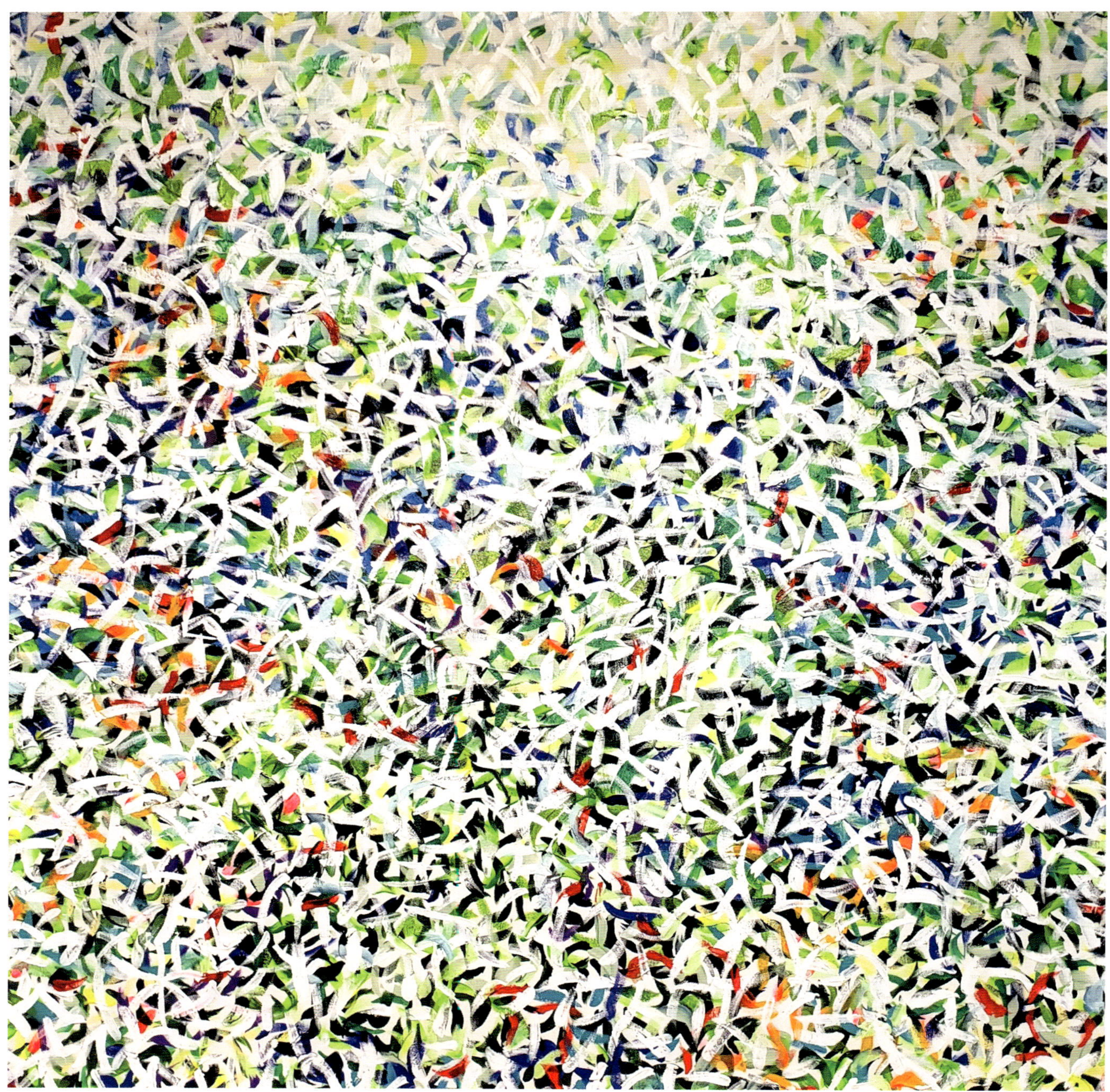

Caren Akers

Caren Akers would like to think her artwork expresses fun and peacefulness. She enjoys creating abstract paintings and utilizing vibrant colors and metallic paints. Her work is inspired by a color, a word, movement, or pattern that she may have seen or heard. Aker believes that art is in the eye of the beholder, and her art allows the viewer to display it either landscape or vertical format, which allows one to view a new, different painting. "I love it when someone tells me something about my work that was completely different than my own impression of the creation of it," Akers says. "To me, that is the beauty of art. After all, I do not believe there is right or wrong in art or in the interpretation of the piece, that belongs solely to you. To me, that is the beauty of it."

No. One
Acrylic
36 x 36 in.

carens.art@gmail.com
caren-akers.com
@carenakers

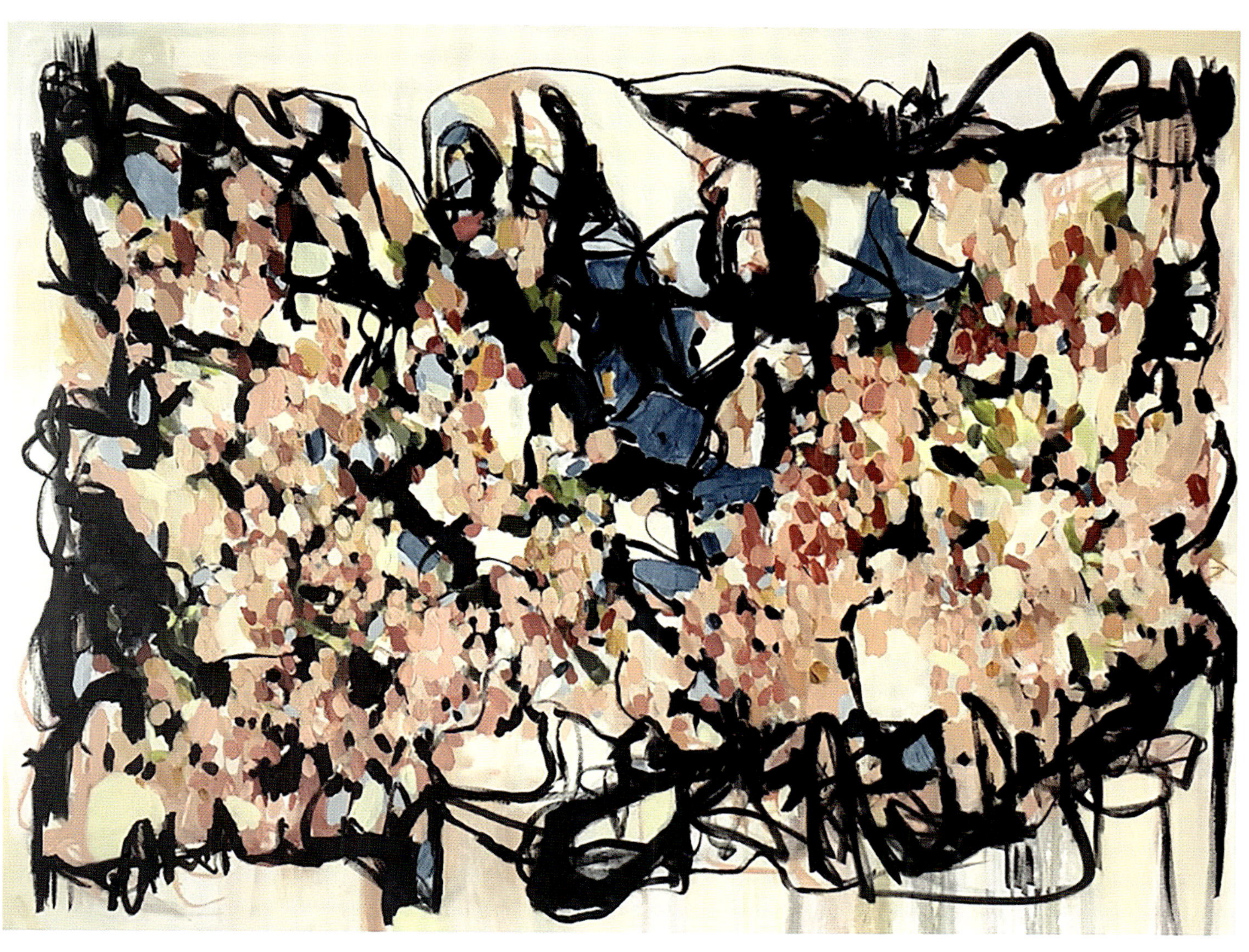

Susana Aldanondo

Susana Aldanondo has become known as "the artist who paints under the rain" because she has included rain as a special part of her creative process. Intuitively, she found beauty in rain from an early age, and it very naturally became a part of her process, as life challenged her to find ways to paint while overcoming obstacles. Rain embraces the idea of expression of freedom; it points to the artist's inner challenge to continue to paint under any circumstances, and it turns the world into an art studio that provides solitude where you'd otherwise be surrounded by a crowd. It is also about life and the chaos associated with life itself. It can be chaotic to paint under pouring rain and windy conditions, and there is an element of excitement about it too, because you never know how it's going to turn out. You just need to go with the flow.

Blue Sky
Acrylic
30 x 40 in.

susanaaldanondoart@
gmail.com
susanaaldanondoart
.com
@susanaaldanondo

PAINTING: TRADITIONAL/ABSTRACT

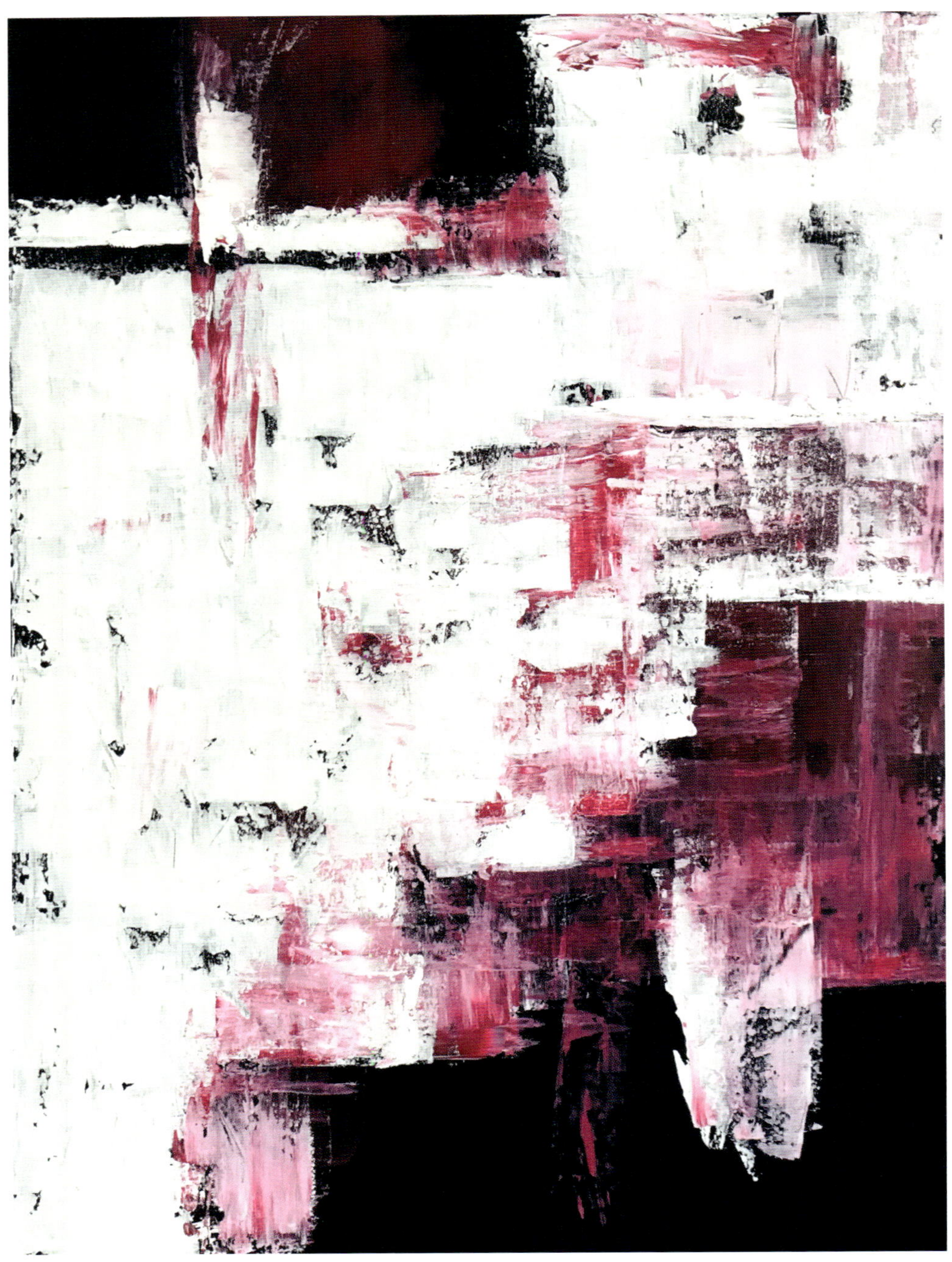

Kelly Aldridge

As an artist, Kelly Aldridge likes to associate her work with high-fashion. Her use of texture and movement is varied as she is drawn to create work that is glamorous yet edgy. Her work has a dramatic vibe as the color schemes are usually heavy and bold and the sizes demand attention. Being a former fashion model, Aldridge believes black is everything in fashion and thinks it spills over into her artistic style because it is her favorite color. Everything from concrete pavements to fashion photography to patterns found on place mats inspires her. Aldridge likes rough textures as she likes her work to resemble the old but incorporate the new, using glossy paints and metallic flakes that often elevate the painting in terms of glamour. Her works are oversized, and she likes to think of them as high-fashion paintings.

Atypical
Acrylic
49 x 37 in.

kellyaldridgeart@yahoo
.com
kellyaldridge.com
@kelly__aldridge

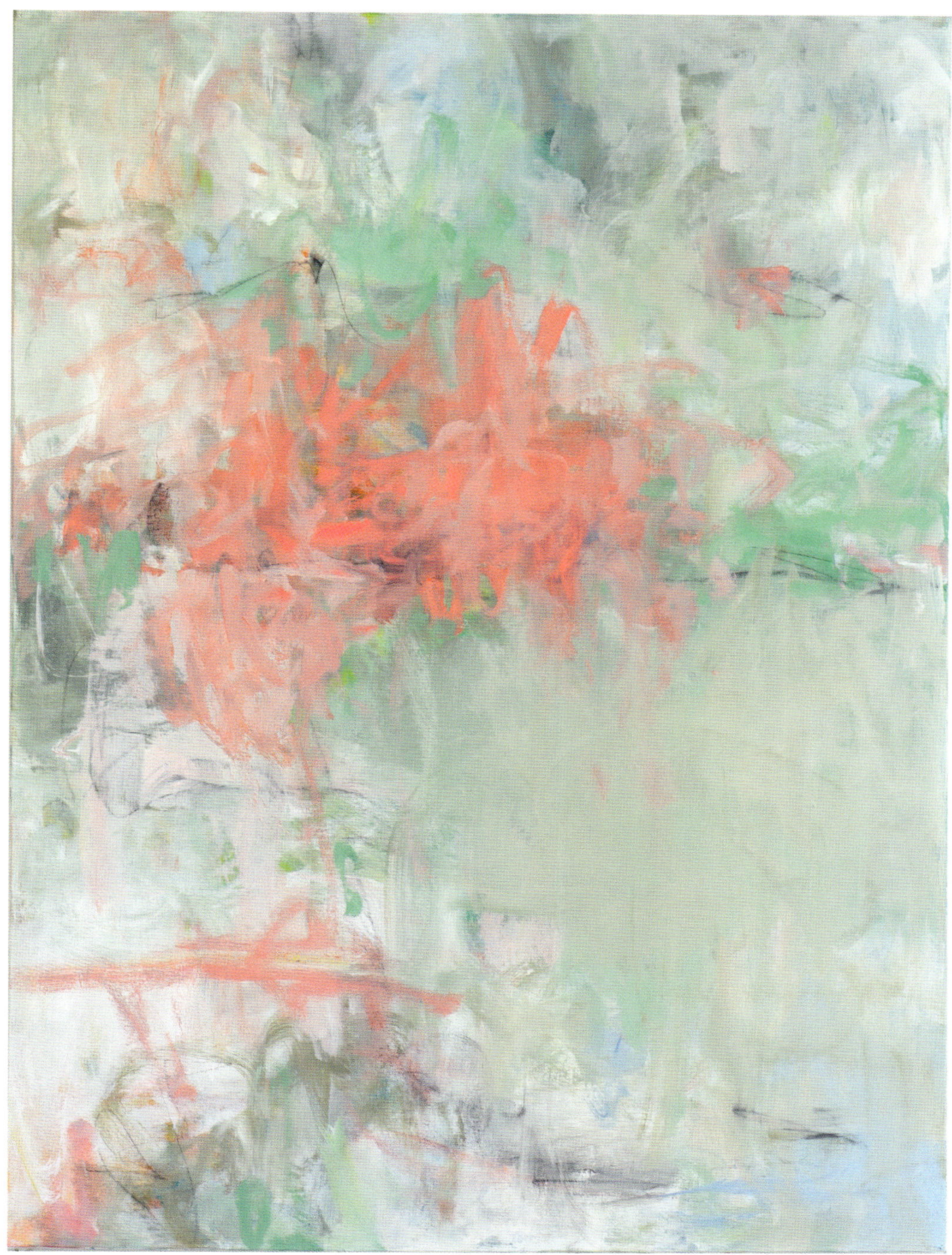

Elizabeth Bernheisel

Elizabeth Bernheisel loves color and light and finds joy in discovering the subtle differences in hue, tone, tint, and shade. She enjoys the activity of energetically making bold marks with her brushes, then softening those marks and blending color as she goes, creating new colors along the way. Bernheisel's mark making can reflect many things: her mood that day, how the view from her studio makes her feel, or a response to what she's put on the canvas. She enjoys exploring and building on the intersections of colors and marks that are created as she works.

Bernheisel is inspired by natural beauty—the shadows a leaf makes, the silhouette of a tree against a sunset, the sun reflecting on water, or the light coming in through a window. The goal with her art is to reflect the peace and joy she feels when she is enjoying nature and then leave that memory on the canvas.

Fragrance of Spring
Acrylic
40 x 30 in.

beth.bernheisel@gmail
.com
elizabethbernheisel.com
@bethbernheiselart

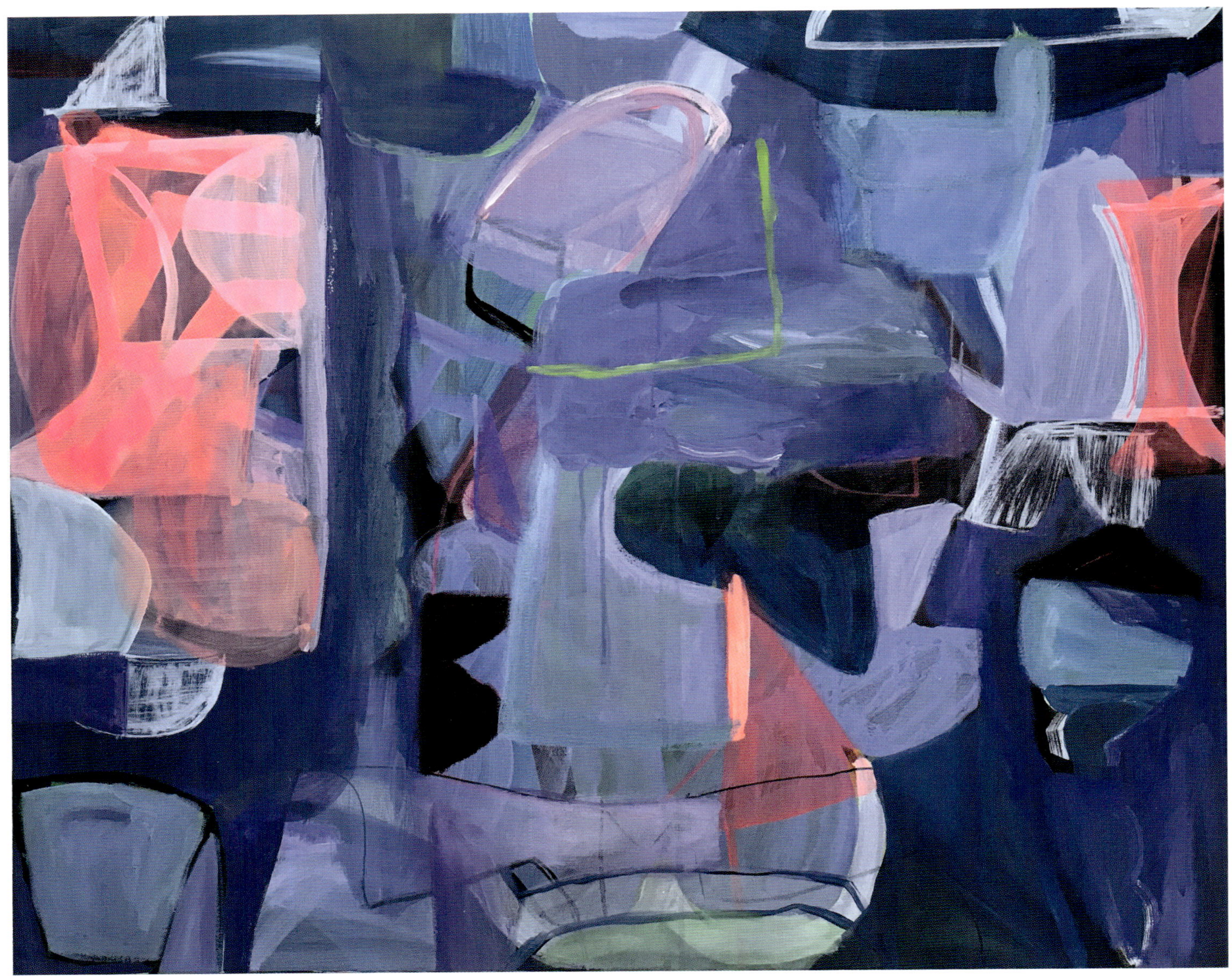

Cira Bhang

From her tiny studio, Cira Bhang loves to tell stories using bright colors harmonized with the layering of lines, shapes, and brushstrokes. Each of these elements is intuitively applied using acrylic paint, medium, and mixed media on various surfaces of media. The compositions are inspired as much by the simple things in her everyday life as they are by more serious and even complex subjects, such as being a woman and wife. While painting, Bhang discovered something unexpectedly interesting that led her to the intention and the process of defining the work. The culmination of her work is successful if the final result allows everyone a personal and unique interpretation. In her opinion, even something imperfect can become attractive.

A Woman Is Sitting In Her Room
Oil stick, acrylic marker and acrylic paint
31.8 x 39.3 in.

info@cirabhang.com
cirabhang.com
@cira_bhang

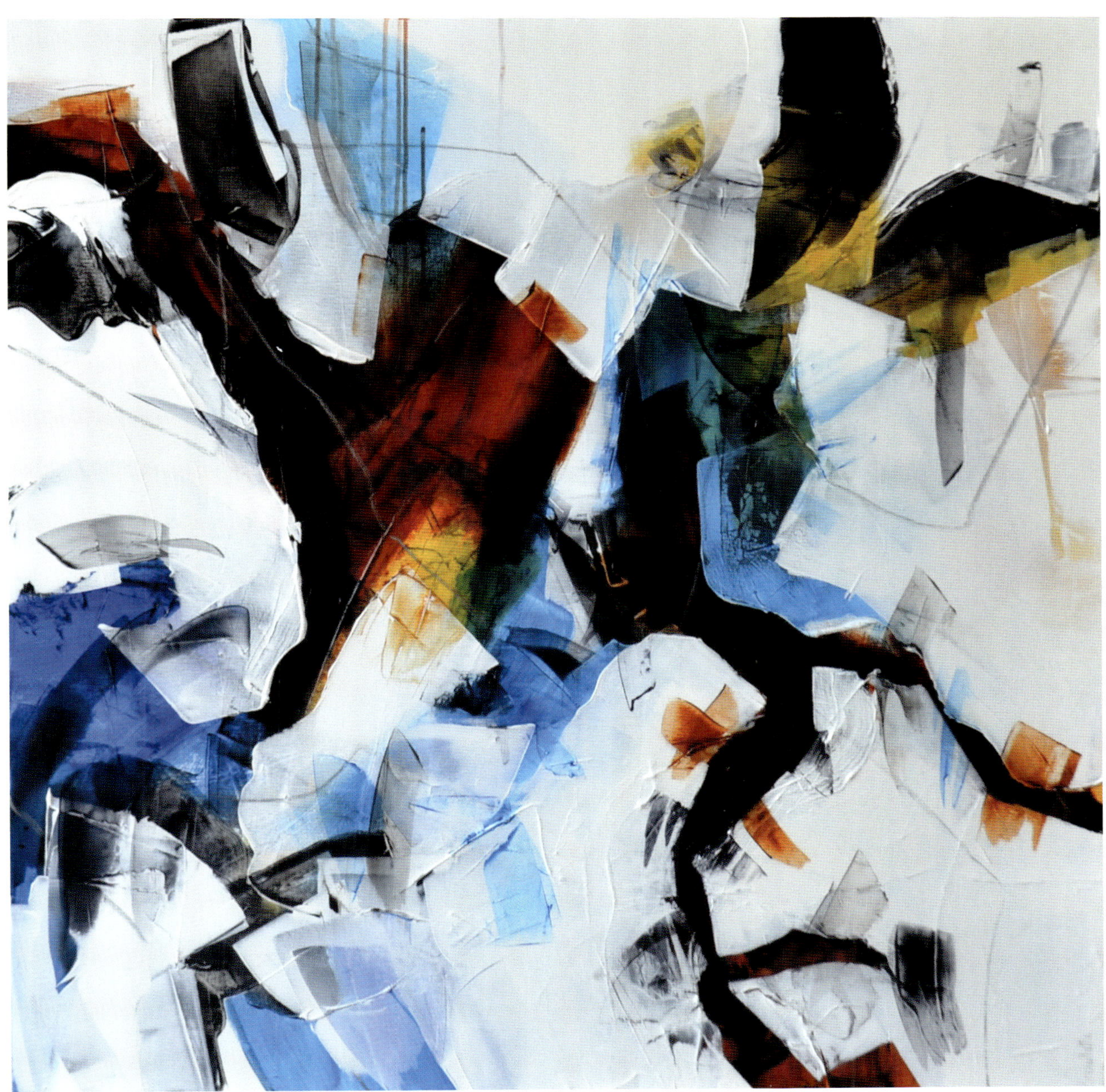

Johanne Brouillette

Having chosen to renounce figurative painting a few years ago, Johanne Brouillette now paints in an expressionist and gestural style. The color palette she uses can be either monochromatic or vibrant. She always includes areas of black for its confrontational and paradoxical effect, which is both grounding and indicative of endless depth. Balance is fundamental in her work. The challenge is reconciling her natural tendency toward perfectionism with her strong desire for freedom and disorder. Evidence is seen in both her process and finished product. Although the initial foundation is applied spontaneously, subsequent layers show a strong influence of her conscious mind. As such, her work mirrors her internal struggle to find balance between the opposing aspects of her personality. Brouillette's paintings incorporate both raw emotion and quiet tranquility and reflect her recent experiences at any given time. Her purpose is to give voice to what is felt but unseen.

Joie de vivre VIII
Acrylic, collage and graphite
40 x 40 in.

johanne.brou@hotmail.com
johannebrouillette.ca
@johannebrouilletteart

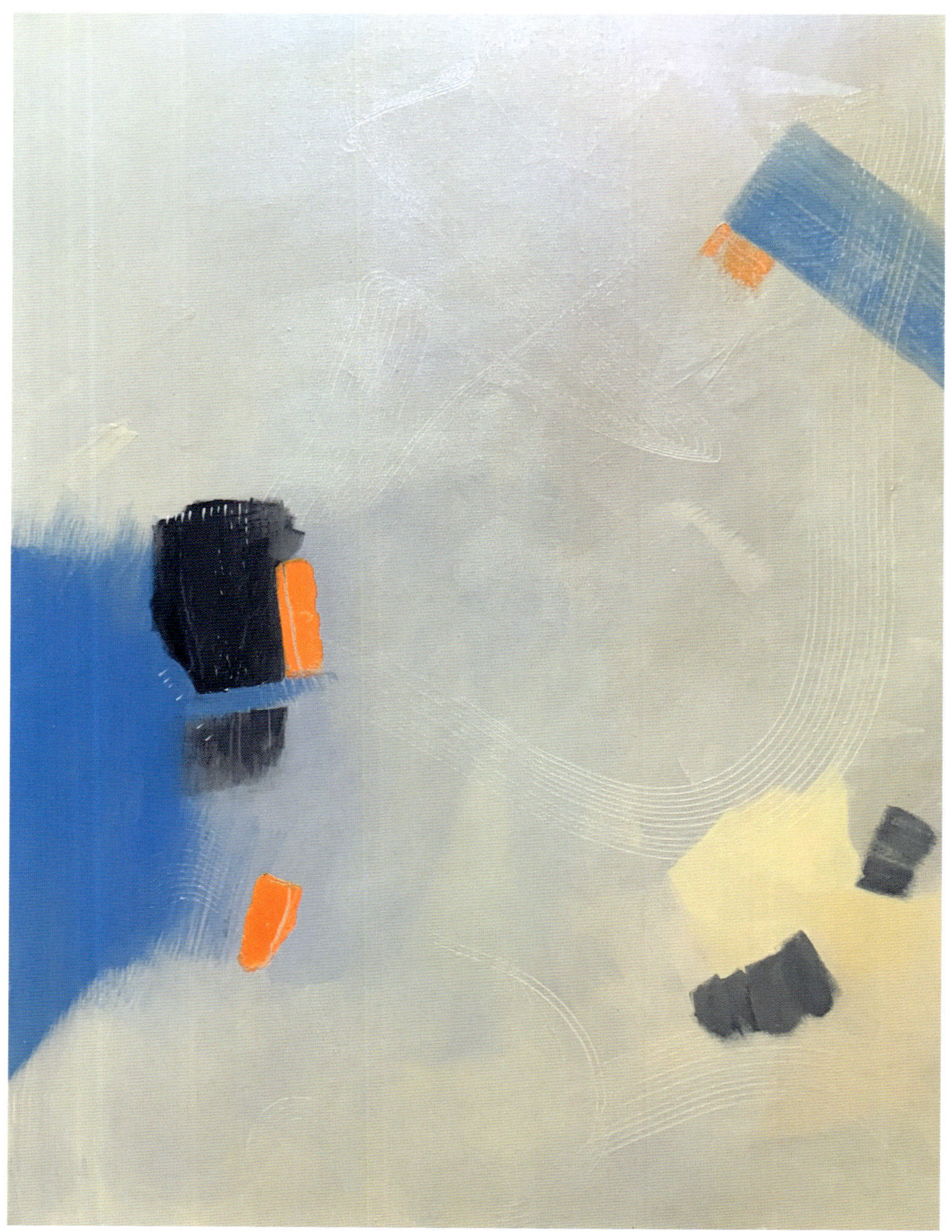

Julie Shunick Brown

Julie Shunick Brown's painting style is always evolving, changing as her life does. Currently, it's strictly intuitive. She starts without any preconceptions or reasons and without any idea of the end result. Usually, her first step is covering up the whiteness of the canvas or panel with whatever color catches her eye. Her process gets more deliberate and intentional as she progresses, but there is no plan or end in mind. She works more as a reaction to what is already on the canvas. Her focus is on the composition and color, working instinctually. The result is always a surprise, but it amazes her how often the work seems reflective of what's happening in her life. Even though her process is not really conscious, it feels like an endless search for calm, making sense of the chaos and urgency about us

Morning at the Market
Acrylic
40 x 30 in.

julieshunickbrown@
gmail.com
julieshunickbrown.com
@julieshunickbrown

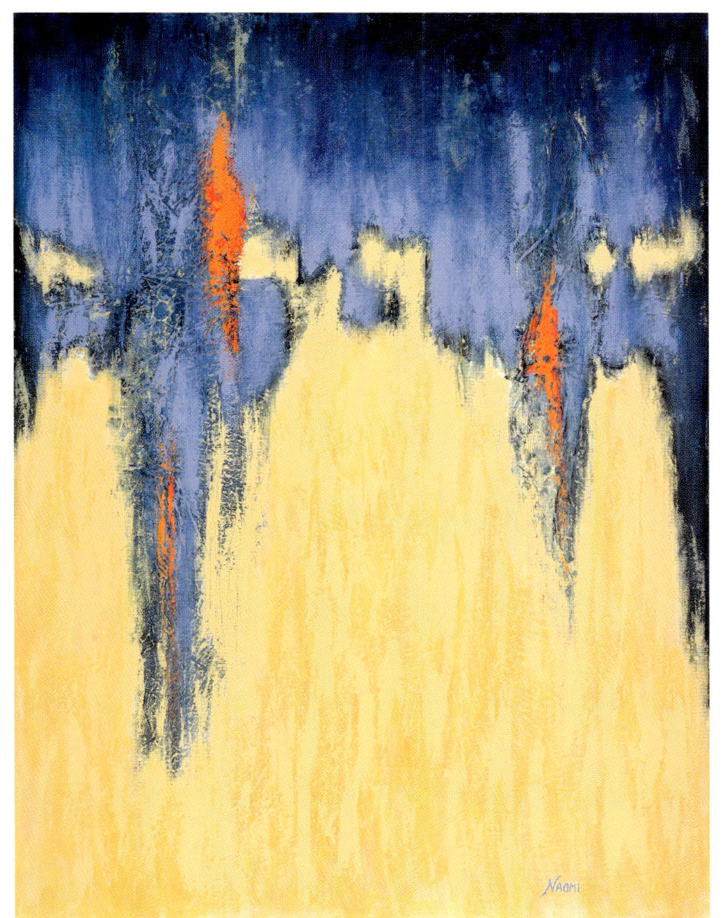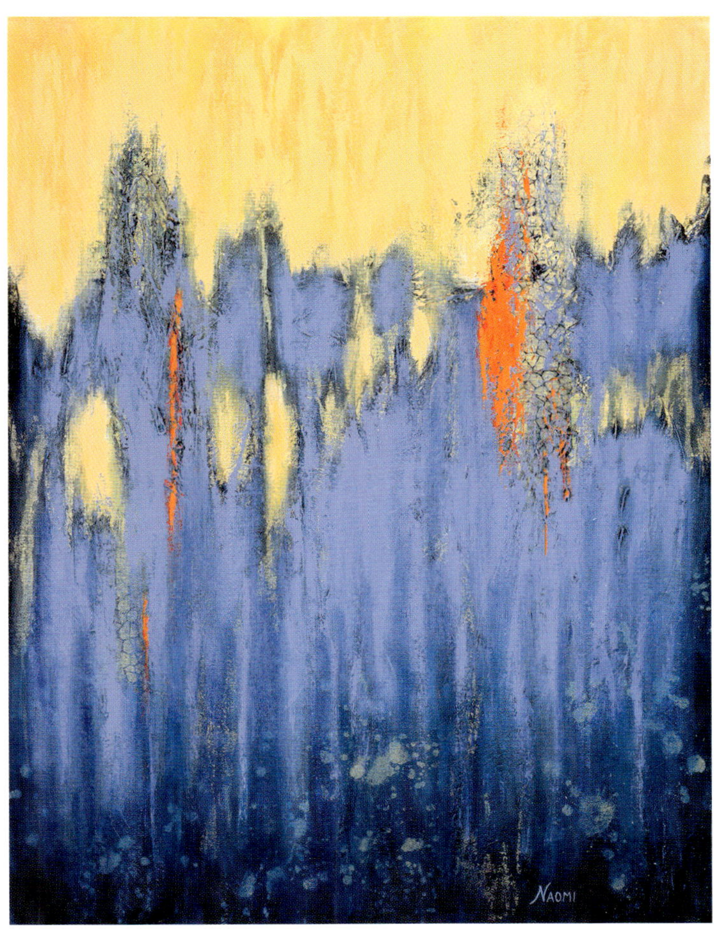

Naomi Butler

One of Naomi Butler's recent bodies of work is a series titled *Choices*, which represents the good decisions we all make. "There are many opportunities to make smart choices, which can give us positive energy. The *Choices* paintings are presented in a reverse effect to portray outcomes from great choices," Butler says.

When viewing her work, Butler wants the viewer to see something new each time they look at the art, such as textures, cells, color values, and different shapes and images through the depth of the many layers. It is her hope that this will excite the viewer, triggering positive feelings and emotions. Texture and paint applied to the artwork in a happy, carefree manner are particularly important in the *Choices* series, creating unique and exciting patterns, shapes, and layers, which are inspired by abstract shapes such as cracks in sidewalks.

Choices #1 and #2
Acrylic and mixed media
48 x 36 in.

info@
abstractartbynaomi.com
abstractartbynaomi.com
@naomi.butler

PAINTING: TRADITIONAL/ABSTRACT

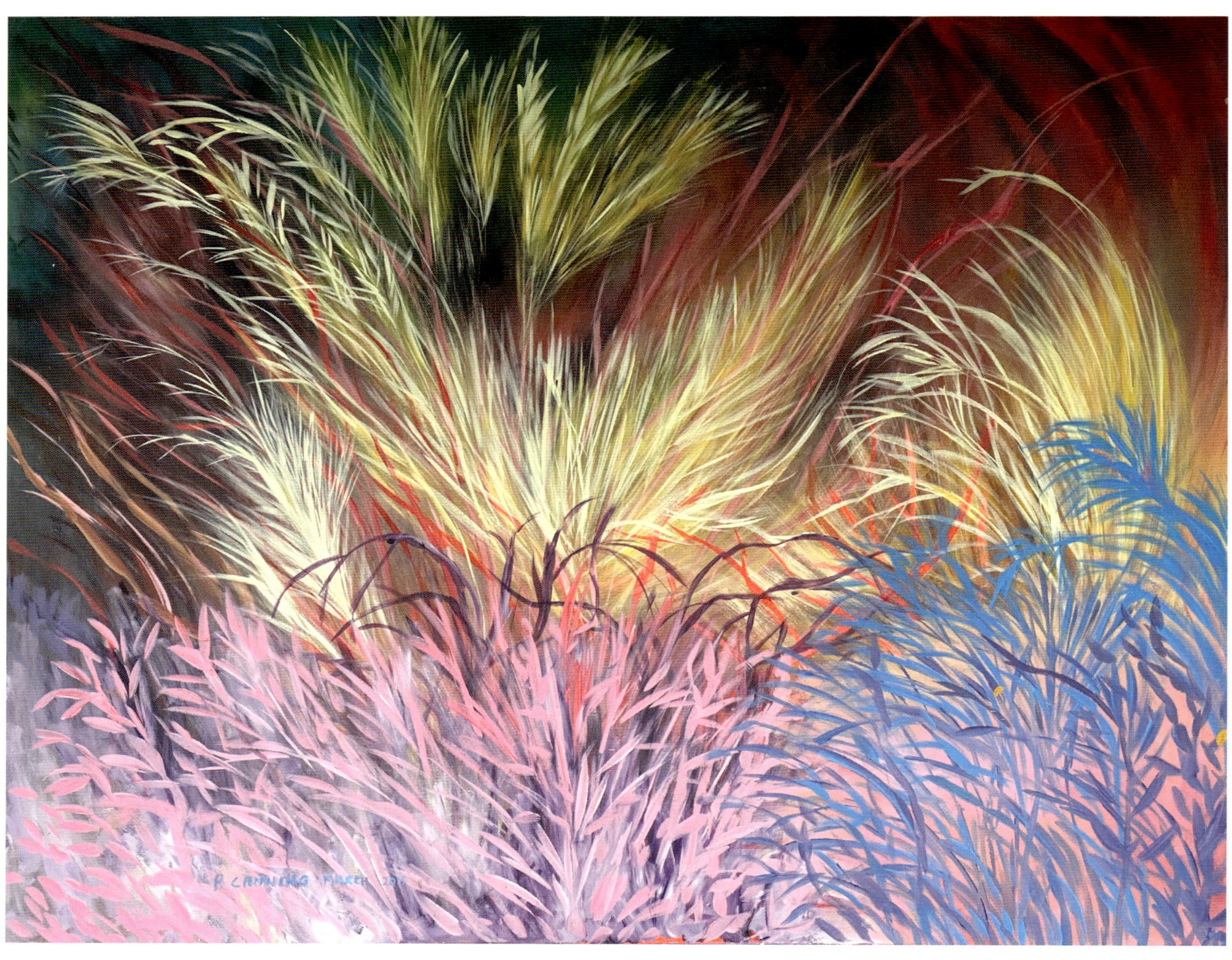

Patrick Canning

As an artist for over fifty years, Patrick Canning says his style of art can be termed as Abstract Expressionist, similar in style to the New York school of the 1950s–60s. Up until the early 1970s, Canning had painted traditional themes. However, he became restless and began a search for fresh ideas. It was at this time he discovered abstract expressionism. Artists like Pollock, Motherwell, Rothko, and de Kooning painted with an expression of complete freedom and vigor that aroused his curiosity. It seemed to Canning that these pioneers were making new and fresh discoveries. When he painted in this fashion, he felt a great deal of exhilaration, akin to jumping off a cliff. He wanted to paint from within, expressing his emotions and allowing his subconscious to guide him as he painted.

Undiscovered Country
Acrylic
47.5 x 59 in.

canningpat7@yahoo
.co.uk
@canningpat7

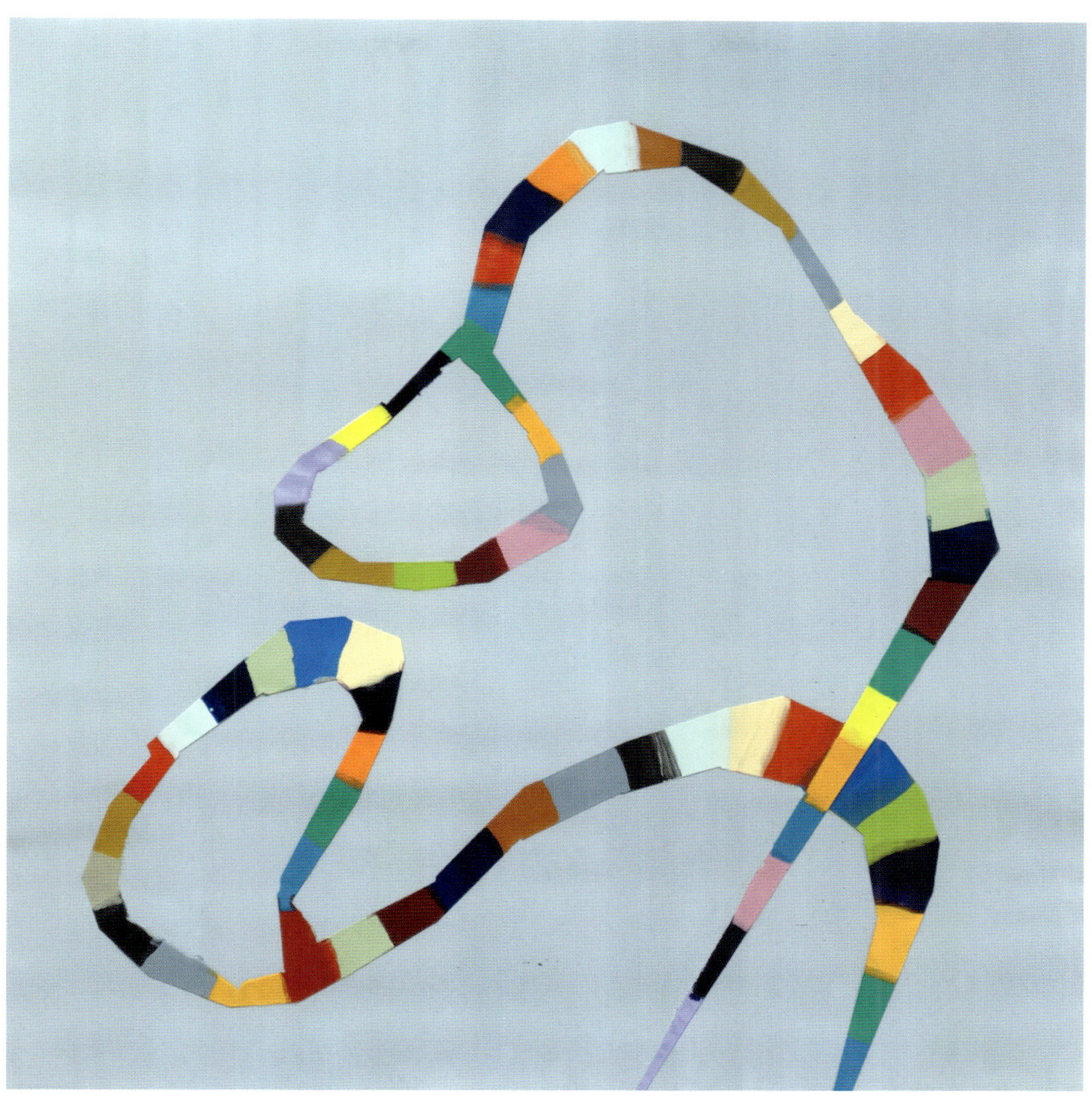

Kathy Cantwell

Minimalism has a quiet beauty that Kathy Cantwell is drawn to. She has derived a great amount of variation in her paintings by working with only a few elements. Staying within the self-prescribed elements allows Cantwell to focus and surrender to the process that she needs in order to progress in each work. A seemingly small change in direction can actually be a huge leap for the artist.

The paintings in the series *Curved* are such a formal and expressive departure from her previous work. The paintings sprang from a curiosity as to where Cantwell might take a previous series with curves slowly taking hold. The artist wanted to see interconnectedness. "What would happen if I started to bend the lines rather than fold them?" Cantwell asked herself. The end result was that the lines became more narrative and almost figurative. The narration sprang from a relationship Cantwell was having and found its way into the paintings.

Swoop
Encaustic
24 x 24 in.

kathy.cantwell@gmail
.com
kathycantwell.com
@cantwell57

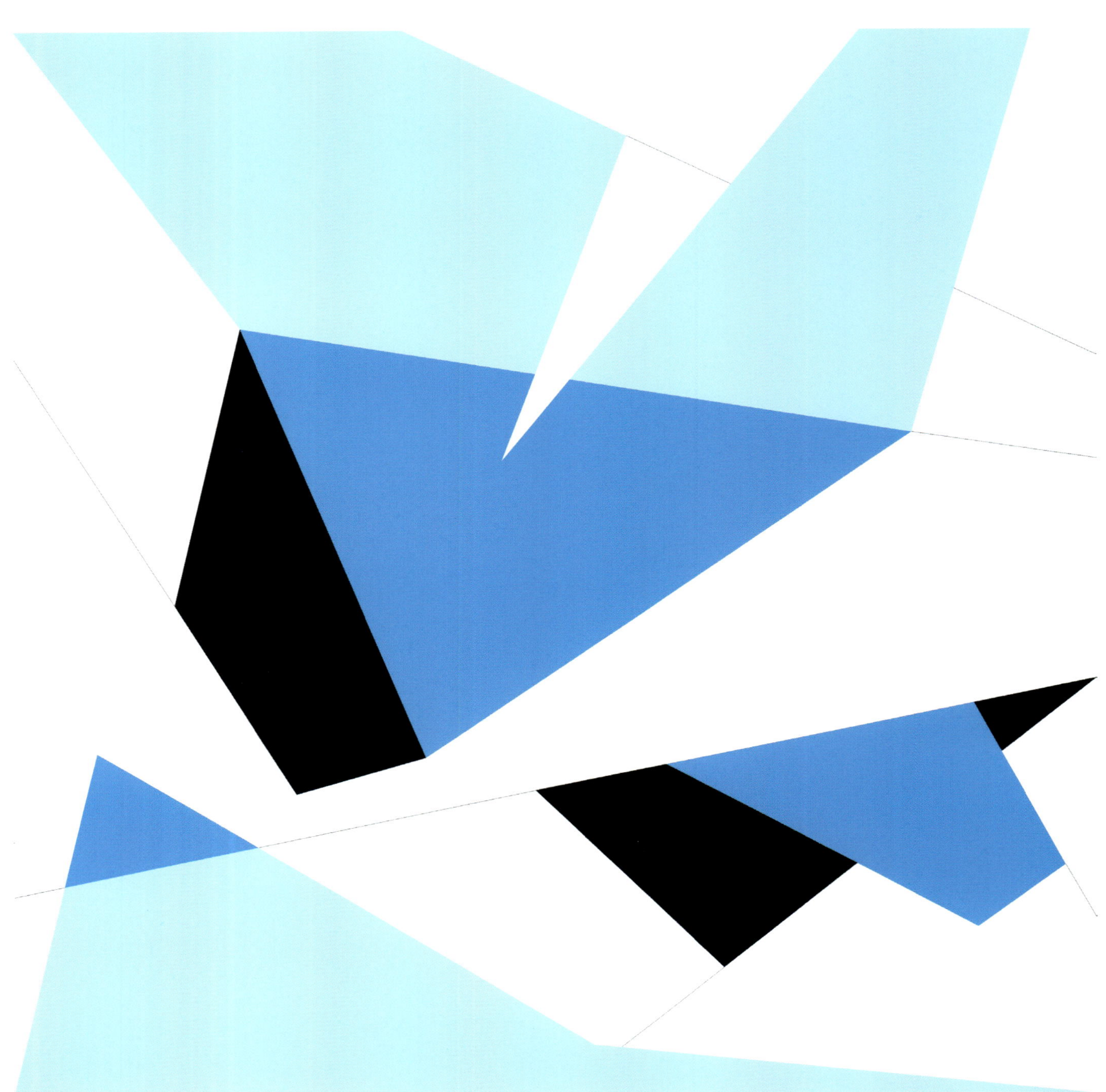

Daniel Sánchez Casado
Daniel Sánchez Casado's current paintings show an intimate and conceptual work full of two-dimensional geometric shapes, textures, and lyrical abstraction. His last series of abstract compositions on flat, colored backgrounds play with synthetic geometric shapes superimposed on each other (in some cases replacing those closed shapes by the open manipulation of space), where Casado uses a limited palette to highlight the work against the background. In this way, the greater the contrast ratio between figure and background, the more the figure will be distinguished. Sometimes, this contrast generates a certain moment when the figure becomes background and vice versa. In other words, the viewer's eyes see, but visual perception composes the image and selects only what has caught our attention.

Waterfront
Acrylic and collage on wood
19.6 x 19.6 in.

danielsanchezstudio@gmail.com
@danielsanchezstudio

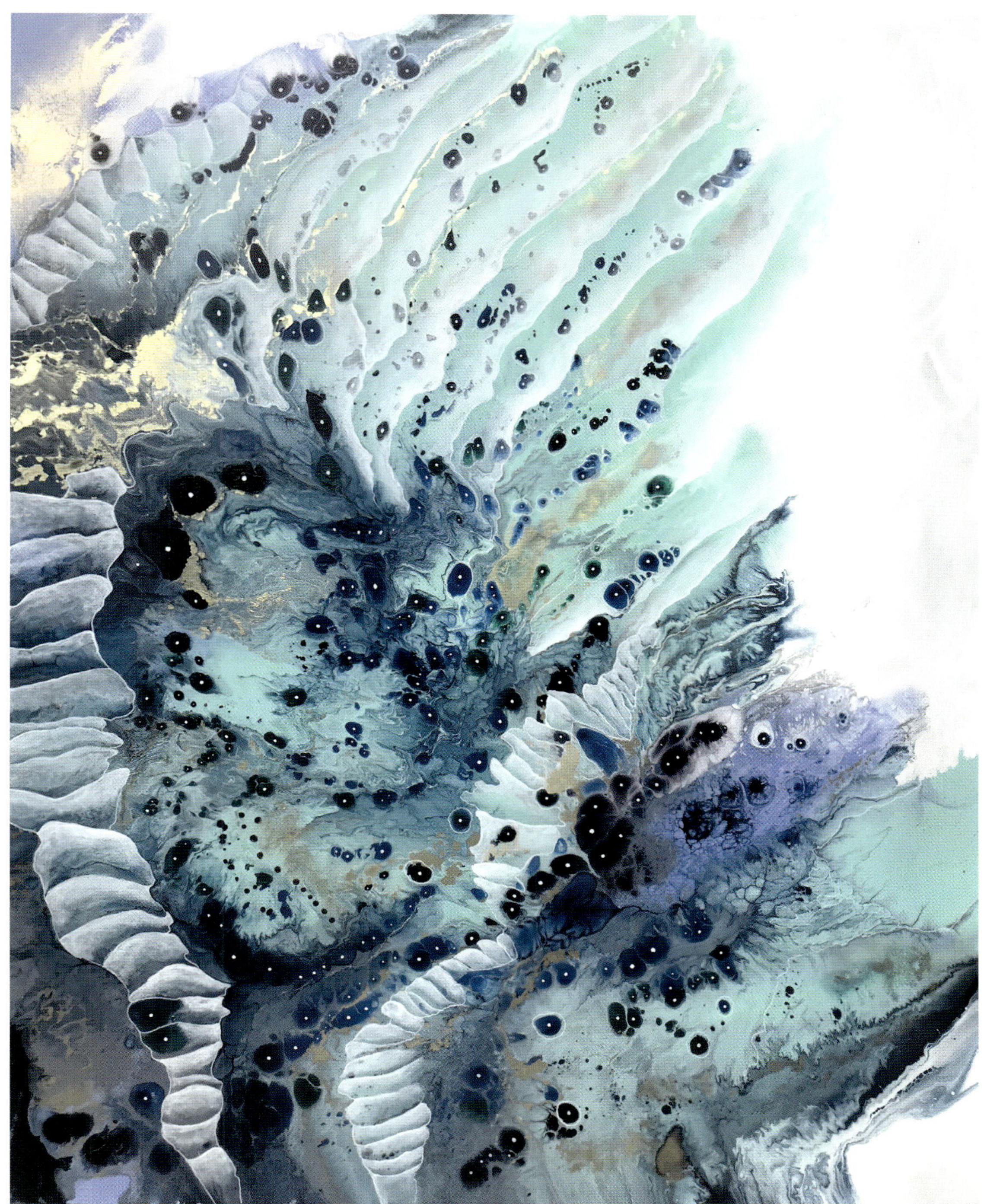

Jessica Chaix

Jessica Chaix's work is her greatest fulfillment. Each piece is a new opportunity to create a unique experience while opening herself up to the world in different ways. Inspiration is everywhere, ready for her to see it and begin creating. Forms, colors, balance, textures all mix together, resulting in a fascinating fusion. This is a never-ending journey for the artist, and in recent years, Chaix felt a strong need to find her own voice. To find an expression of herself as an artist in a way that truly expressed herself— her soul, her journey, and her experiences. In each brushstroke, in each color and line of her paintings, she tries to capture the feelings of light, texture, shape, and forms of nature combined with the universe, hoping it expresses to the viewer her most intense emotions.

Jellyfish II
Acrylic
60 x 48 in.

jessica_chaix@yahoo
.com.mx
jessicamchaix.com
@Jesschaixart

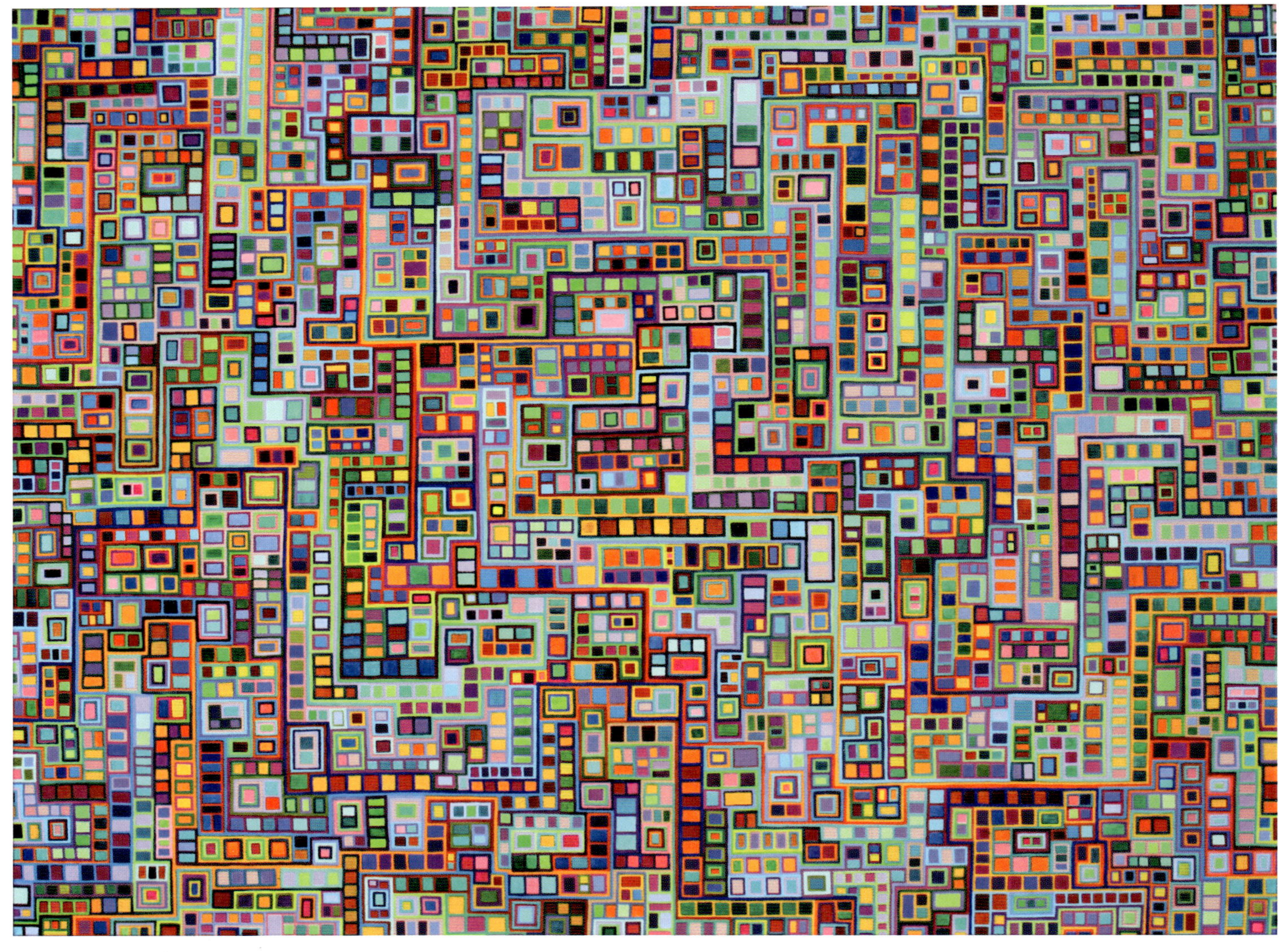

Andrew Chalfen

The ripples, radiance, fractal blooms, and clustered shapes of Andrew Chalfen's paintings, drawings, and mixed-media pieces reference aerial views, cartography, architectural renderings, musical notation, urban-like densities, and other natural and man-made patterns, many spilling out over edges, suggesting unseen continuations. His process mirrors that of his songwriting and music arranging, involving the repetition of a small selection of formal elements, subtle variation, the timbre of color palette, rhythm, and randomization strategies.

Chalfen's work shows a sheer joy in precise, dense patternmaking. The viewer may not know what to focus on first and become overwhelmed and subsequently absorbed in the details, which is akin to the experience of mediation or a divine/psychedelic experience.

Screaming Windows
Acrylic
3 x 4 ft.

andrewdchalfen@gmail
.com
andrewchalfen.com
@i.think.like.midnight

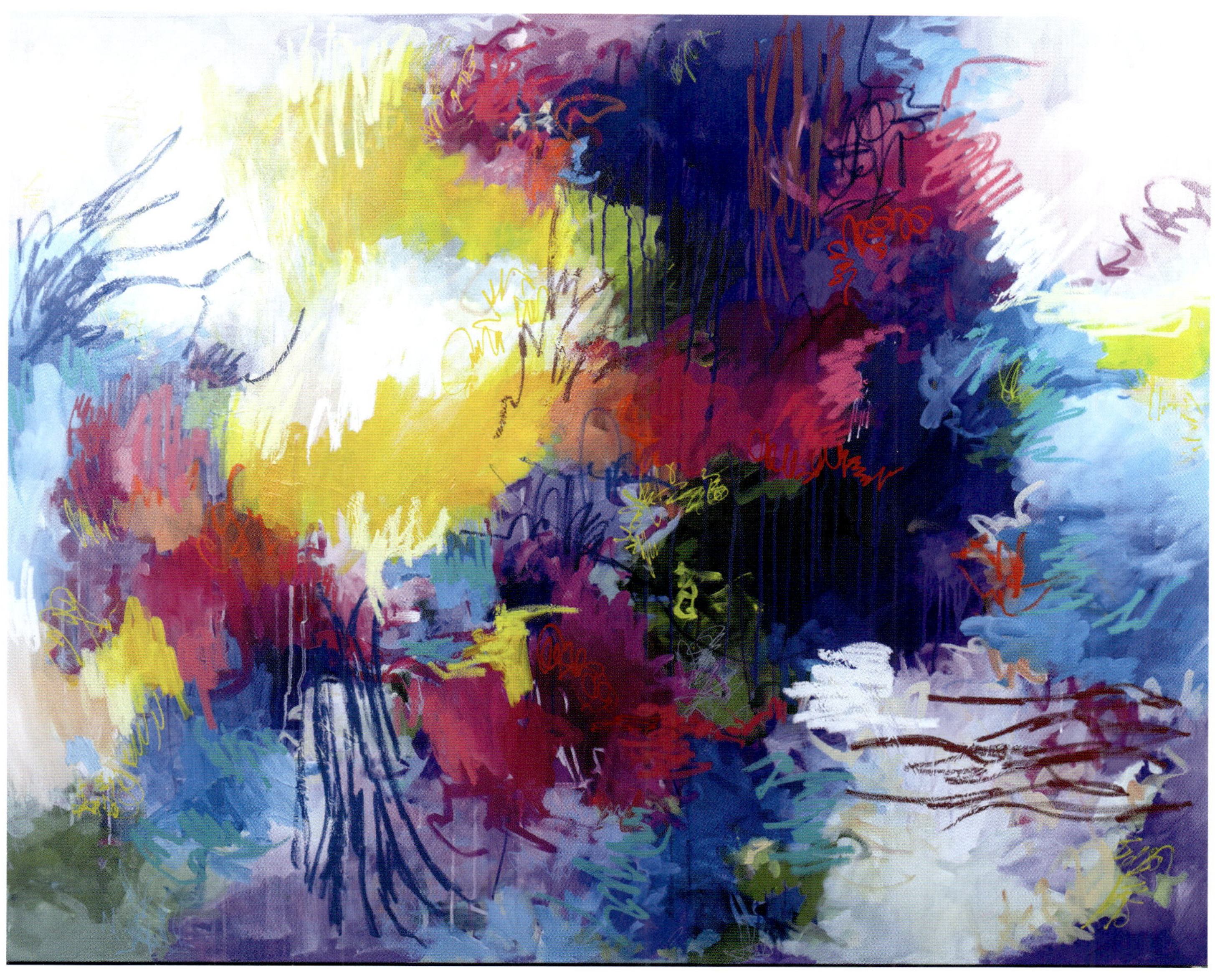

Lavanya Challa

Lavanya Challa grew up painting and drawing. When she began, she was always learning to perfect her skill or forms, causing her to repeatedly feel constrained and restricted by the need to stay true to the subject or the theme. That's when she discovered her love for abstract art.

The artist works on a painting for several weeks, constantly tweaking and teasing it out. This allows her to incorporate several ideas into a work, and the painting grows along with her. This method also allows Challa to keep her work current and updated. She experiments and plays with different materials and discovers how they complement each other, often leading to her next painting. Challa channels all her frustration and pain into her work, which is surprising considering how bright and cheerful the work is.

A Very Texan Sunset
Acrylics and mixed medium
48 x 60 in.

lavanyaschalla@gmail.com
lavanyachallaart.com
@lavanyachallaart

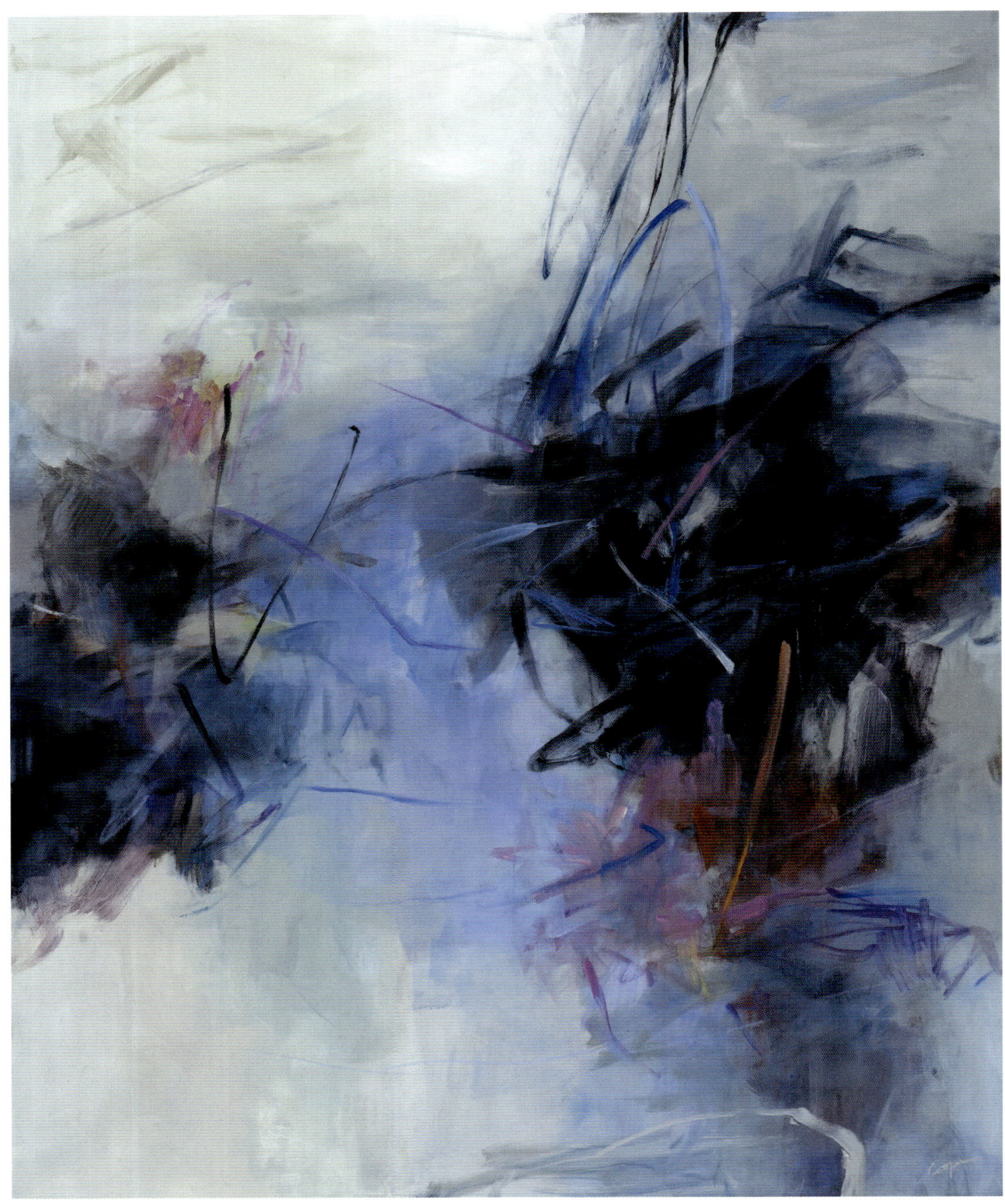

Sally Cooper

Nonobjective painting allows free expression of Sally Cooper's emotions, feelings, and individuality. Her work is about a creative process rather than a specific image or place. Following intuitive promptings, Cooper applies a vigorous, gestural linear mark or brushstroke that comes from deep within. The surface is built, destroyed, and erased, again and again, creating a subtle and sensitive history to what has been. Working in this quick, intuitive manner makes the unexpected a centerpiece of her work. The freedom of this style of painting is essential to Cooper's approach because she enjoys the direct experience of the art-making process, the spontaneity, and the surprise elements of painting. Many of her paintings are suggestive of depth and water, with luminous colors and floating, lyrical mark making.

Blue Rhapsody
Acrylic
72 X 60 in.

sallycooperart@gmail.com
sally-cooper.com
@sallycooperart

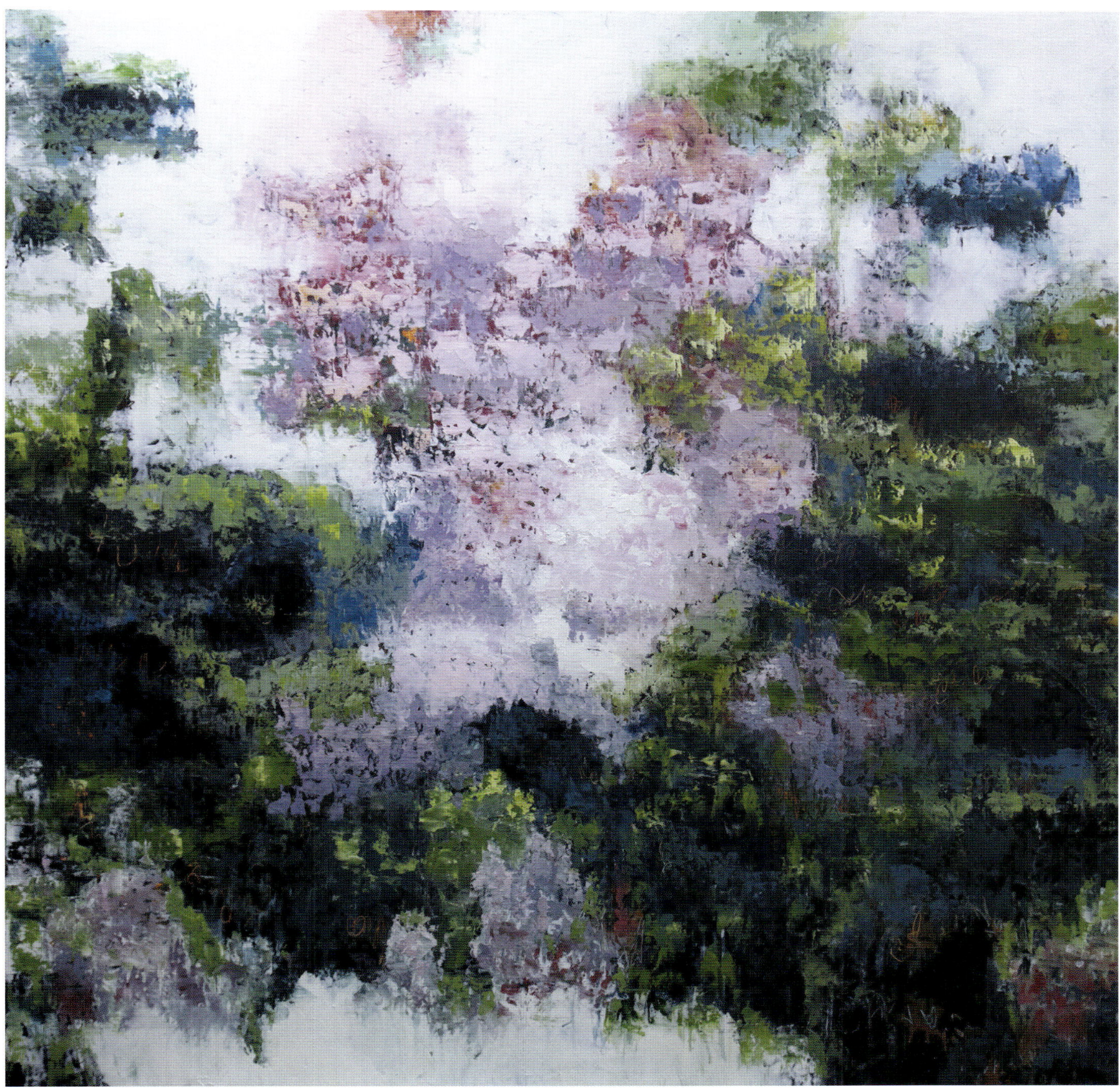

CT Cummins

"Abstract painting is a personal exploration. Through the painting process, I let intuitive color guide my emotional realm into a perceptible domain. My work uses a language brought on by my love of nature in its most abstract form," says CT Cummins.

By way of a painter's lexicon—color, form, space, texture, and line— Cummins finesses those elements through layers of transparent paint, giving a depth to the painting. Her search is for the moment of synchronization between how she feels and what has been revealed on the canvas. It is the artist's hope that she has created a painting that is both beautiful and emotional.

Prairie Queen
Oil and cold wax
48 x 48 in.

ctcummins@gmail.com
ctcummins.com

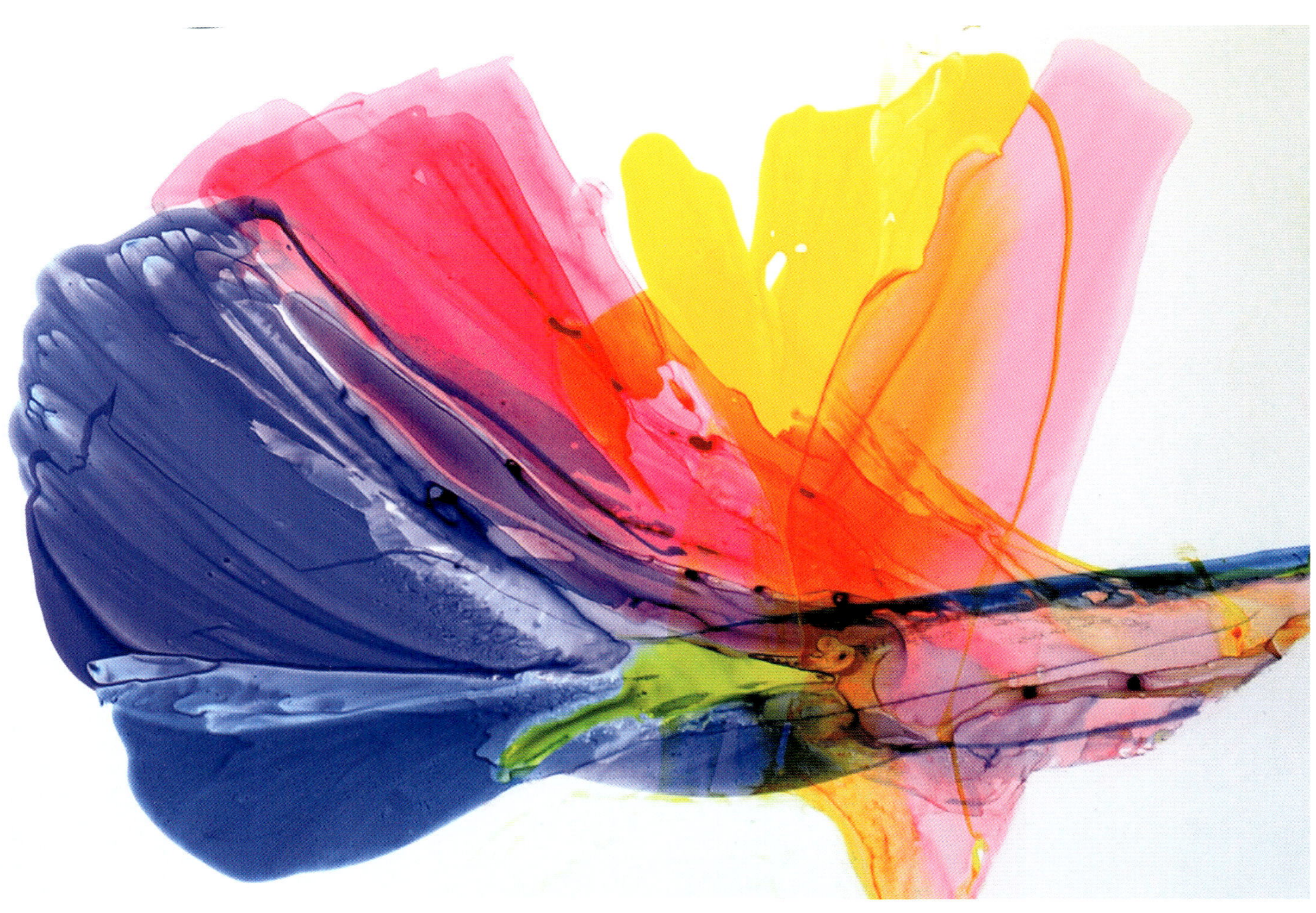

Joy Daniels

Joy Daniels is a self-taught artist who has always enjoyed exploring visual mediums. She studied at the Haliburton School of Art & Design, and it has given her the confidence to push forward, explore, and use paint in different ways.

"It's the movement and flow that excites me. Pouring, painting, and directing the flow of paint can produce gorgeous works on paper and canvas," Daniels says. "I'm always on a quest to produce a piece of drama with strong elements of composition, great value contrast, and good rhythm."

Daniels is endlessly curious and stimulated to experiment with color, texture, and design in ways that connect with the world around her.

Flying
Acrylic
28 x 30 in.

joydanielsvisualartist@
gmail.com
joydanielsvisualartist
.com
@joydanielsartist

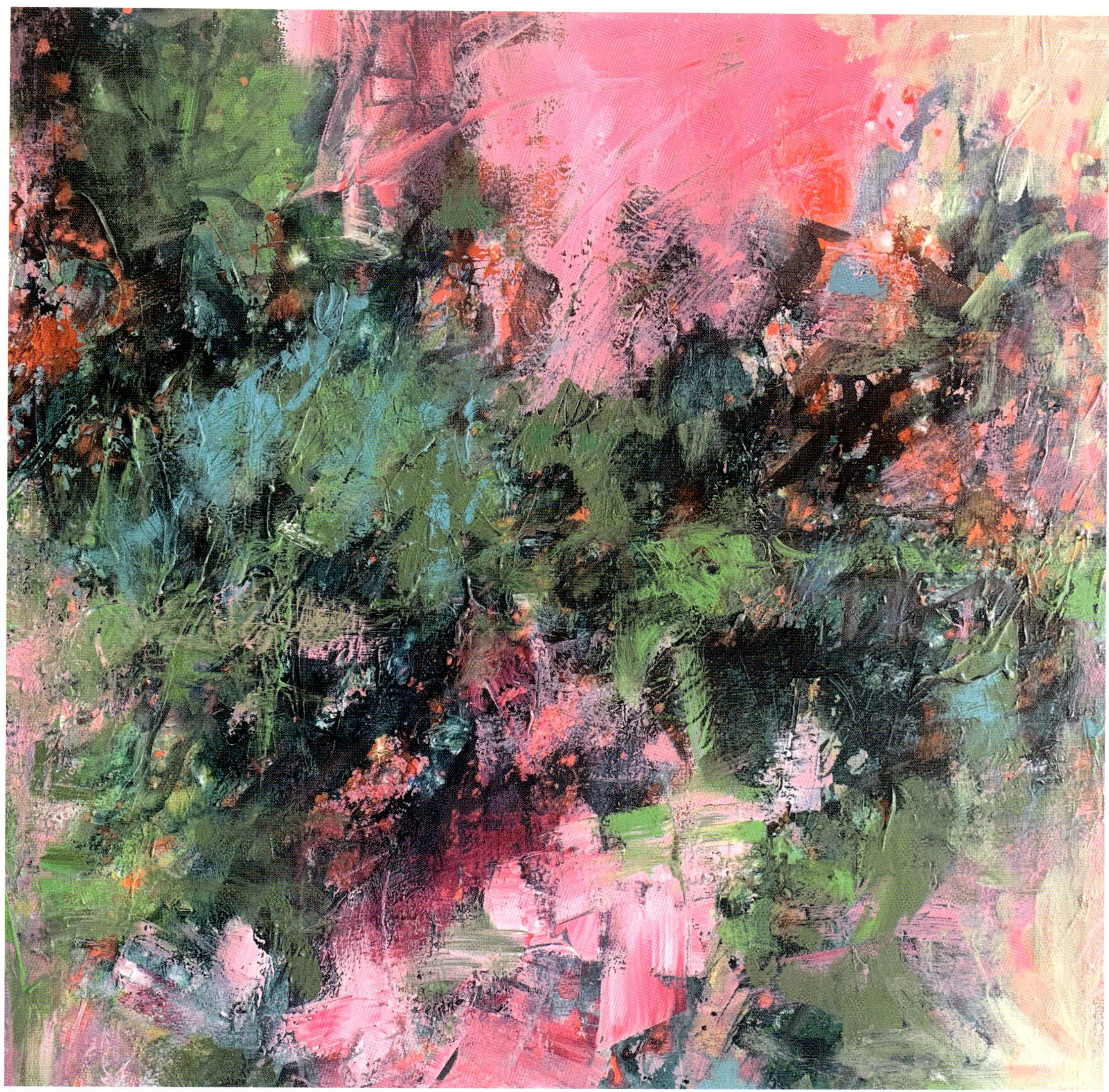

Sami Davidson

The world is different now, and color is Sami Davidson's happy place. She is inspired by the magnificent Florida sunsets, the luscious colors of the flowers in her garden, and the translucent turquoise hue of the ocean. She wants to immerse herself in these colors and create beautiful, joyful paintings. For Davidson, creating a painting has always been an exciting and unpredictable adventure. As a nonobjective abstract artist, she works intuitively. Creation comes from within. Her process is one of impulsive and sometimes compulsive experimentation. Davidson begins her paintings with random bursts of bright colors. Then she applies layers of opaque and transparent hues, gestural marks, handmade papers, drips, stamps, and stencils. A final image gradually emerges.

Dalliance
Acrylic
40 x 40 in.

samidavidson@gmail
.com
samidavidsonart.com

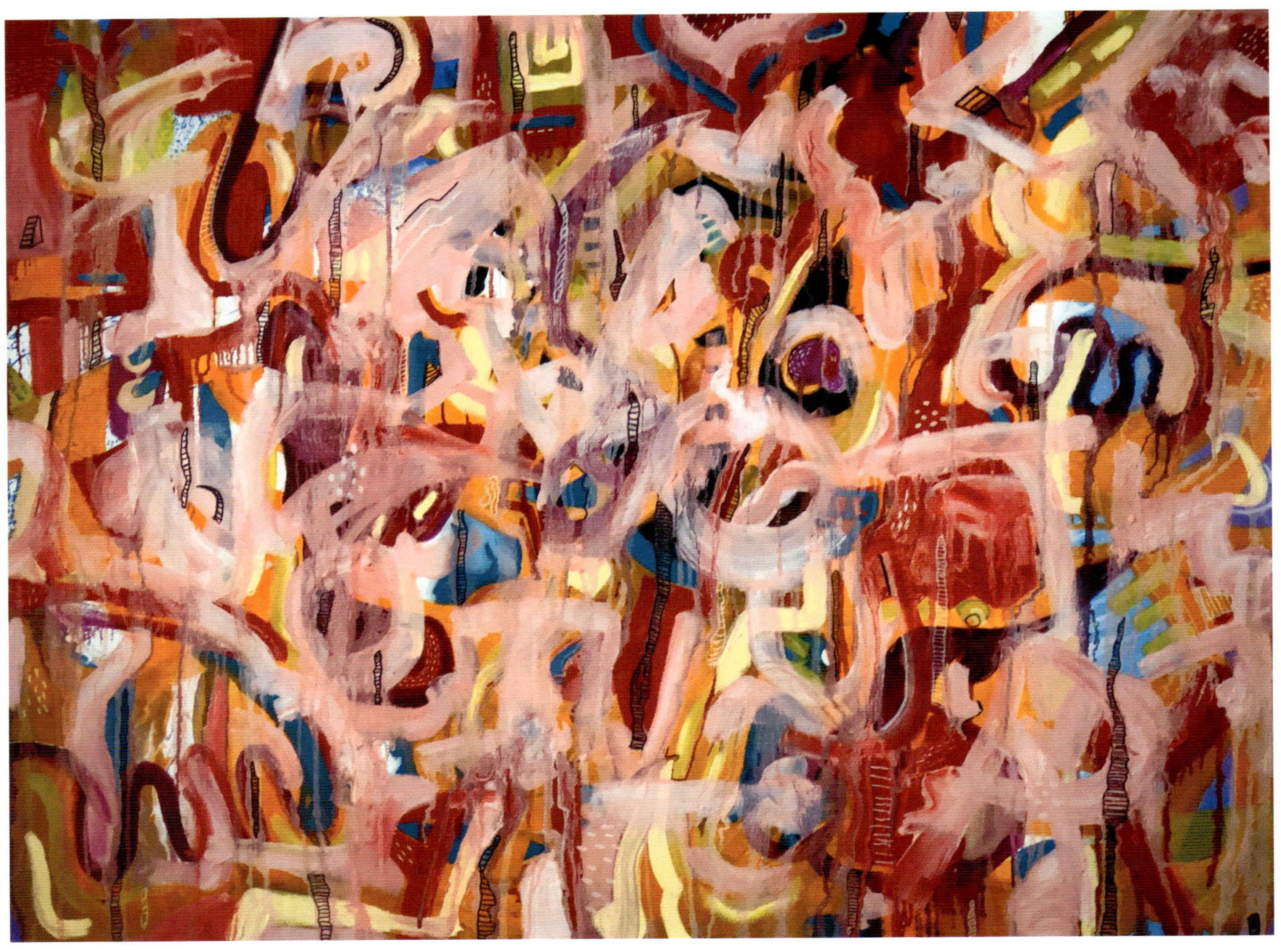

Mcat Davis

When viewing paintings, the experience generally exists in two realms. One with the observing viewer, and the other is the artist's created world within the format of a traditional canvas. Mcat Davis' work generally strives to break that frame and merge the worlds of the artist and viewer. The electric colors are influenced by moments of remembered energy and movement that are utilized as an invitation to the viewer. Once accepted, the form is able to invade the spectator's space, forcing them to change locations in order to view the piece in its entirety. This allows moments of movement mimicked on both sides of the observation. Davis is committed to the idea of unifying the spaces in which the work and viewer exist. By melding the two, she hopes to give life and form to both sides of the art-viewing narrative and promote an emotive mirroring.

Snakes and Ladders
Oil
36 x 48 in.

davism31@gmail.com
mcatdavisart.com
@mcat.davisart

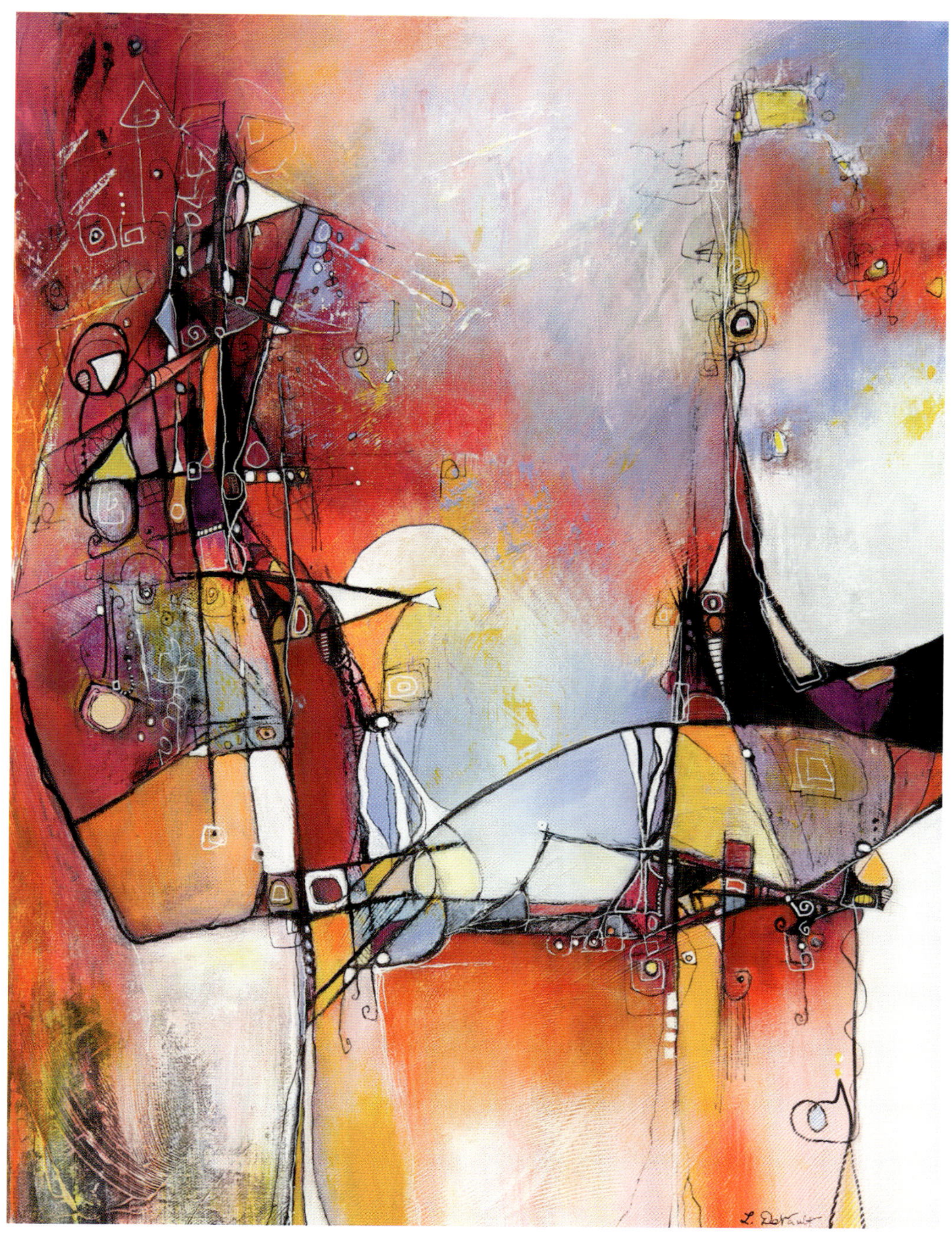

Laurie DeVault

Laurie DeVault's creative process is a lot like her favorite way to travel: unplanned and open to new possibilities. It's a journey of exploration and discovery as she plays with colors, shapes, textures, and mark making. The artist uses a variety of tools, such as palette knives, scrapers, paint markers, pencils, and oil pastels. Each painting is an authentic creation by the artist in that moment, and different days bring forth different moods and desires. DeVault's intention when she enters the studio is to honor her process and trust her intuition, free of worries about the final "product." If she focuses on the final destination rather than where she is, it can create a tension that robs her of the joy of the creative process. DeVault is happiest when she stays in the moment and trusts the painting to lead the way.

Voyage
Acrylic
24 x 18 in.

lrdevault@icloud.com
lauriedevault.com
@lauriedevault

PAINTING: TRADITIONAL/ABSTRACT

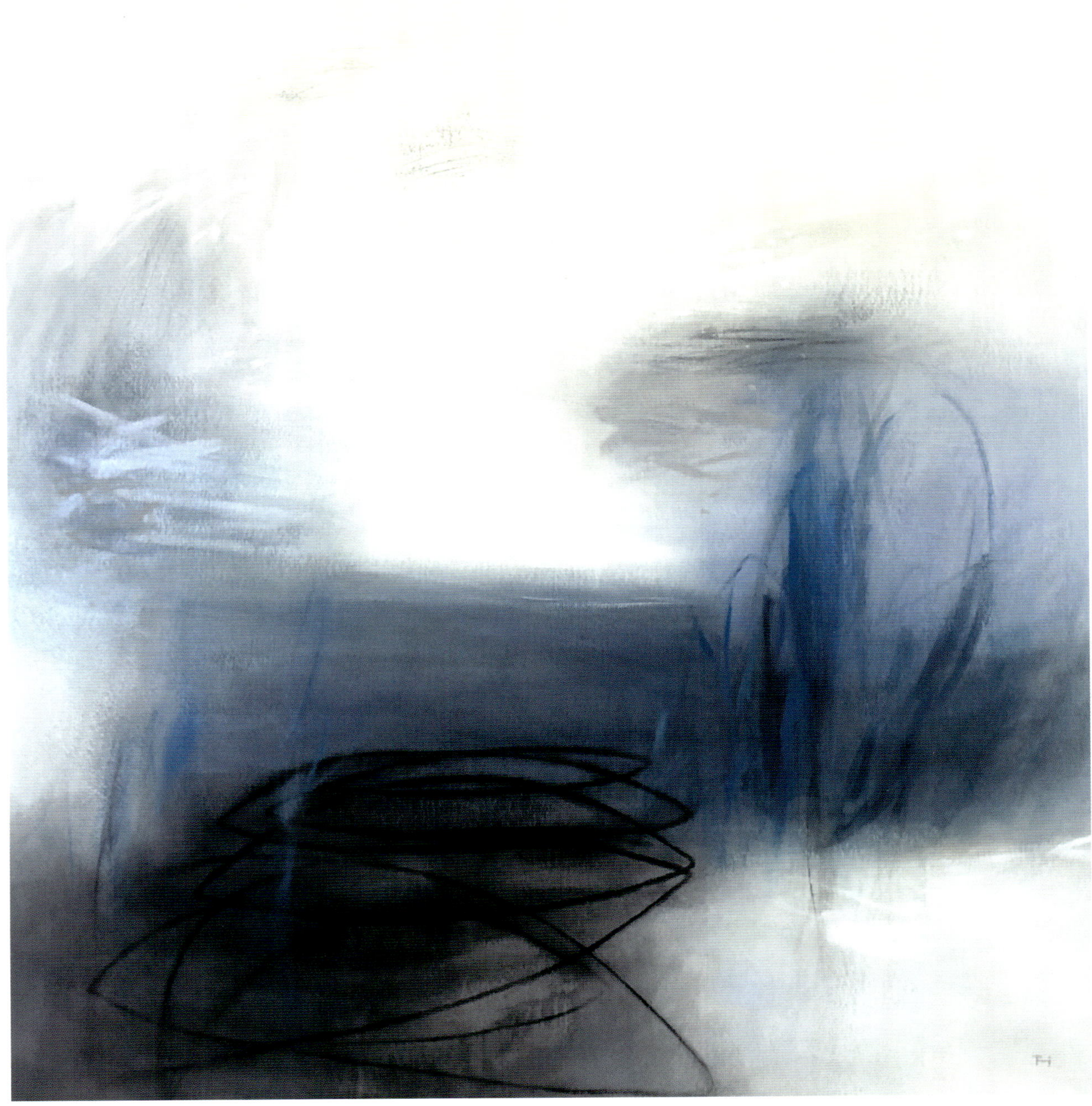

Terri Dilling

Terri Dilling is inspired by the beauty and complexity of the natural world, especially its structures, patterns, and cycles. Through gestural marks and organic forms, she makes reference to the landscape around us and also to the emotional landscape within. Her work is a metaphor for being in the world and feeling alive. She is interested in using expressive marks and color relationships to create a mood or feeling. For the artist, it is a way of searching for balance in this crazy, complicated, and yet beautiful world. She is intrigued by the transformation of an artwork during its creation. Some elements get pushed back and covered over, while others are pulled forward, and when a painting is finally complete, it contains a rich history. For the viewer, Dilling hopes her art is something you can look at for a long time and always see something new.

Cairn Cove
Acrylic and mixed media
54 x 50 in.

terri@terridilling.com
terridilling.com
@terridilling_art

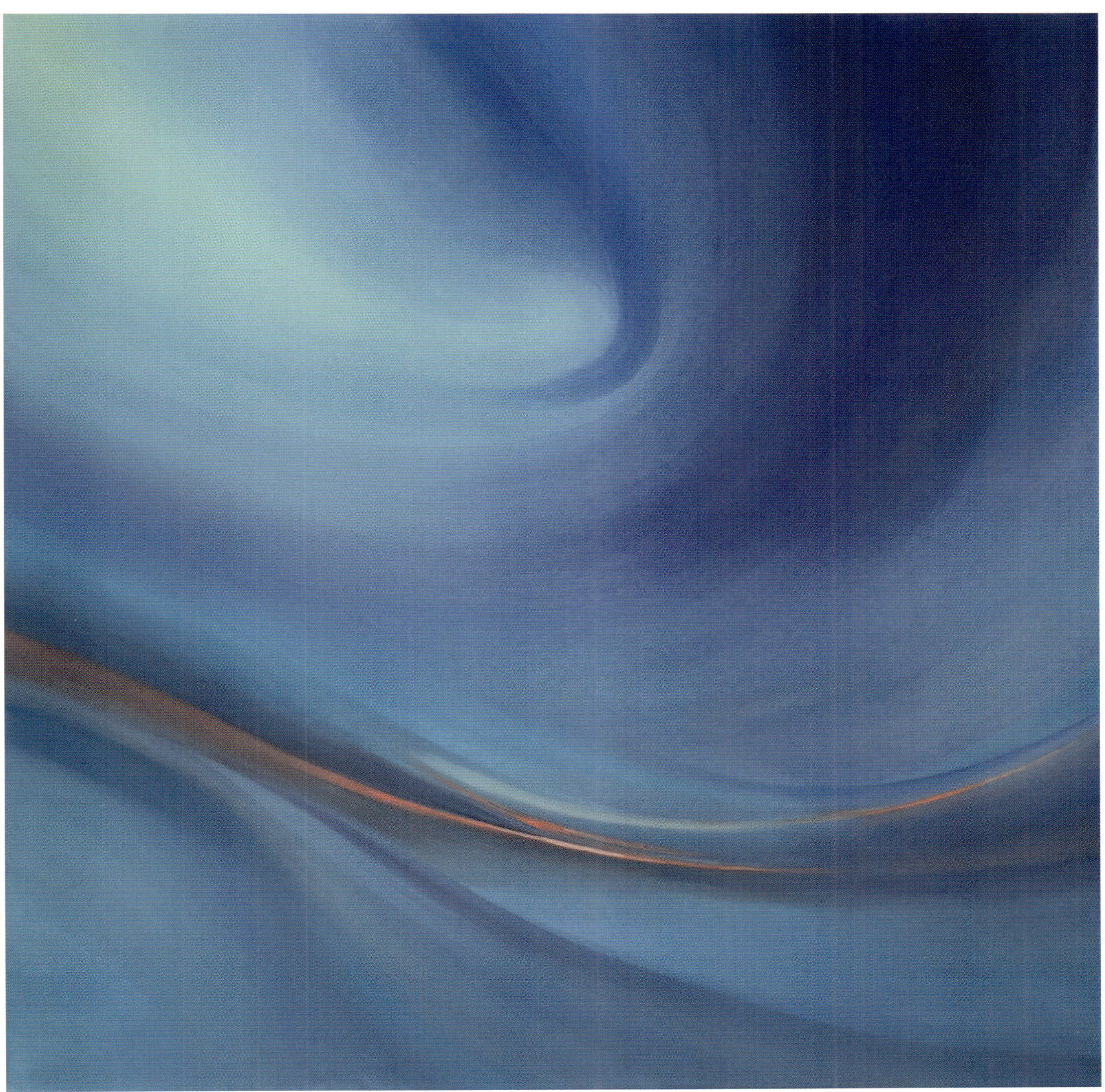

Olga Doberstein

Olga Doberstein works mostly with oil paint and digital art. In her abstract paintings, one finds forms of energy represented, which are continuously developing or standing in polar opposition of "light" and "dark" to each other. In her interpretation, energy is in continuous motion and able to transform itself. That energy often appears in the different psycho-emotional states. The artist is reflecting the form of energy into her art, where the viewer can not only see that but also feel the atmosphere. The feeling of movement in the painting is the most important tool, which shows the continuously developing form of energy. It is a constantly moving form from one stage to another. Doberstein's goal as an artist is to express these stages as precisely as possible.

Winter
Oil
90 x 90 in.

olga-doberstein@gmx
.de
olga-doberstein.com
@olka_daheim

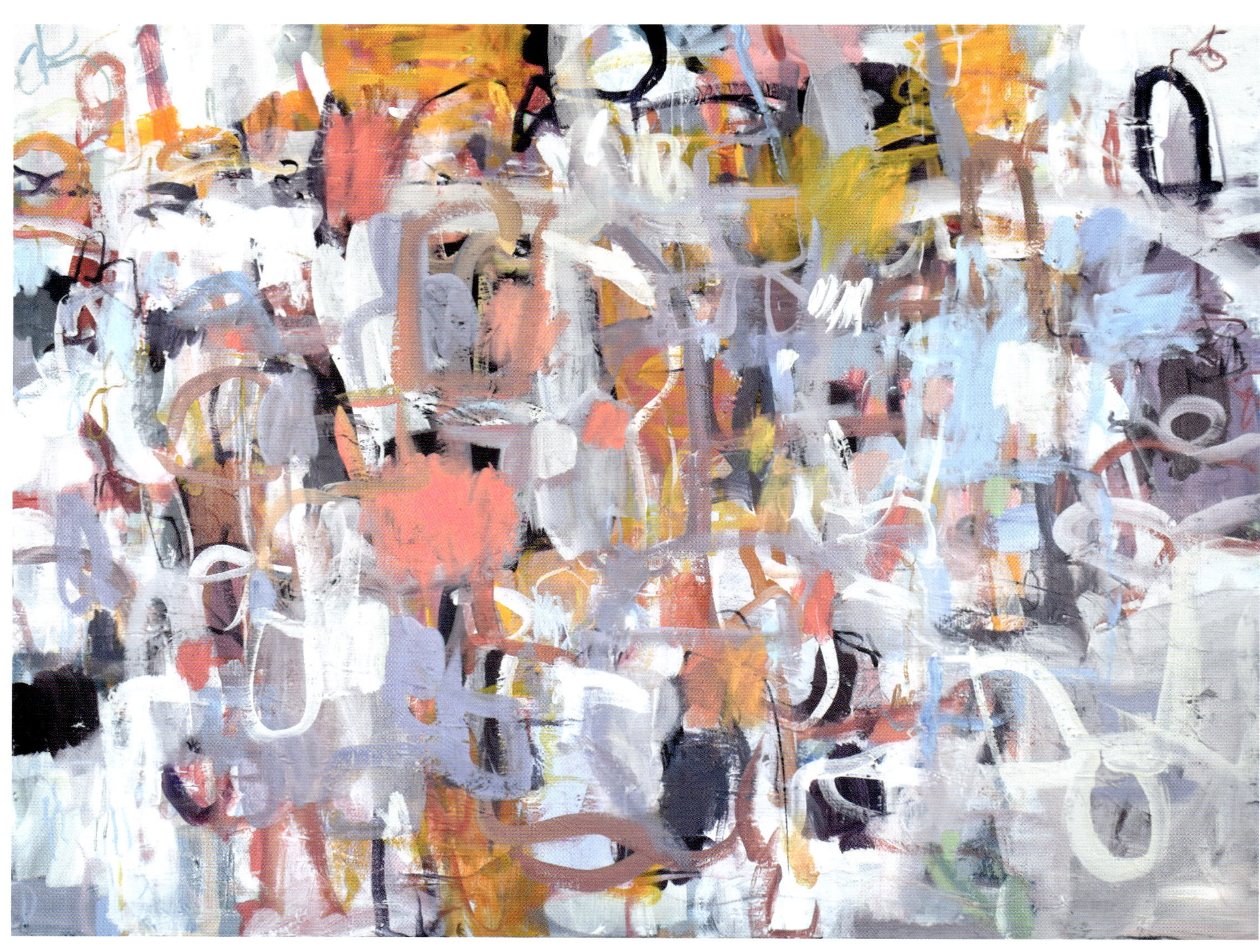

Mark Dunst

Through the expressive and formal language of painting and drawing, Mark Dunst's abstract art explores the messy, imperfect, sometimes contradictory, always transitory, and ultimately beautiful struggle to discover what exists in the space between thoughts. His work is a pursuit to catch a glimpse of the sublime in a flux of uncertainty. Dynamic compositions employ veiled layers of sweeping lines, impressible shapes, and improvisational brushstrokes, creating a rich conversation. The color palette is sophisticated and uncomplicated; the marks are hurried and raw. Serendipity is sought and mistakes are not hidden, rather they help reveal the path forward.

In his work, Dunst finds himself intentionally getting lost, wandering in uncharted territory, and then scrambling to find his way to a place he's never been. Often, the not knowing is an uncomfortable space riddled with uncertainty and doubt. But Dunst is constantly striving to document the search for harmony and beauty in the vastness and strangeness of the shared human experience.

Paradox of silence
Acrylic
36 x 48 in.

art@markdunst.com
markdunst.com
@markdunst.art

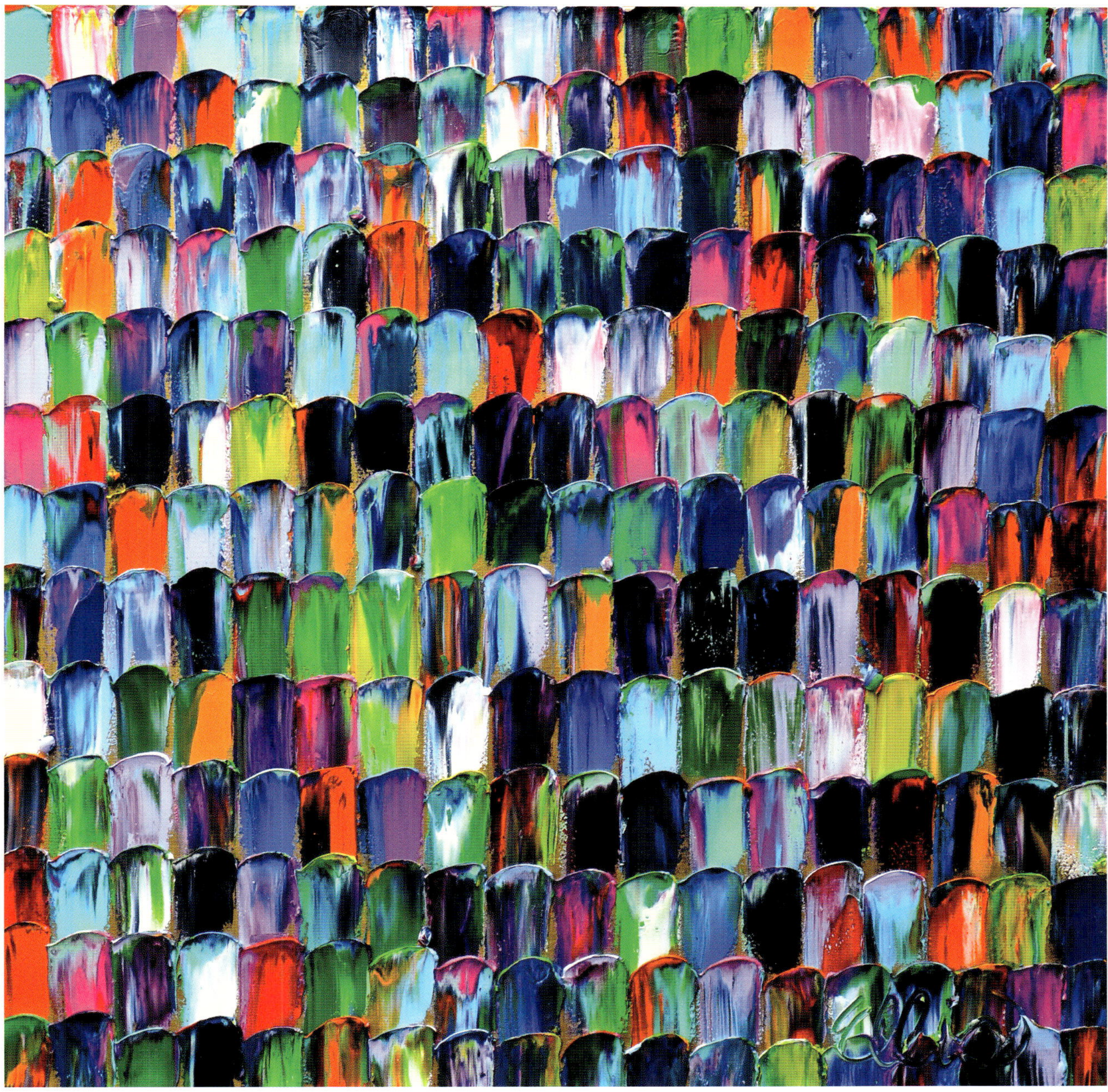

Melissa Ellis
Native Texan Melissa Ellis specializes in bold, sculptural oil paintings. She plays with spectacular color palettes to create brilliant patterns by applying thick oil paint to the canvas with her unique style of impasto palette knife painting. This original and imaginative technique that she developed instantly became her signature style. Often described as "organized chaos," Ellis' work is a dichotomous celebration of spontaneity through the highly calculated and meticulous methods she uses to create organic motion, shadows, patterns, texture, and depth in all of her paintings. Her palette knife skills turn simple oil paint into wild and incredible shapes and patterns. Constantly pushing the boundaries to see how the paint will mix, mold, and sculpt, she creates new forms of motion and texture in each of her pieces, all while playing with unending combinations of color.

Greenville
Oil
36 x 36 in.

melissa@melissaellisart.com
melissaellisart.com
@melissaellisart

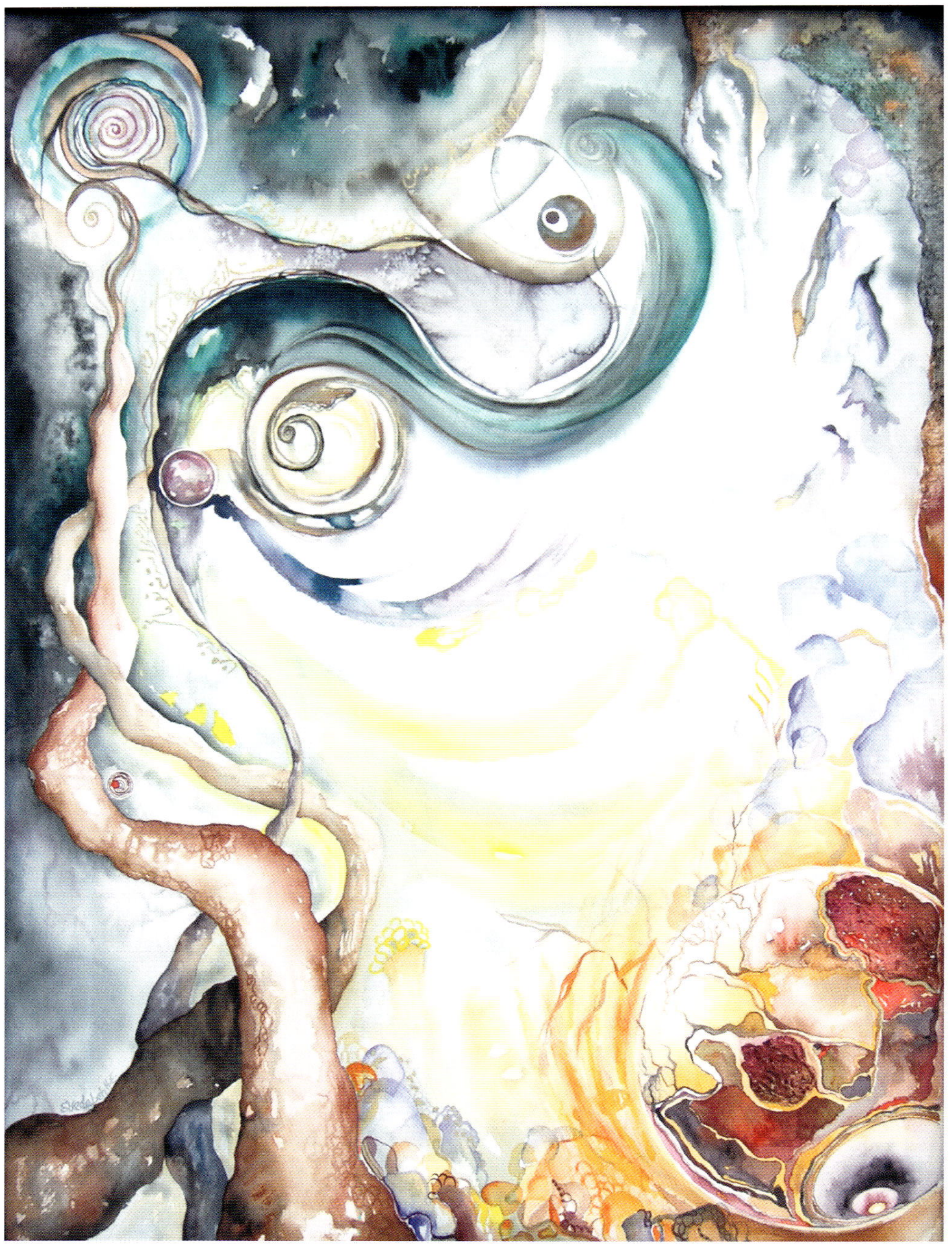

Suedabeh Ewing

Eternal Mysteries is a series of watercolor paintings inspired by a rubaai (a four-line poem) by Persian poet Omar Khayyam. In the rubaai, Khayyam talks about the mysteries of eternity and claims that the secrets of eternal life will not be revealed to any of us in this world. This poem has been written into Suedabeh Ewing's works. The verses blend with the other elements, such as lines, shapes, textures, and colors, of the painting and in a sense become part of the artwork.

Aerial photos of Earth are used for inspiration to create an unknown atmosphere that emphasizes the ambiguity concerning eternal life. Colors that are hardly juxtaposed in nature pinpoint this uncertainty. Although the atmosphere and colors are intended to be mysterious and represent the unknown, textural values are incorporated to give a tangible aspect to each image.

Creation
Watercolor on paper
24 X 18 in.

suewing2014@gmail
.com
suedabehewing
.blogspot.com/
@suedabeh_art

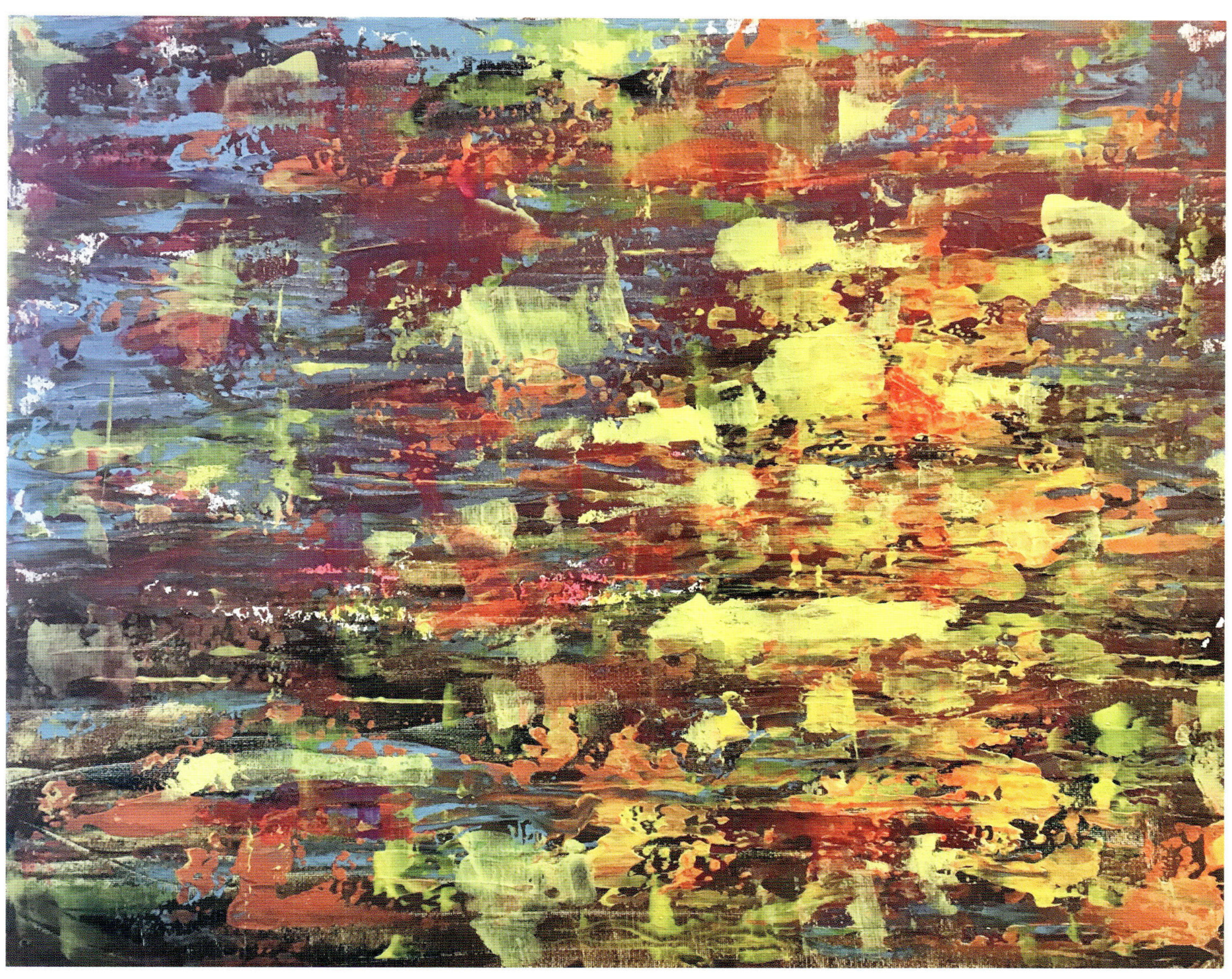

Ty Fawley

Painting is Ty Fawley's alter ego—his "me" zone. Within this zone Fawley observes not only the subject matter of the painting, but he also surveys the surroundings, light, color, and atmosphere around him. "Painting is a progress of creativity, limited within the work in which I am forming," he says. "I find the beauty in nature and seek to respect that visualization on to my canvas. At times it's challenging. I am not looking to paint exactly what I see, but endeavor to craft my impression enthusiastically on the canvas."

Color is everywhere, even where you may not see it. Fawley's energy is to bring those colors to the visualizer's eye and the mind's eye. He seeks to generate emotion and endeavors to spark an inspired creative dialogue with the viewer as a participant within the painting.

Abstrakta
Acrylic
16 x 20 in.

jlfthree@gmail.com

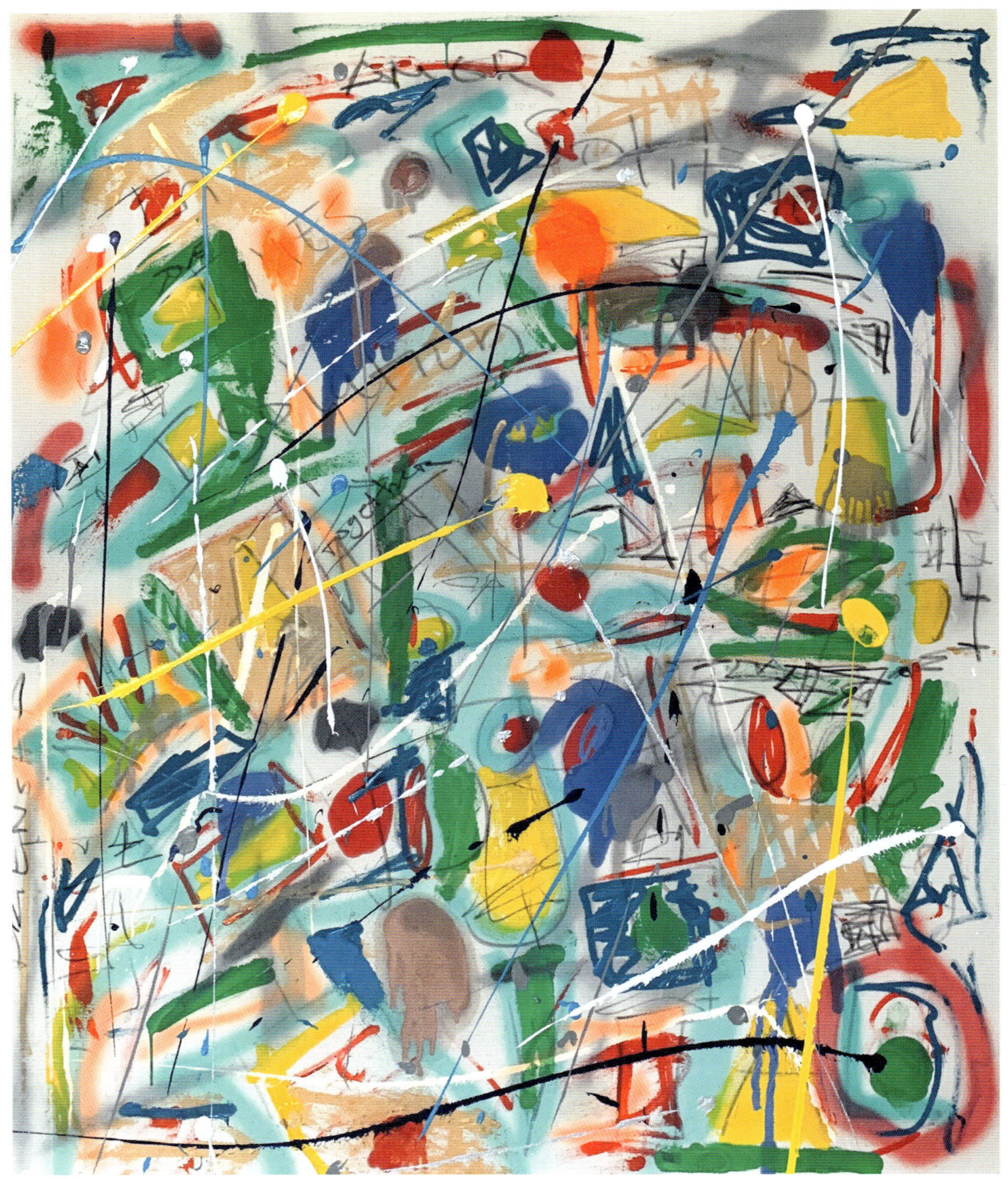

Ben Fluno

Art is the fullest expression of Ben Fluno's personality, the outer workings of the inner musings released onto canvas. Working in an abstract expressionist style, the artist creates each painting so that it has a unique and one-off character to it. Using different media for contrast and texture, Fluno is drawn to bold colors that explode onto the canvas in an eruption of emotion and passion. Working mainly in large-scale, abstract mixed-media paintings, he uses many different mediums, including oil, acrylic, resin, pouring medium, gold leaf, and canvas on canvas, as well as with other repurposed materials. With a background in architecture, real estate, and design, he blends his love for design with abstract art, in turn creating modern and contemporary artworks that work in many different styles of homes and commercial properties.

Connection is Vital
Mixed media
48 x 40 in.

benfluno@gmail.com
benflunoart.com
@benfluno

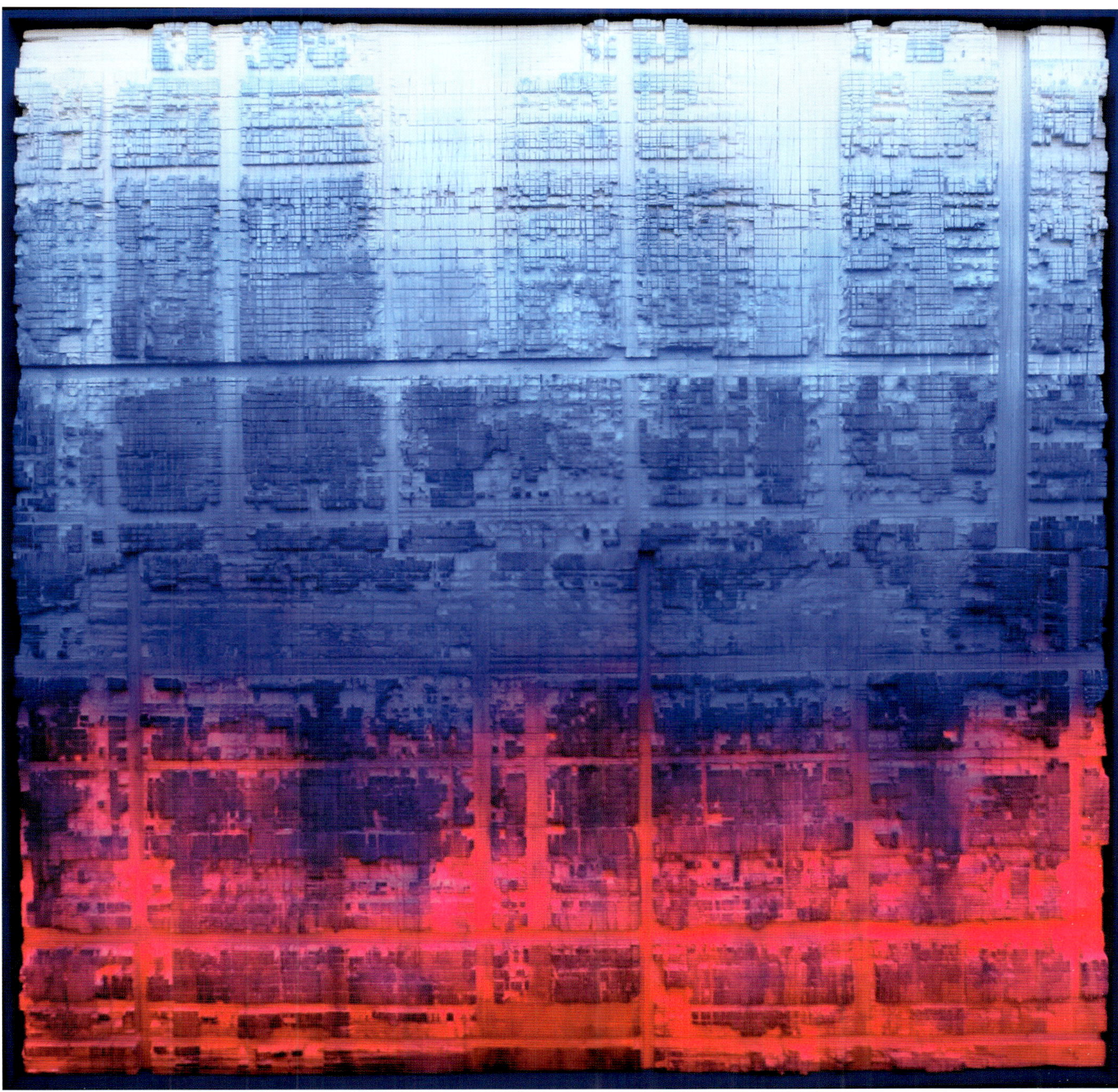

Peter Foesters

In the mid-1990s, Peter Foesters started painting forms and objects in combination with gesso. For the past five years, he has only been painting abstract art. He has always been fascinated by both sculpting and painting, which he finally ended up combining into his work. As most of his work is made on canvas, the material has to be exceptionally light, which is the reason why he uses polystyrene. He is fond of using bright fluorescent colors, especially combined with black. Nevertheless, he is also passionate about monotone paintings. Foesters always tries to bring depth to his work, mainly by using straight lines. This makes his work sleeker and creates an extra dimension as well. His calls this style "Straight Dimensions." Above all the artist is inspired by modern architecture (buildings, bridges, monuments) and contemporary artists like Klein, Mondrian, Hockney, Warhol, Lichtenstein, and Johns.

The Destruction of Ankaris
Mixed media
47 x 47 x 4.7 in.

P.foesters@telenet.be
straightdimensions.com
@peter_foesters

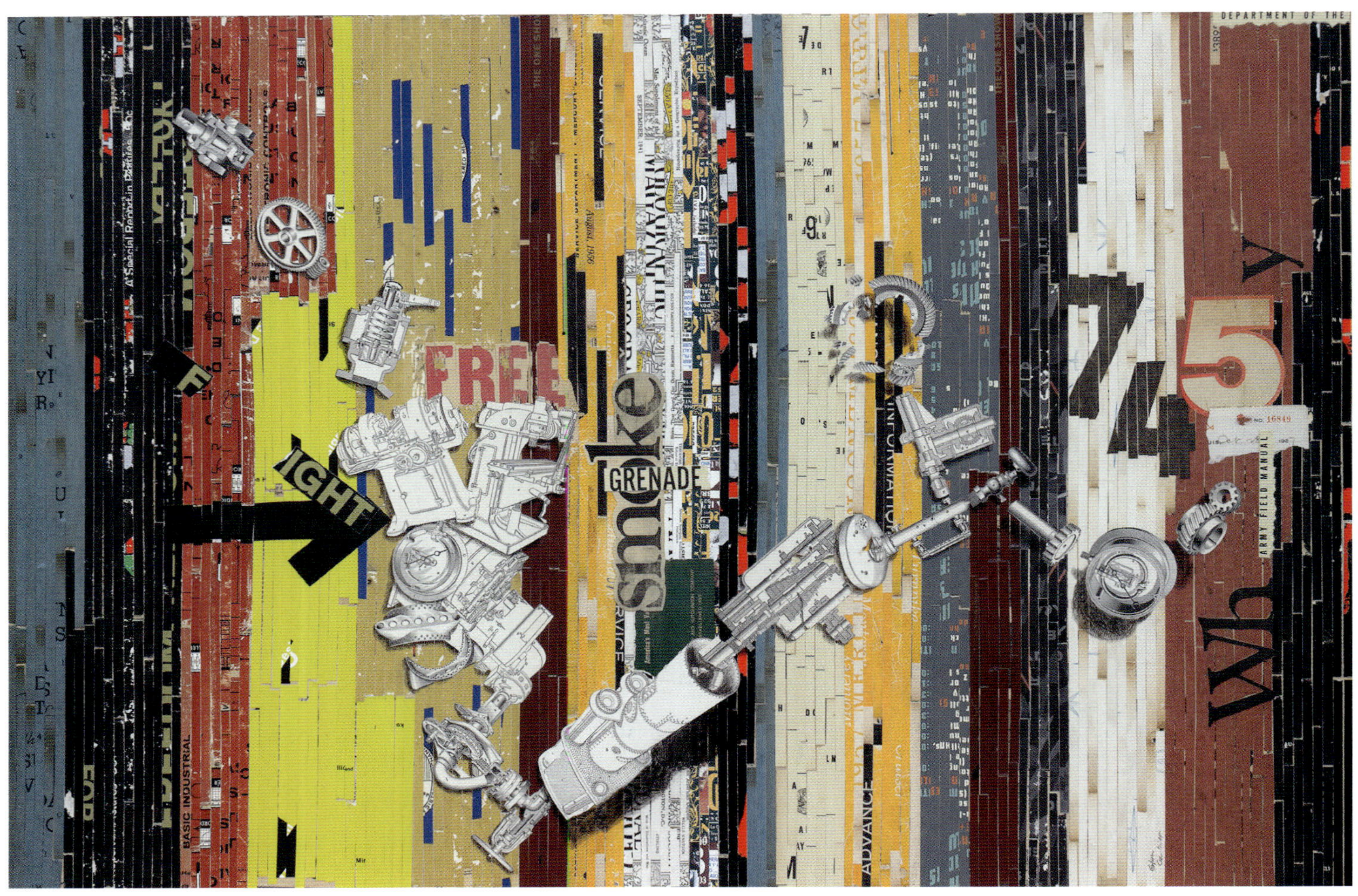

Glen Gauthier

Glen Gauthier's collages utilize printed ephemera to serve as a time machine. The drama of the Cold War, the eclectic nature of old books, brochures, and documents—all of these are fascinating to him and help to inform his work. These bits and pieces have been stuck in the dark in these places, and he gets to uncover them and combine them to give them new life. Combing through these materials, the seeds of ideas are planted. Gauthier then creates thumbnail sketches, trying to make sense out of them. Patterns start to emerge, then images and stories rise to the top as he is working. Other pieces are often the result of visual connections between previously unrelated images, which when combined, create more interesting visuals. Themes that the artist explores include the Cold War, military defense, and space travel, as well as human and mechanical relationships. His work is an ongoing conversation between past, present, and future.

Fragile Machinery
Collage on masonite
24 x 36 in.

glen@streetfairstudios
.com
streetfairstudios.com
@glengauthier

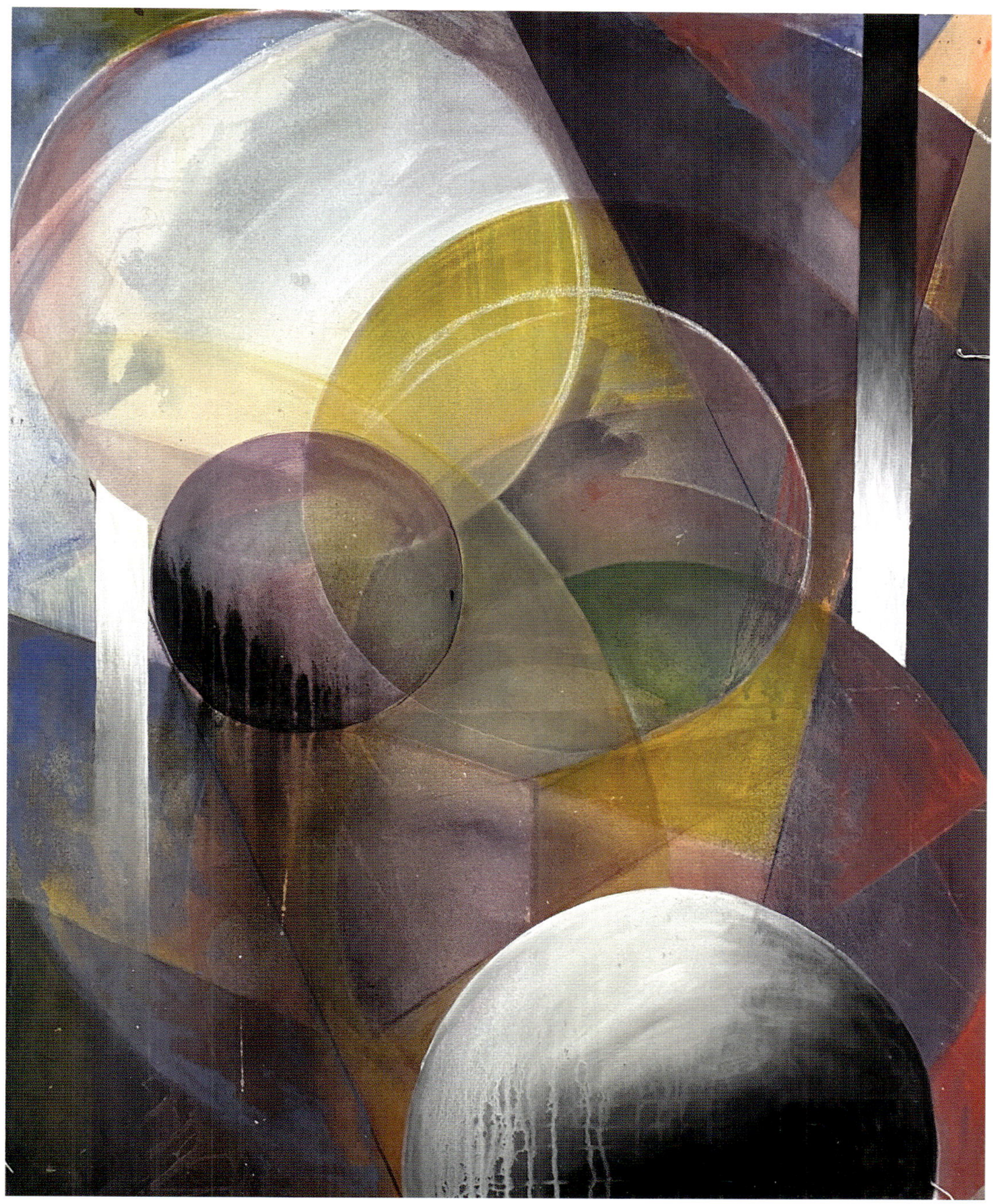

Jenna Girolamo

Jenna Girolamo's work is a never-ending search for transparency. She works with layers and stages, allowing the canvas to breathe and then build some more. Every step of the way, no matter the context, is undoubtedly important. Transparency is universal; it allows one to reflect and acknowledge where you've come from. It is the nourishment of the canvas, scraped layers of pigment, saturated colors, and shapes that want to be confronted. It is the visibility of each step and the patience that is needed to give each layer time to breathe. It is in that moment that, with love, one is able to appreciate where the transparency has come from. The intent of Girolamo's work is to create a conversation between the viewer and the painting. "We try to understand transparency by reformulating new information, to shift perspective," says Girolamo. "It is a perspective that introduces a new way of experiencing reality."

Transparency
Acrylic and chalk pastel
42 x 35 in.

jgartbuzz@gmail.com
jgartbuzz.com
@jgartbuzz

PAINTING: TRADITIONAL/ABSTRACT

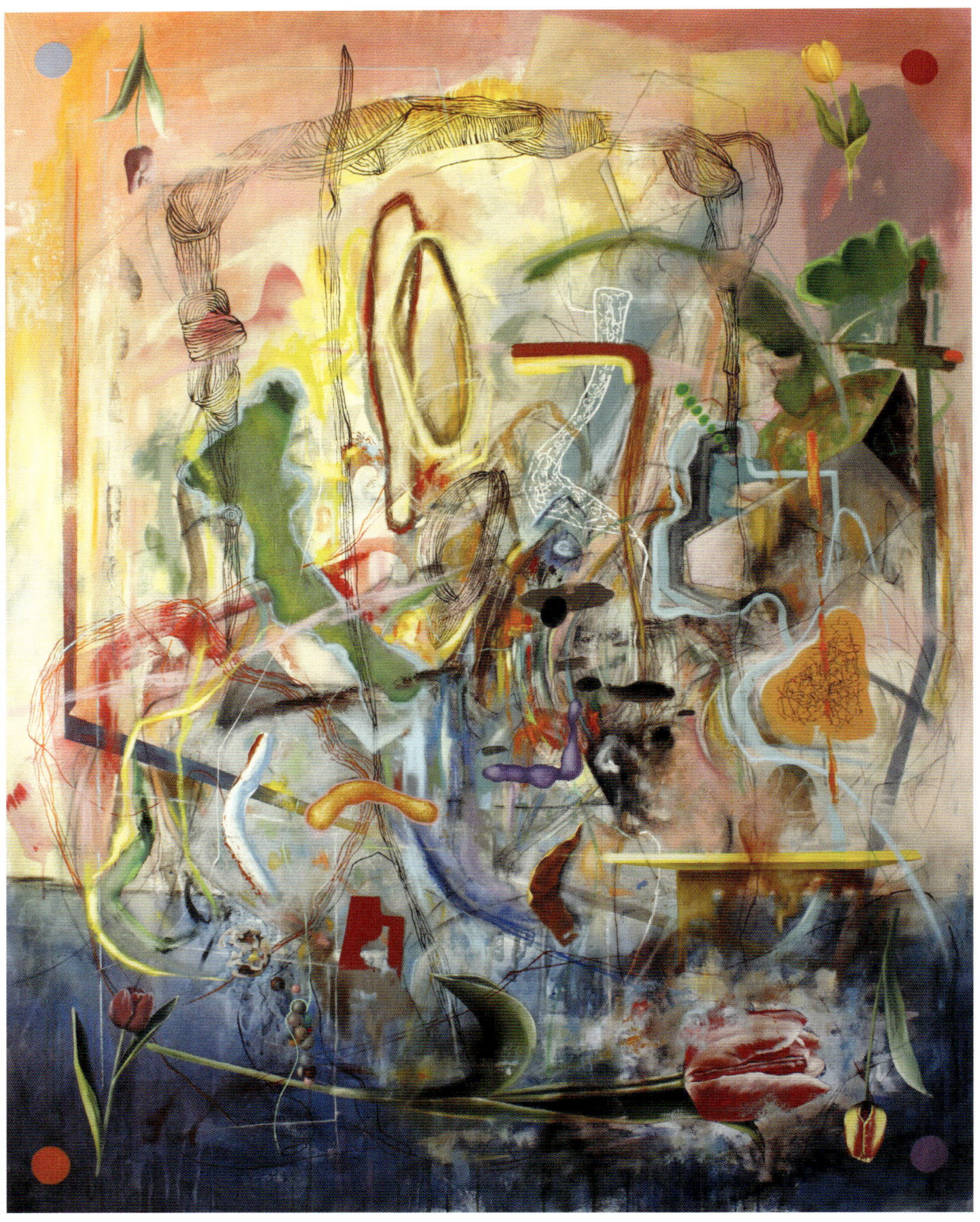

Detlef "Dego" Gotzens
Making art and the reason behind it is an impulse, or drive, for Detlef "Dego" Gotzens. One that is not always clear. "The desire to make art has always been there and is very powerful at the same time," he says. Gotzens is constantly in the process of finding a visual language that continuously seems to be changing from one series of work to the next. Every piece is leading him to another place, where he wonders, yet again, what is behind the next painting or sculpture he makes. "It feels like a never-ending, winding road, where the journey is all that matters anyway," the artist says. Gotzens believes there are elements of free expression in his paintings and sculptures as well as controlled form and order, which is certainly a manifestation of his personality showing through or reflecting in his work

After Easter Excavations
Acrylic, charcoal, ink, oil, and oil pastel
68 x 54 in.

dego@degoarts.com
degoarts.com
@degoarts

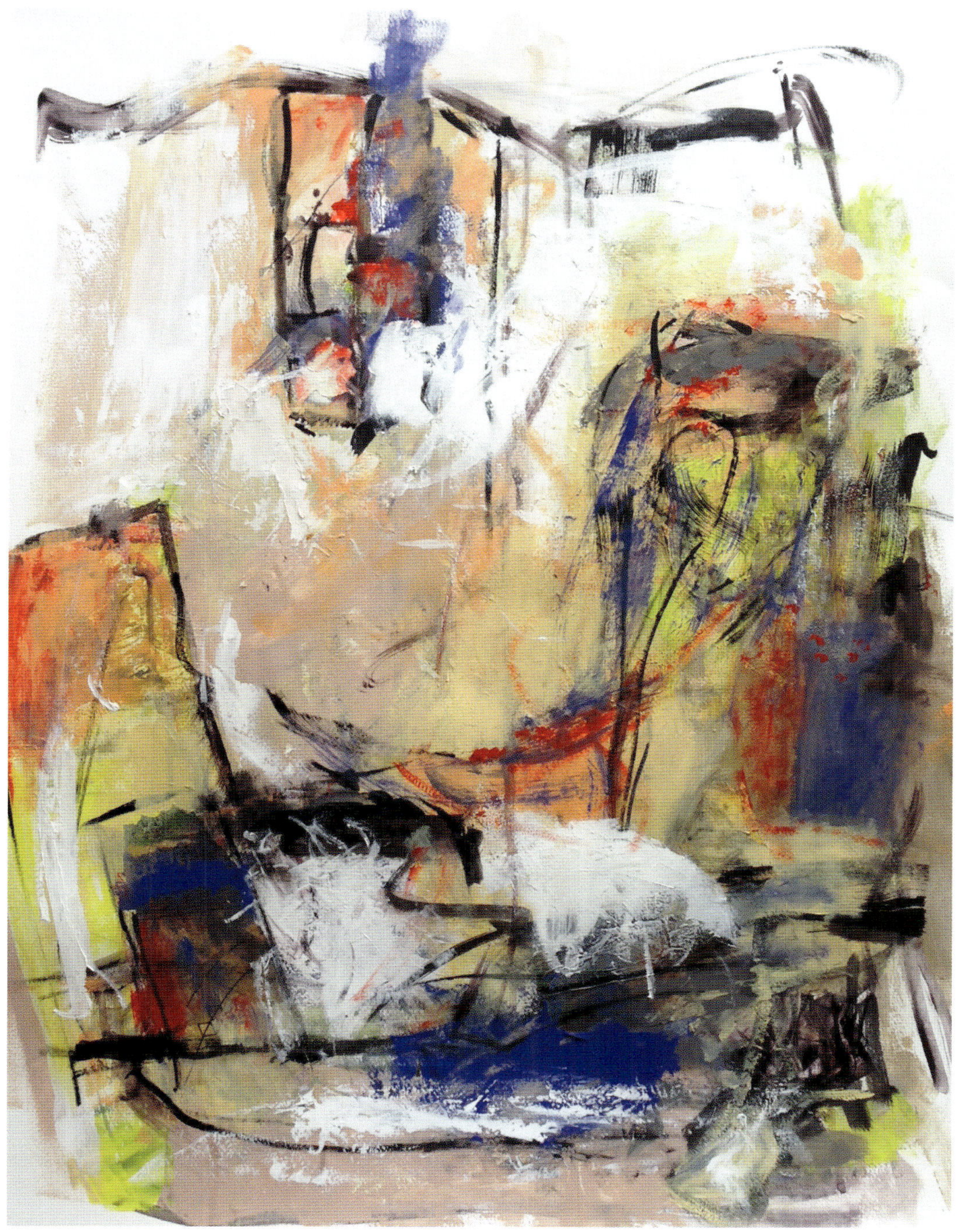

NC Hagood

NC Hagood's art is like a dream where fleeting moments in time have been captured. She uses glimpses of what she recalls from her dreams as inspiration. She starts by doing strong and quick marks of what she remembers in a raw and fundamental manner. Once she has formed the foundation, she begins adding shapes and further designing the piece with paint, paper, and any other media that the piece demands. She allows herself to intuitively start following the direction the piece starts taking. There are many layers of paint, paper, and mixed media used through this process, and many times the fundamental design will change, but its underlying structure will be implied. Hagood does not strive for perfection, but rather she wants to show the hand of the artist and soul. In short, she catches fragments of her dreams and transfers them for the viewer to observe.

Amber Light
Mixed media
28 x 22 in.

hagoodnancy@gmail
.com

PAINTING: TRADITIONAL/ABSTRACT

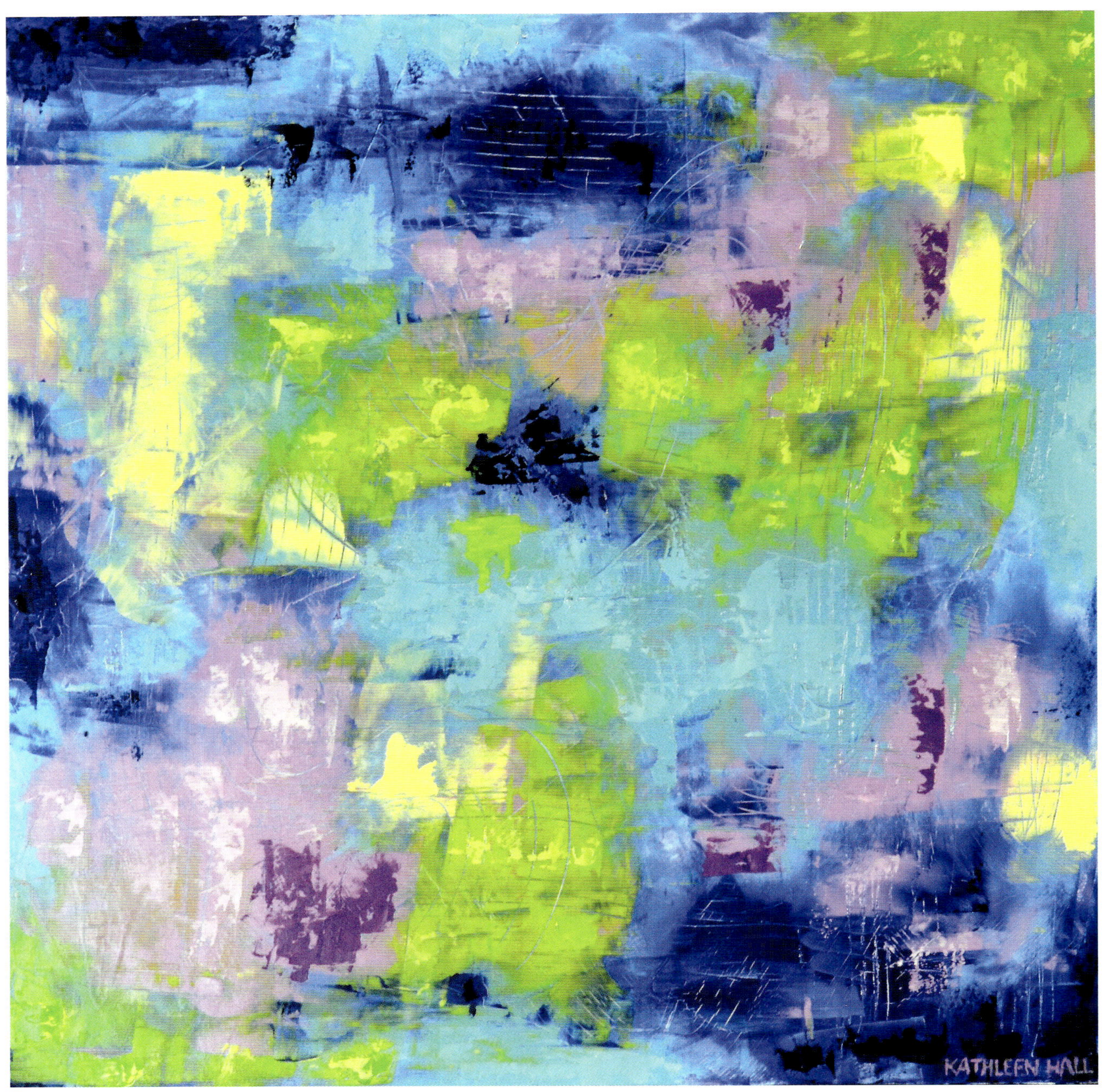

Kathleen Hall

Kathleen Hall loves the physicality of creating art and the process of mark making. Her painting toolbox includes palette knives, spatulas, dough scrapers, bubble wrap, and containers (such as glass jars) for imprinting shapes. She paints primarily with oil paints and sometimes with cold wax. What people notice most about her paintings are the texture, dimension, and vibrant colors, often complementary hues, juxtaposed to create energy and build tension. She sometimes observes viewers studying her paintings from multiple angles, tracing her journey through the layers. As an artist, she finds it fun to see how an abstract painting develops, listening to her inner voice, trusting her intuition to know what comes next, and recognizing when she has taken a painting as far as it should go. Hall is deeply inspired by nature and, in particular, the magnificent rocky coast of Maine in and around Acadia National Park.

Reflecting Pool
Oil and cold wax on cradled panel
16 X 16 in.

kathy@kathleenhallart.com
KathleenHallArt.com
@KathleenHallArt

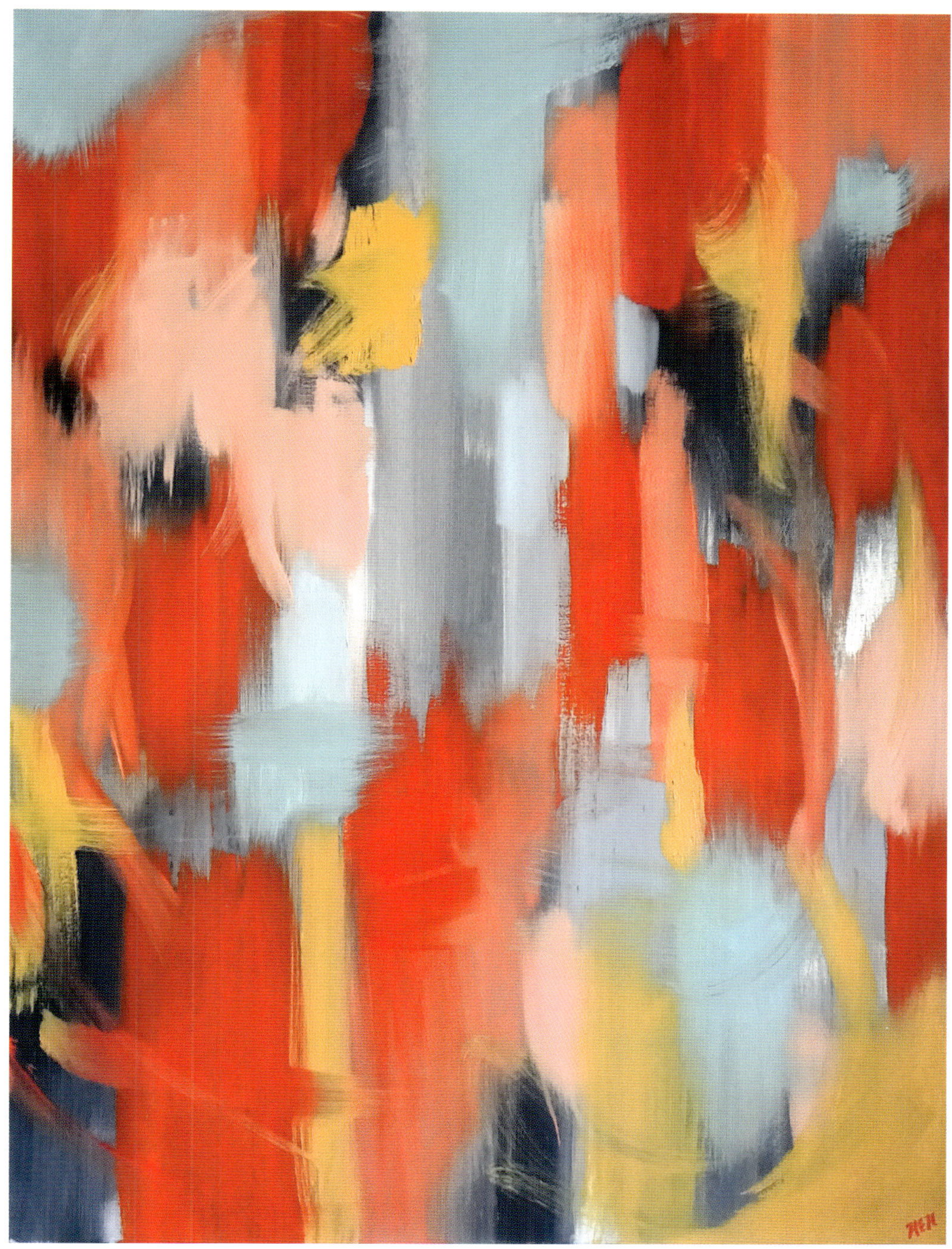

Hallie Hamilton

Hallie Hamilton's work has evolved from realism early in her career into pure abstraction. Her exploration of color is evident in the dreamy, impressionistic land and seascapes she produced early on and in the gestural paintings on which she is currently working. Her work clearly borrows from early abstract expressionist artists, even drawing on similar themes, like the spiritual and the unconscious, but Hamilton's unique background brings freshness to the genre. While her emotive paintings may appear effortless, her sophisticated color palettes, adept paint handling, and balanced compositions are evidence of her formal training. Her paintings, often large-scale, are striking in their apparent simplicity and aesthetic beauty. Hamilton primarily works in oil, acrylic, and mixed media.

Take Me to Neiman's
Mixed media
40 x 30 in.

halliehamiltonart@gmail
.com
halliehamiltonart.com
@halliehamiltonart

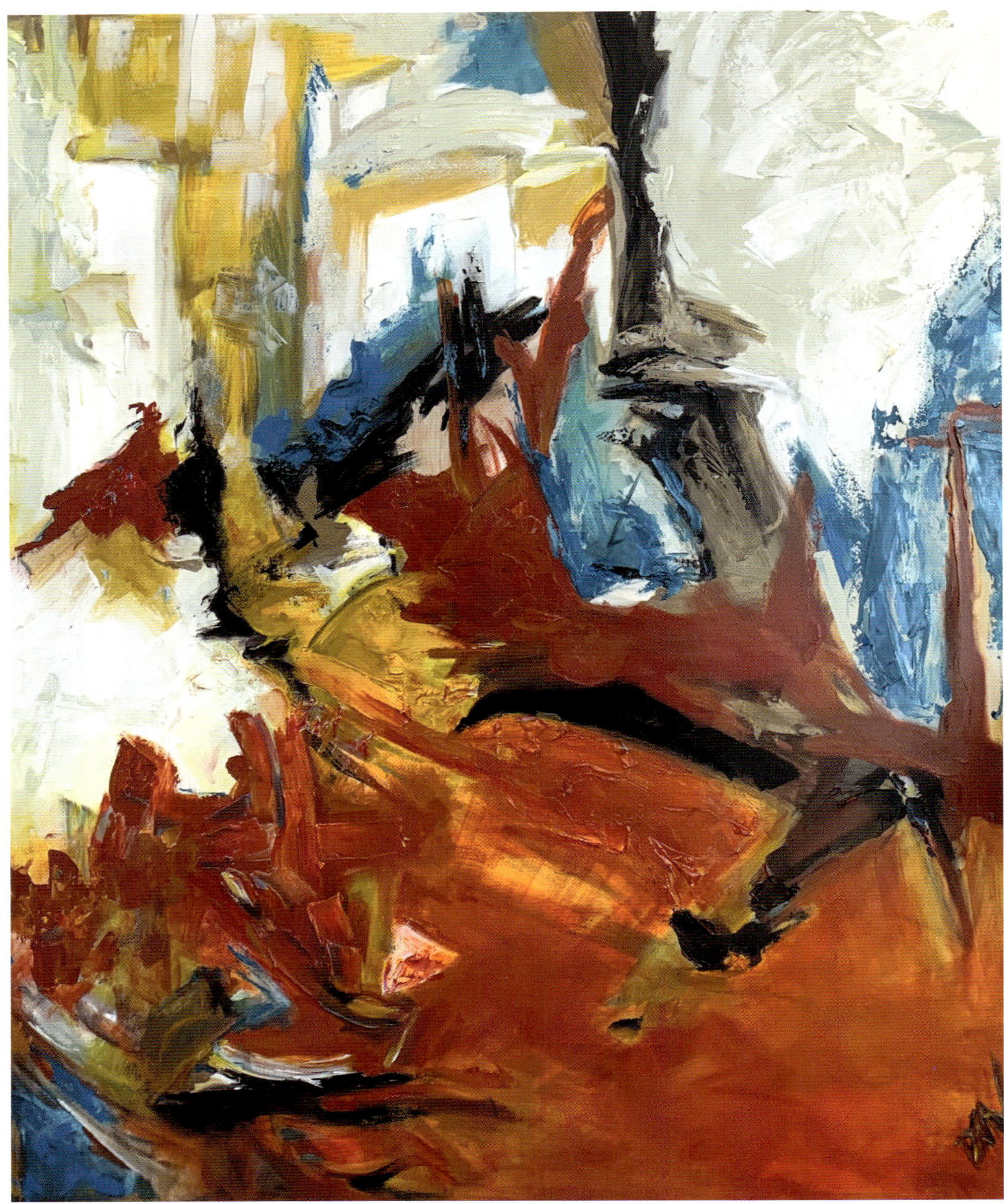

Deborah Hartigan Viestenz

Much is revealed about Deborah Hartigan Viestenz through her artwork. Known for her large-scale, multimedia abstract paintings, Viestenz seeks to translate nature into feelings. Always fascinated with the often-overlooked beauty of nature, Viestenz began her studies in oil painting at the age of ten.

Given her admiration for minerals, stones, landmass, and the sea, these elements became the subject matter of her work.

"We see these every day: birds, grass, trees, lakes, oceans, stone," she says. "We are touched by these elements every day. Water on our hands and bodies. Sunlight warming our skin. Rocks and grass beneath our feet. Darkness making us seek light. We hear these every day. Birds speaking to each other. Wind rustling the leaves. The cacophony of storms and thunder. My goal is to express the emotional feelings of wonder and admiration of these natural elements, events, and occurrences—to have the viewer experience a different way of seeing."

The Road
Acrylic
72 x 72 in.

dhvartworks@gmail.com
dhvartworks.com
@dhv_artworks

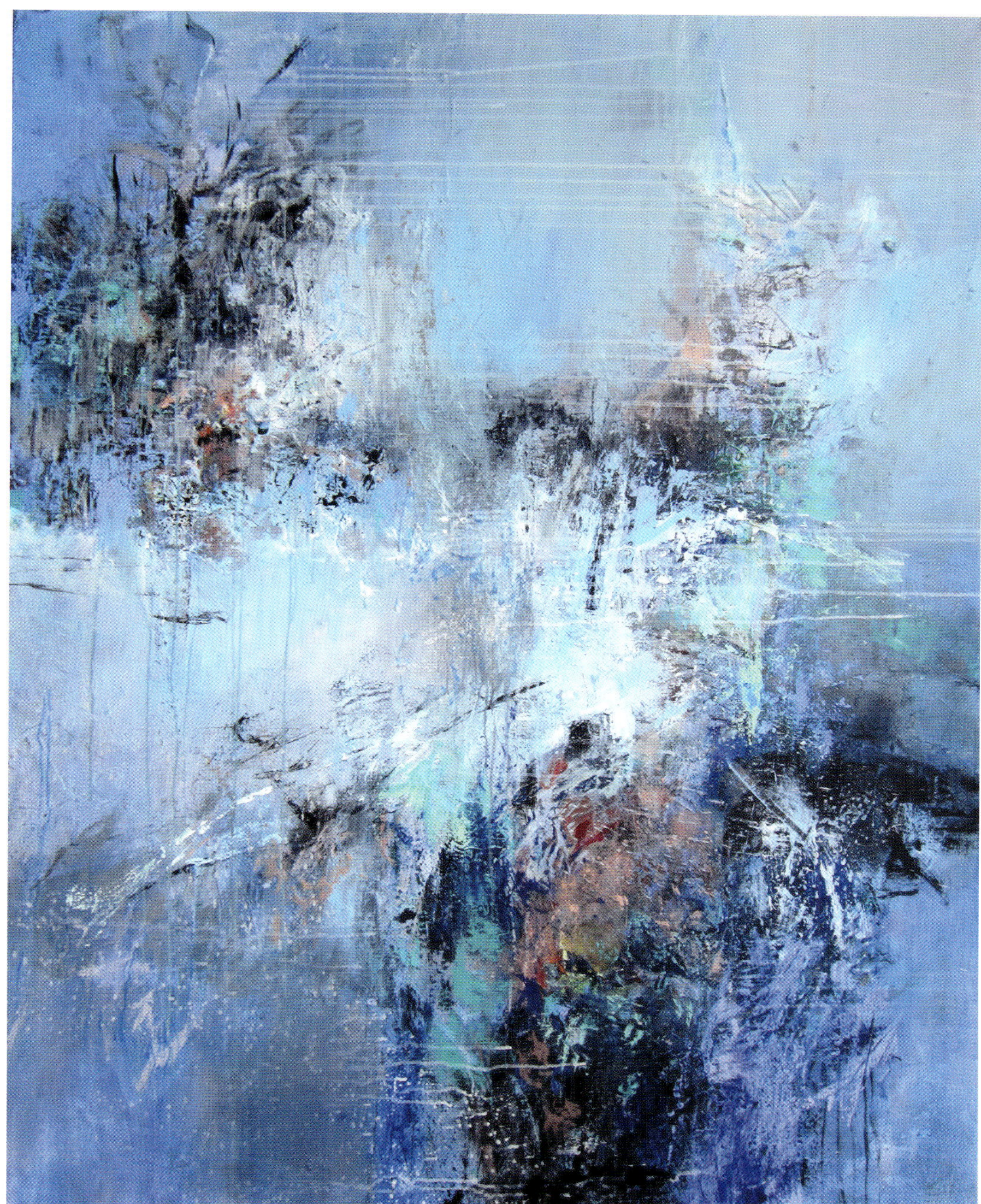

Kristin Herzog

Kristin Herzog's work is about color and its power to convey emotion. On another level, it is also about preserving a feeling or a moment. Viewers can use her images to enter their subconscious and dream. The artist builds up the surface of each painting with many layers to create a complex and engaging image and finds great joy in unexpected results. Herzog's interaction with each piece is guided by intuition and exploration so that every step of the way becomes a surprise.

In her work she is particularly interested in atmosphere and light, exploring the relationships of spaces and layers, some appearing to fade off into the distance while others come forward. She likes the overlapping of lines on the forms and the depth and mystery she can create with many glazes. Illuminating various sections of the painting makes the work come alive as different colors help support each other.

Light on the Water I
Acrylic
60 x 48 in.

kherzogart@hotmail
.com
kherzogart.com
@Kristin_Herzog_Art

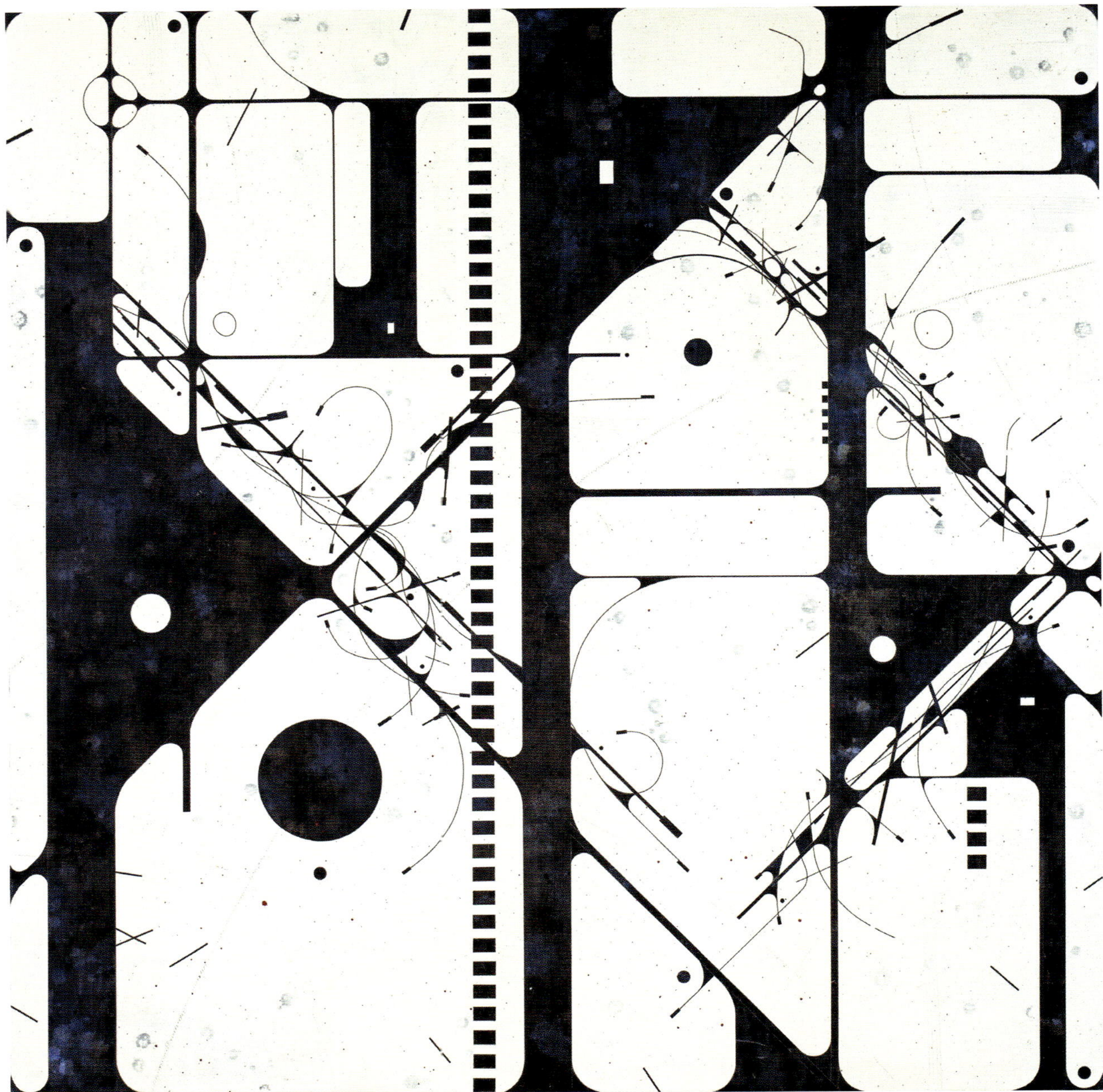

Lee Hill

Devoid of pictorial motifs and narratives, the work of Texas-based painter Lee Albert Hill follows a strictly process-driven formal vision. The understanding is contained within each painting, and Hill's interests lie in the essentials: strong relationships of form, composition, color, line, and geometric flourishes that impart the work with unique character.

Hill uses a technique that combines a foreground of rigorous, hard-edged mark making with an informal assemblage of composition, background, and texture. His sleight of hand hovers between these elements, resulting in images that obscure the true nature of their handmade production. Upon closer inspection, each piece reveals a sense of genealogy, language, and inscribed time, imparting a quality of permanence.

Bluestem 25
Acrylic on canvas with cold wax finish
72 x 72 in.

lee@leeahill.com
leeahill.com
@Studioleealberthill

Benjamin Hoffman

Since Benjamin Hoffman painted his first abstract work of art in 2008, he has been working exclusively with black paint. For the artist, the process of creating a work has to happen relatively quickly, since he mainly concentrates on the contours; multicolored elaboration of the remaining surface would be disruptive to his dynamics. Hoffman uses monoprinting to fill the surface, which he can either keep in the structure of his collages or reduce by washing off the paint. Hoffman chose to make collages because the possibility of different assignments within the composition complements his passion for intuitive painting. The attributes of his style, in part, result from his intention to express his melancholy. From the beginning, the most important factor in his stylistic development was his enthusiasm for what fascinates him most about art and, above all, about abstract expressionism— the creation of a raw aesthetic that remains constant even after repeated consideration.

Collage 4
Watercolor on paper
11 x 8 in.

b.b.hoffmann@gmx.de
@gangraen

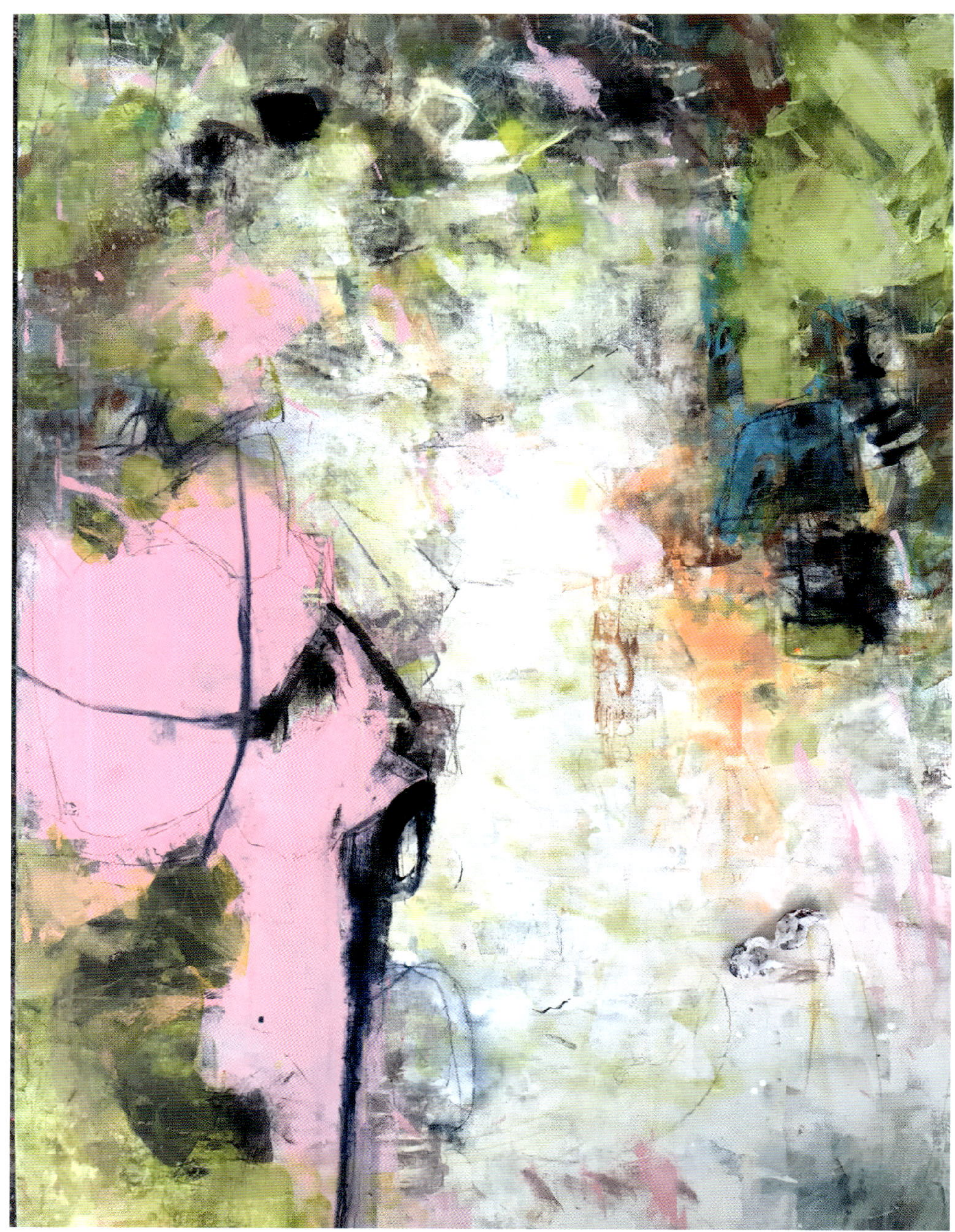

Christy Hopkins

Christy Hopkins is a self-taught, intuitive painter. Her work is moody and bold, with striking marks and lines that are uniquely hers. She works with acrylic on canvas and often paints in seven to ten layers per work. Hopkins typically includes hidden messages and symbols in her pieces, and the collector can sometimes find a hint of a letter or number that is special to them. She uses bright, thick color and includes deep values in her work. Hopkins creates with a carefree, wild painting style and will often show her process and how her paintings evolve with each layer on social media.

Broken
Acrylic
40 x 30 in.

kurcreative@gmail.com
@christyhopkins_art

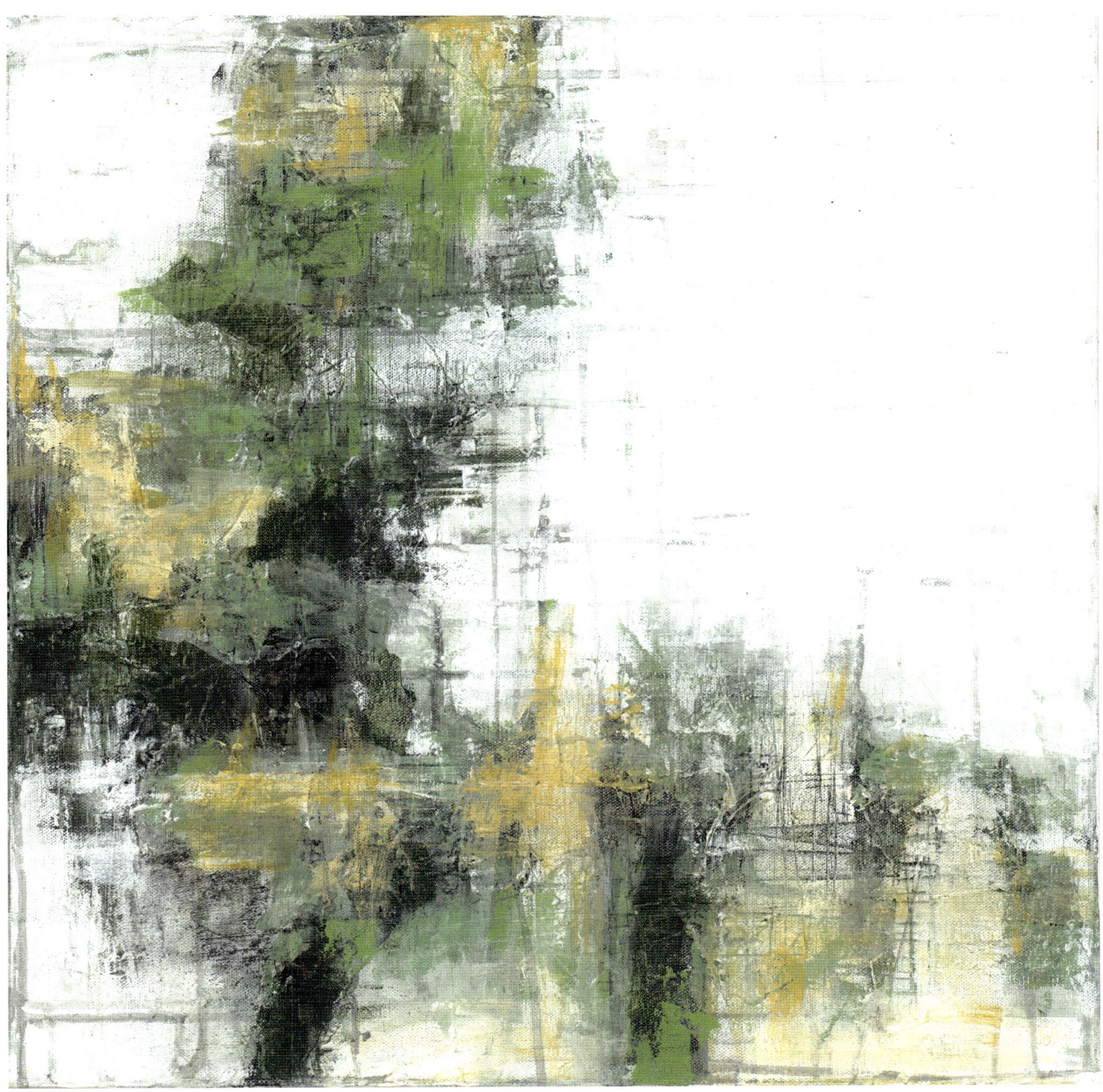

Tonda Howard

In 1993, Tonda Howard and her husband welcomed their daughter to the world. She was born with an extremely rare and profound chromosomal disorder. "We were stunned. Our world was shattered," says Howard. "It's difficult to describe the devastating pain and fear we experienced. I learned that there are many things in life that I cannot control, but I can still find beauty and profound meaning."

This life experience connects Howard on a deep level with the style of art she is drawn to. She can only control part of the creative process, and she feels a partnership with the creative spirit that exists outside of her. Working together with this spirit, the artist enters a meditative state where healing and transformation occur. Sometimes, the final work is not pleasing to Howard, but the journey, the process, was beautiful. Other times, the final work is beautiful, and as she looks back on it, she feels a deep sense of peace and contentment.

Distant
Acrylic
20 x 20 in.

tondahoward59@gmail
.com
tondahowardart.com
@tonda_howard_art

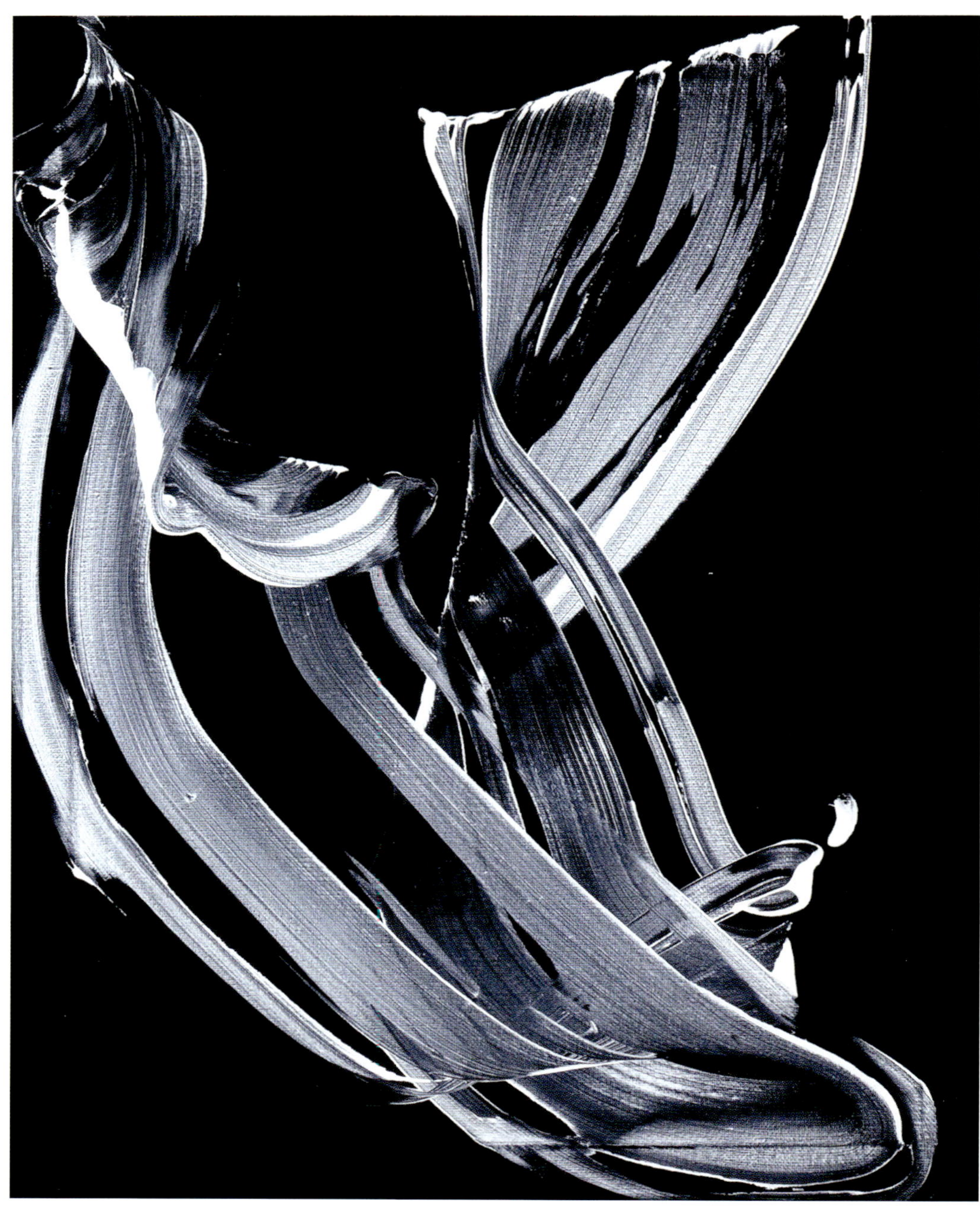

Newel Hunter

Newel Hunter paints almost exclusively in acrylic on a variety of surfaces, employing a selection of nontraditional painting tools, many of which the artist makes himself, to produce arresting images with a sense of depth and sculptural form. His technique merges action painting with bold calligraphic styling to create art that is contemplative, contemporary, and compelling. Hunter considers his best work, which is highly physical, gestural, and interpretive, a whole-body exercise in storytelling. He often paints in black and white, inspired by any number of European Art Informel artists and American abstractionists, among them Kline, Motherwell, Still, Hofmann, Richter, de Kooning, and especially, Pierre Soulages.

After Hours
Acrylic
20 x 16 in.

newelh@hotmail.com
newelhunterart.com

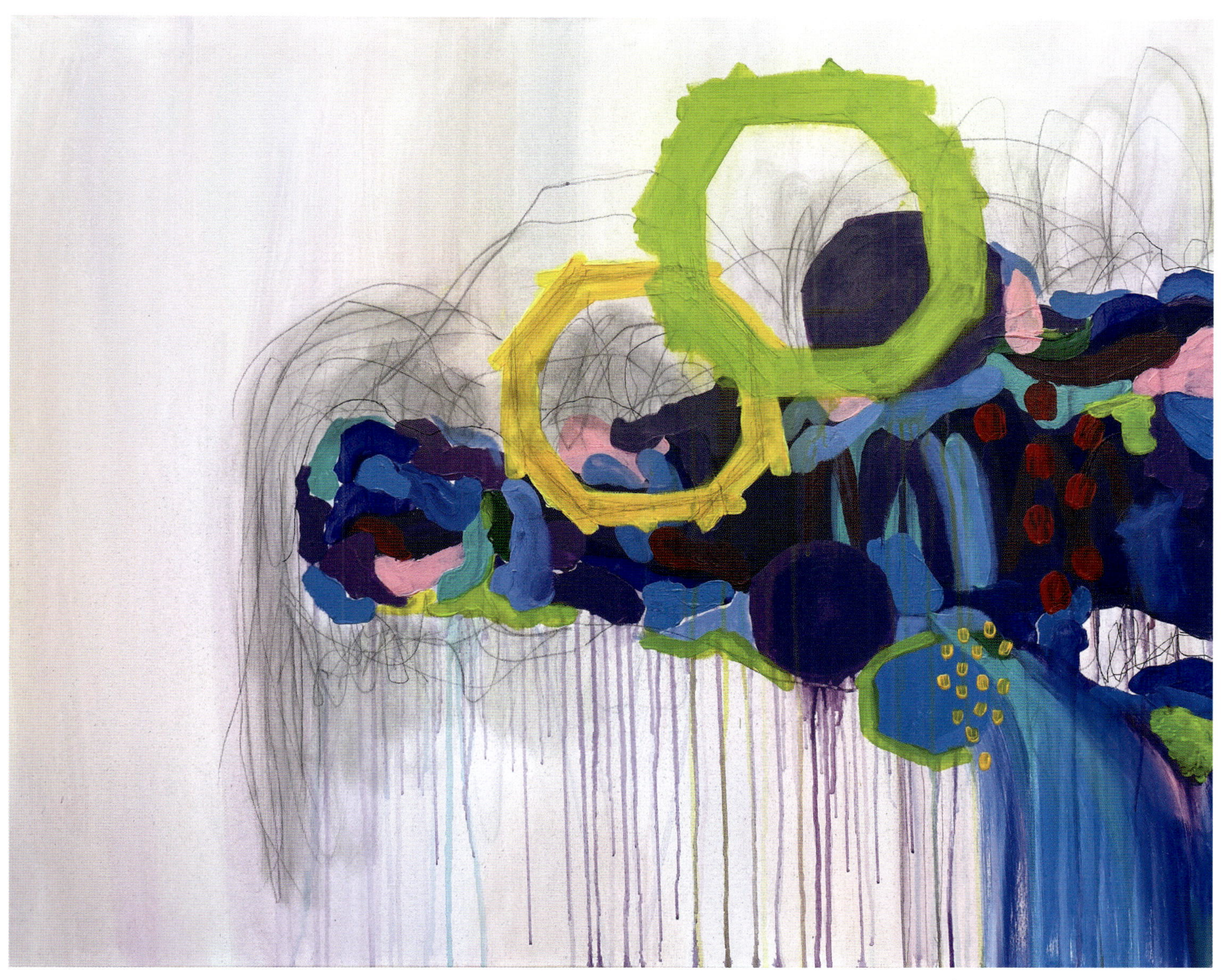

Ewa Jaros

As an educated art critic, Ewa Jaros wishes for her art to be open to interpretation, and she also wants it to offer a happy and aesthetically pleasant experience to the viewer. Jaros has a master's degree in art history and is working on her PhD. During the 2020 pandemic lockdown, Jaros realized how much the creative process brings her pure happiness, and it is her desire to share this with her collectors and those that view her work. Sometimes chaotic, other times elegant and soothing, her work is predominately an abstract concept, thus it appeals to one's subjective perception in the best imaginable way. She considers color to be the subject and object of her art.

Springpops
Acrylics and pencil
39 x 31 in.

e.jaros@onet.pl
ewajarosart.pl
@ewajarosart

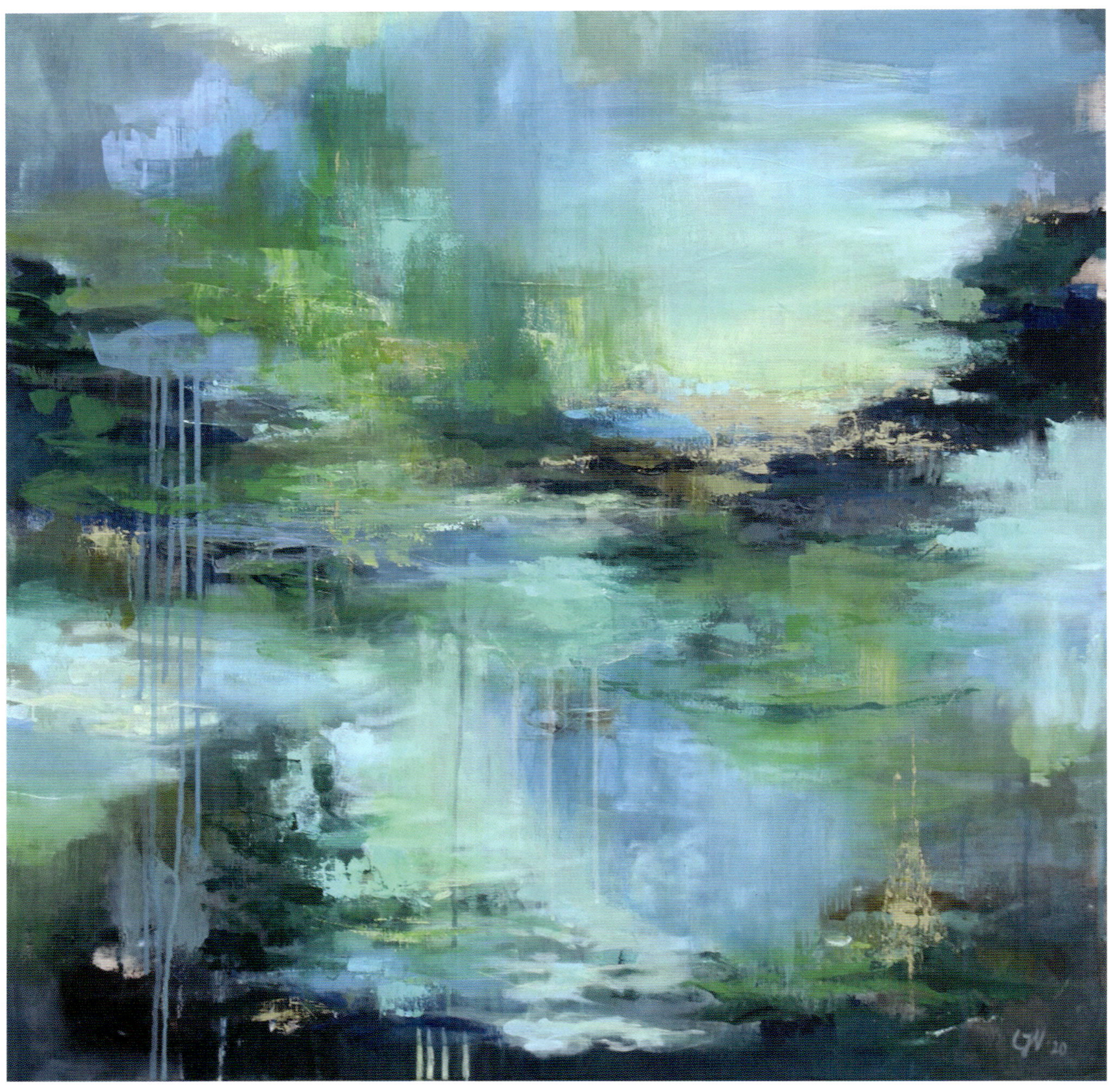

Nikolina Car Jergovic
Fascinated by the nature that surrounds her, Nikolina Car Jergovic likes to observe its colors and forms and the way it transforms itself through cycles. Drawing inspiration from those visual impressions, the artist creates abstract paintings in a processual manner, experiencing them as emotional interpretations of a subject. The process begins with a loose concept, an idea, or a memory that is developing and taking its own course. It is an intuitive, responsive process of building a painting with many layers of colors and texture. As the work evolves, the artist experiences many emotions, ranging from inner struggle to joy. It is very important to Car Jergovic that her finished painting evokes emotions in a viewer. "I see my work as introspection and exploration," she says. "As the painting grows, the connection and communication establish between me and the image, and finally with the inner self, which the painting reflects, grows."

Oasis
Acrylic and gold pigment
31.4 x 31.4 in.

ninanein@gmail.com
@nikolinacarjergovic

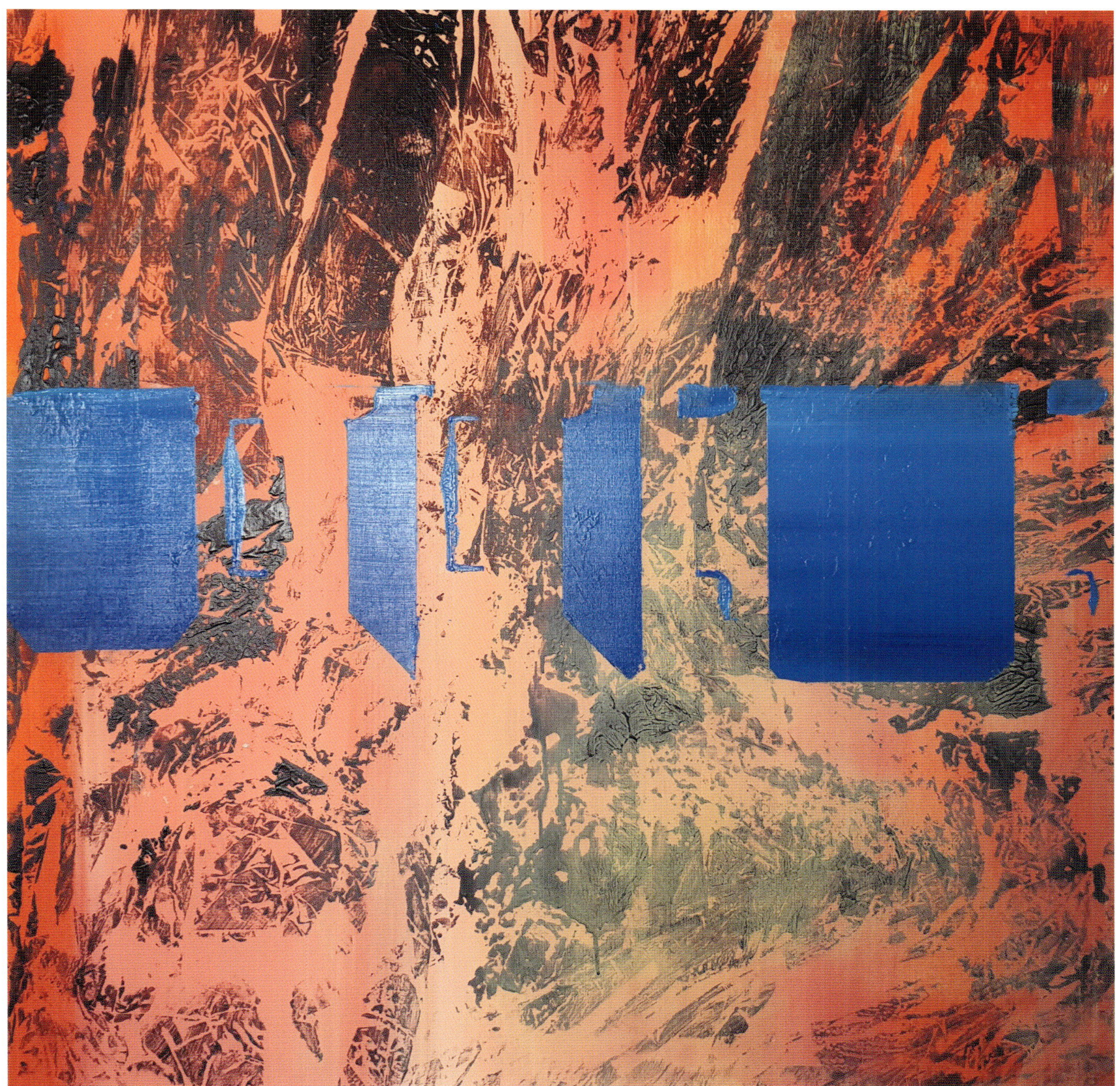

Stefanie Kamrath

Stefanie Kamrath's paintings are the visualization of her personal perception of the present, the intense dealing with an exciting interaction. Nothing is completely isolated. During her process of painting, she reveals the invisible in strong colors, using her whole body for strong motions.

"Everything is in motion at any given time. Everything is in context with something else right here and right now," Kamrath says. Body movement and dancing have always been central elements of Kamrath's education and life. She studied architecture in Paris, France, and in Aachen, Germany, and fine arts in Essen, Germany. Working as an architect, she loves creating spaces. While working as an artist, she loves revealing the invisible in between.

New 2
Acrylic
47 x 47 in.

skam.arts@gmail.com
skam-arts.de
@stefaniekamrath
@jessicaeichman

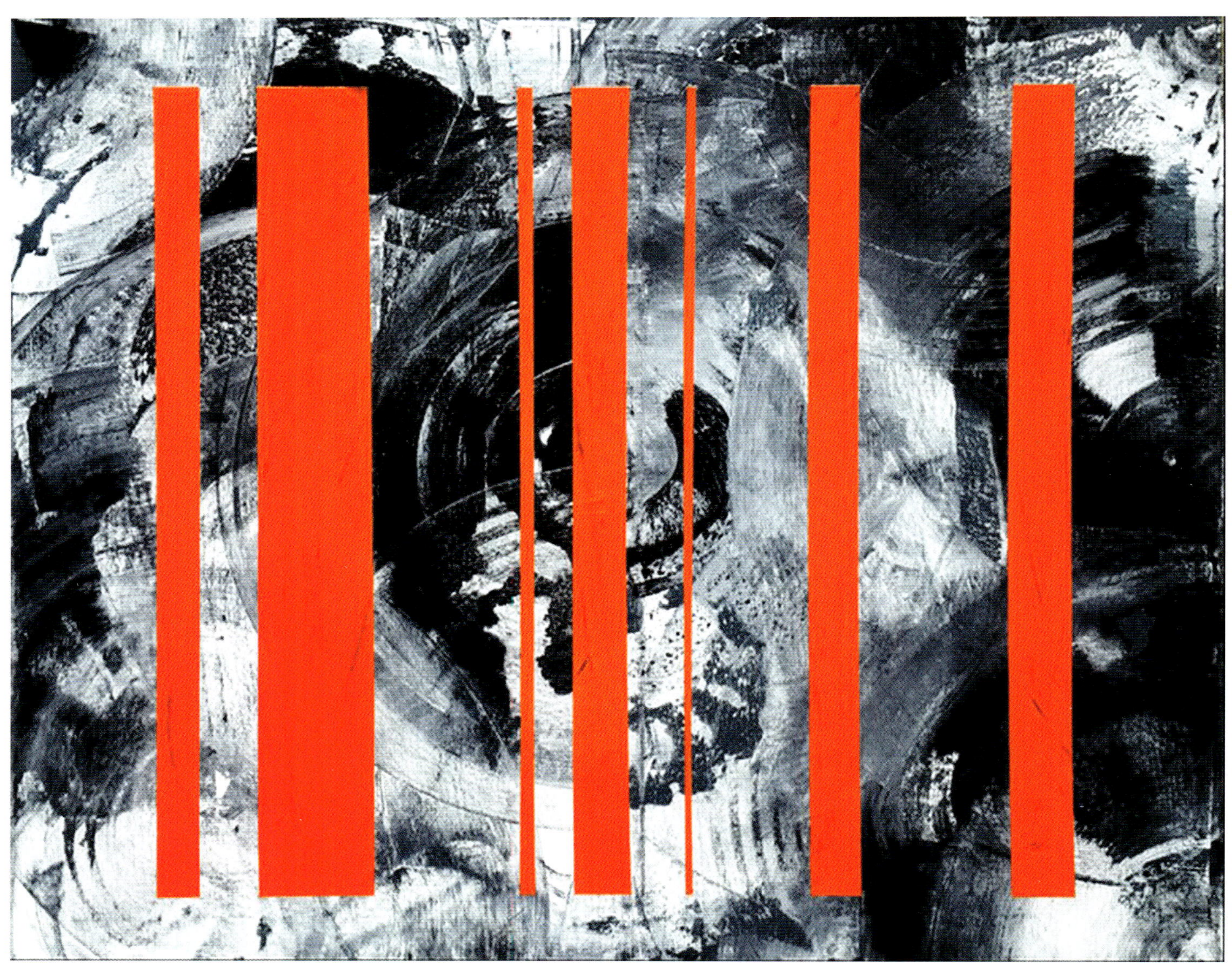

Rebecca Kaushal (aka Becks)

Becks is an abstract contemporary artist specializing in works of acrylic, oil pastel, spray paint, and watercolor on canvas. Her work encompasses a fine balance between integrating layers of precisely calculated placement of color schemes, shapes, mediums, and techniques with spontaneous techniques that may arise in the process. Her aim is to emulate abstract ideas surrounding nature, society, spirituality, and the cosmos through contemporary and mixed-media layering techniques. Her creative process entails tapping into her intuitive self, with no real destination or plan around how the piece will turn out. Much of her work features geometric shapes, floating lines, and vibrant colors, as seen in the works of Wassily Kandinsky. "Art is a strong contender of how we share our thoughts and ideas," Becks says. "It holds the opportunity to influence thoughts, allowing new ideas to emerge. Just one new idea can change a person's perception, inspiring me to continue to create."

Meditation
Acrylic
24 X 30 in.

beckstudioart@gmail.com
beckstudio.ca
@beckstudio

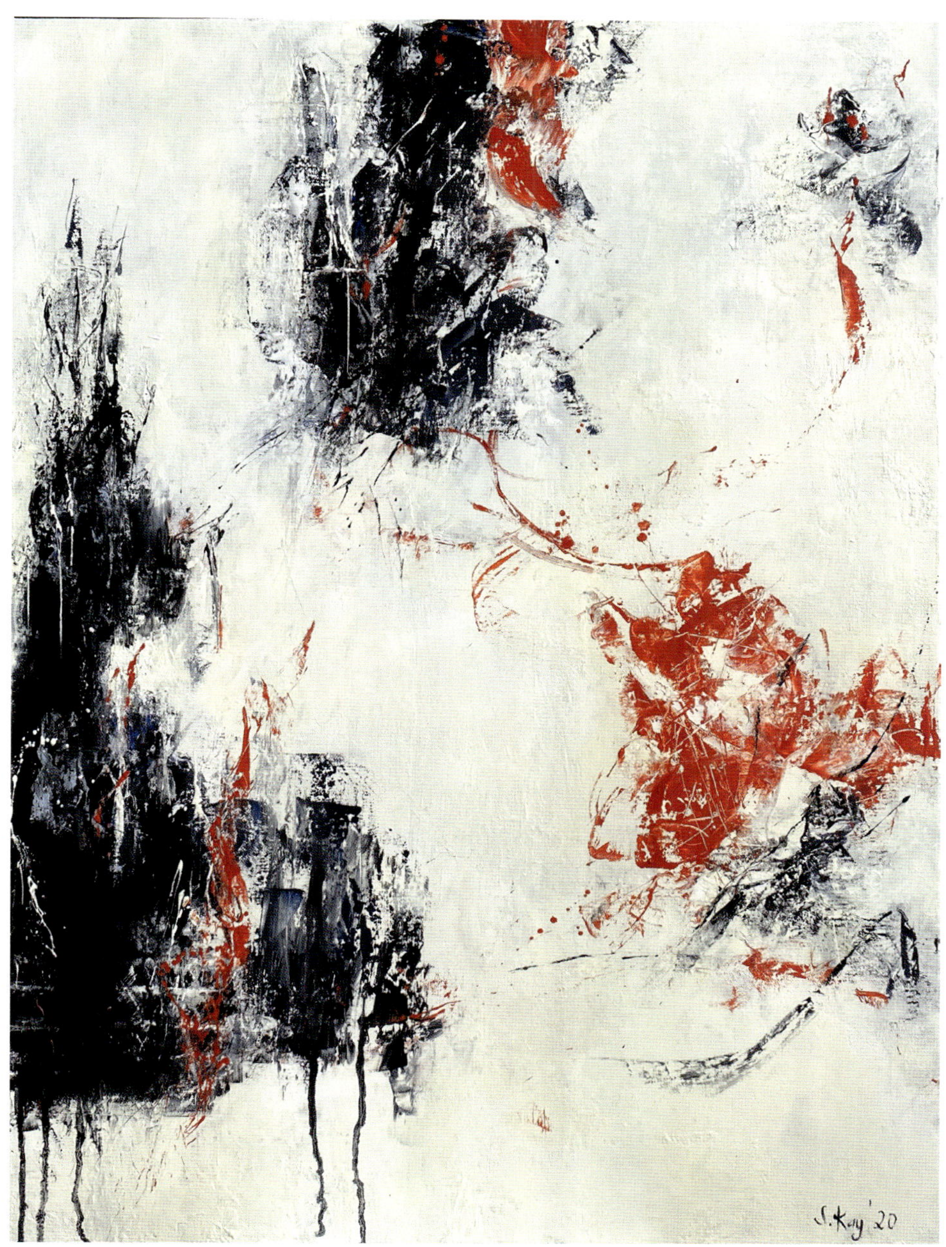

Sabine Kay

Sabine Kay loves to create art, and with her contemporary abstract oil paintings, she hopes to reach the hearts of viewers and bring them happiness and joy. In the beginning, Kay worked realistically, but over the years, she learned that she can better express herself through abstract painting. Her abstract landscapes reflect her love for color and nature, which is also her source of inspiration. While painting Kay builds several layers of oil colors using a palette of soft and serene colors with those that are vibrant and invigorating. Colors are important for Kay because they can show the full range of human emotions and experiences. Her expressive technique is based on her wish to achieve balance and to reach beauty in the contrasting forces that exist everywhere. Kay's creative process is an interplay between accuracy and intuitive impulses, revealed especially in thin splashes of paint made with the spatula, which give every work its characteristic touch.

Red Whisper
Oil
31.5 x 23.6 in.

sabine.kay3@gmail.com
emergingartistplatform
.com/sabinekay
@sabine.kay3

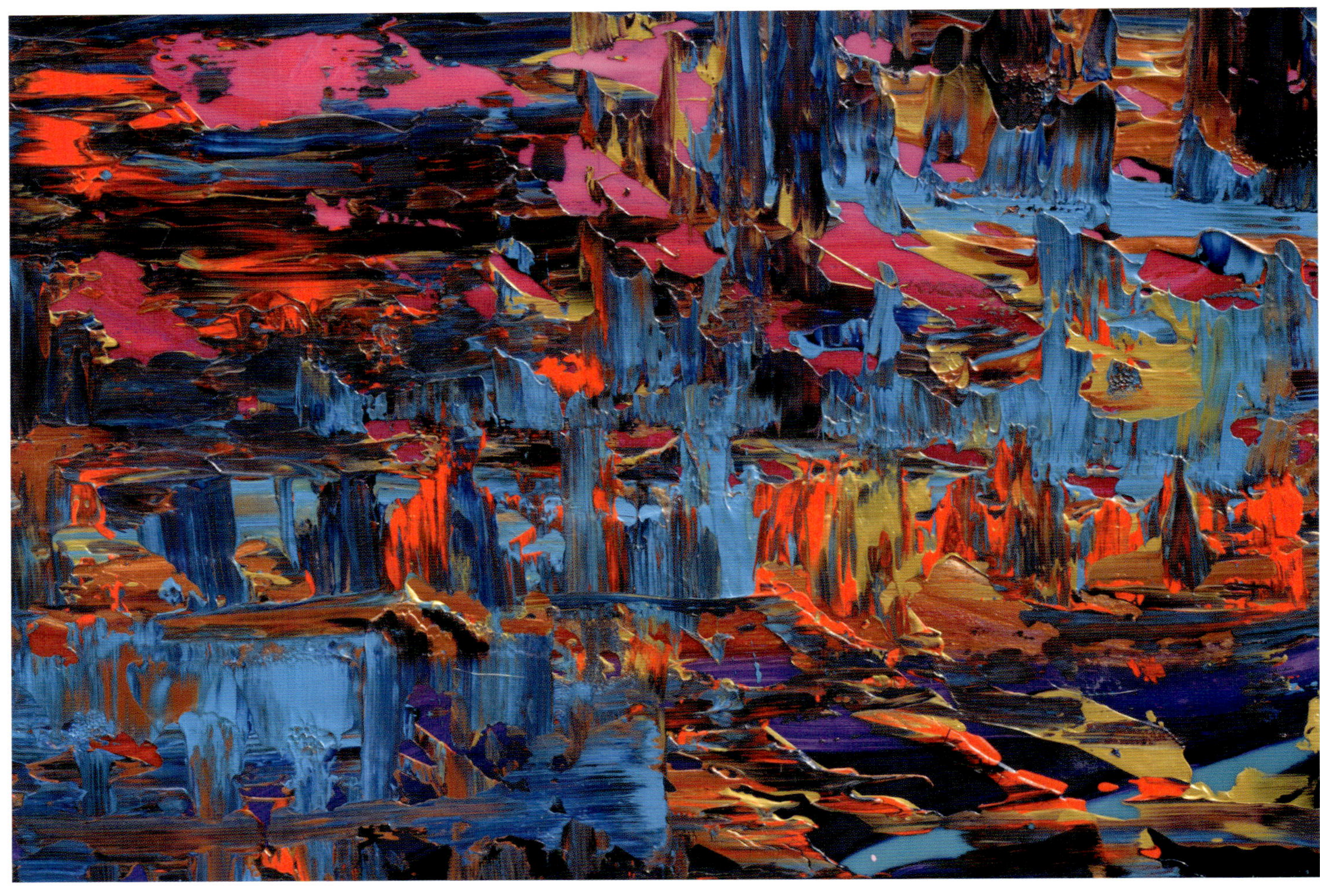

Robbie Kaye

Inspired by all things in nature, society, and life, Robbie Kaye creates photographs and paintings. In her abstract work, her intention is to create a narrative through the emotion of each piece. She works with acrylic paint in a way that feels more like sculpting. She creates layers and layers with spackle knives and paintbrushes. The layers are not predetermined. Most times, she creates a piece and, thinking it's done, she will set it aside but return to the work three or four times, building more layers and creating texture while the colors from previous renditions can still show through. At times, Kaye begins with a resin formation on wood or aluminum, underneath the painting, which protrudes through the paint if the layers are not too thick. She loves the process of experimentation, as it takes away any pressure for perfection, and she finds it easy to let go of the frustration when a piece doesn't work.

Rainbows in Windows
Acrylic resin on
aluminum
16 x 20 in.

robbie@robbiekaye.com
robbiekaye.com
@robbiekaye

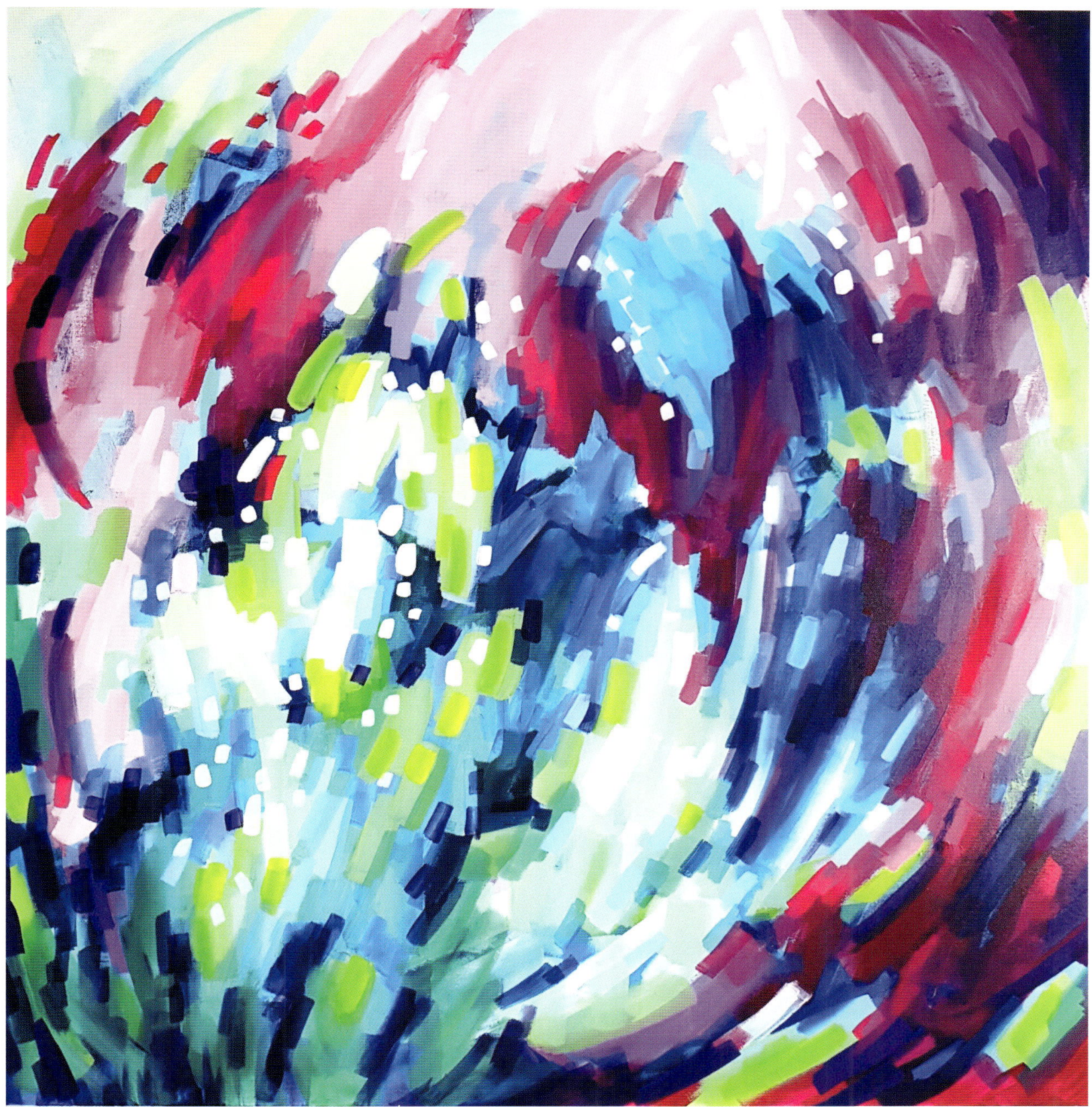

Jennifer Keeney-Bleeg

J.K. Bleeg's first and most vivid memories are of colors—a canary yellow balloon her parents bought for her at a parade when she was two, a shimmering aqua swimming pool, her cherry red tricycle. Colors have always triggered a visceral response in the artist, and in her painting practice she likes to examine and experiment with how color impacts mood and energy. Since a color is defined by the colors surrounding it, Bleeg likes to test the boundaries of a shade on canvas by partnering it with neighbors that can elevate its drama. Her work incorporates many layers of acrylic paint and touches of pastel. These media help her to create depth, build texture, and develop a backdrop for bold pops of color. Bleeg's aim for each painting is to draw viewers inside and escort them through a range of emotions or states of mind.

Waking Dreams
Acrylic
40 x 40 in.

jennifer@jkbleeg.com
jkbleeg.com
@jkbleeg

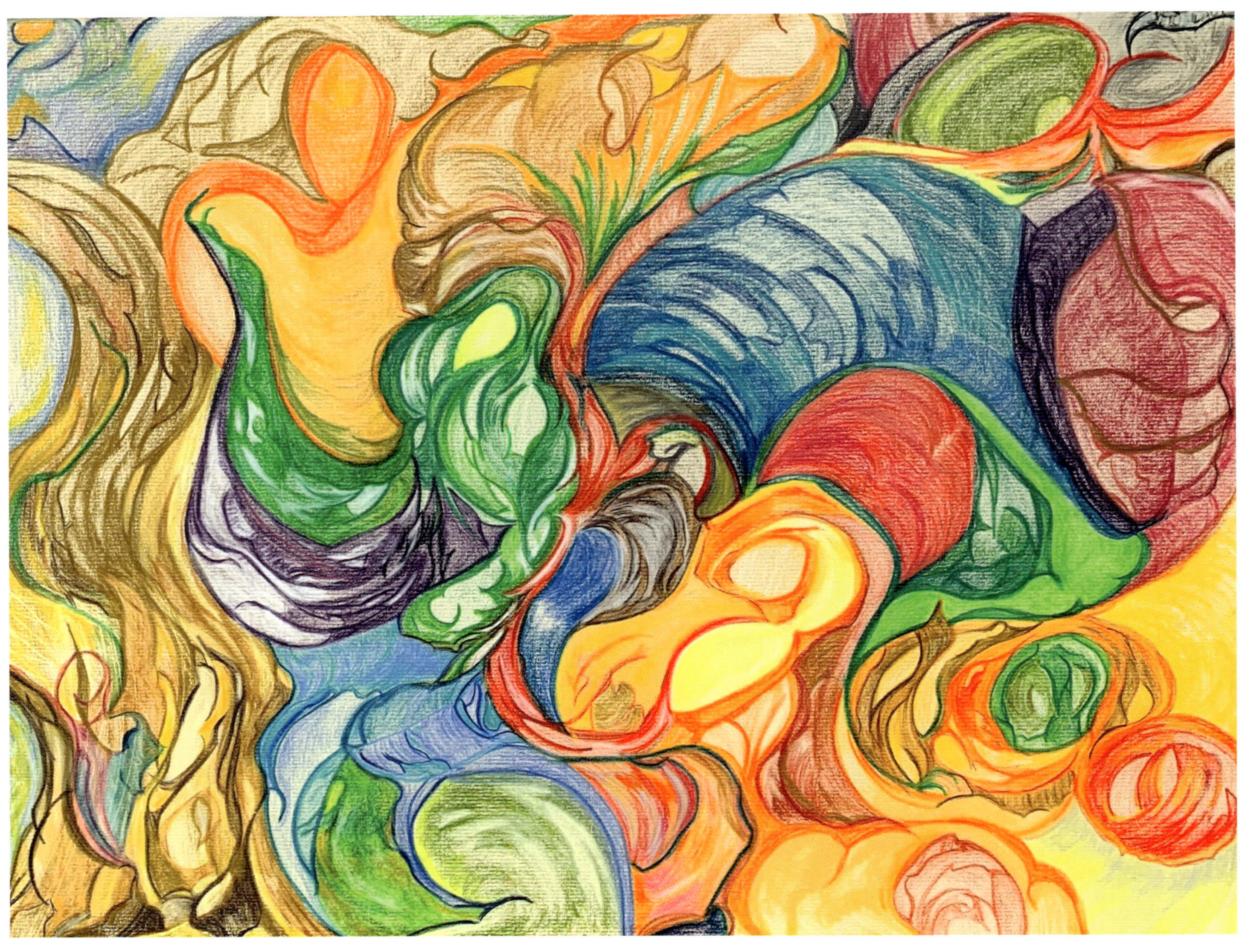

Viviane Laut

Art has always been part of Viviane Laut's life. It is her way of expressing herself. When she draws, she has to let go of all her worries to allow all the space for her creativity and imagination. Laut likes the motion of drawing. It allows her to refocus on herself, to release her emotions, and to convey her state of mind through colors and various shapes. Laut's inspiration comes from immersing herself in what surrounds her and her story. Her process is spontaneous. She draws for a period of time then goes back over her drawings several times to complete them. Currently, Laut is interested in a drawing method called neurographica, which helps to refine her line and allows her to evolve personally.

Charibari
Colored pencil
29.7 X 42 in.

laut.viviane@orange.fr
@viviane_laut_17_

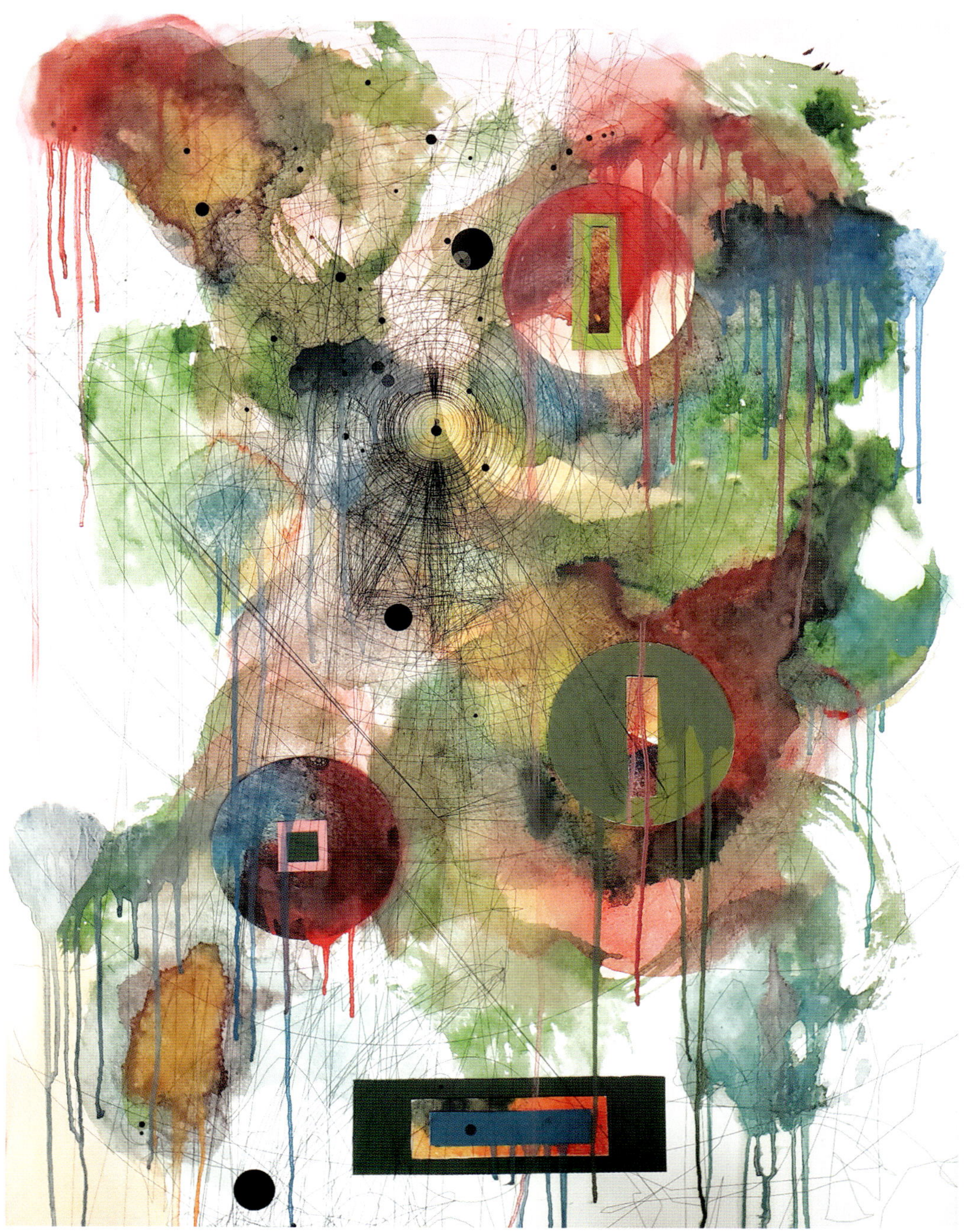

Taylor LeBlanc

Creating interesting nonobjective designs that are a combination of digital and traditional processes is Taylor LeBlanc's primary focus. She creates pieces that contain different types of mediums, which help maximize the contrast of each piece. She uses a mixture of watercolor, collage, digital, and oil painting together in one design. LeBlanc's process is especially important to her since it allows her to start with a handmade piece, enhance the design digitally, and then perfect the design with oil on canvas. She enjoys not letting the viewer be aware of what is digitally created or made by hand. This mixture of progressive and traditional methods is what pushes art forward.

Selah 3 v2
Oil over digital
40 x 30 in.

Trleblanc88@gmail.com
trldesign.com
@trl__designs

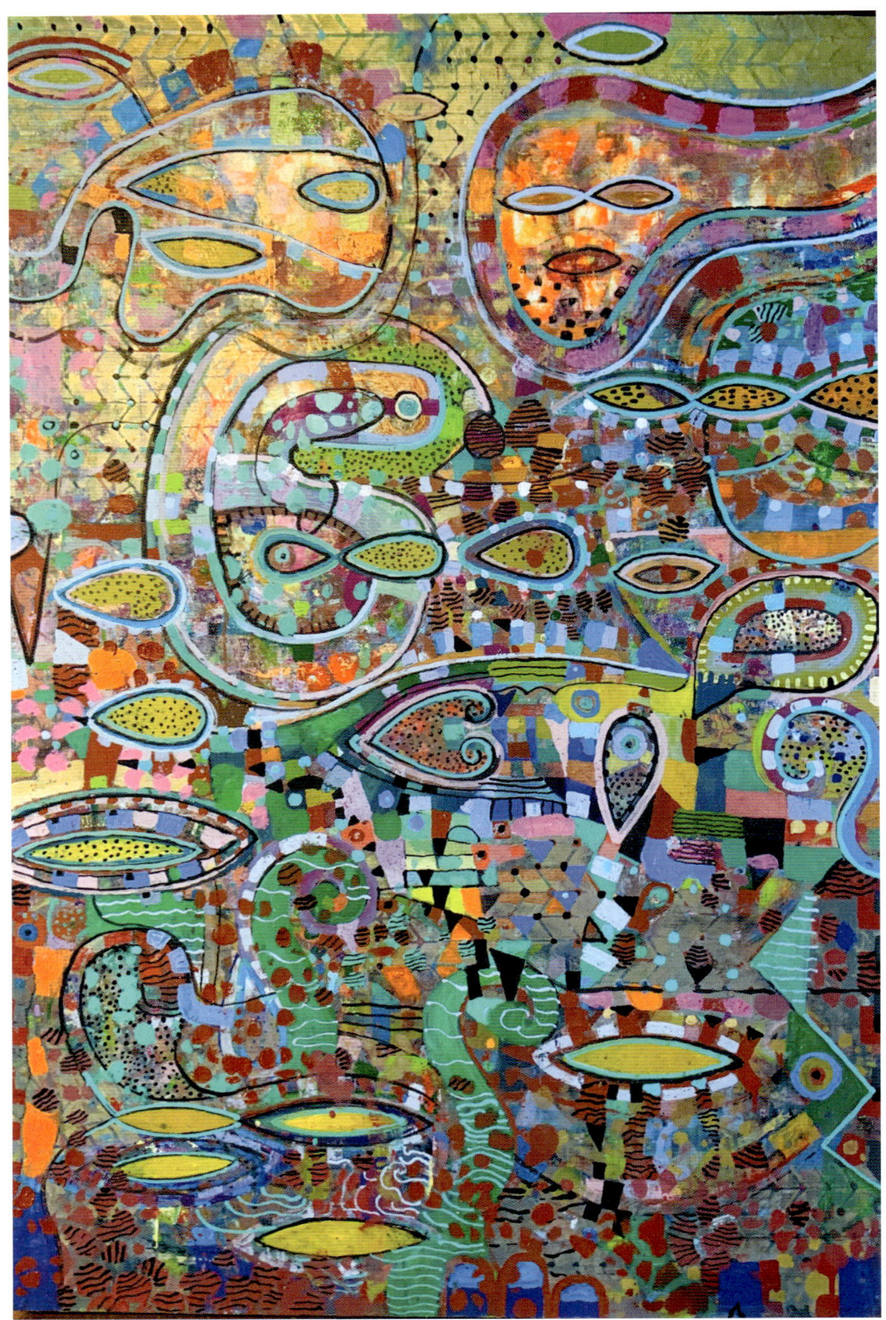

Alise Loebelsohn

Alise Loebelsohn's painting career emerged from a desire to transform surfaces into a new reality. Her work is about the patterns and images that randomly appear in nature, like memories that can fade but then come to the surface when sparked. She is interested in those murky areas where there are no clear truths. It is here where she tries to imagine the laws of imaginary worlds and how she can make sense of the universe in which we live. Loebelsohn is sensitive to how materials can be used to create patterns in new and undiscovered ways. It is her wish to use the two-dimensional space as a way of breaking through the boundaries of time, space, perception, and dimension. Loebelsohn begins each painting by preparing the surface with many layers of plaster, oil paint, and resin. It is her wish for the colors to reflect a luminosity by using a variety of materials.

Orange To Green
Oil on panel
36 x 24 in.

aliseloebelsohn@nyc
.rr.com
alisemloebelsohn.com
@alise_loebelsohn

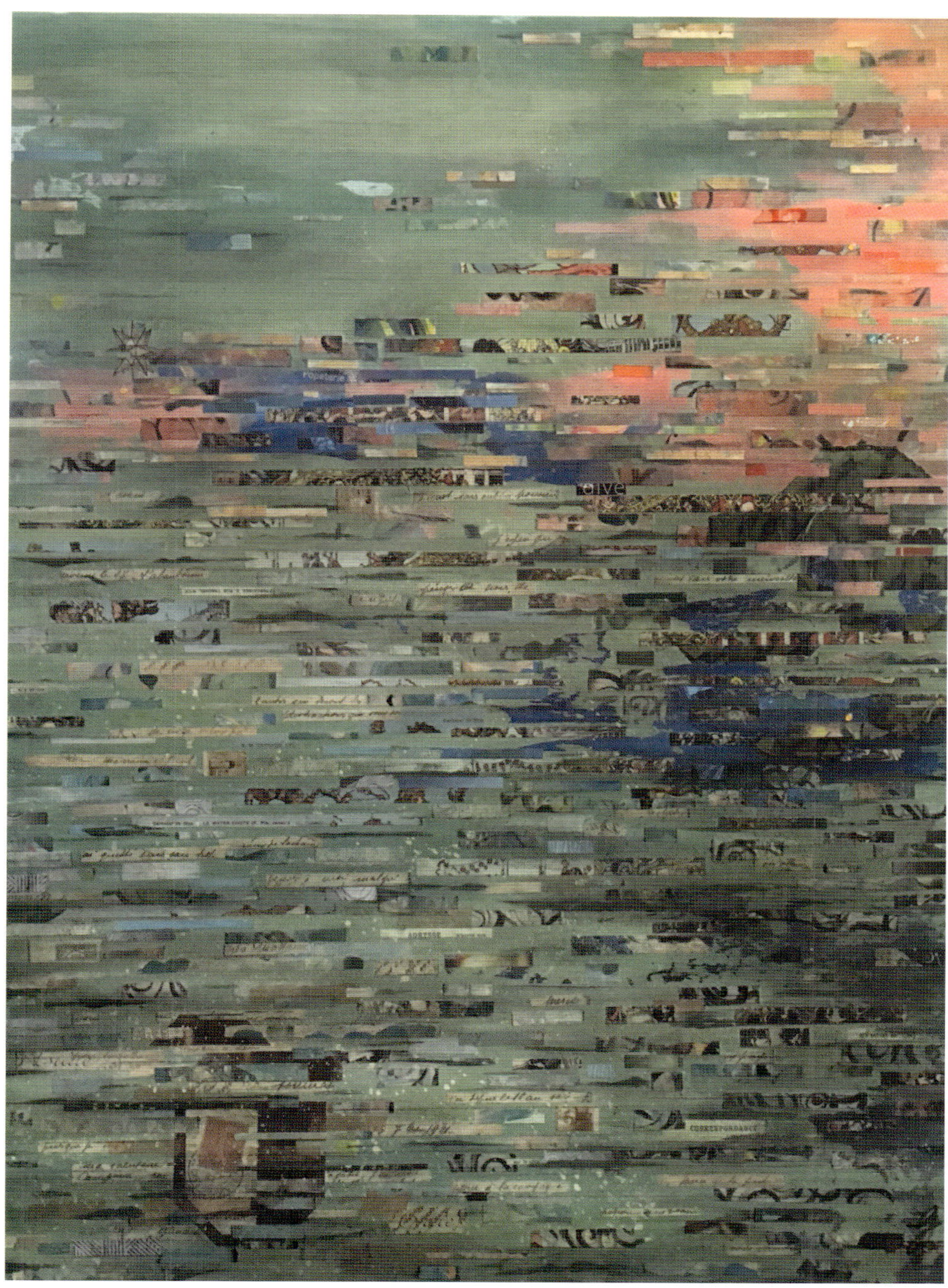

Gillian Loop

Gillian Loop began her education as an art major, but a naive fear of poverty led to a career in fashion with a focus on form and construction as well as logo, textile, and storyboard design. Textile design informs her work; she utilizes printed elements derived from labels, packaging, and magazines to create typically irreverent but sometimes earnest artwork. However, a dual perspective exists and is consistently evident in her work, one is detailed and the other is a more generalized image or theme.

Carnavale de Nice
Acrylic and mixed media
24 x 18 in.

gillianloop@hotmail.com
gillianloop.com
@gillianloop_the_art_of

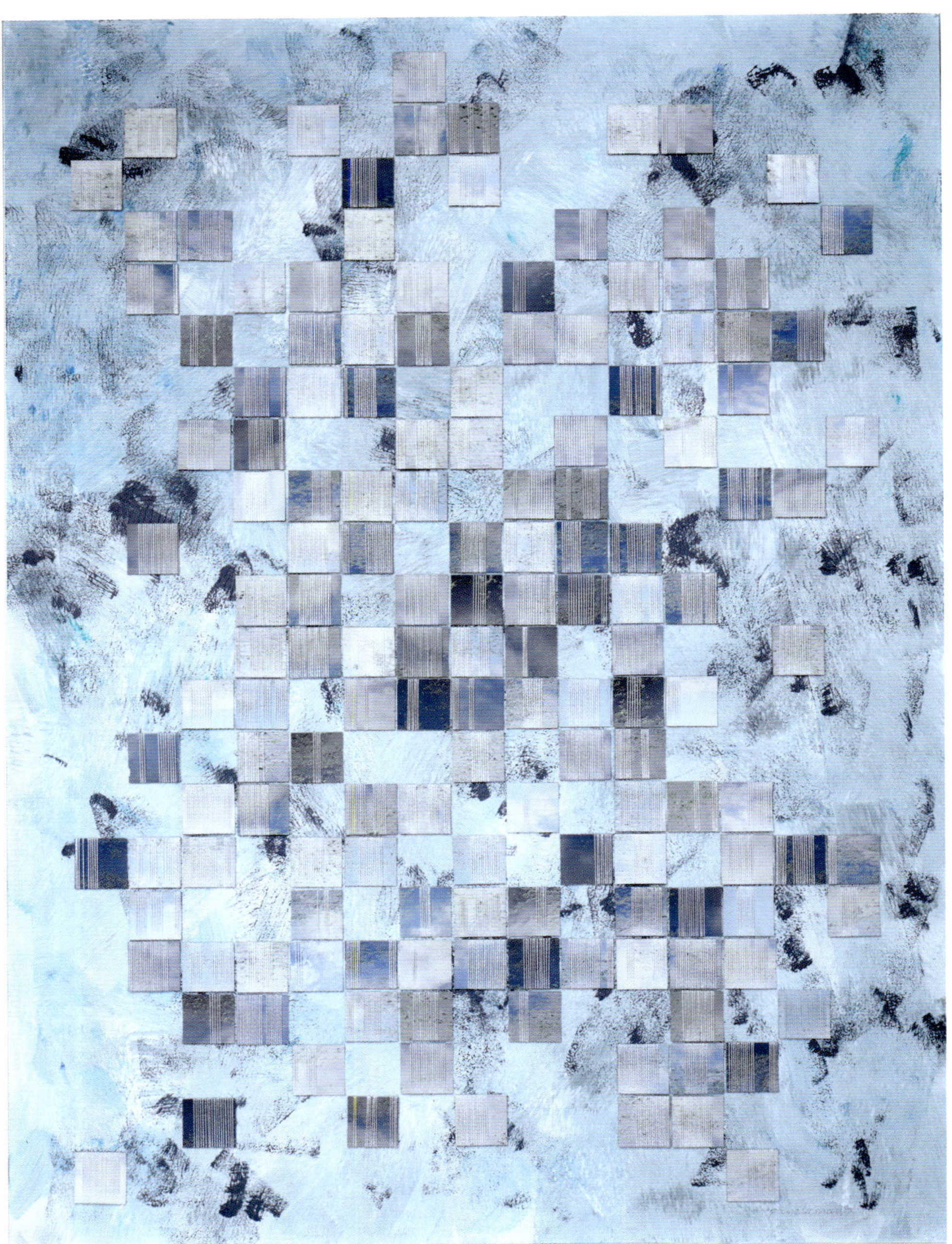

Paméla Maria

The beauty of everyday life and nothing is what it seems to be are leading themes in Paméla Maria's work. Nature is an important source of inspiration. Maria enjoys zooming in on the endless wealth of patterns, structures, shades of color, and light in the (urban) landscape. Her work depicts how these impressions slide over each other and yield new compositions with endless shades of color. Her reliefs are made with yarn, acrylic paint, paper, and photos that portray the tranquil landscape of Holland.

"For me, working is a changing process, shifting from reality to geometric or expressionistic proportions," Maria says. "The seemingly flat surface changes into a relief with several dimensions. The yarn picks up details, directs the eye, and adds a third dimension."

A Rainy Day in Spring
Acrylic paint and yarn on paper and canvas
31.4 x 23.6 in.

studio@pamelamaria.nl
pamelamaria.nl
@pamela_maria_1234

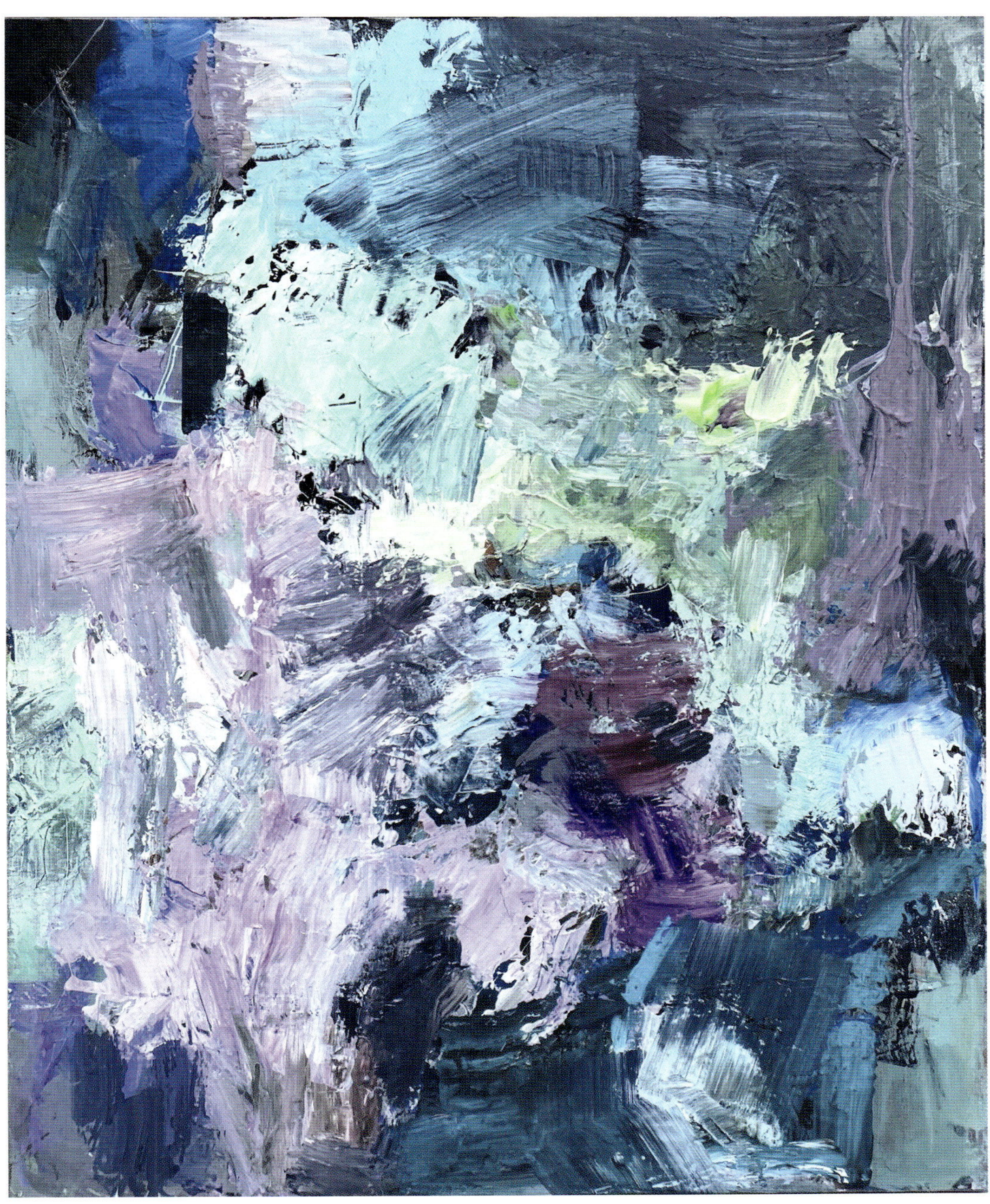

Michelle Marra

As far back as Michelle Marra can remember she had a paintbrush in her hand. Her mother recognized her obsession and enrolled her in private art lessons throughout her childhood and into high school. Art took a back seat while she made a career and then a family. Marra took up the brush in earnest while spending time in Florida. There she started working in oils and realism but knew she was missing something. Attendance in an acrylic and abstract painting workshop in 2012 changed her focus, and it allowed her to give a visual voice to her inner feelings. Marra sees in swaths of color and light. Painting has become a form of meditation set into motion. She allows the colors and the initial marks to take her to the next step. It can be a complete joy and a complete challenge at the same time. She often says a bad day painting is better than a day of not painting at all.

Scurry in Place
Acrylic
30 x 24 in.

michellemarra@
comcast.net
michellemarrastudio
.com
@michellemarrastudio

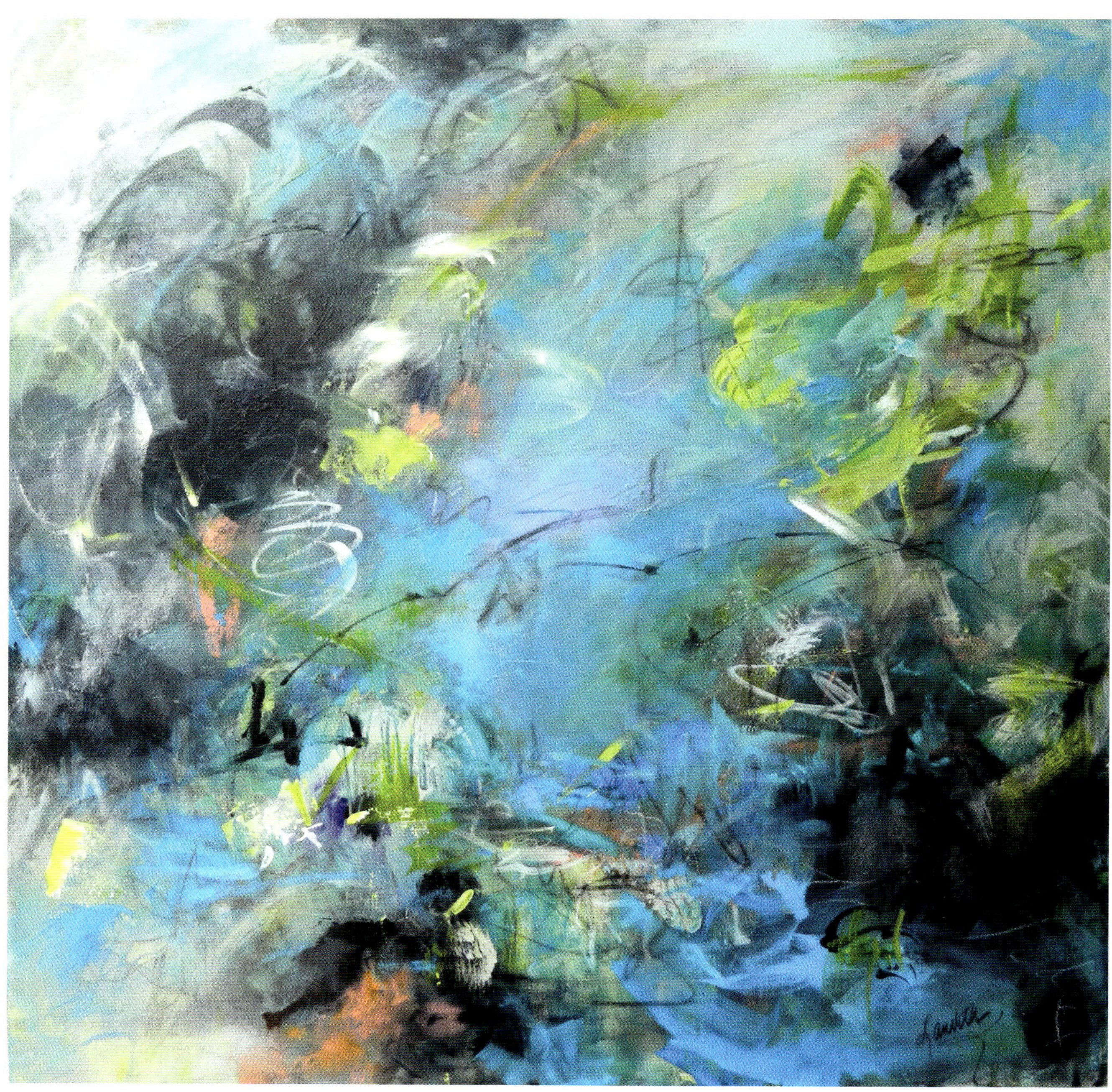

Lambeth W. Marshall

Lambeth W. Marshall has had a passion for art for over forty-five years. She focused heavily on clay during the early part of her professional career, all the while maintaining her interest in painting. Years ago, Marshall was encouraged to begin painting in a more abstract fashion. She has been experimenting with different drawing and painting materials and exploring the abstract realm regularly ever since. Her tools include charcoals, inks, pencil, acrylic paints, pastels, and sometimes alcohol-based inks. She is constantly intrigued by the playfulness and freedom of making abstract art. It feeds her soul. Her work represents her experiences with water, the ocean, mountains, and her gardens. She wants people to enjoy her artwork, knowing that each one is made with love and enthusiasm for life. Her abstract paintings offer something special: a chance to explore your imagination and use the creative side of your brain.

Bajo el Oceano
Acrylic
36 x 36 in.

lambethpottery@
windstream.net
lambethpottery.net
@lambeth marshall

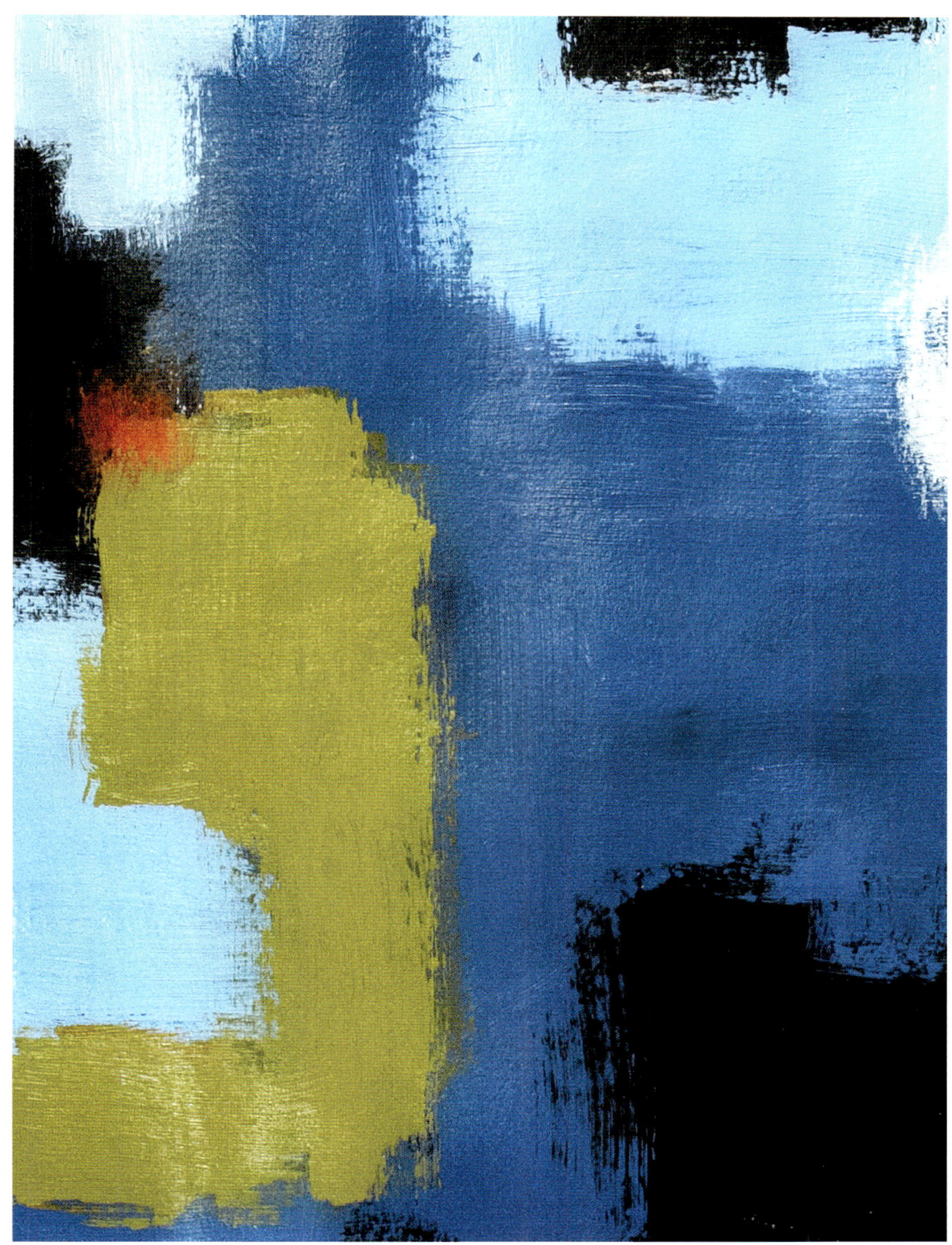

C.S. McIntire

C.S. McIntire is both thankful for, and frustrated by, his extremely vivid imagination. He has always been a visual person. He likes to look at color, shapes, and how color and shape change in different light or while in motion. Nature always centers the artist. A simple hike sparks creativity and inspires his palette. For McIntire, creating is all about connection. The deeper he gets into creating, the deeper he drops into and connects with his own open and authentic space. Whether he is pairing intense colors, bold brushstrokes, or subtle mark making, McIntire wants to convey the energy and emotion in that moment, to connect with the viewer. He draws inspiration from artists such as de Kooning, Pollock, Diebenkorn, and Van Gogh, as well as from colors and forms found in nature.

Azul
Acrylic and oil pastel
10 x 8 in.

craigmcintire@hotmail.com
csmcintire.com
@c.s.mcintire

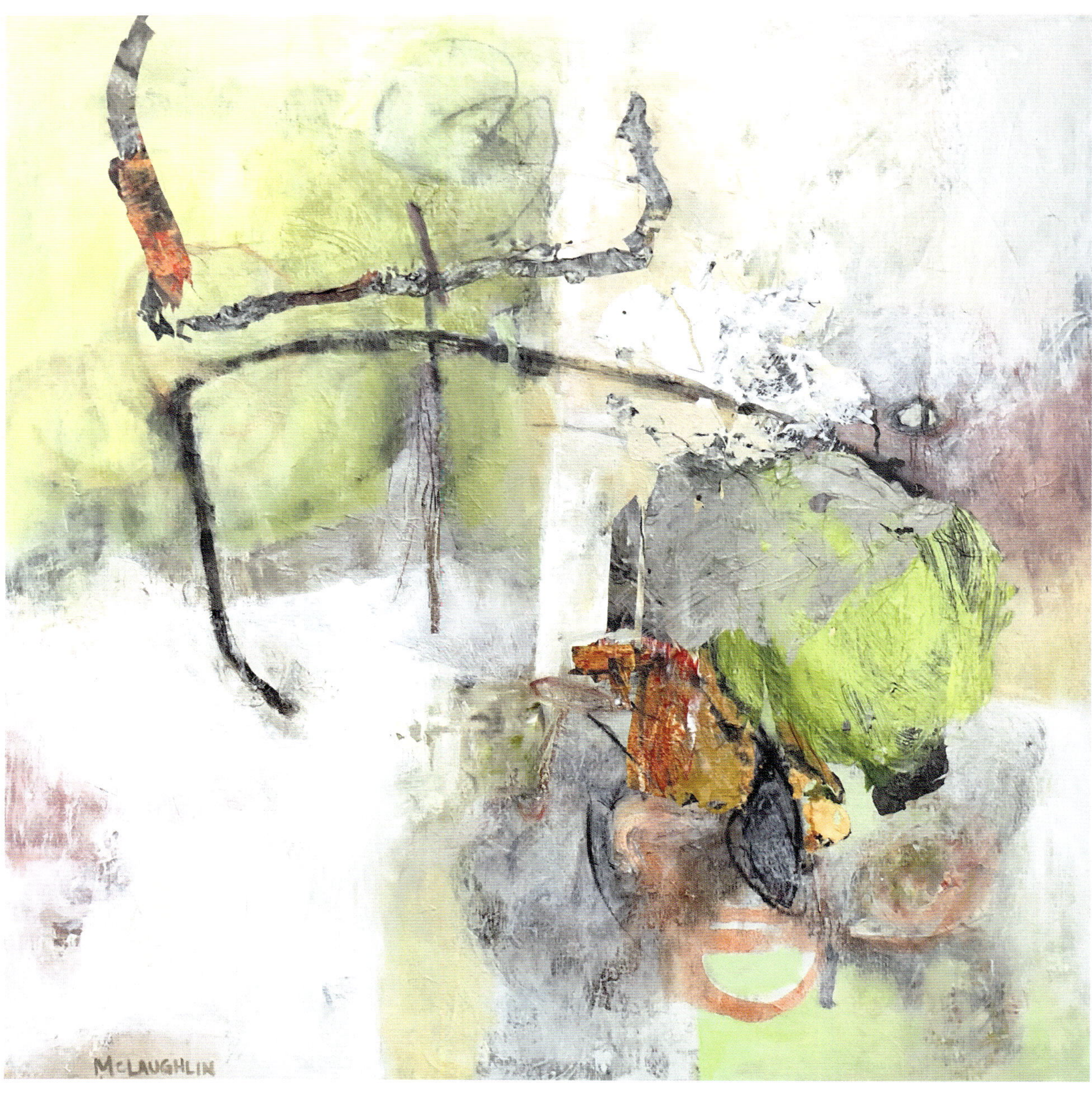

Lisa McLaughlin

Lisa McLaughlin can't remember a time in her life that she wasn't creating. She was fortunate to have parents and teachers who encouraged her as a child, as well as The Toledo Museum of Art, with its world-class collection, to inspire her. McLaughlin studied design, fine art, and art history at university and now is blessed to travel extensively for work and pleasure. Her full-time job in the music business keeps her on the road 200 days a year on average, so any chance she gets, she visits the local museums. As the pandemic temporarily shut down the music industry, it has forced her to slow down, stay in, and shift gears, but McLaughlin is taking a glass-half-full approach. She has been using this extraordinary time to paint and to organize the thousands of photos she has taken as resources for artistic inspiration.

Libra
Acrylic
24 x 24 in.

info@lisamclaughlinart
.com
lisamclaughlinart.com
@lisamclaughlinart

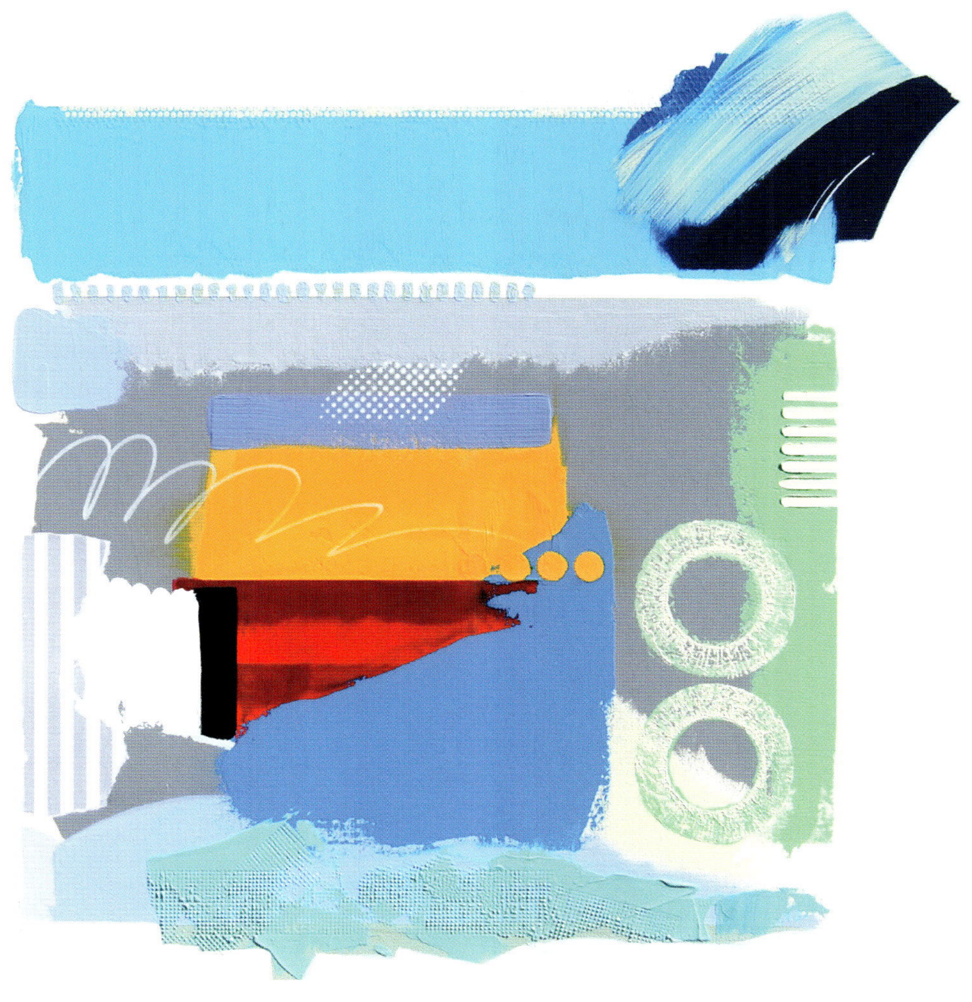

Kevin Megison

Kevin Megison's approach to painting is direct. He looks around his studio and makes decisions as to scale, orientation, and color choices based on what's available that day. There is a discipline to setting the stage for making art. Megison established an environment for the purpose of creativity, and he is prepared to engage with focus and determination while still remaining flexible enough to react with spontaneity and abandon. Sometimes he will start with a rough composition but will alter it as he works, allowing new developments and layers to influence decisions moving forward. Megison admits he struggles with the concept of inspiration. Motivation seems more tangible to him. He is motivated out of a need to create. In the end, his artwork is a product of enjoyment. If it doesn't spring from joy, it just doesn't happen. The viewer may not be able to identify why there is an affiliation with a particular work, but it is felt and that is the point. To consider his work a success, Megison is looking for an emotional response of "it just feels right."

Unhinged #02
Acrylic
36 x 36 in.

kevinmegison@att.net
kevinmegisonart.com
@kevinmegisonart

149

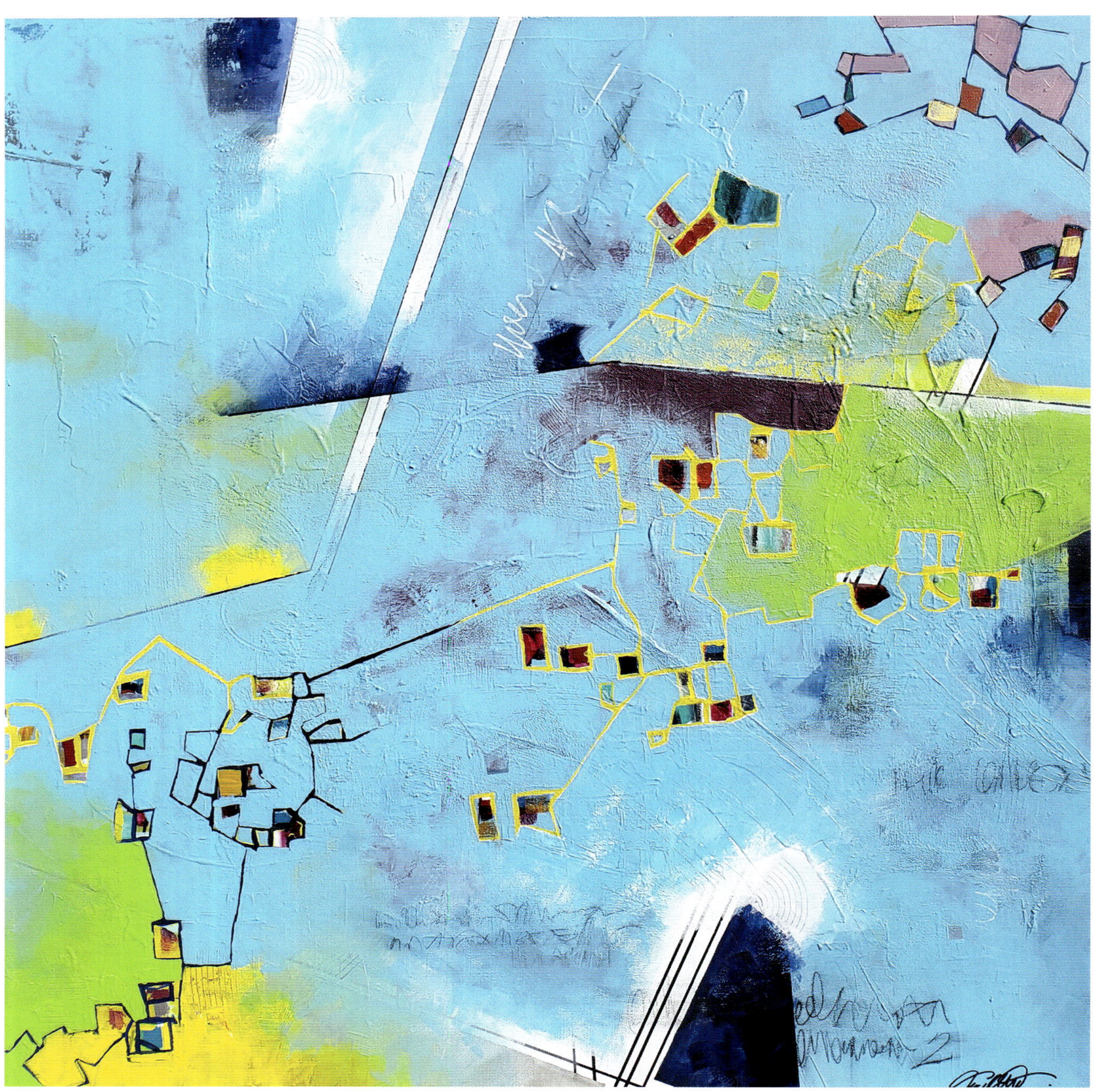

Traci R. Meitzler

As an artist, Traci R. Meitzler works hard to develop a work that speaks both to herself and to others about her emotions and frame of mind while creating. Each piece has a story, a moment in time, a feeling. The direction at the start of a project can be monumentally different compared to the conclusion. Documenting that process is the best way to see that evolution. Meitzler takes many photos throughout the process and keeps a diary on what has inspired her or the music she's been listening to. Going back and reading what she's written always gives her a baseline to come back to. Meitzler classifies her style as chaotic architecture. She enjoys the juxtaposition of straight edges with organic curves. She believes that a painting or any design cannot have just one element, but that each exists in harmony because of the other.

The Lies We Tell Ourselves
Acrylic and mixed media
36 x 36 in.

mad7artstudio@gmail.com
mad7studio.com
@mad7studio

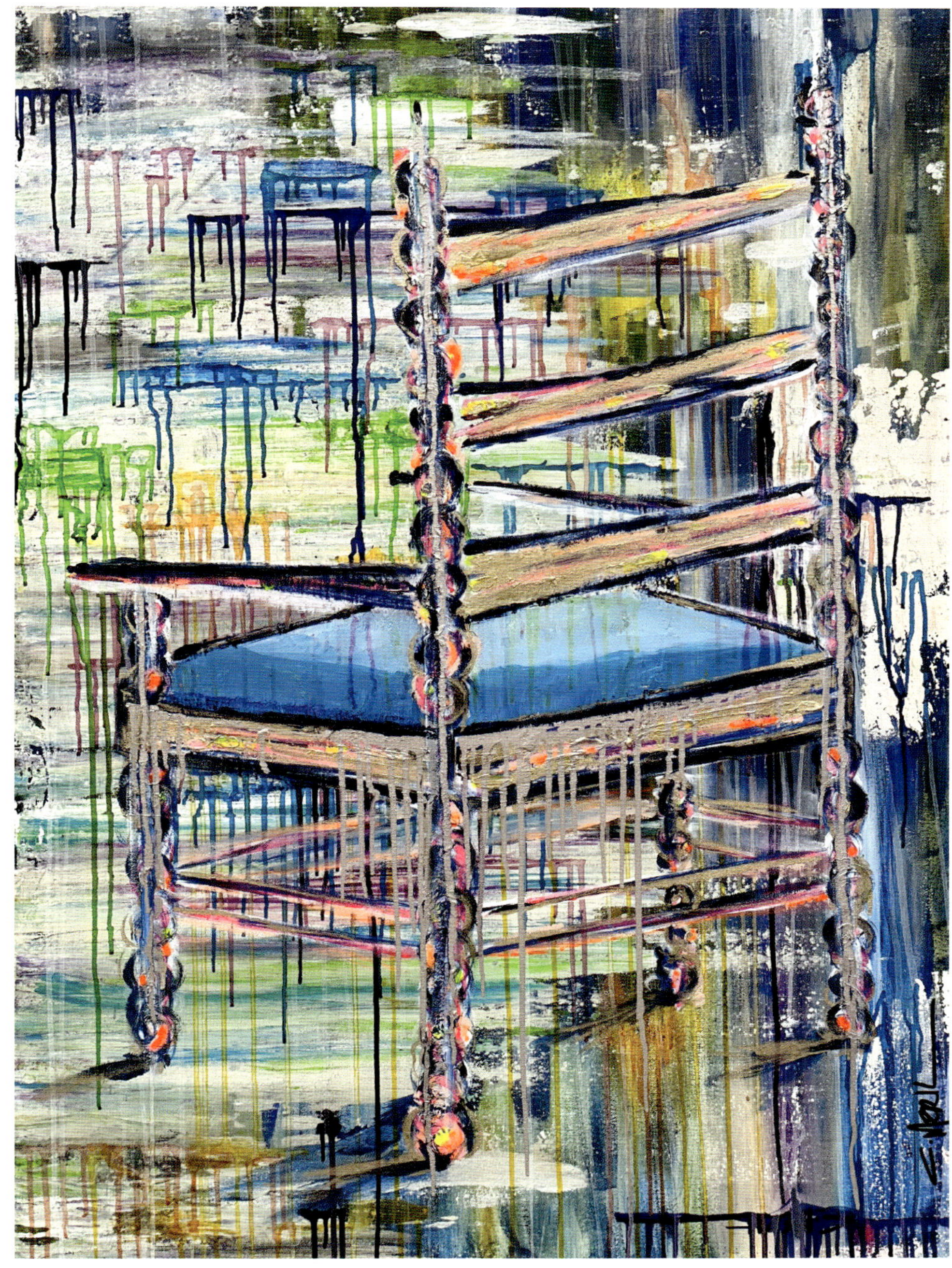

Christi Meril

Christi Meril is a contemporary artist who creates abstract works on canvas, wood, and paper. With expressionistic style, Meril uses bold color and texture by combining mediums such as oil, acrylic, pastel, watercolor, and ink. In addition to pulling together diverse medium combinations, the artist will often include text and custom neon light to convey meaning. Her work is filled with vibrant color, movement, and texture that create her message for the world. It is Meril's hope that her work will both communicate and reinforce love, compassion, optimism, and the powerful strength that equality and inclusion give to us as individuals and as a society. Her artistic ethos is "art with purpose" and it revolves around acts of compassion and pursuing equality for all people.

Home at Last
Acrylic and ink
40 x 30 in.

christimerilart@gmail
.com
Christimerilart.com
@christimerilart

PAINTING: TRADITIONAL/ABSTRACT

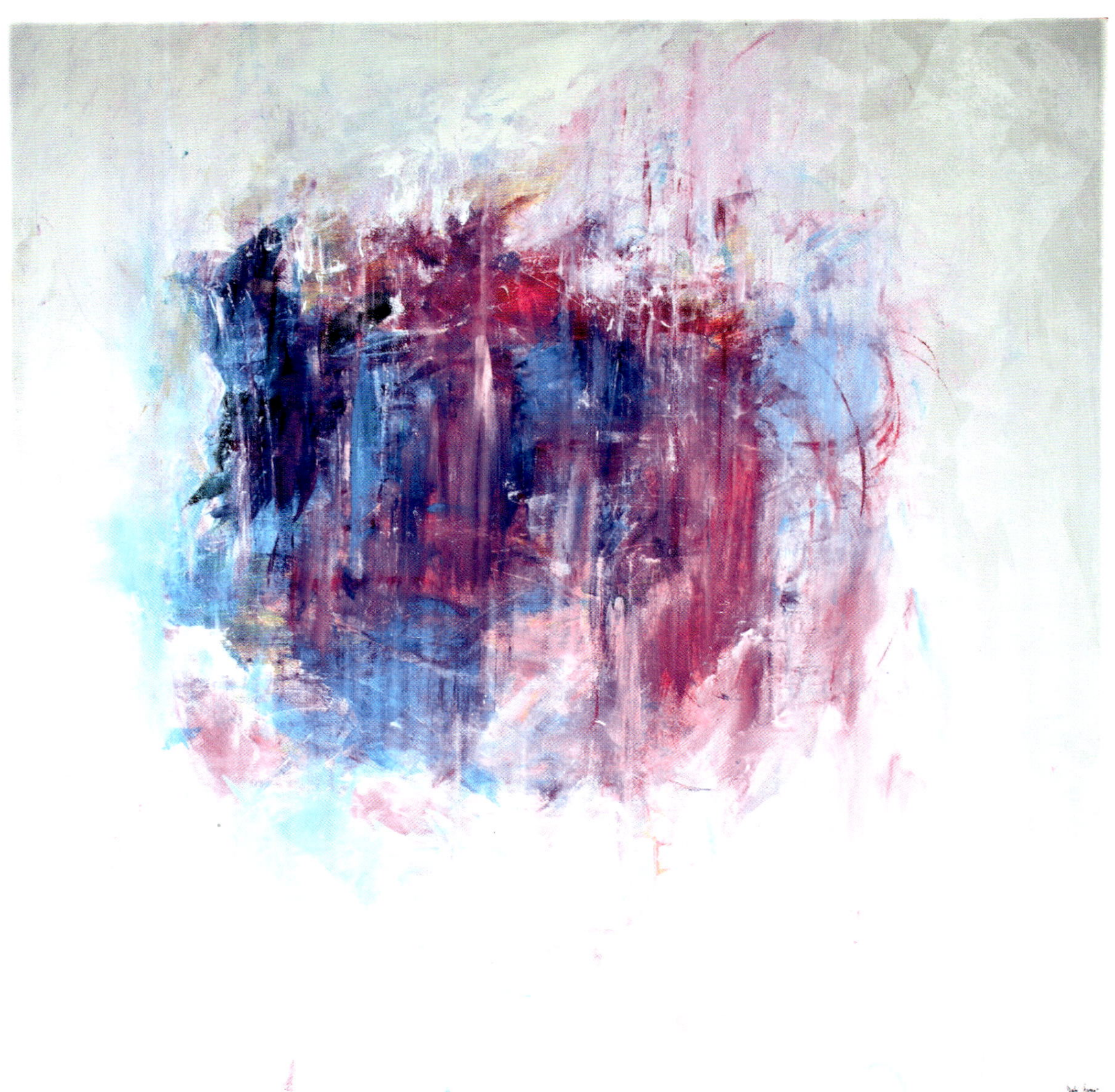

Meghan Noonan

Meghan Noonan is a self-taught visual artist who started to paint about five years ago. Her journey into painting was slow and meaningful. It was deeply connected to changes in her world view, specifically how we are all connected to each other and nature. She believes art has the power to connect us all to what it means to be human; it touches the parts of us that cannot be reached with words.

Noonan paints for the joy of the creative process. It is her emotional outlet and place of peace. For her, the process of painting is very intuitive, free-flowing, and unattached to an end goal. She likes to describe her paintings as a vulnerable and spiritual journey within the self.

As an artist, she aspires to empower people through her own vulnerability and creativity. She truly feels she has succeeded when viewers are able to find something of their own in her pieces.

Into the Deep
Acrylic
30 x 40 in.

meghnoonan@hotmail
.com
intuitivepaintings.
wixsite.com/
meghannoonanart
@meghannoonanart

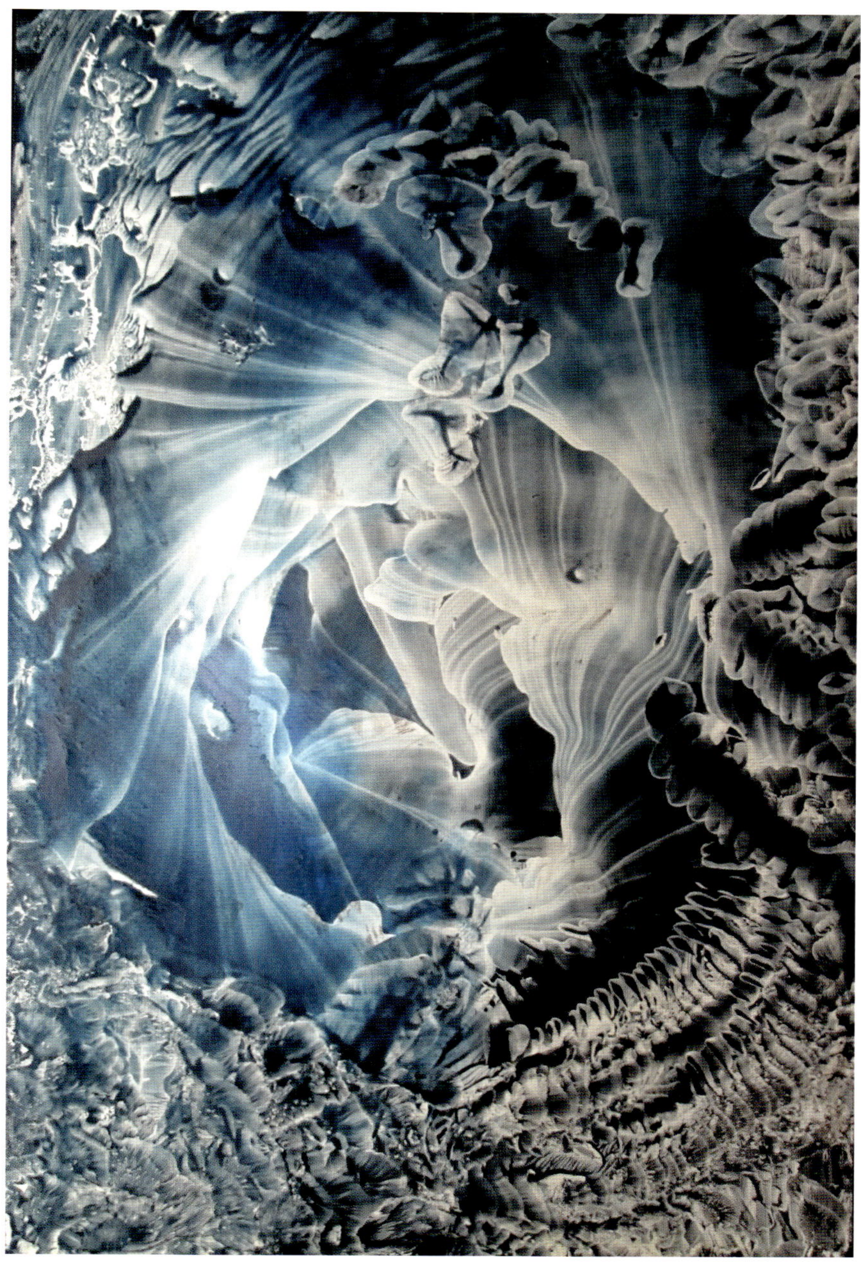

Bill Oakes

What most characterizes Bill Oakes' art is openness and experimentation. He uses a variety of media, including acrylics, inks, pastels, sands, powders, metal, cloth, and bark. The one constant is that he always paints to music. His art is often a translation of the music. Consequently, his nonrepresentational paintings emerge from the intuitive side of thought. To Oakes, art and visual thinking can be used as creative problem-solving tools. His artistic methodology is designed to stimulate himself and others to push beyond preconceived self-limitations and to rely on the innermost being to be flexible, spontaneous, and open to new ways of thinking and seeing.

For Oakes, art must include philosophical and metaphorical thinking. Oakes' goal and passion when creating these works are to nurture creativity, intuitiveness, and flexibility of thought—to stretch the imagination of artist and viewer. As an artist, his aim has always been to be a facilitator of discovery.

Cynosure
Ink on paper
48 x 34 in.

billo@mindleaps.com
mindleaps.com
@artofbilloakes

153

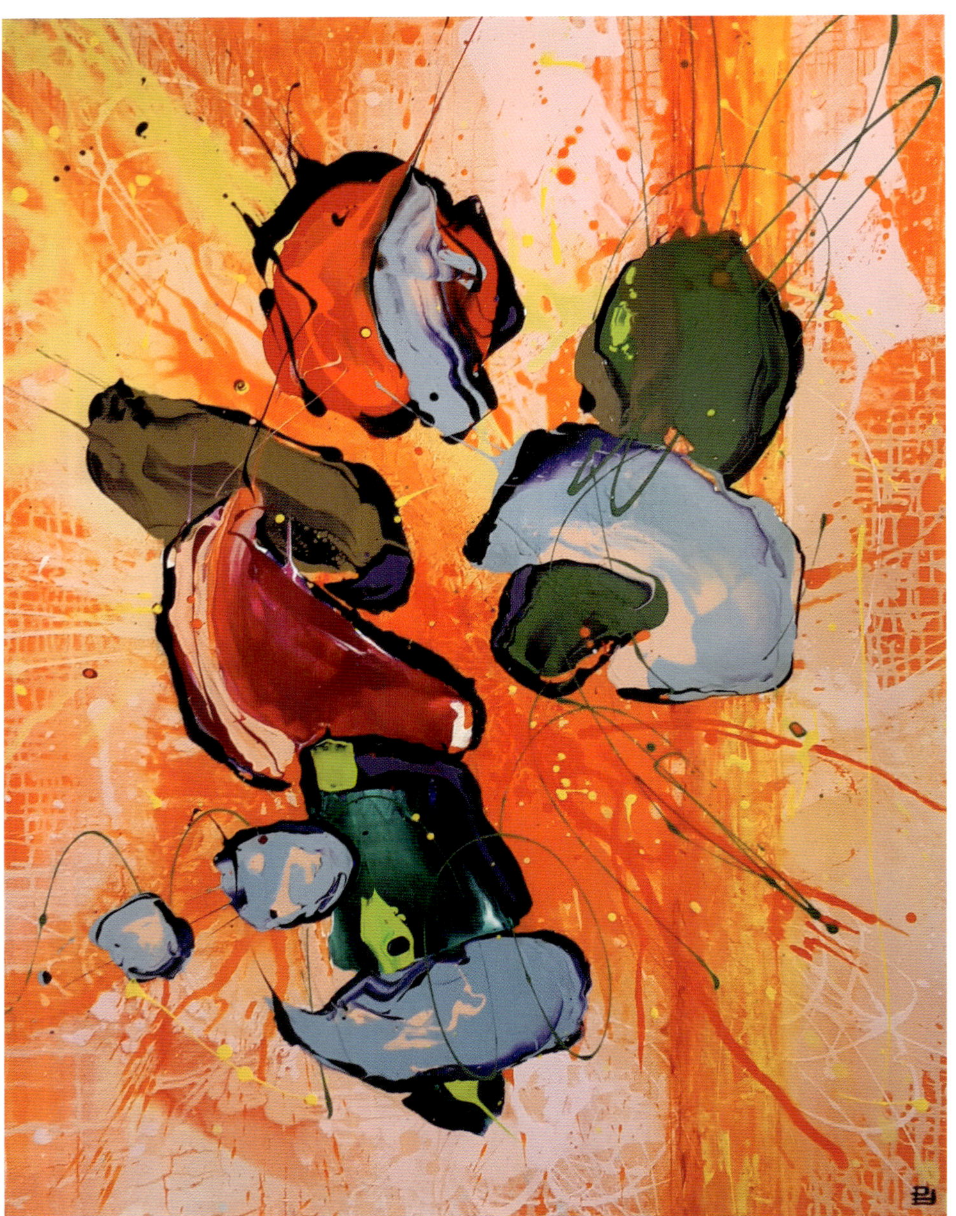

Florence Pages

Florence Pages' work, which she calls "Art Arithmetic," deals with society and human relations. The forms of her work represent humans inscribed in rectangles and trapezoids and are, therefore, imperfect. They meet, jostle each other, move apart, and no longer understand each other. They are like these mathematical forms that arouse emotion by their beauty, their external colors, but they have no soul. They wander around having lost all reference. They collide and don't stop. Humans no longer understand their neighbors, strangled by their egocentricity and selfishness. "Do we have affinity by connecting abstract forms to each other, thus connecting our souls and understanding each other better?" Pages asks in her work. "This is the meaning of the thread that runs through the web between the forms."

Orange is Nice
Acrylic
45.6 x 35 in.

flo.pages@orange.fr
florencepages.net
@pages.florence

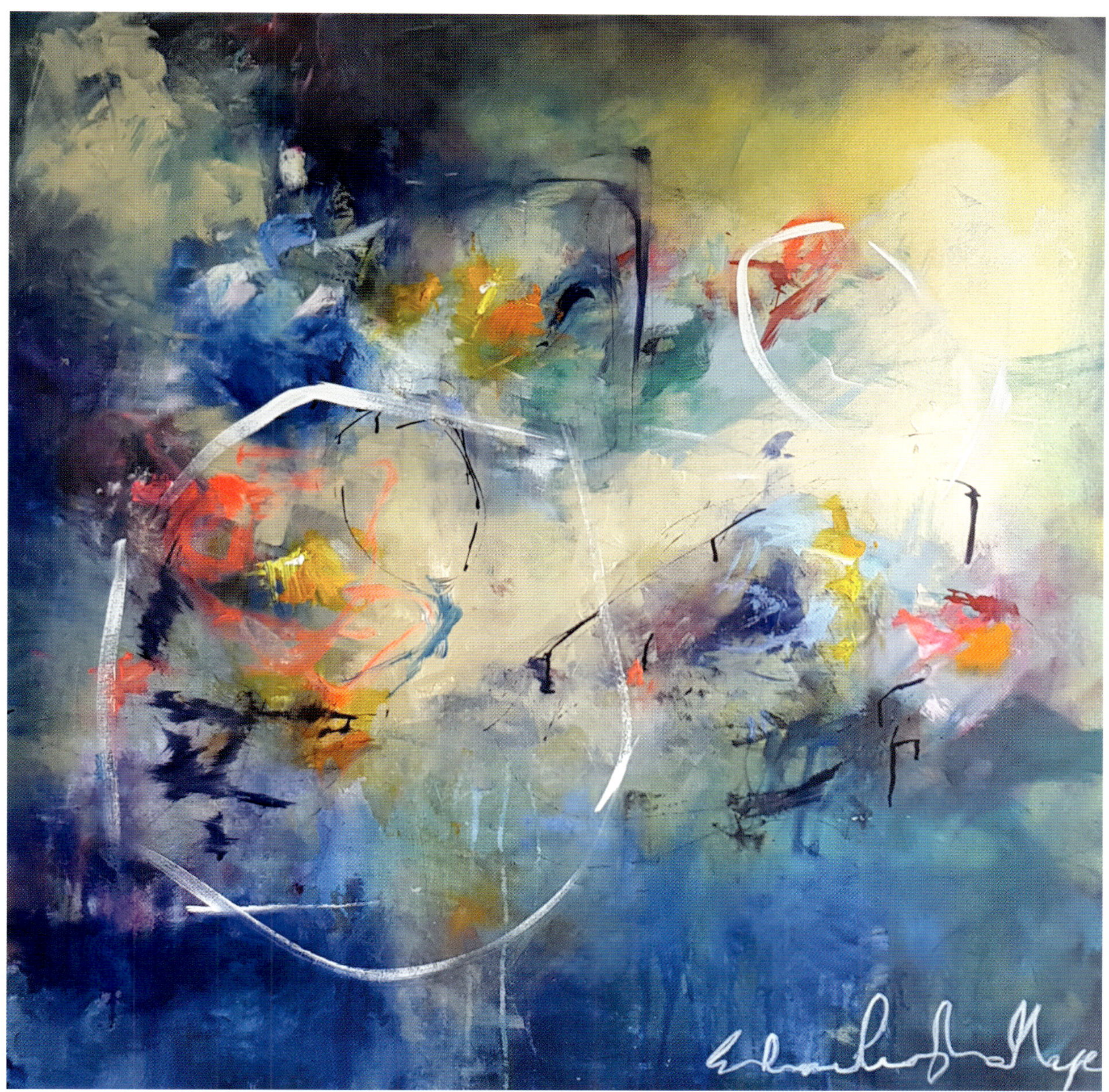

Catherine Pennington-Meyer

Catherine Pennington-Meyer's work concentrates primarily on Abstract Expressionism. She sees her painting as a kind of language, translating what she feels or experiences to those viewing it. She is innately drawn to create raw, emotive, expressionist pieces, mostly abstracts, which distill a subject down to its feeling. "I don't only want my art to be beautiful but for it to reach out and touch the person who is viewing it on an immediate, intuitive level," she says. "I want my paintings to speak to their audience in their own visceral language."

Pennington-Meyer is influenced by nature, particularly the multifaceted nature of water, and memories of growing up in particularly beautiful landscapes in North Yorkshire and Scotland. She also finds human psychology fascinating. She sees compositions everywhere, whether in the flowers in a park, the way smoke curls, bottles in a bar, books on a library shelf, or a street market. Everything is made up of shapes and colors. For the artist, the world is made up of influences every day.

Perspective
Acrylic and ink
39 x 39 in.

cpm@galleriewhite
.space
galleriewhite.space
@galleriewhitespace

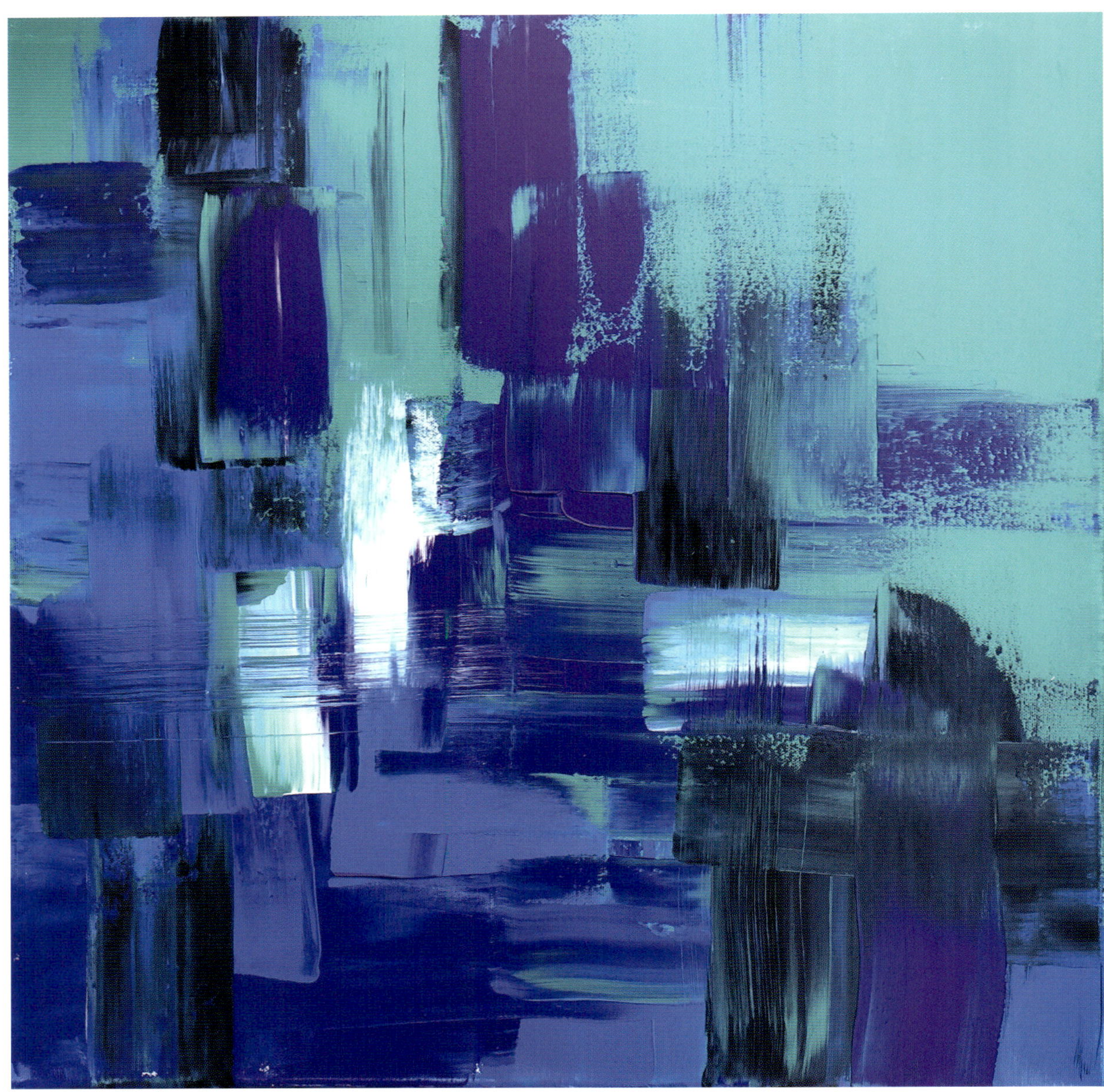

Ludwika Pilat

Ludwika Pilat graduated from architecture to painting and says her past influenced the composition and use of color in her works. After being committed to technical drawings and developing concept sketches, Pilat felt that she needed to bring more feelings into her art. She was always good at following reason while confusing what she wanted with what she thought she should want. Ultimately, she needed a way to better illustrate her emotions in art. She has learned to listen to herself and slowly unlock that heavy-duty container where her feelings were kept. She admits she is not striving for perfection anymore. "I want to provoke thoughts and questions and express something more with textures, colors, and ambiguous words," Pilat says. "I began experimenting with abstract acrylic painting, often including collage elements. The process to understand that art doesn't have to be accurate and perfect. It has now developed into a distinct aesthetic."

Dynamo
Acrylic
19.6 x 19.6 in.

ludwika.pilat@gmail.com
ludwikapilat.art
@il.lu.str

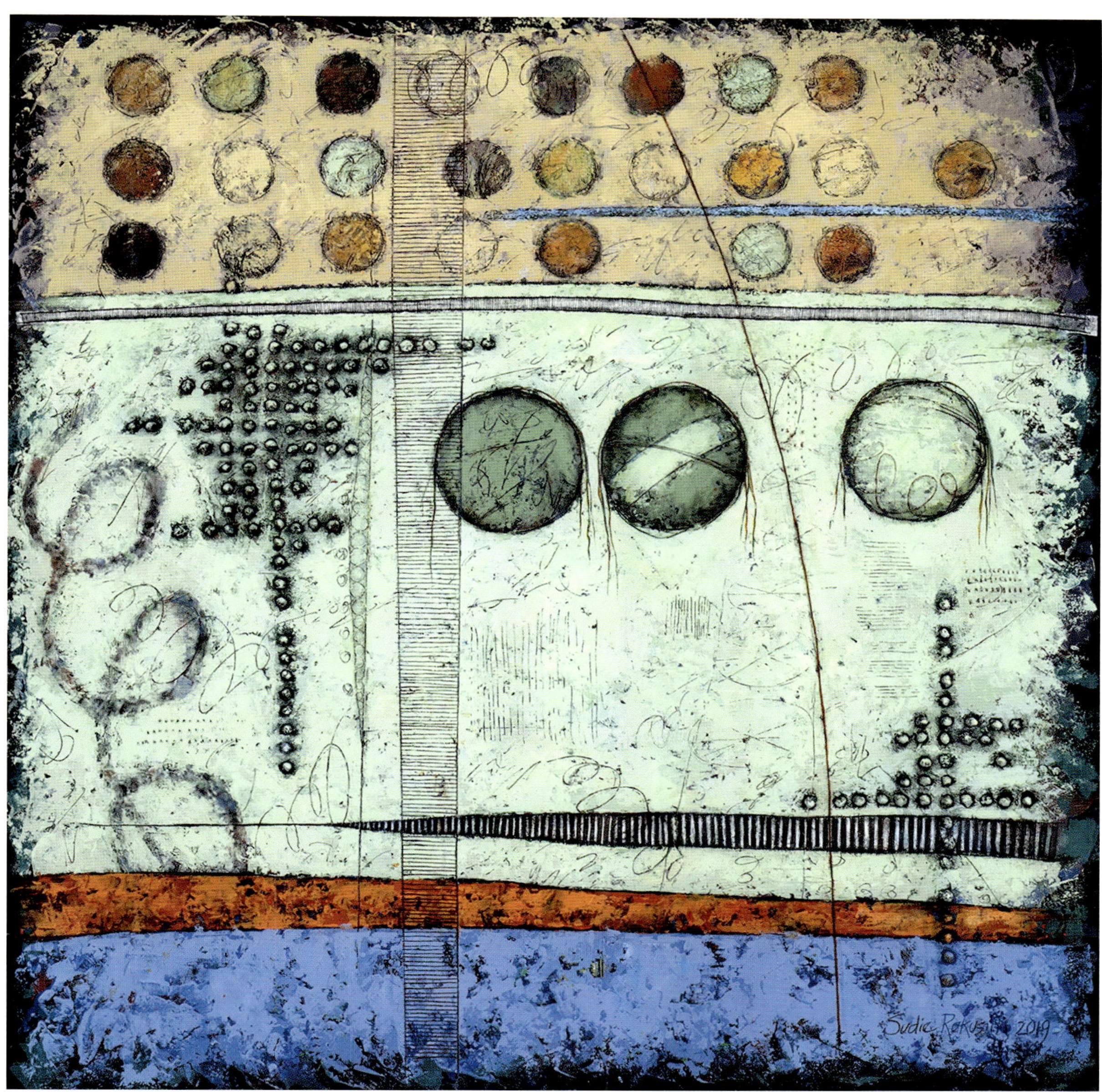

Sudie Rakusin

Sudie Rakusin's artwork flows from what moves her and from where she finds beauty: women, animals, the earth, color, patterns, and light. Her art represents the deep connection she feels with these elements. Through her artwork, she creates the world as she would like it to be, where harmony exists between animal and human, and where nature thrives. Her body of work consists of pieces created using cold wax along with oil on wood panels, where the focus is on color, pattern, and design. The properties of cold wax fascinate her and keep her curious. The underlying layers inform and alter the layers applied over them, and incising, scraping, and glazing make more changes. Rakusin wields the palette knife and mixes the colors, but what happens on the panel is beyond her control.

She is learning how to be fine with the state of not knowing how a finished piece will look.

Ecliptic Series No. 11
Cold wax medium and oil paint on wood panel
36 x 36 in.

info@sudierakusin.com
sudierakusin.com
@sudie.rakusin

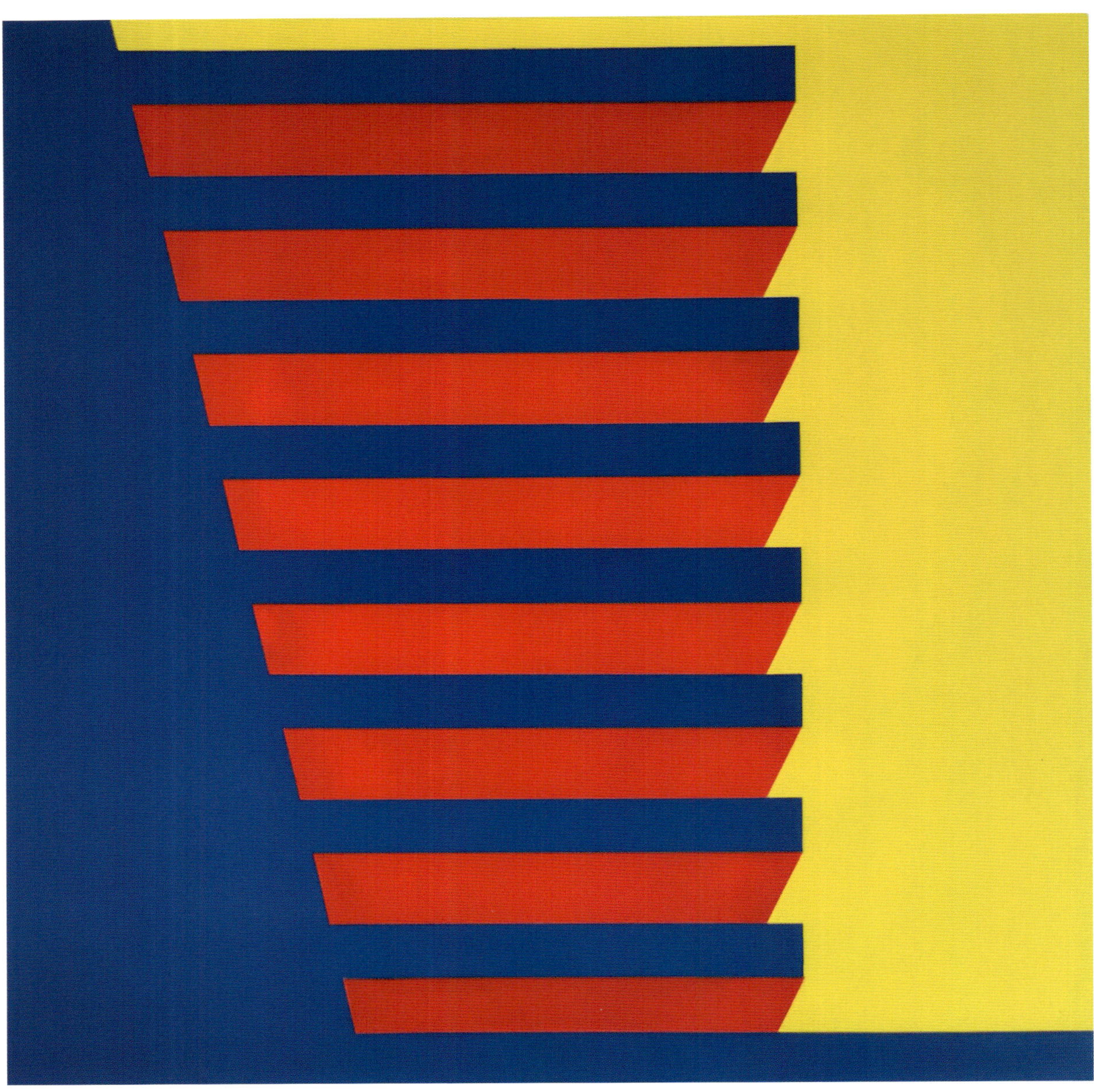

William James Ramsay
William James Ramsay's focus and interests lie within the modernist aesthetic of hard-edged painting, geometric abstraction, and the minimalist movement. His creative intention is to develop the basic concepts of visual aesthetics: line, color, form, scale, and perspective, to explore, interpret, and communicate architectural spaces that he finds inspirational or he has personally experienced through travel. This creative approach and mindset have previously led and developed into both minimal and complex outcomes, ranging from drawings, hard-edge acrylic paintings, three-dimensional wooden sculptures, site-specific installations, and paintings made with vinyl tape. In 2020, Ramsay began to primarily focus his attention on the process surrounding hard-edge painting, trying to further develop the aesthetic and striking style he envisions. With each piece, the intention is to develop abstract two-dimensional compositions that when used alongside carefully chosen colors and basic design elements, communicate the sense of perspective and three-dimensional depth often found in modern architecture.

Breakwater I, 2020
Acrylic on cradled wooden panel
11.8 x 11.8 in.

william_ramsay@live
.co.uk
espyartistry.com
@espy_artistry

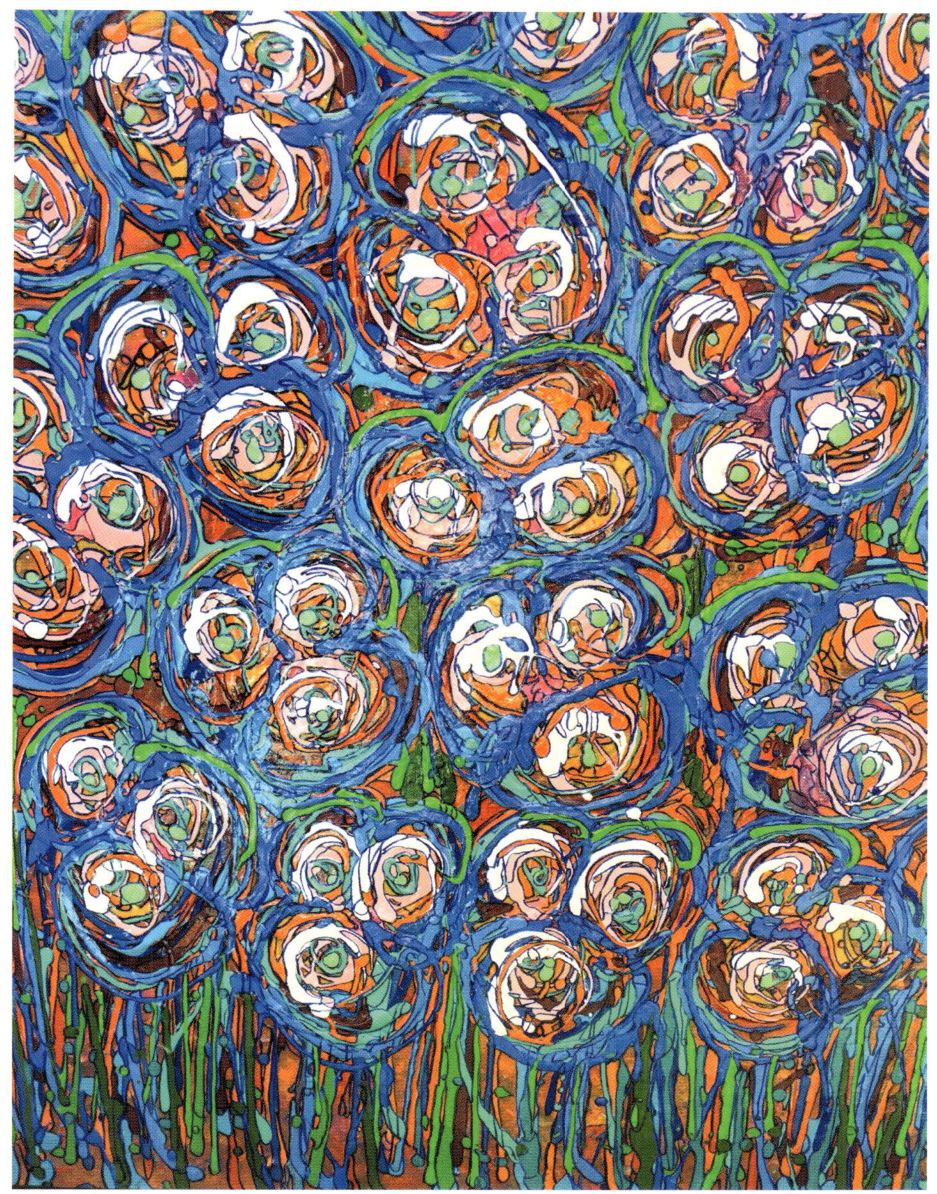

Margaret Schumacher Rehwinkel

Margaret Schumacher Rehwinkel has been on a creative path for most of her life. She thoroughly enjoys creating and creativity—whether painting, designing an interior, creating a beautiful garden, or just choosing a wall paint color. Commercial art and interior design have comprised most of her career, and they fuel how she approaches painting. Like many artists, nature and the natural world inspire her artwork. Her collection of paintings focuses on organic subjects, textiles, and shapes, often featuring bold colors and design. Unique shapes and colors characterize her abstract art, while nature and organic matter strongly influence her Meadows series. Strong attention to detail shapes all her work.

Blooming Colors
Acrylic and ink
48 x 36 in.

shoe1955@aol.com
@margaretschumacher-rehwinkel

159

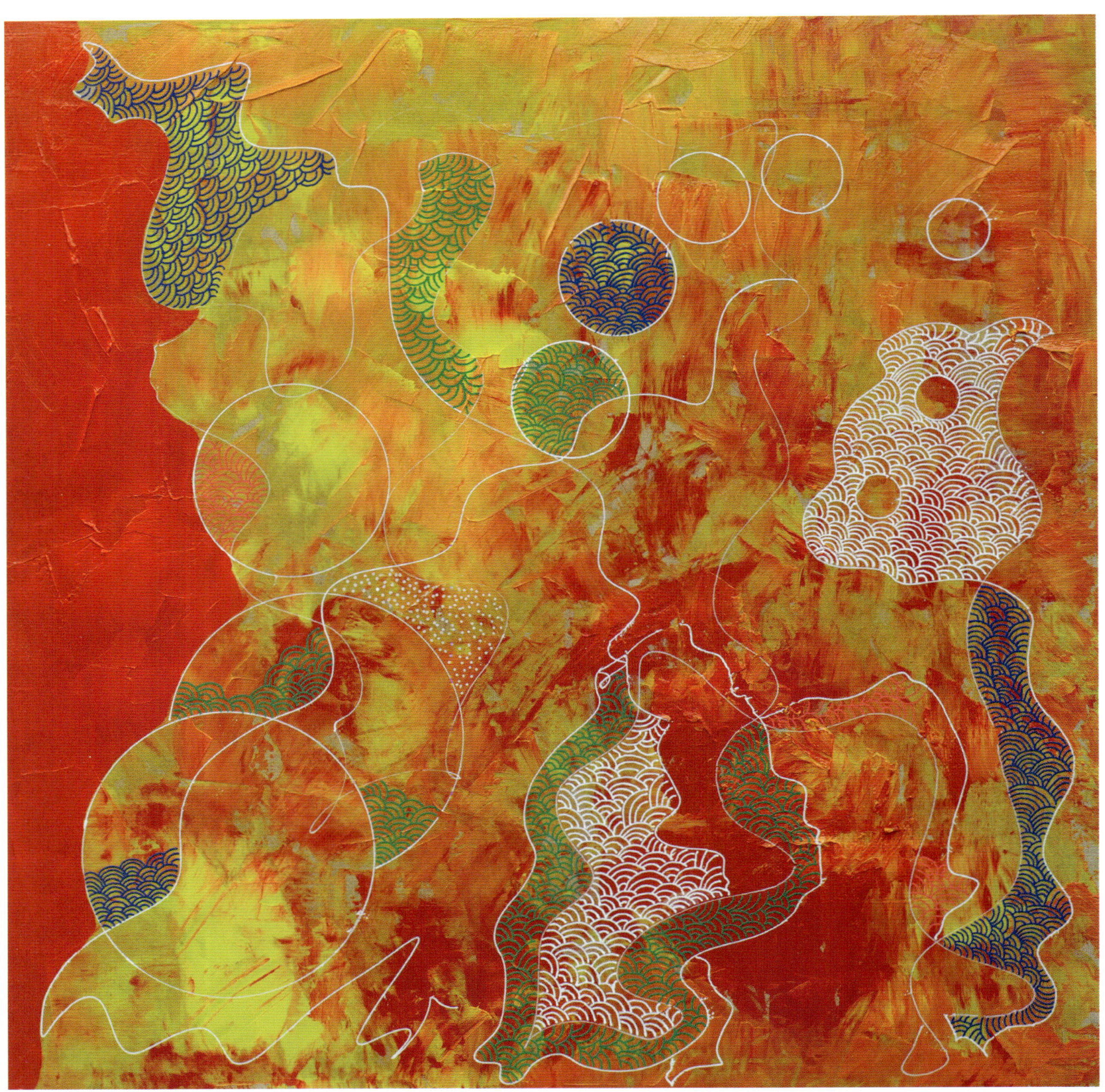

Carole-Yvonne Richard

Carole-Yvonne Richard paints from her daily life—the encounters and events of ordinary, extraordinary, and common life. She paints a human landscape woven with encounters, friendships, and events of all kinds. Her work focuses on the emotions and feelings associated with certain life experiences that we all face at one time or another in our human journey. To her painting, she adds elements of collage, photos, words, and symbolic objects that she staples, knots, ties, wraps, or glues to a work. She also works by accumulation of pictorial elements, assembling several pieces to form a larger artwork that she calls a mosaic. Her paintings develop from spontaneous and constructed gestures. The spot, the line, the repetition, and the shape become her guides. By suggesting landscapes, portraits, and abstractions, her work evokes different styles or conventions of art history. In sum, it is her intent to capture the human presence that allows us to collectively experience the feeling of being alive.

La vie n'est pas une Droite Ligne!
Acrylic
18 X 18 in.

Carole-Yvonne@
CyRichard.com
cyrichard.com
@cyrichard

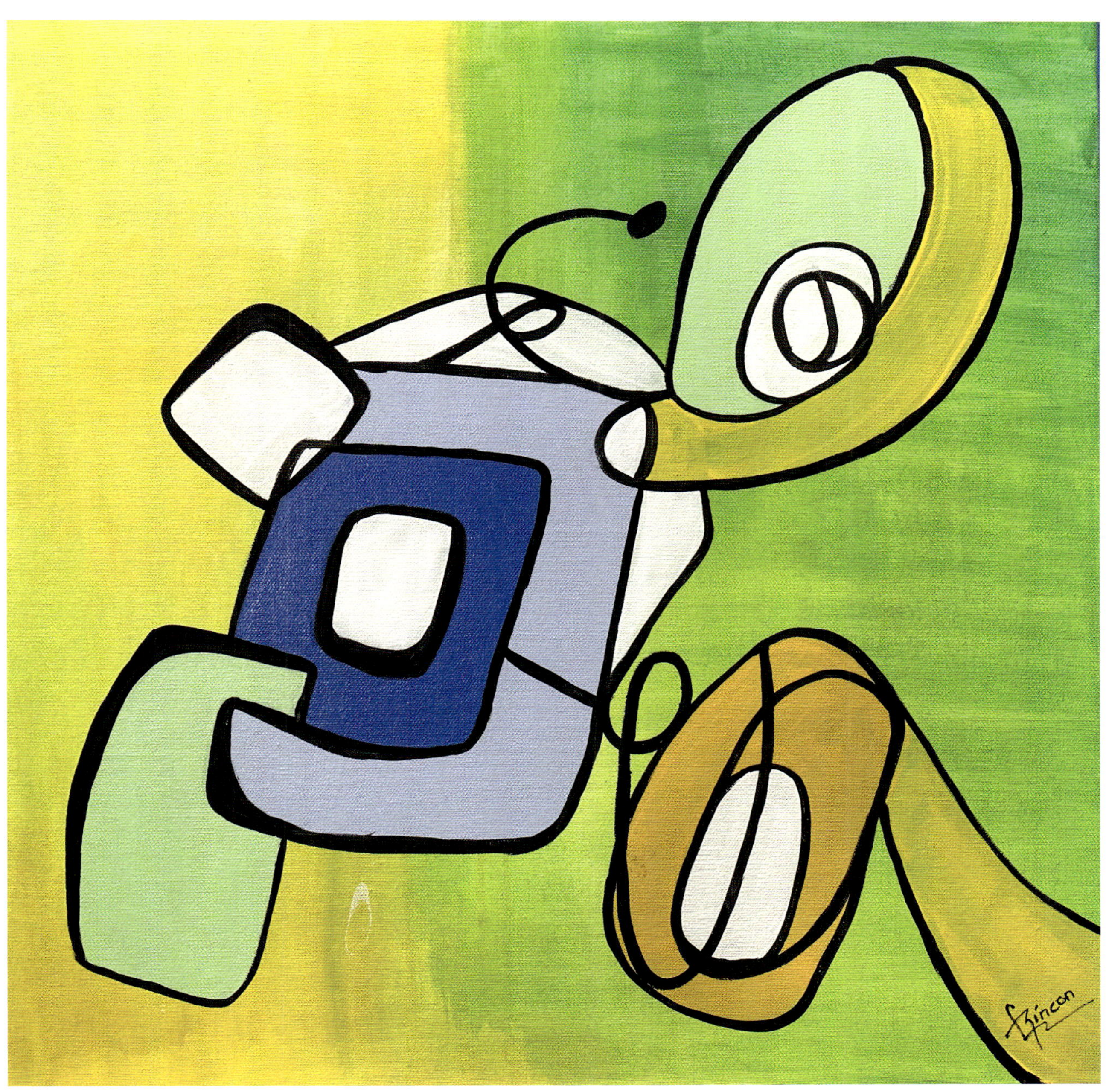

Lina Rincon-Hoover

Since she was a young girl, art has always, in one way or another, been Lina Rincon-Hoover's way of communicating with the world. She happily spends many hours in front of the easel in order to bring her paintings to life.

She enjoys the time she spends focusing on the most basic details and being able to see the transformation from concept through simple brushstrokes into a finished painting. Through her artwork, Rincon-Hoover seeks to explore the beauty in the simplicity of nature. To appreciate every day like it's the last, because just like that, we're here today and we can be gone tomorrow. Lately, the artist has been focusing on romance and love. "Creating art is a way to reflect my soul and to appreciate where I am in life," says the artist. "My main focus is to bring something to life and express my feelings in such a way that the viewer may do the same."

Turbulence
Oil and acrylic
24 x 24 in.

linarincon75@gmail.com
artitudeart.com
@artitudeartist

PAINTING: TRADITIONAL/ABSTRACT

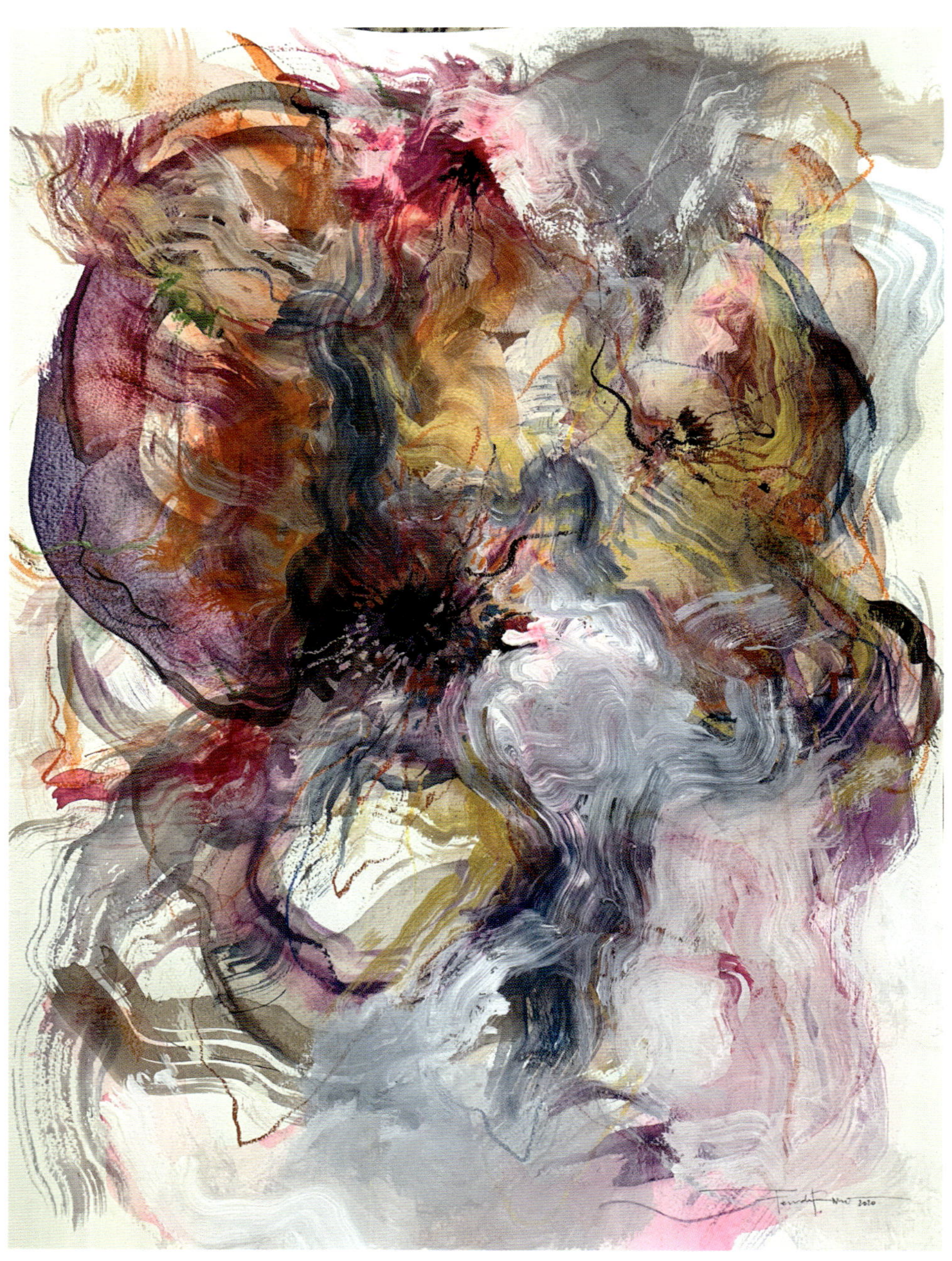

Fernanda Rivero

"Art has become my most authentic form of expression and freedom," Fernanda Rivero says. "The studio is a place of artistic exploration that is constantly evolving in the personal search for growth and self-knowledge, both personal and artistic."

From the first day Rivero took up a brush until today, the result has been the expression of her deepest feelings and thoughts, which inevitably show a more authentic, original, and honest part of her. From the beginning, she fell in love with acrylics because it is possible to work with them in different layers much faster than with oils, but she likes to mix the materials, giving them space to converge and flow. In her work, you will find mixed media within the same piece, usually charcoal, pastel, acrylic, and oils.

Minimal Studies
Watercolor, acrylic and pastels on paper
25.5 x 19.6 in.

cherrystudio.art@gmail.com
fernandarivero.com
@fernandarivero_arte

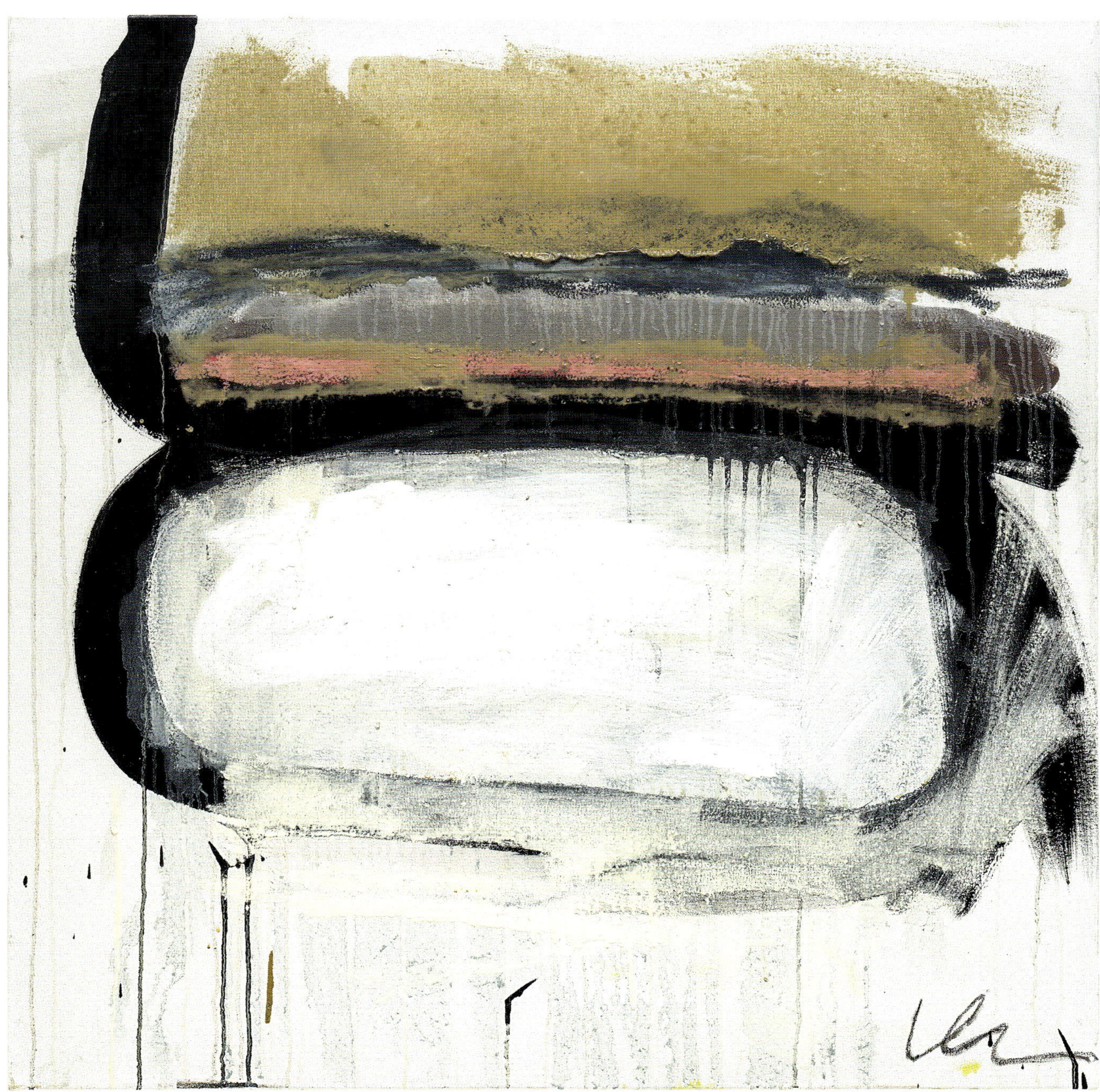

Laura Roebuck

Laura Roebuck's art seeks to expand boundaries. It needs space, depth, air, height, and light for exploration. Through intuition and movement, Roebuck explores the interplay of color, shape, and texture using palette knives, paintbrushes, and assorted household and construction tools. She makes paintings of varying sizes but is especially drawn to making large-scale works. Her process is largely unconscious but coherent. When she begins a painting, it is often without a specific plan, making the evolution of the painting unpredictable. She layers, scrapes, reveals, removes, and builds a painting, mixing focus and abandon. In this way, her paintings evolve, often over months, sometimes over years. While much of the process is spontaneous, it is disciplined by the emerging structure of the painting as a whole. Each mark leads to the next while suggesting a series of subsequent steps. In the end, Roebuck wants to enjoy looking at the painting, but more importantly, it has to feel true.

Porter on a Cross-Country Train
Oil
36 x 36 in.

studiolr@att.net
lauraroebuck.com
@roebuckstudio

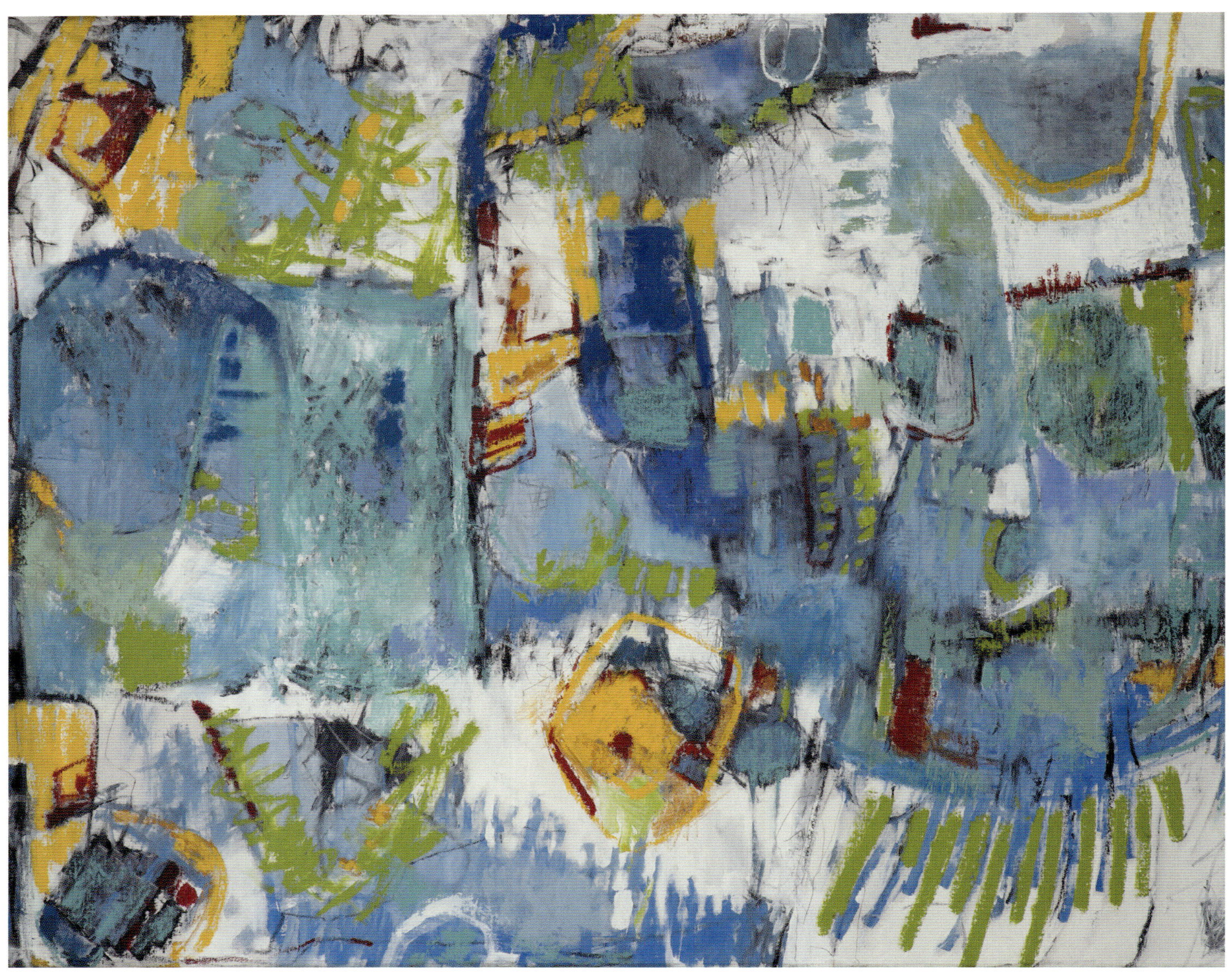

Leslie Rolnick
Painting has been a lifelong pursuit and means of expressing Leslie Rolnick's interior life, influenced by her external reality and experiences. Painting is her personal form of spirituality—the only place where time, conscious thoughts, worries, or other preoccupations are completely suspended.

She is only involved in the immediacy of the artwork and the excitement of the process. Mixing color; experimenting with mark making; creating textures, patterns, and forms; applying and pushing paint has been an endless source of fascination since she was a child. While she was trained traditionally, her transition to becoming an abstract expressionist painter has been a revelation. "I use stronger colors and feel freer to experiment differently on any given day, letting mood, intuition, the time of year, dream imagery, travels, nature, memories, and unconscious material all come to the fore while working on each piece," she says.

Wild Grace
Oil
48 x 60 in.

leslierolnick@gmail
.com
@leslierolnick52

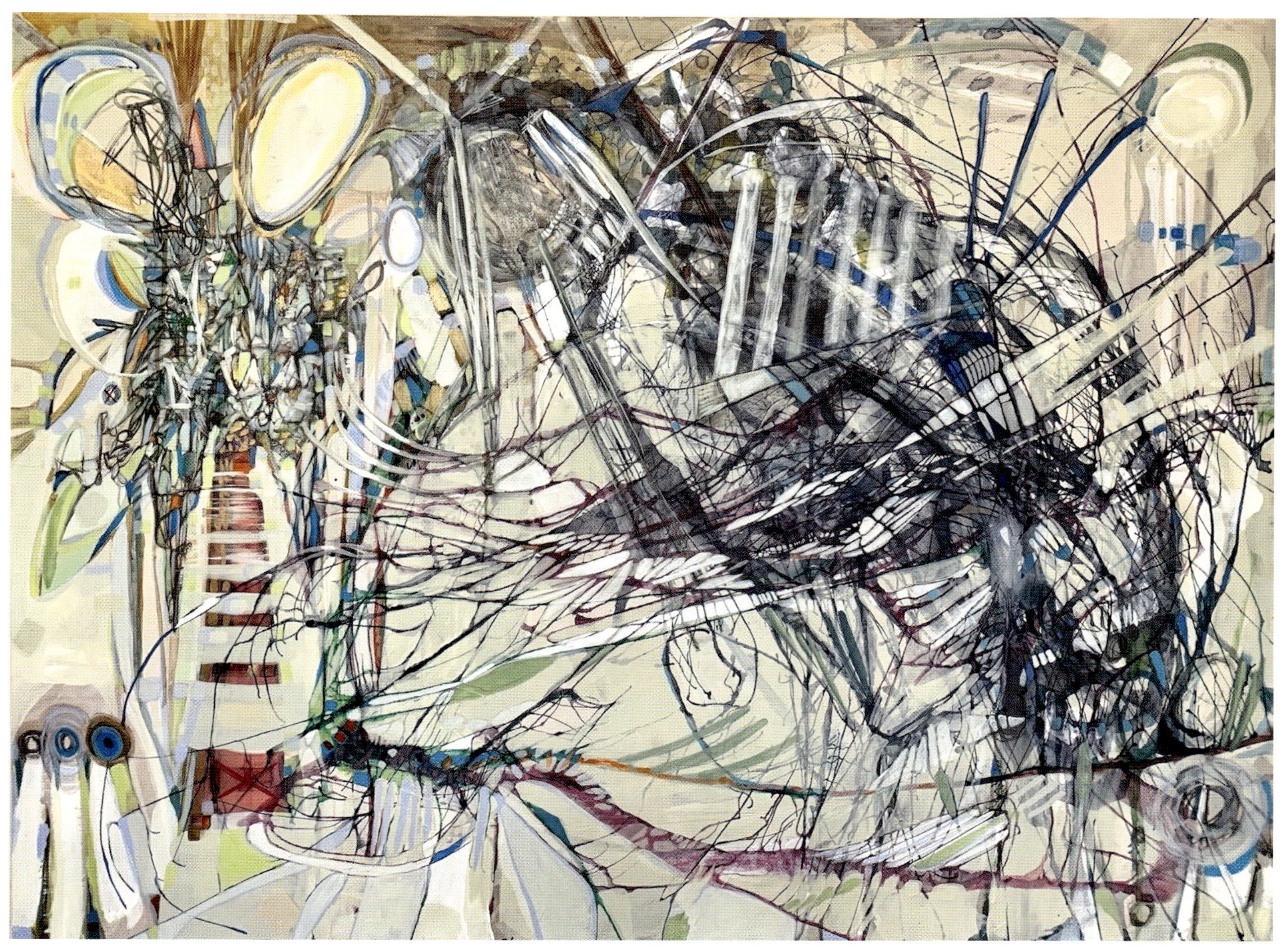

Anastacia Sadeh

For Anastacia Sadeh, her work reflects her love of the abstract process and mark making as an emotional conduit. She is drawn to the visual presence of feeling within most marks and colors. Behind her own marks rest a myriad of emotions and thoughts—some concrete, some subconscious. Her objective is to gather a deeper awareness of her emotions' existence and then process this construct through her work. She is deeply interested in the universal importance of mental health and how it is shaped by human emotions. The artist uses acrylics, Indian and alcohol inks, water-based oils, graphite, charcoal, and Venetian plaster on either paper, stretched canvas, or wood panel. Sadeh loves the optimistic echo of how purposeful and accidental marks can work together as visual harmony is achieved. Each work stands as a clip of her human existence, much like a vintage film's individual frame captures just a moment.

Leaning Into Trust
Acrylic, Indian ink, graphite, and Venetian plaster on canvas
36 x 48 in.

anastacia_sadeh@ yahoo.com
anastaciasadeh.com
@sadehstudioarts

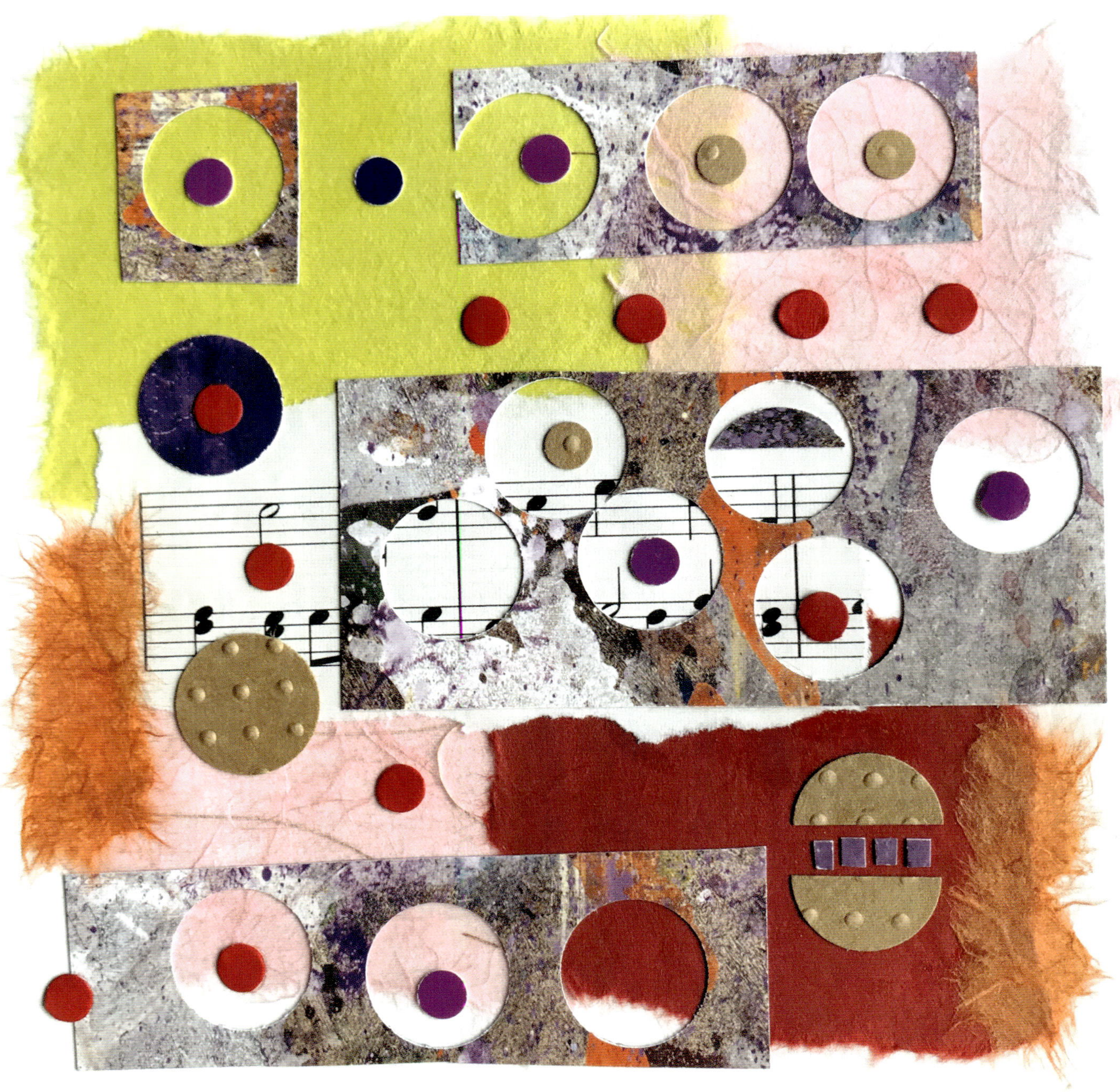

Deborah Saks

Deborah Saks' work includes abstract collage using all types of paper, vintage maps, sheet music, and French ribbon. She uses vivid color, paper with pattern and texture, and geometric shapes to create her designs. Saks loves the feel of paper—the smooth surfaces and the ripped edges. Scissors and glue are her tools. She is constantly cutting out images from magazines for future use. She tends to make small pieces, six inches square, with a focus on explosions of color. Her compositions are intricate and draw the viewer into the piece. She hopes that her collages evoke a feeling of happiness while also provoking thought.

The Blue Dot
Collage
6 x 6 in.

d_saks@yahoo.com
deborahsaks.com
@deborahsakscollage

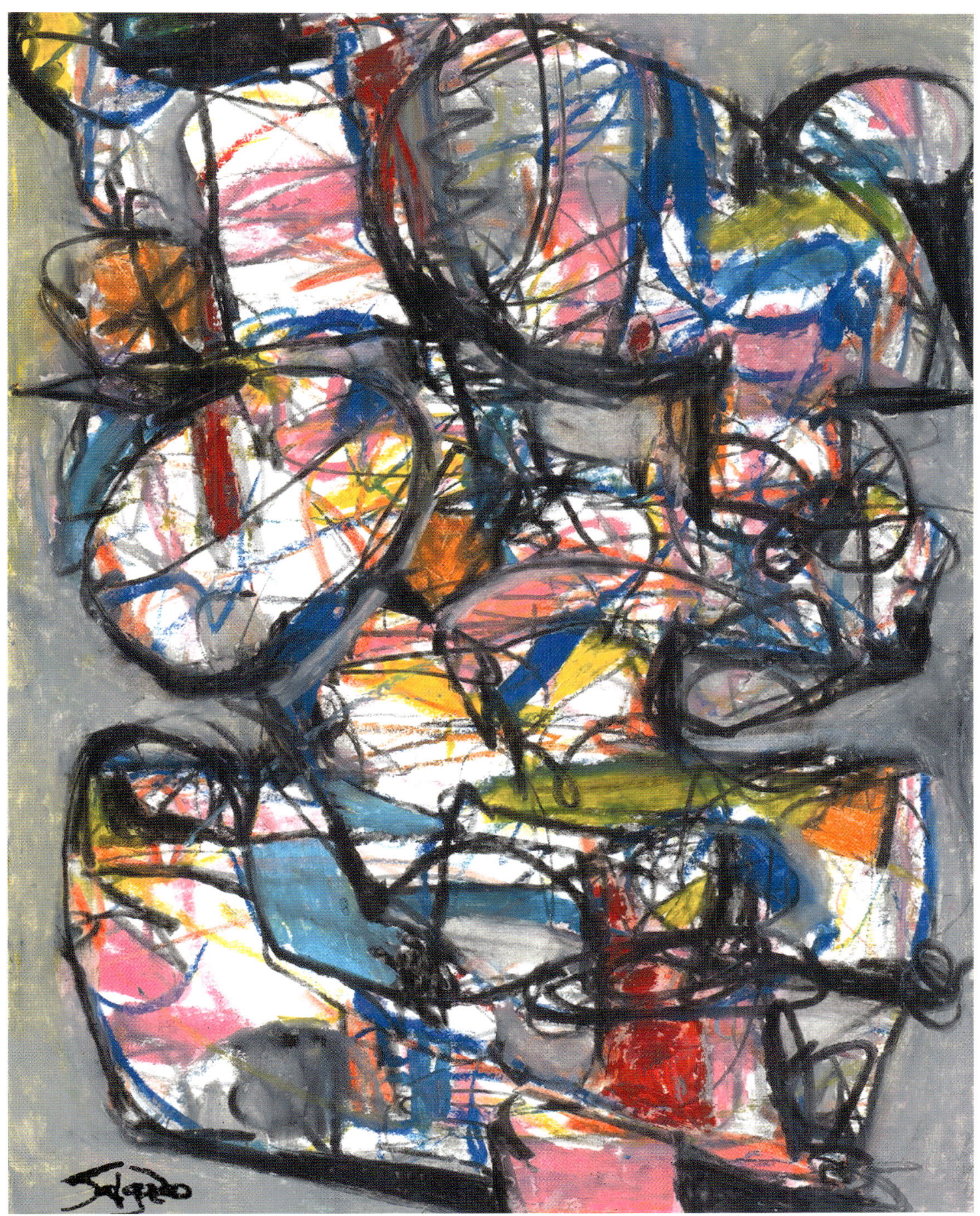

Antonio Salgado

Antonio Salgado's work comes to life in a very loose and fast way. A critical part of what he does happens in the first ten minutes of starting a piece. He has to build a scaffolding that will be present the whole time it takes him to finish whatever he is working on. If that doesn't happen, this very often means it's a total redo. Salgado has been strongly influenced by the New York Abstract Expressionist movement of the '50s. He considers himself groomed by de Kooning, Pollock, Still, Rothko, etc. "I go back and forth between color and black and white," says Salgado. "I'm not concerned about my paintings relating to each other, I would rather have them relate to me. The more different they are from each other, the more I feel the growing pains of being an artist."

Gen Pop
Oil pastel and wax crayon
12 x 9 in.

antoniosalgadostudio@
gmail.com
antoniosalgadostudio
.com
@semperpictorem

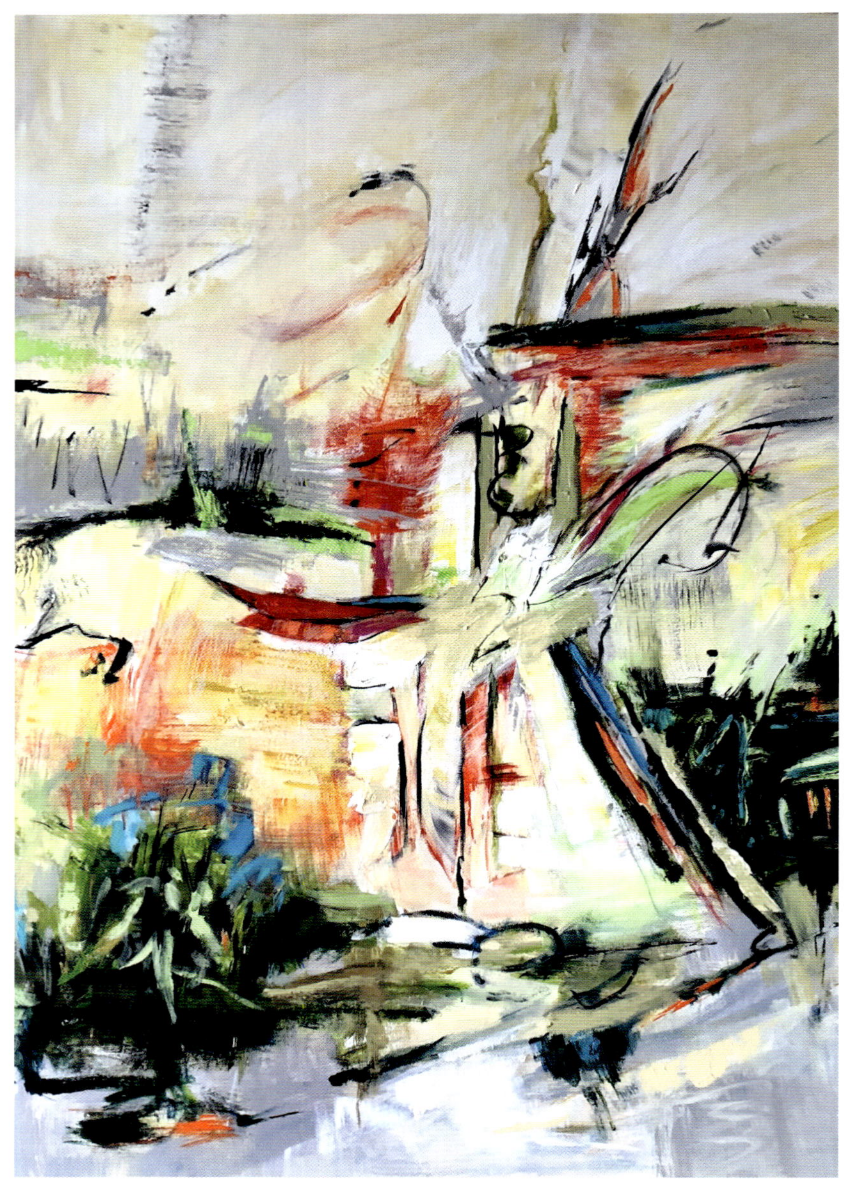

Karen H. Salup

As a painting evolves, Karen H. Salup is composing intuitive images that reference nature. There is a vocabulary that she has developed, consisting of visual poetry. Her work develops over time. She finds image secondary to the art making. Although abstract in nature, there is an underlying visual order that gradually seems to emerge in her work. Working intuitively, she enters a realm of the unknown, where there is more of a calling than any real choice. "I seem to be forever altering and adjusting the core of the painting and some invisible reality that appears," she admits. This self-imposed repetitive process, as she builds, erases, and paints layers, becomes a definite chaos through which the work evolves, and it seems to return repeatedly to its beginning. With each revival to the surface, there are the markings, forms, subtleties, and sensitivities that appear in her work.

Reflections of the Garden
Mixed media
48 x 36 in.

monet12@bellsouth.net
karenhsalup.com
@salup

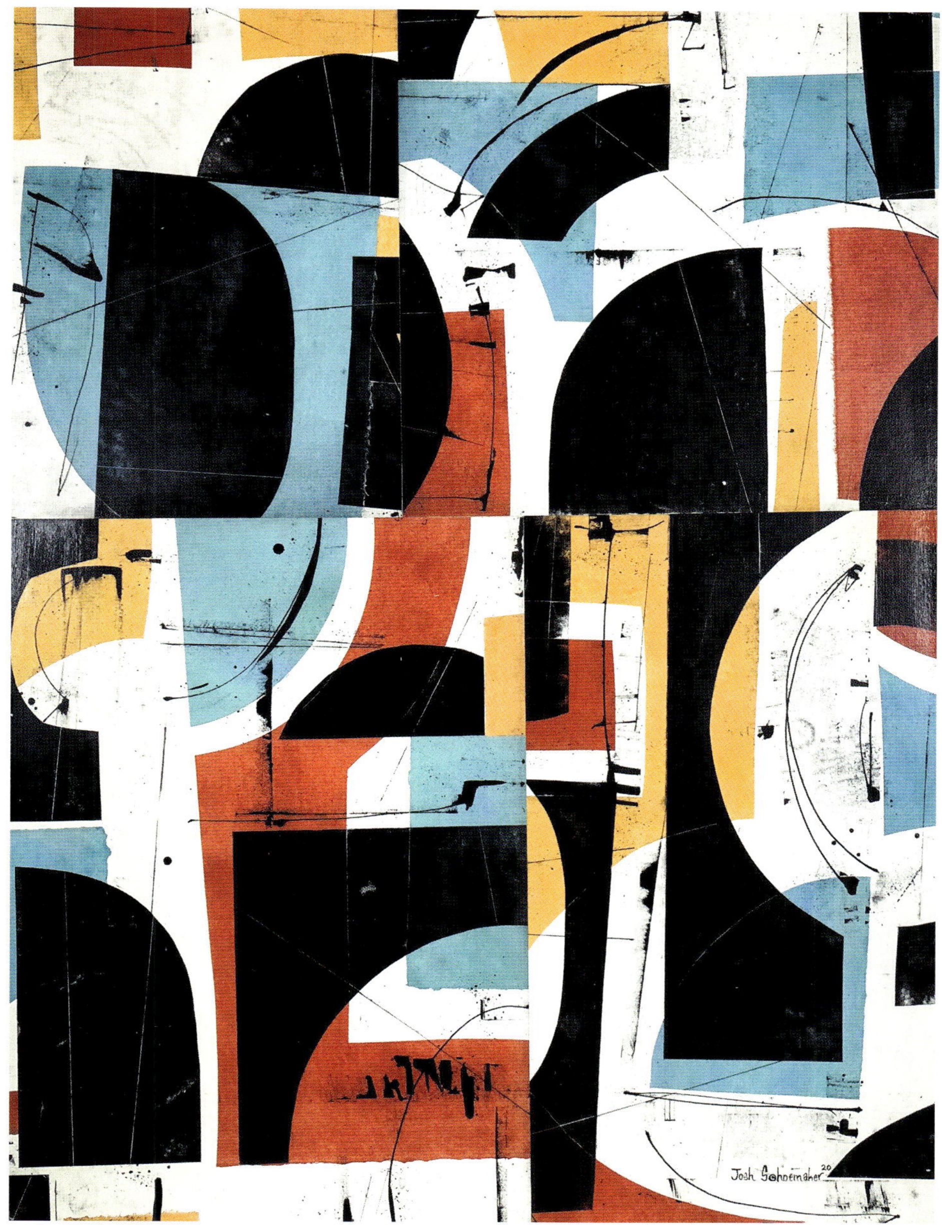

Joshua Schoemaker

Joshua Schoemaker's inspiration comes from the purity and simplicity of Zen painting, which uses brushwork and bold marks to convey spiritual awareness. Even without knowing the literal translation of the symbols, these ink paintings have always stirred something deep within him. The combination of deliberate, accidental, and even subconscious brushwork creates something totally unique and expressive, and Schoemaker aspires for his art to speak to others in much the same way. The artist's aesthetic is influenced by his background in traditional printmaking techniques. Every piece he creates utilizes elements of traditional printmaking, from contrasting line widths and smudge marks to speckled ink and misaligned color layers.

Schoemaker continues to explore new techniques for creating his art, and he finds that there's something interesting that occurs when happenstance leads him down a path—flaws become bouncing-off points, imperfections redirect the focus. Every piece Schoemaker creates is the result of his journey as an artist to discover the perfect composition or a fresh new aesthetic.

Fragments
Remembered Two
Mixed media collage on
wood panel
48 x 36 in.

art@carbonandcotton
.com
carbonandcotton.com
@joshschoemaker

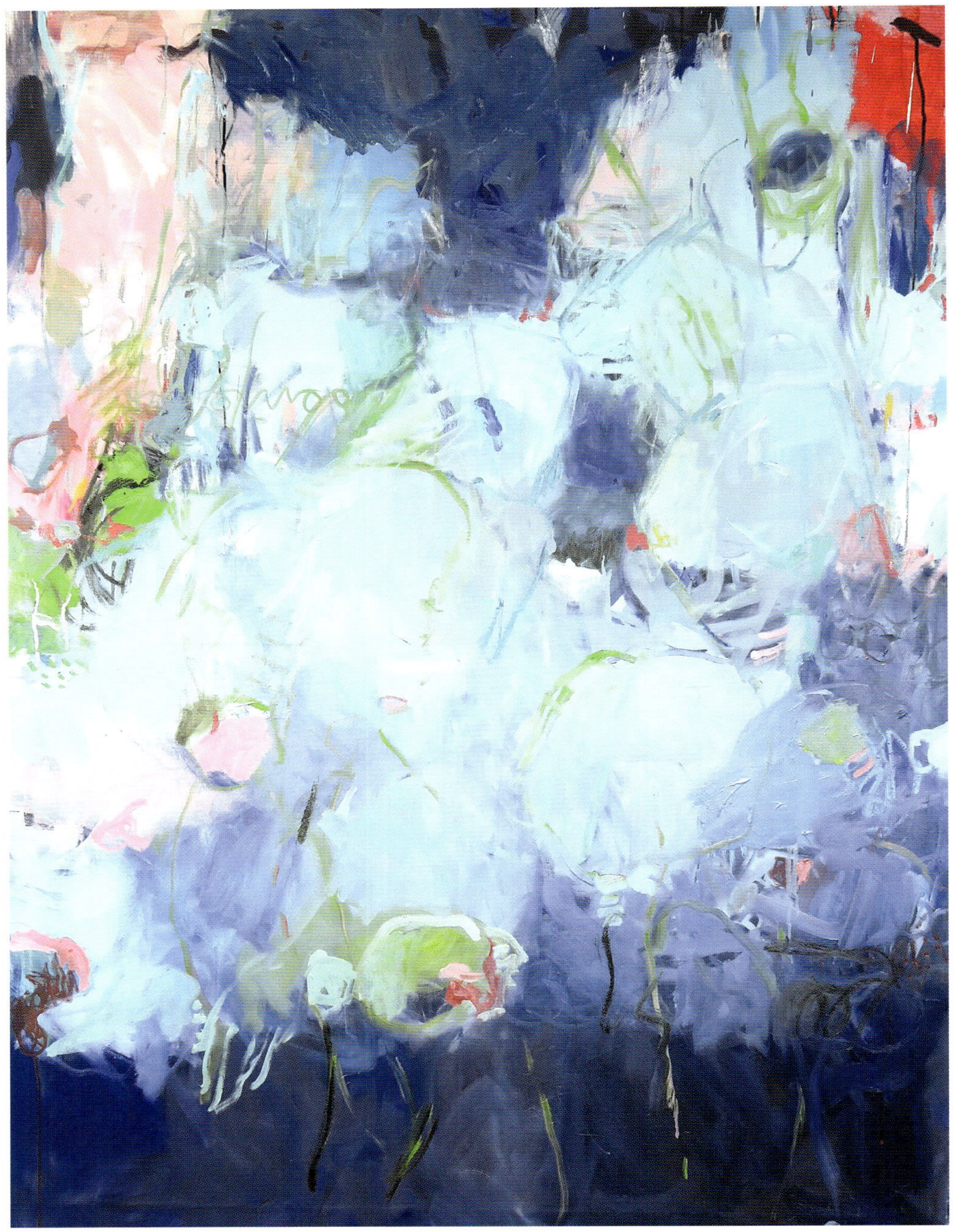

Petra Schoot

Painting for Petra Schoot is the way to explore the world and express herself in a way that cannot be expressed through words. She feels inspired by colors and shapes and lines that surround her daily. She takes them and transposes them into the more abstract language of painting.

Schoot finds it very fulfilling to express herself by oscillating between figurative and abstract painting.

Schoot works in cycles and series. She may use only one range of colors and one common idea in a group of paintings. She feels the colors or the language of lines want to express themselves and be explored further, and she lets them come and go as they will. She lets the painting decide where it wants to go.

Honouring the waters
Oil and oil pastels
57 x 43 in.

Petra.schott@gmx.net
petra-schott.de
@schott.petra

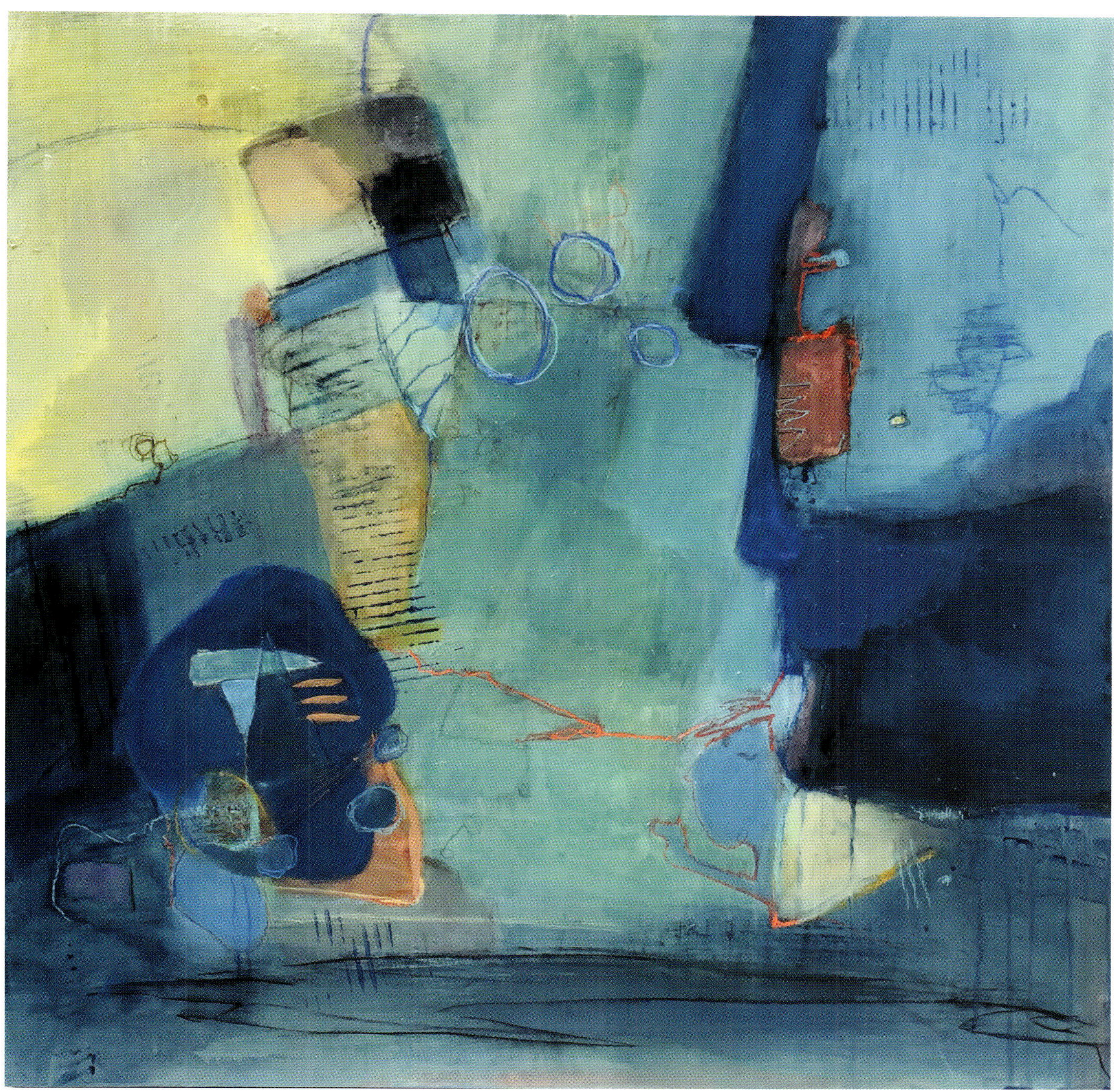

JL Schwartz

Just as a mystery writer or poet slowly reveals the plot or underlying meaning, JL Schwartz strives for her paintings to do the same. Her goal is to draw the audience into a world that envelops them and ultimately stimulates thought and feeling. In order to achieve that goal, she uses nature and all that it encompasses as her inspiration. Exploration of the shapes, composition, and color, as they appear in the world around us, and the emotions that they generate are exciting to Schwartz and something she strives to convey to the viewer. A close-up view of the bark on a tree, an insect, or the wider panorama of a forest, water, or sky can provide new insights and a sense of awe. As with the many layers that can be identified in natural objects, her work is comprised of different layers and techniques in order to develop art that people want to continually explore.

Facing Our Challenges
Acrylic
24 x 24 in.

jlschwartzart@att.net
jlschwartzart.com
@jlschwartzart

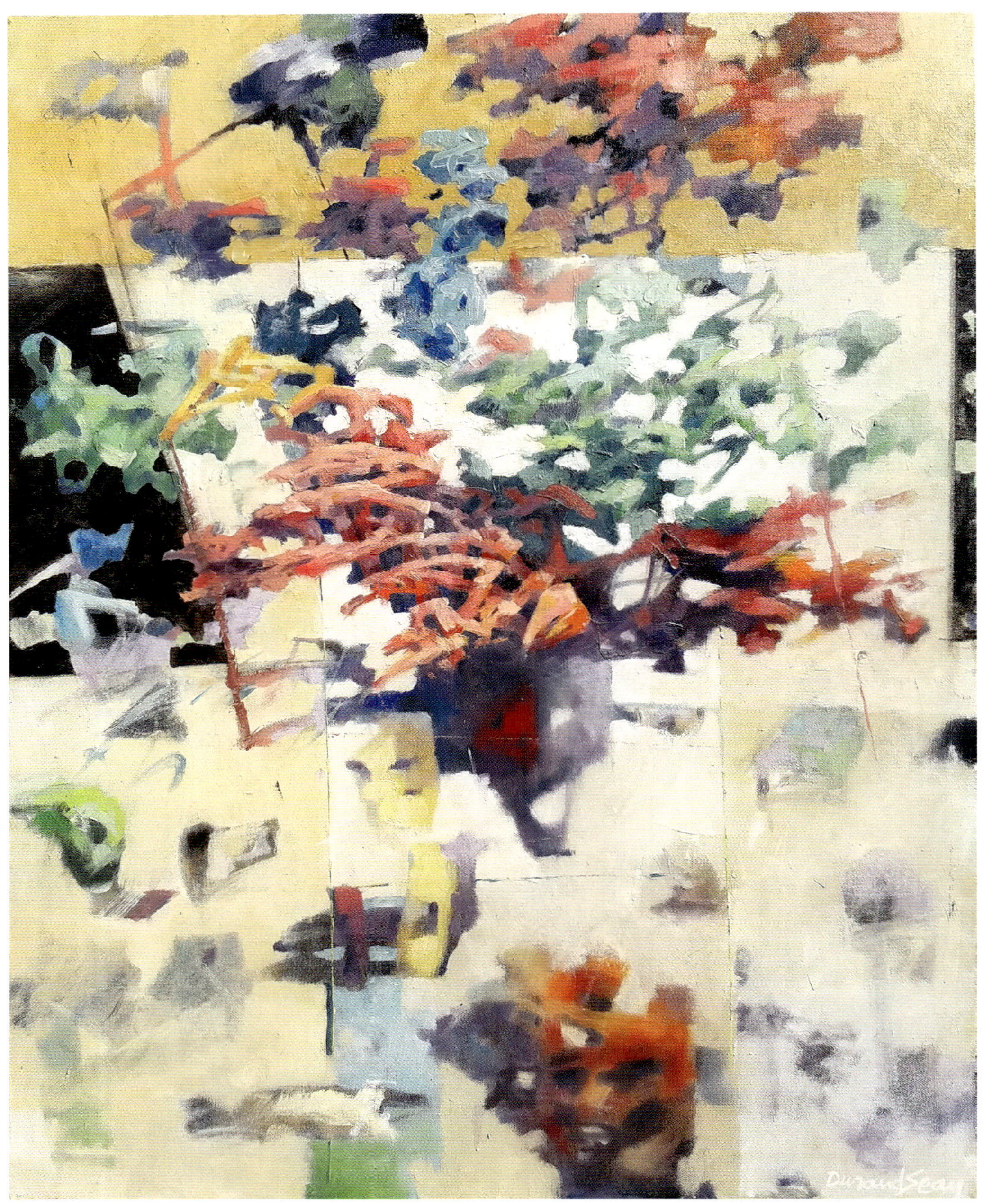

Durand D. Seay

An artist from the Deep South in Alabama, Durand Seay escapes the traditions that label artists by location. His paintings search for a flowing and unpredictable expression, ever changing, like water in a stream or the fluidity of waves. There is a search for a connection to the soul. Time and movement are essential factors used to affect the participant. As an architect, Seay builds these expressions from structures intuitively found in nature. There is a language with a quantum perspective— past, present, and future all at once. He harnesses a viewer's subconscious to instill awareness, insight, achievement, and the ascendancy of understanding. Seay employs symbols such as horses for freedom, blue roosters for vigilance, or dancers for human emotions like satisfaction or regret. Seay's illusionistic field creates a moment of disintegration and formation at once.

For Those That Play
Oil
30 x 24 in.

durand@durandseay
.com
Durandseay.com

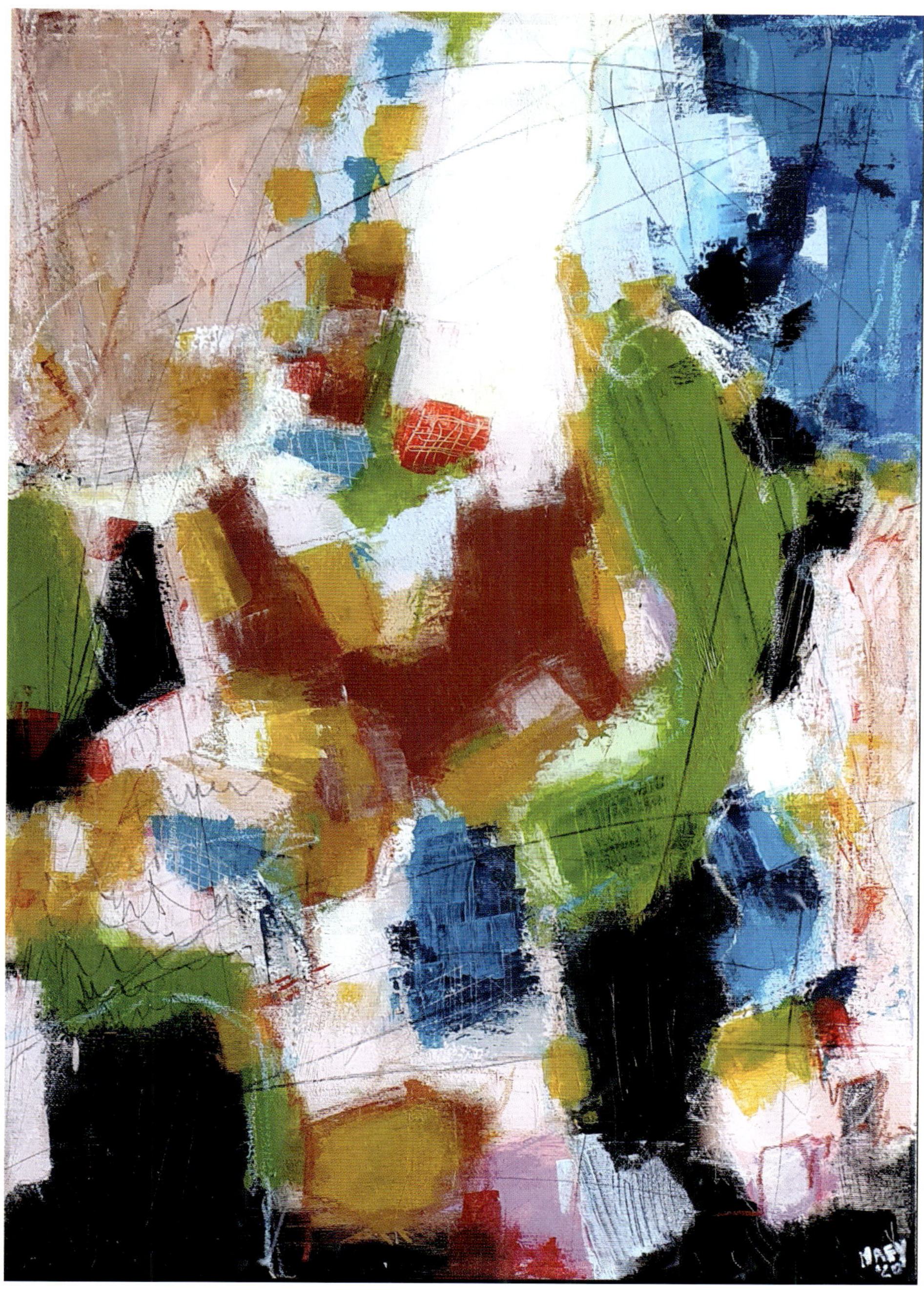

Mafy Signo

From the beginning of 2010, Mafy Signo chose to follow a new artistic path dealing with abstract and informal painting. She is influenced and attracted by Italian masters such as Afro Basaldella, Alberto Burri, Tancredi Parmeggiani, Lucio Fontana, and Emilio Vedova, as well as American Abstract Expressionism. Signo is a shy and reserved person who, through an acute introspective analysis, begins to create abstract works based on blends of color and informal elements, shadows, and light, dictated by the freedom of an intense creative passion. Often her work is stimulated by literary works of contemporary and classical poets and writers from '70s American rock music, especially the work of Leonard Cohen. Signo prefers to use acrylic paint in her artwork because she finds it extremely versatile. "My art is almost always rough, edgy, and I would say brute in some respects," she says. "I don't like perfection. I try to find beauty and harmony in imperfection."

Mankind
Acrylic
27.5 x 19.6 in.

artisthereason19@gmail
.com
@mafy.signo

PAINTING: TRADITIONAL/ABSTRACT

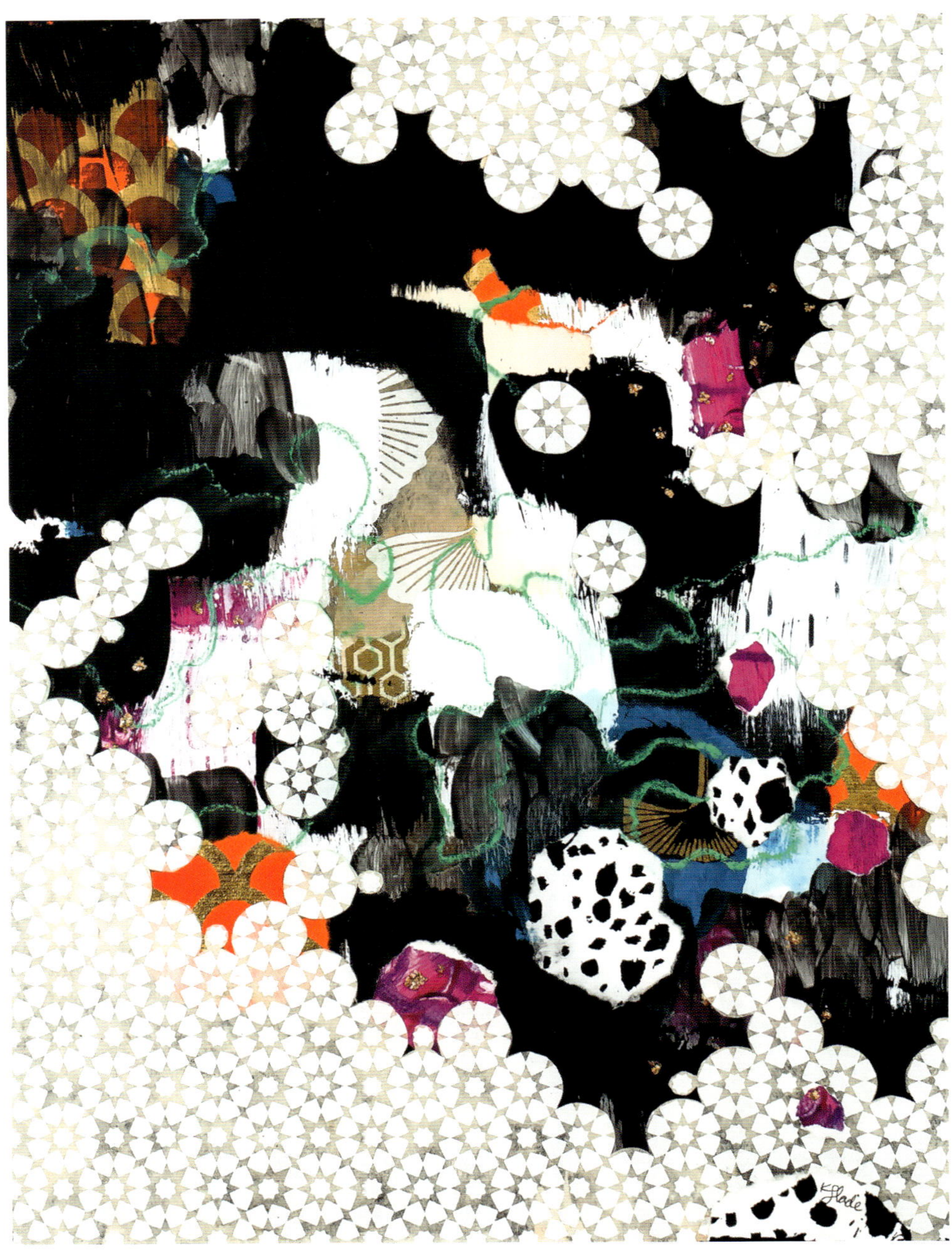

Katrina Slade

Katrina Slade's art practice is rooted in mindfulness. She creates abstract paintings for creative fulfillment, as well as to process anxiety and cultivate a mindset of abundance. When she paints time stops, the outside world slips away, and she is blissfully present in the moment. The color and composition of her work are rooted in the emotions she feels in that moment of creation. Her creative process begins by simply sitting and letting her intuition guide her as she meditates on a subject. She usually finds her muse in the intangible, such as the revitalizing energy of nature or feelings of interconnectedness. The power and beauty of nature are greatly inspiring to Slade. Organic and repeated elements are often found in her work. Her medium of choice is acrylics because she likes to work fast. She loves to incorporate mixed-media elements into her work in order to hint at the complex or ethereal qualities of her muse.

Crown
Acrylic, collage, pastel, and mica on panel
12 x 9 in.

hello@katrinaslade.com
katrinaslade.com
@katrina.slade.art

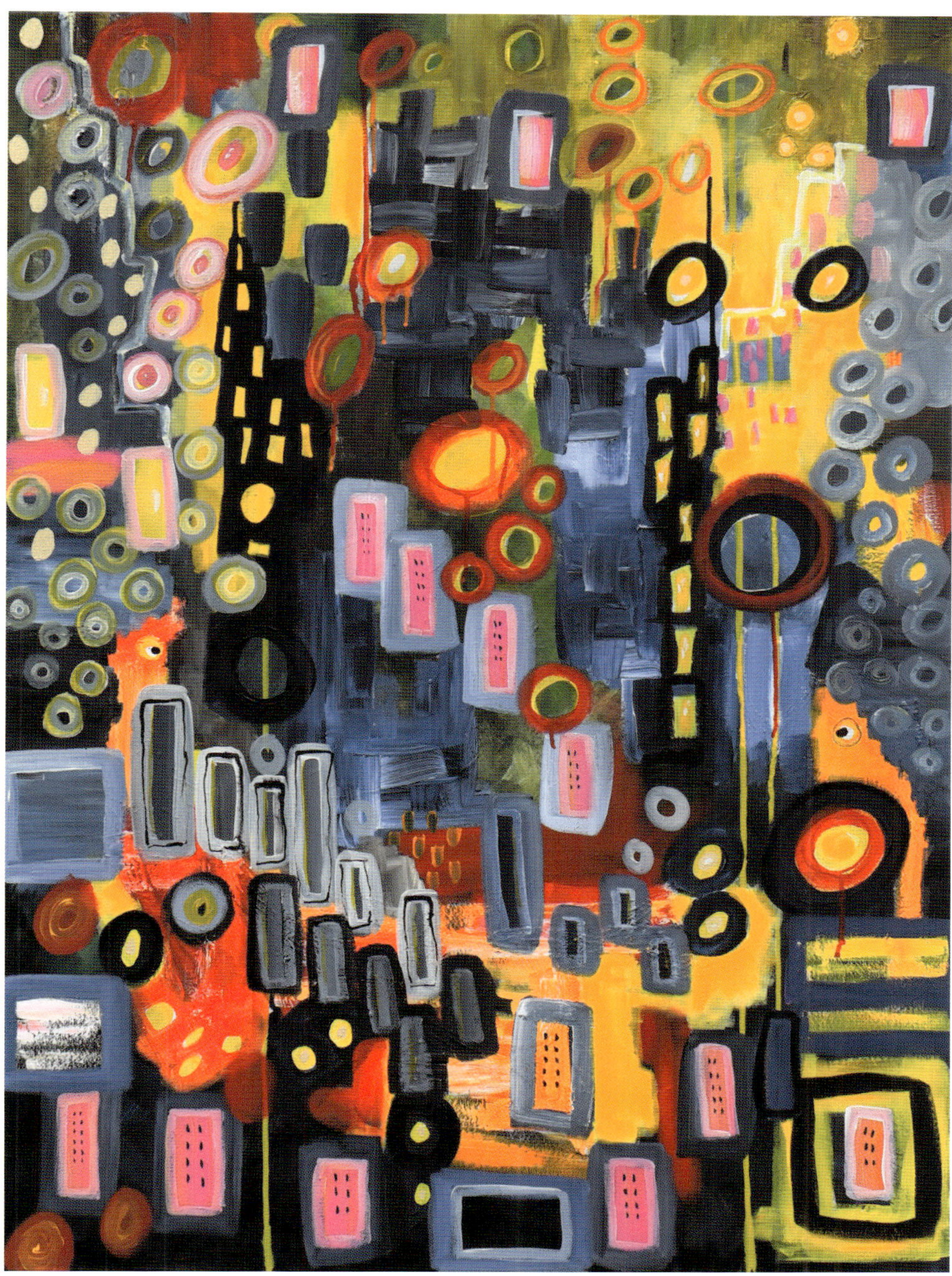

Roxanne Smit

For Roxanne Smit, painting is her drug. Rather than destroy and anesthetize her feelings, her art allows them to be released and infused into her art. She finds her inspiration and motivation in the need to express herself outside politically correct societal imperatives. She takes all the risks on her canvas, where her audacity requires neither justifications nor excuses. "Art is creativity. It offers a safe space to express emotions and explore personal style," Smit says. "Limitation of style, material, and method is the antithesis of the original purpose of true art."

Smit's abstract artwork is intentionally left open to all imaginary interpretations. Each piece of work evokes a response depending on the personality, mood, and emotion of the viewer. When asked how she explains her work overall, she answers with a question of her own: "How do you interpret the different emotions of your life or the colors in your dreams?"

City of Light
Acrylic
39 x 27.5 in.

roxsmitty@gmail.com
rxtexture.com
@Rx_texture

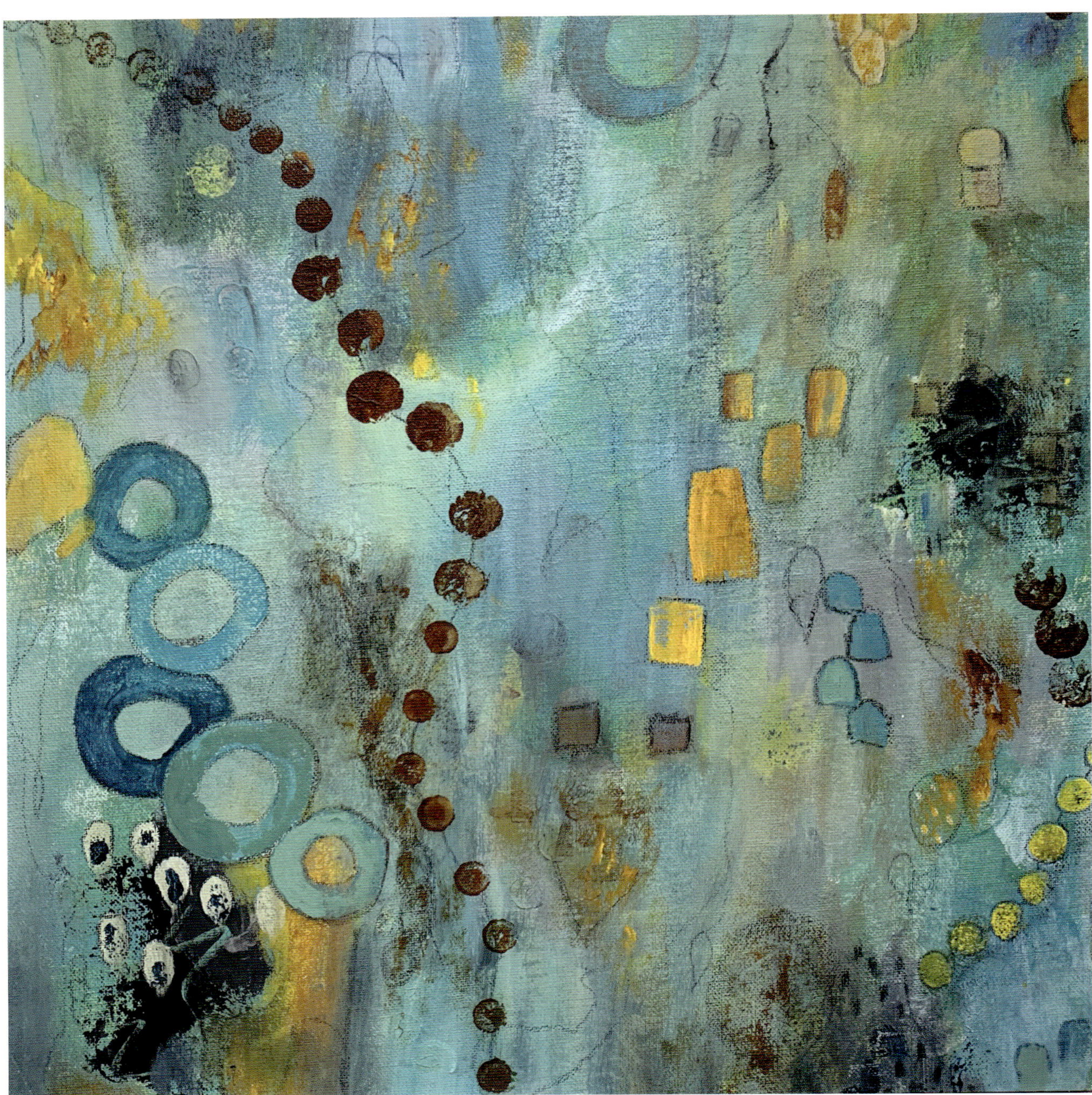

Martha Smith

Martha Smith considers abstract art as an avenue to encourage involvement and imagination, allowing each individual to see their own message in her work. She considers it a privilege to enable the viewers a visual and emotional journey. Smith is passionate about using new techniques and methods, and she employs acrylics, textures, collage, photography, and other forms of mixed media. Abstract art has given her an appreciation for the beauty of imperfection.

Smith was born in Havana, Cuba, where she lived until her family emigrated to the United States after Fidel Castro declared Cuba a communist state. After a successful corporate career, Smith discovered her gift of self-expression when she enrolled in a series of modern art classes at the Boca Raton Museum of Art. She finds inspiration in her travels and surroundings.

Moments in Meditating
Acrylic and mix media
16 x 16 in.

mmgsmith@gmail.com
marthasmithstudio.com
@marthasmithstudio

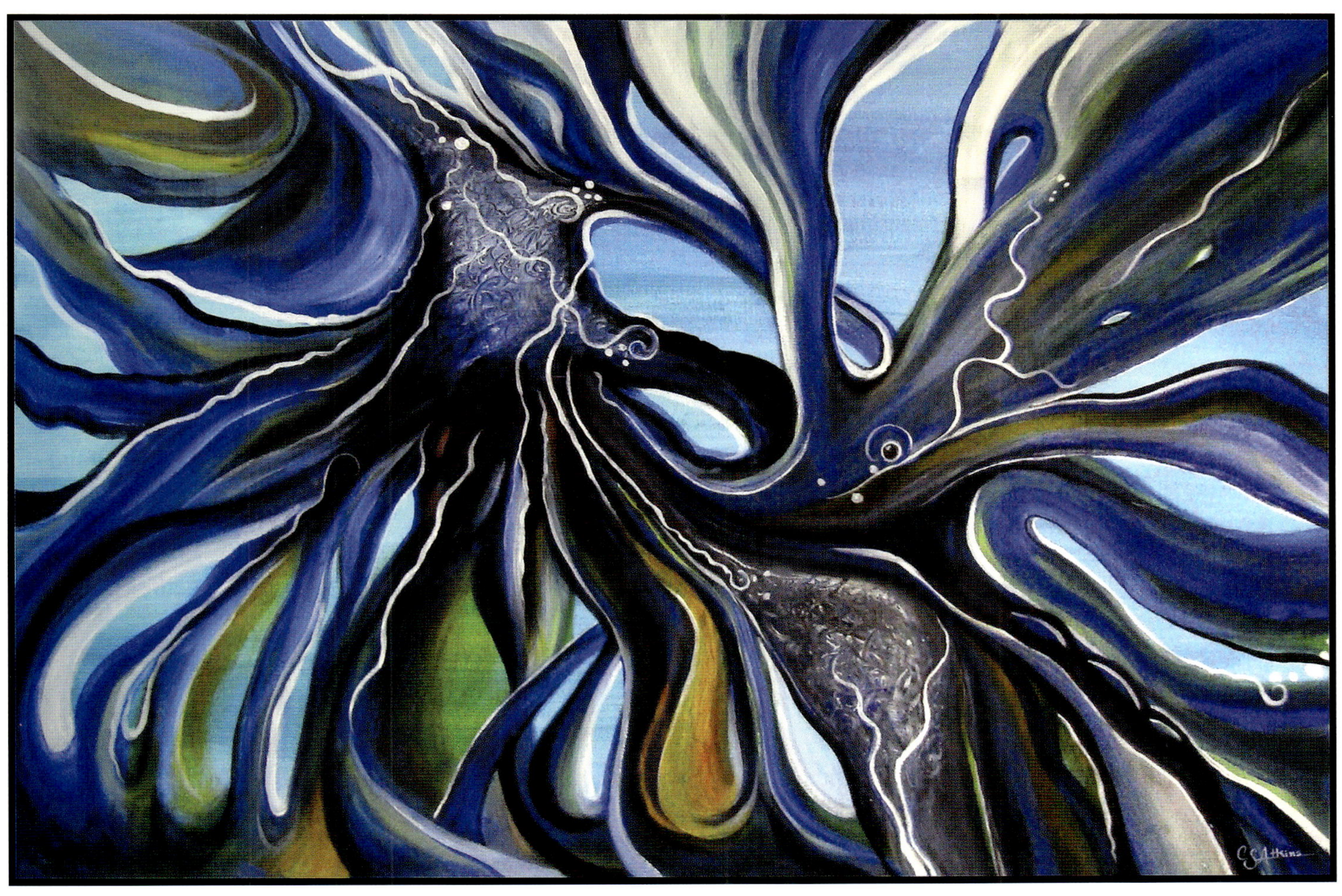

Christine Smith-Atkins

"Often, the process of pushing oneself as an artist involves a journey and a penchant for discovery," says Christine Smith-Atkins. "With abstract art, in particular, it's also a certain amount of surrendering yourself to the process, allowing your intuition to drive the creation, and assisting the art to evolve." She admits that abstract work is possibly the most subjective type of art there is because it doesn't always show an artist's full technical ability. Rather, it embodies emotions and passion through the use of color, form, and lines, yet still depends on the artist's skill and talent to intuitively create a compelling composition. Smith-Atkins likes to think of looking at abstract art as an experience that connects the viewer directly to the heart and soul of the artist. "It's a baring of the soul that allows people to see a part of me that is very personal," she says.

Wateresque
Acrylic
24 x 36 in.

christinesmithtechart@
gmail.com
CSAtkinsArt.com

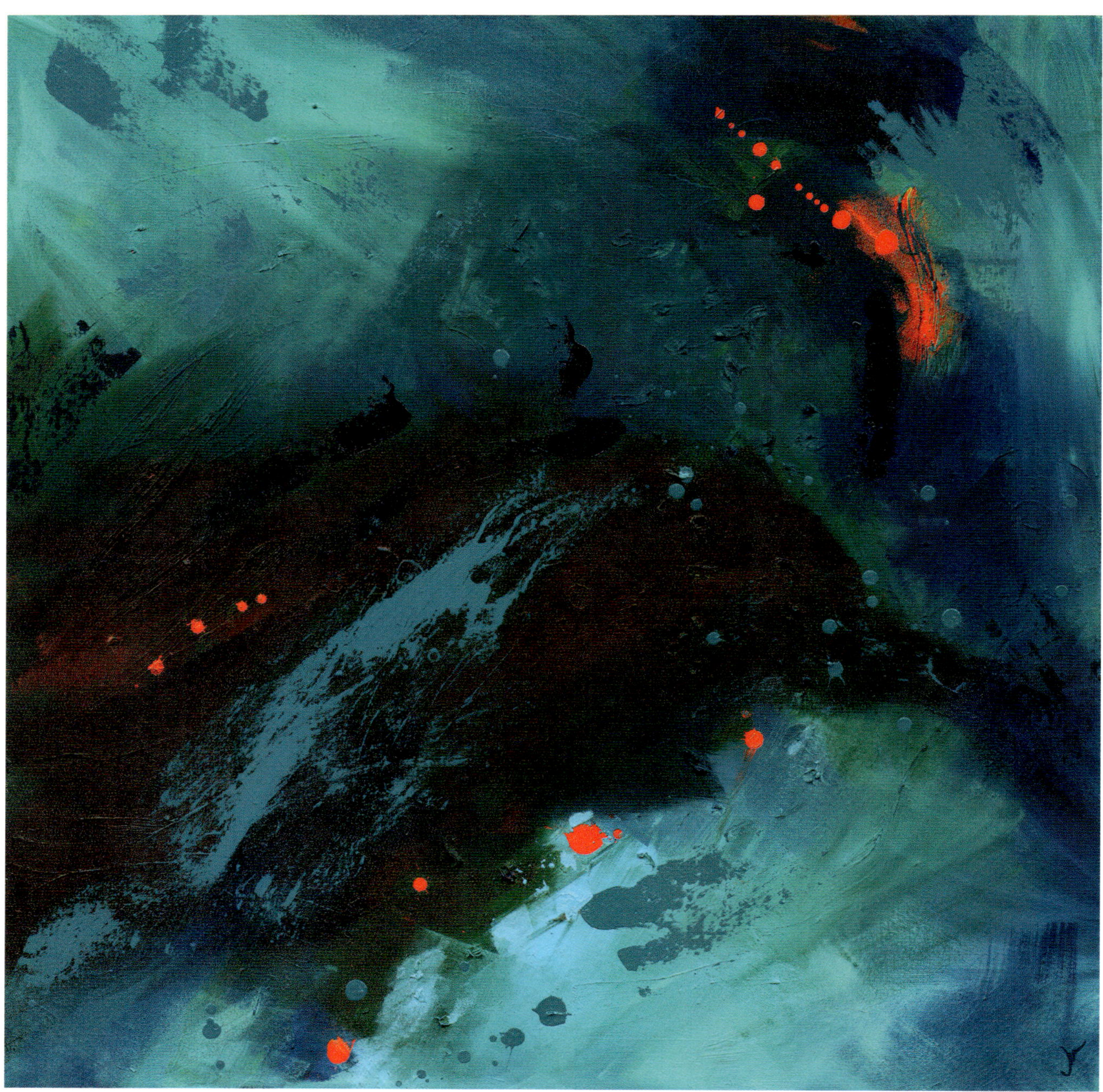

Jen Sterling

Color has always had a profound effect on Jen Sterling's mood and state of mind. She can feel an entire shift in her thinking and emotions when viewing a strikingly bold and colorful piece of art. The goal of her work is to inspire energy and excitement from within and to empower the viewer to do something bold and take risks to achieve their dreams. Sterling's paintings are not meant to be "vanilla" or just match someone's couch. Her work is meant to make you feel strong and powerful—to help you feel the excitement she had in creating them. "My art is meant to burst into your morning with a zing, to prod you into action when you reach your midday lull, and/or to invigorate your senses after a long day," she says. Ideally, her art evokes a reaction and reminds you that life is for feeling and stretching and living.

Under the Wave #3
Acrylic
36 x 36 in.

jensterlingart@gmail
.com
jensterling.com
@jensterlingart

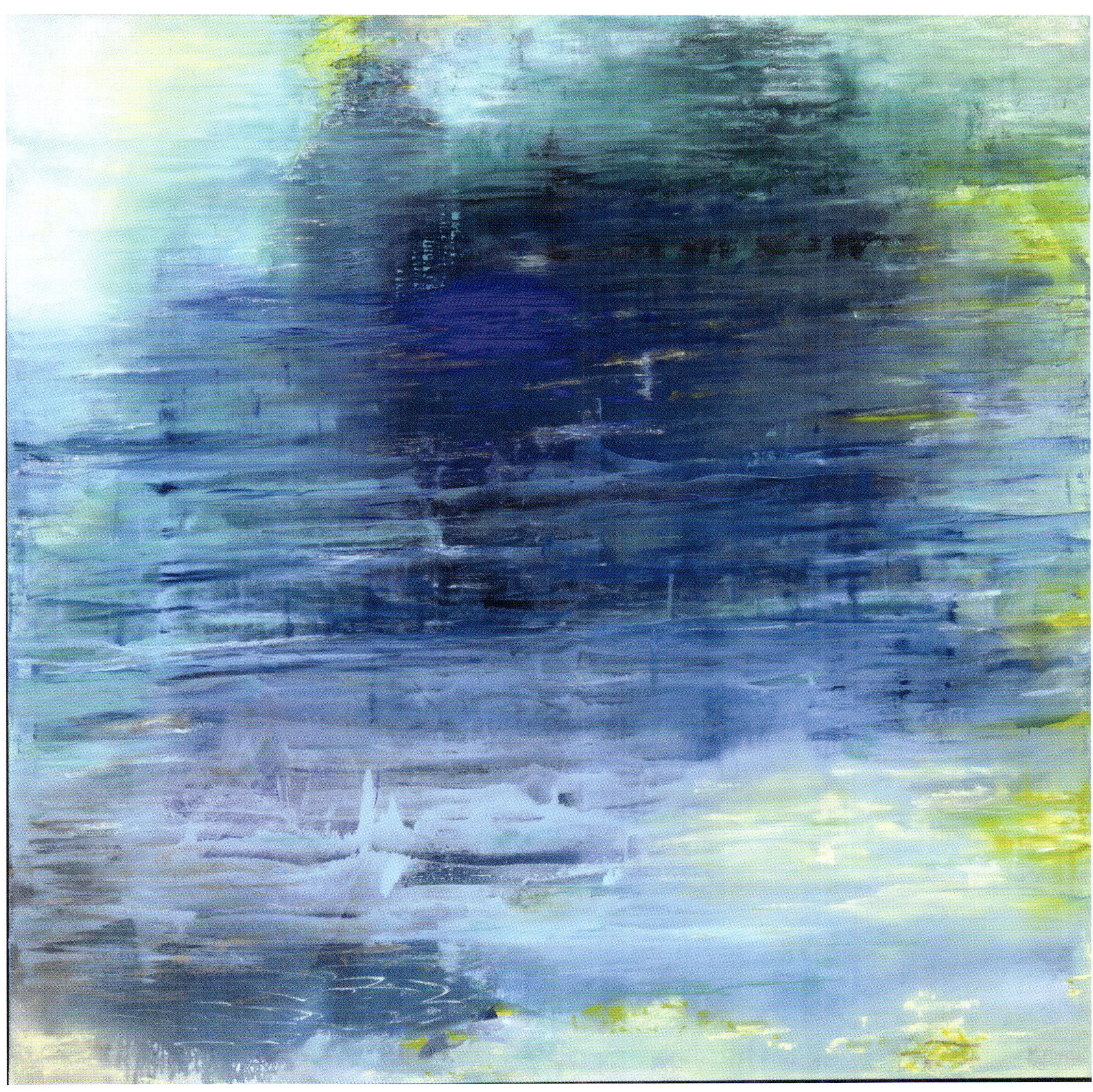

Marine Strage

Marine Strage's mission is to explore the relationship between what we see around us and what we experience internally. Her work is about translating perceptual states into visual language. Strage is particularly interested in creating atmospheres that awake our sense of wholeness. She uses blurring effects and expansive fields of colors as well as vibrating and dissolving light to evoke energy, serenity, and interconnectivity. She draws inspiration from the many landscapes she has encountered, from the windswept coast of Brittany to the radiant vistas of California. She begins with her memories of the colors and atmosphere she experienced, then she lets the process guide her to create an image that links her memories with the present moment. Strage's intention is to encourage the observer to ponder what he or she is looking at and connect to their own feelings and inner life.

Légèreté de l 'Etre (Soft Power of Being)
Oil
60 x 60 in.

marinestrage@gmail
.com
marinestrage.com
@marinestrage

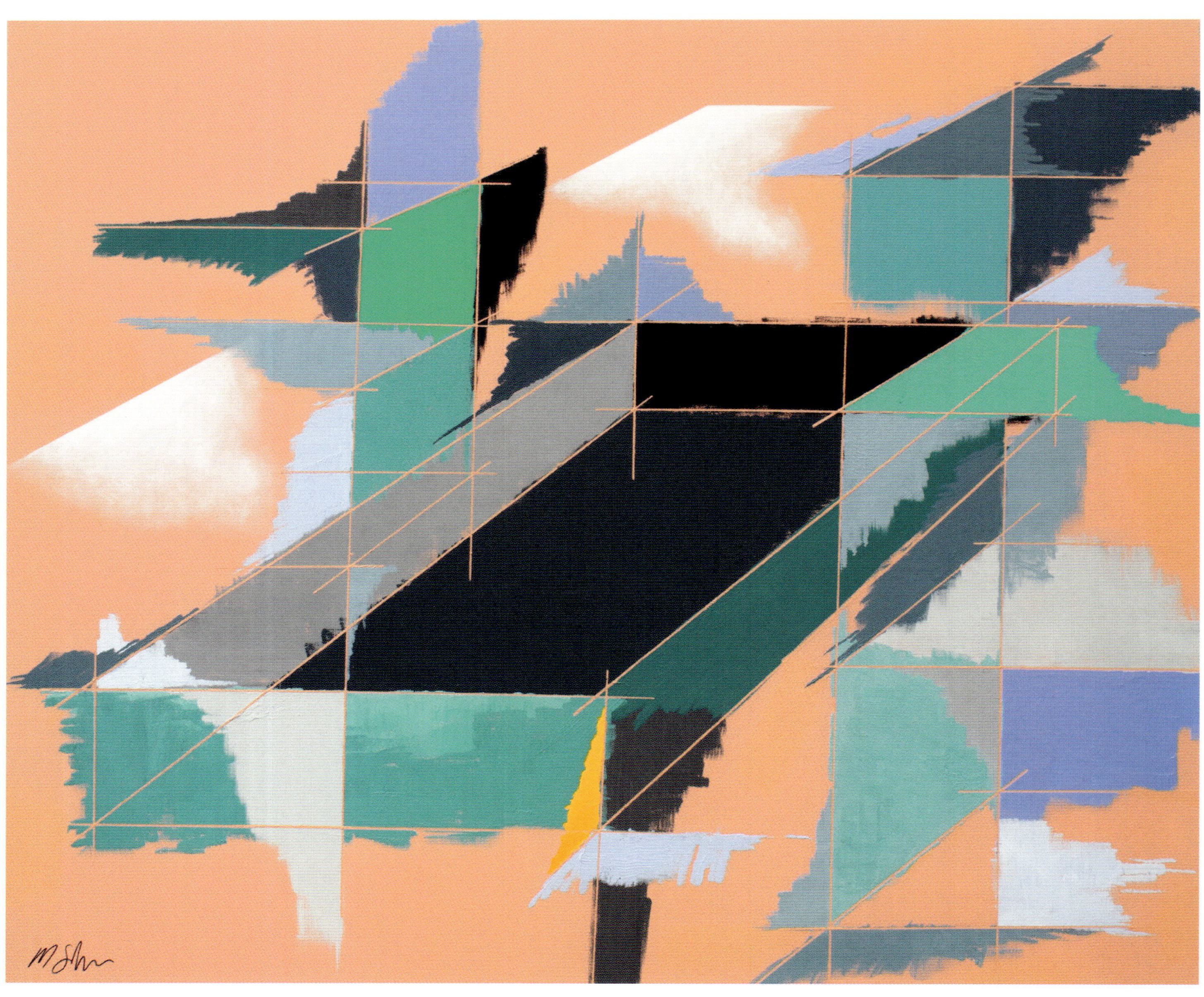

Martin Sullivan

Martin Sullivan (Sully) took to drawing and painting at a young age. He graduated from the Edinburgh College of Art with a bachelor's degree in visual communication. Sully describes his work as abstract geometric. Using heavy brushstrokes and straight lines, he pieces together the subject matter in an original way. His work is also an insight into himself as a person, or at least the person he tries his best to be every day: bright, bold, colorful, energetic, and above all, honest. He believes that art is for everyone and tries to convey that message through his work. His approach to painting and marketing is a combination of what he loves about the art world and what he dislikes about it, and the lessons he's learned on his journey.

A Loading Bay
Acrylic
39 x 42 in.

martinsullivanartist@
hotmail.com
sullyartist.com
@sullyartist

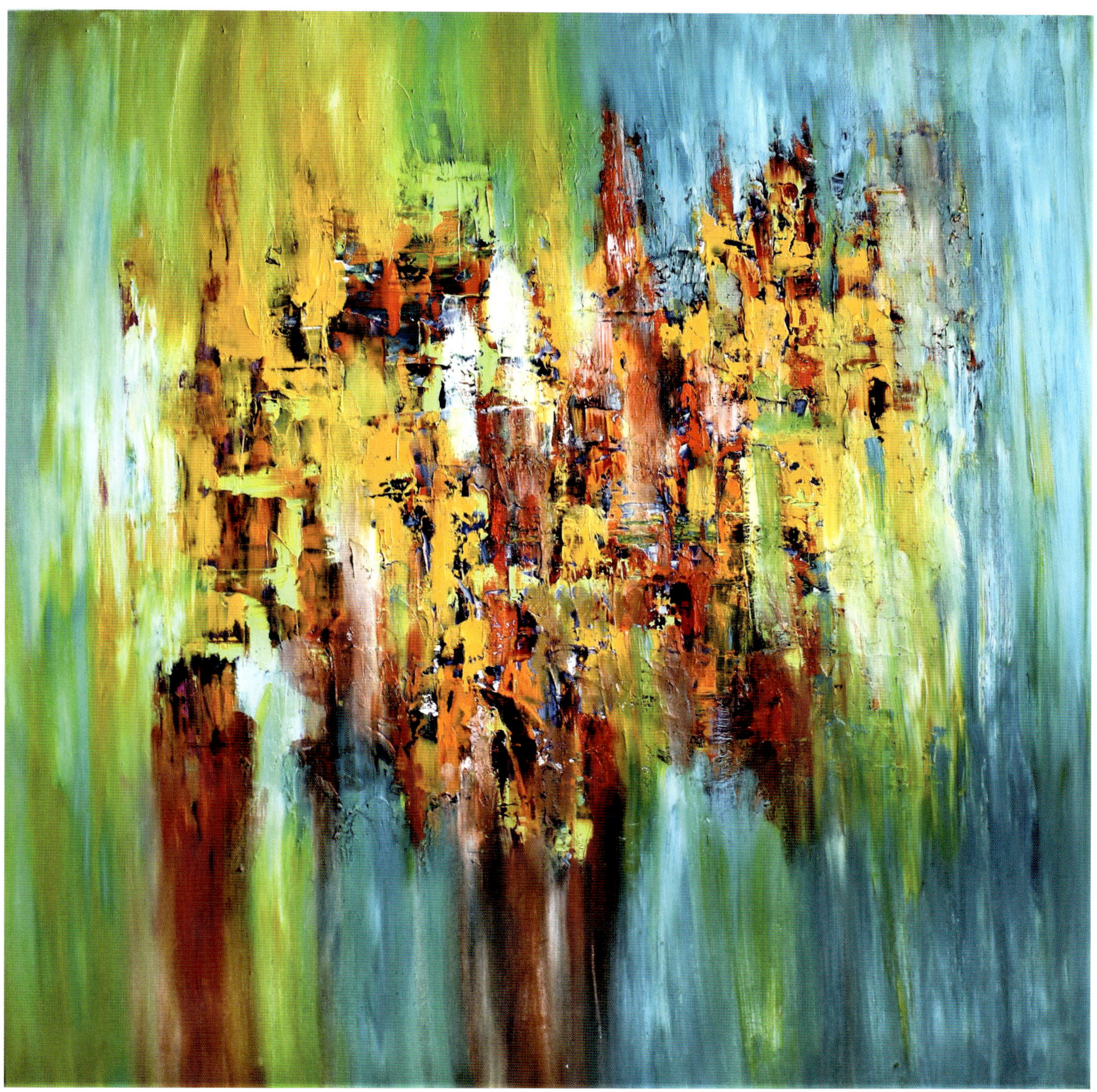

Hanna Supetran

Creating a piece of art is embarking on a journey into the unknown. Mainly abstract in style, all Hanna Supetran's artwork is painted intuitively using oil. Every stroke heightens the anticipation. Every scrape fuels the excitement. Every color mixed suspends time. Each creation is an exhilarating ride, making the once invisible visible, giving the once intangible a tangible form. "There is nothing like transforming a blank canvas into a timeless art piece," Supetran says. "Painting is a fulfilling and rewarding creative expression that adds beauty and quality to life."

Each of Supetran's paintings reflects the vibrancy of life, a balance of intense texture and soft movements, between dark and light, cold and warm. Each work pulls the viewer toward self-reflection, toward an inward journey, toward an adventure of the soul. The paintings can emotionally evoke or mentally provoke. Either way, it communicates to the soul in a manner that is only known to the one viewing it.

Masterpiece
Oil
48 x 48 in.

hanna@
hannaintuitiveartist.com
hannasupetranartgallery
.com
@h_supetran

PAINTING: TRADITIONAL/ABSTRACT

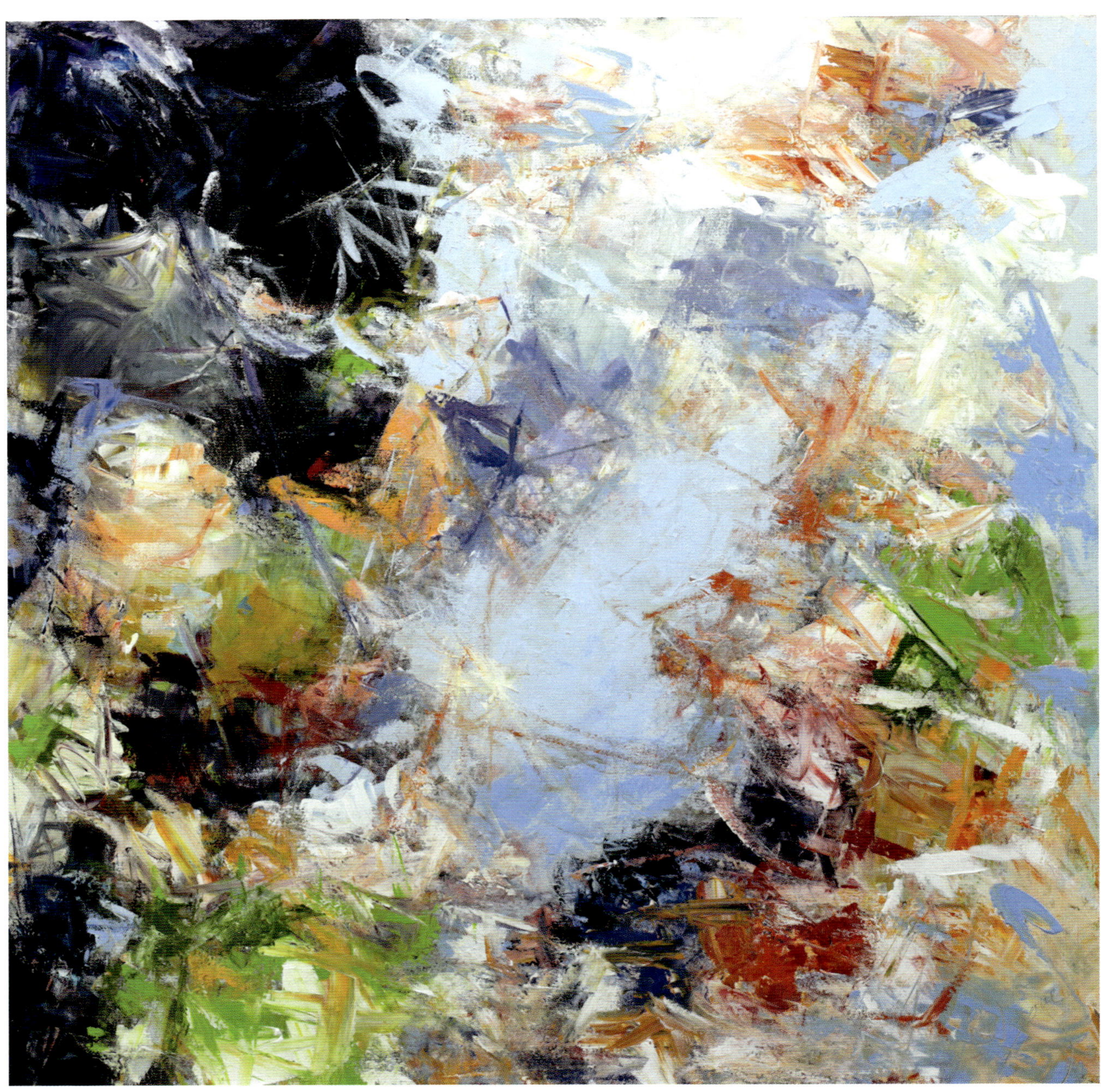

Nancy Teague

Having encountered an internal wellspring of joy, Nancy Teague's abstract paintings flow from adventure, playfulness, freedom, wonder, intrigue, and risk. These dynamics bring abandonment and fun to her canvases. Teague begins with a very dark color mixture on a blank canvas, quickly and freely expressing several black areas. For the artist, it is the beginning of "deep unto deep." Next, bright colors move into and out from the dark areas to create new aspects of themselves and direction for the work. Cutting into the wet paint spontaneously and intentionally adds intrigue. Delightful surprises happen in the lively interaction. "Connection and reflection are important dynamics in my work, as they mirror our true being," Teague says. "Fullness of life means really connecting to relationships that we enjoy, value, enrich, and enlarge one another." Teague's expressive abstracts reflect these beautiful occurrences. When viewers sense a happy feeling in her work, they are tapping into a bit of her wellspring.

In the Moment
Acrylic
30 x 30 in.

nancy@nancyteague
.com
nancyteague.com
@nteague_abstracts

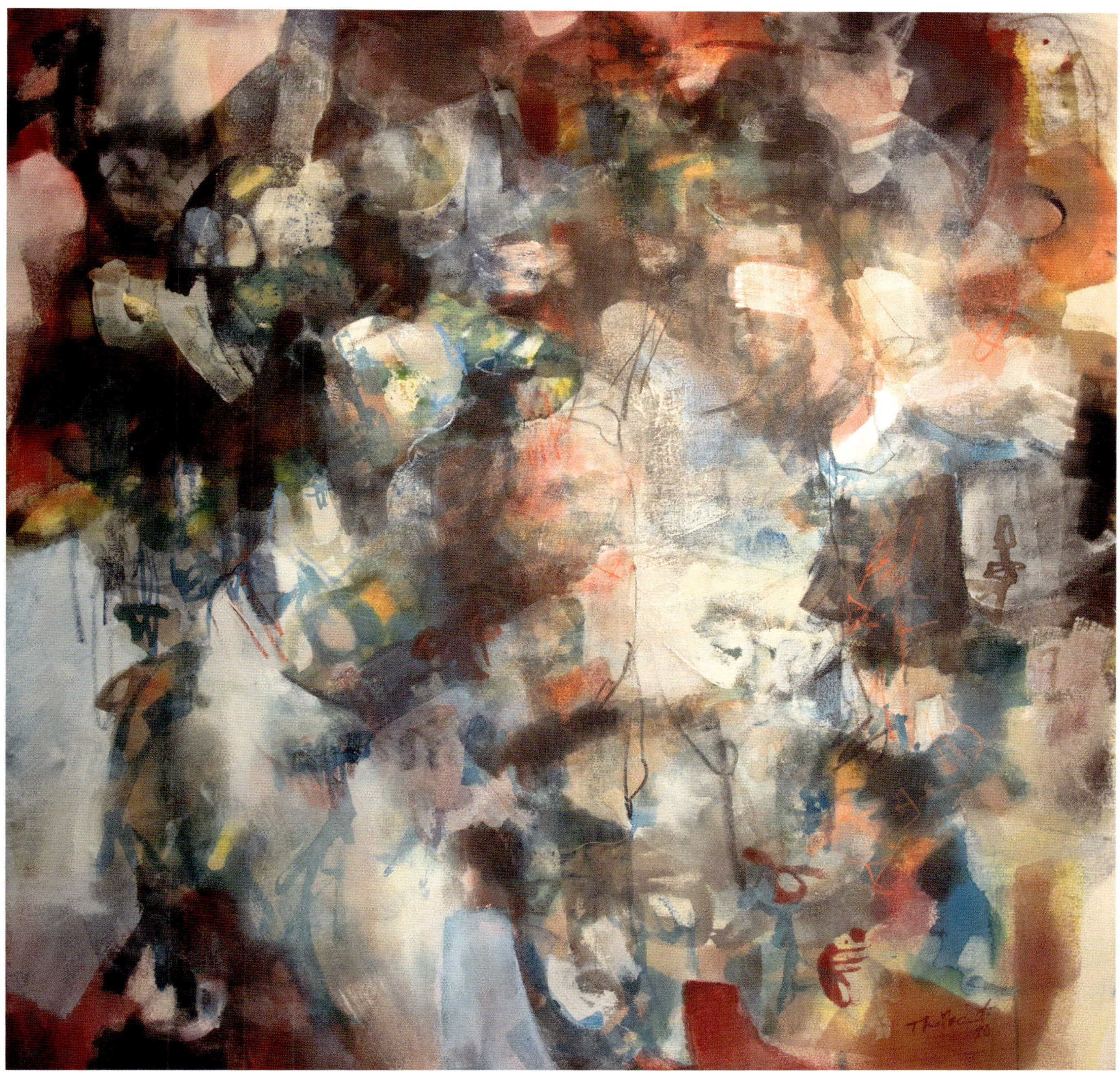

Mark Thibeault

Mark Thibeault is inspired by the intuitive process. Improvisation in music and abstractions in painting are surreal narratives where, in an instant, stories are pieced together. Distant yet familiar melodies and visions are tempered by a passing intuition. Seemingly disparate ideas are collected to find new meaning. Thibeault's practice extends across music and painting. His approach to abstraction is informed by the role of chance in musical improvisation. His abstract explorations in painting combine interests in improvisation, the painted gesture, and the notion of home with a concern for environmental sustainability. Thibeault often refers to objects and surroundings for lines and shapes to start a painting. The mood and composition of each piece are governed by the previous line's influence and effect. His work is an intuitive unveiling of the inherent linear compositions woven through our perception of the world and our interactions within it.

Confluence
Acrylic, ink and wax stick on raw canvas
26 x 25 in.

mark@markthibeault
.com
markthibeault.com
@markt_art

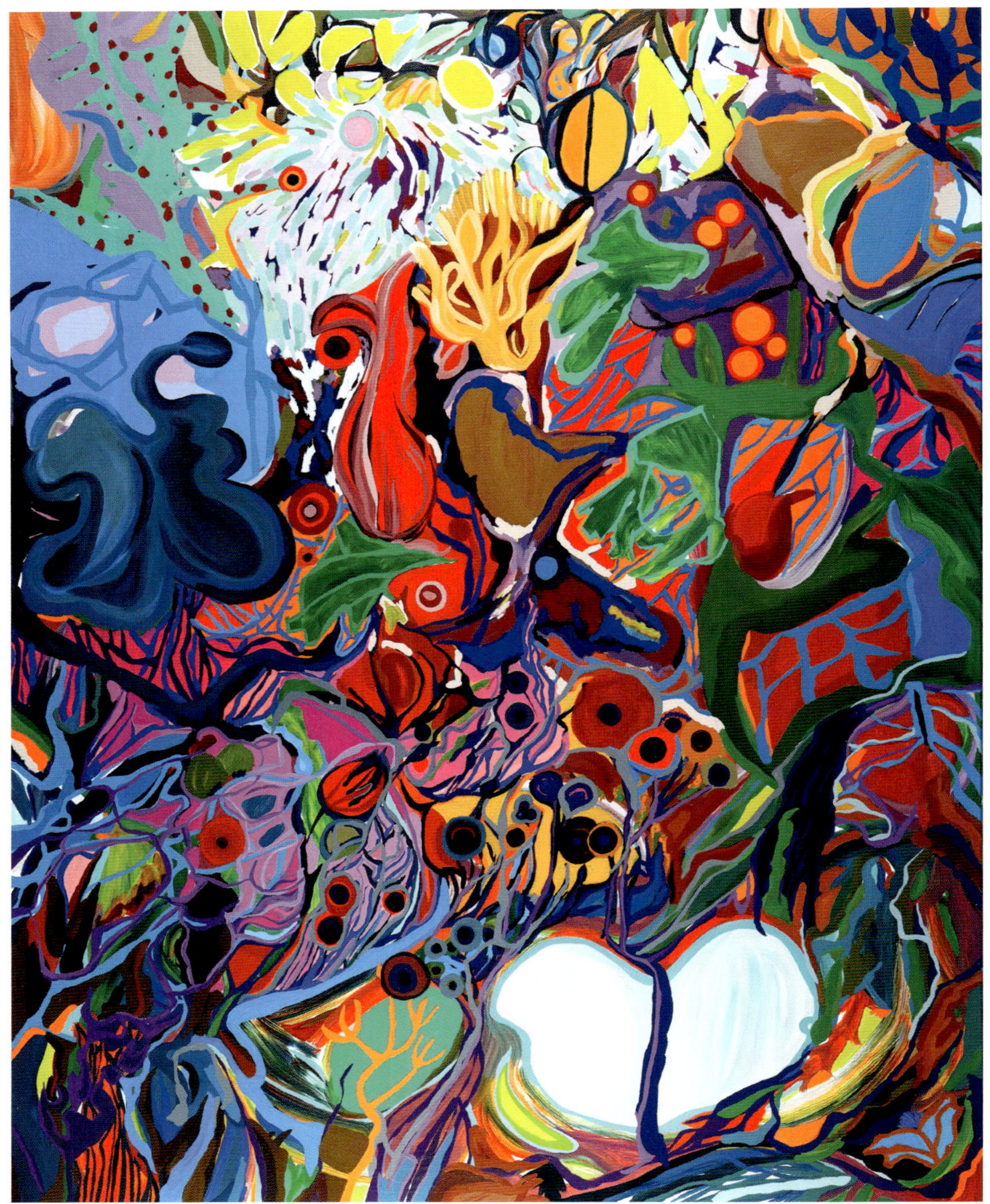

Özlem Sorlu Thompson
Özlem Sorlu Thompson obtained an undergraduate degree in biology and completed her master's degree in botany. After graduating, she decided to listen to her inner voice and concentrate on her art. She lives in the same flat where Mondrian painted before the start of the Second World War. While drawing was always something she enjoyed, Thompson realized that she wanted to make her mark as a painter. Her background in biology and organic structures became a strong influence on her work, and key to her process is the abstraction of forms from nature to effectively describe the concepts that flow from her subconscious. While she views her work as a reflection of how she sees and interprets the world, the impromptu flow of strong colors and shapes is intended to affect user-defined feelings and impressions and to facilitate a wide range of interpretation and interaction between the viewer and the artist.

Flowers III
Acrylic
60 x 48 cm in.

ozlemsorluthompson@gmail.com
@ozlemsorluthompson

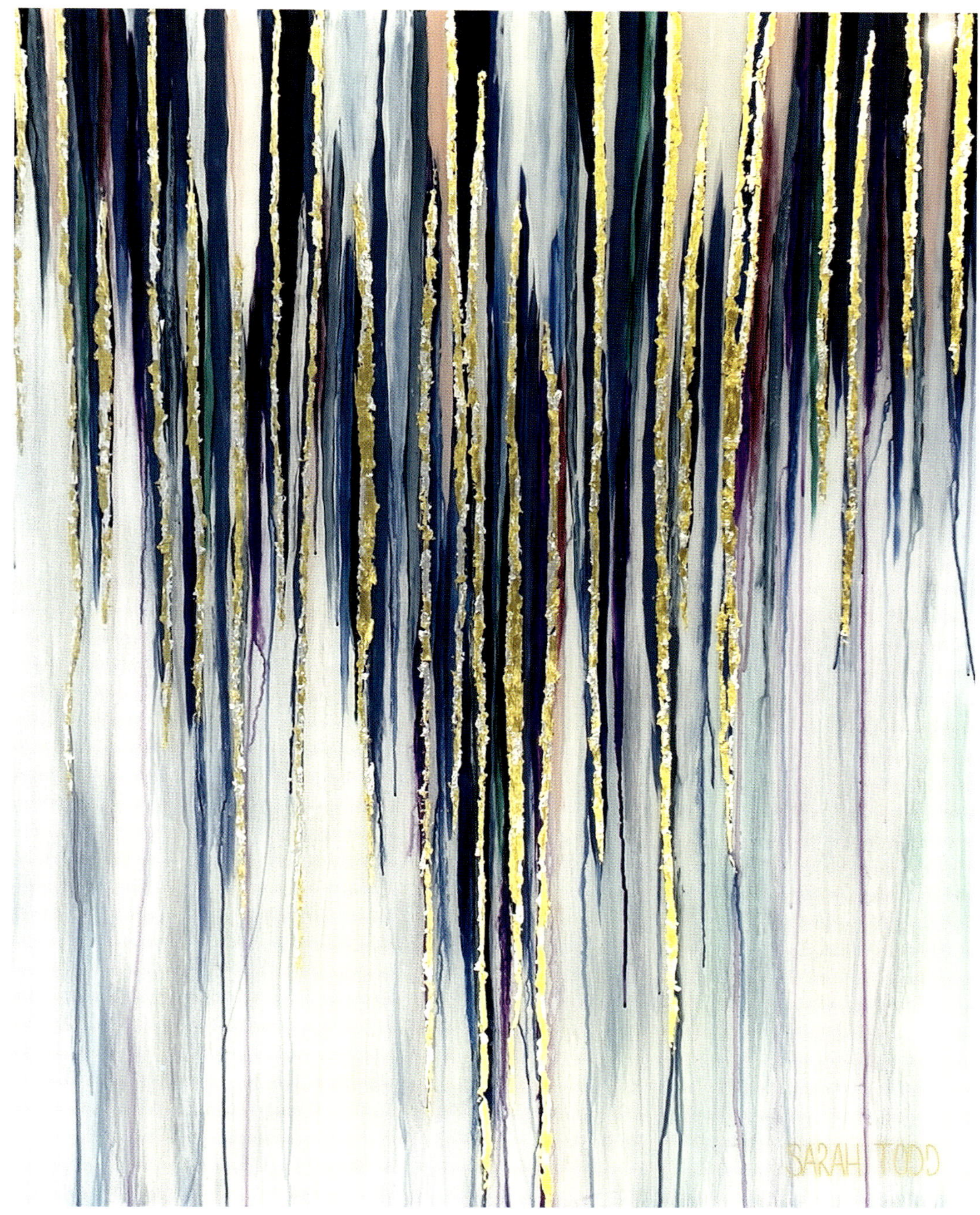

Sarah Todd

Sarah Todd feels blessed to use her skills to create art that is both reflective of this world yet exists in its own realm. Her work is inspired by her travels, organic formations, and light reflecting on surfaces. The contrast of the 24K gold leaf and vibrant paint mimic the way the warmth of the sun and coolness of the water interact with each other. The vertical and organic movement in her paintings, along with the use of resin, emphasize the natural beauty of water. The contrast of the metallic gold and bold colors do not compete but rather complement each other to create harmonious visions. Todd's desire is to evoke a sense of wonder and peace in the viewer as they engage with her art and use their imagination to discover what the painting means to them. She considers it an honor to leave her mark on this world through her brushstrokes.

God's Promises
Acrylic, 24K gold leaf, genuine silver leaf, and resin
54 x 42 in.

sarah@sarahtoddart.com
sarahtoddart.com
@sarahtoddart

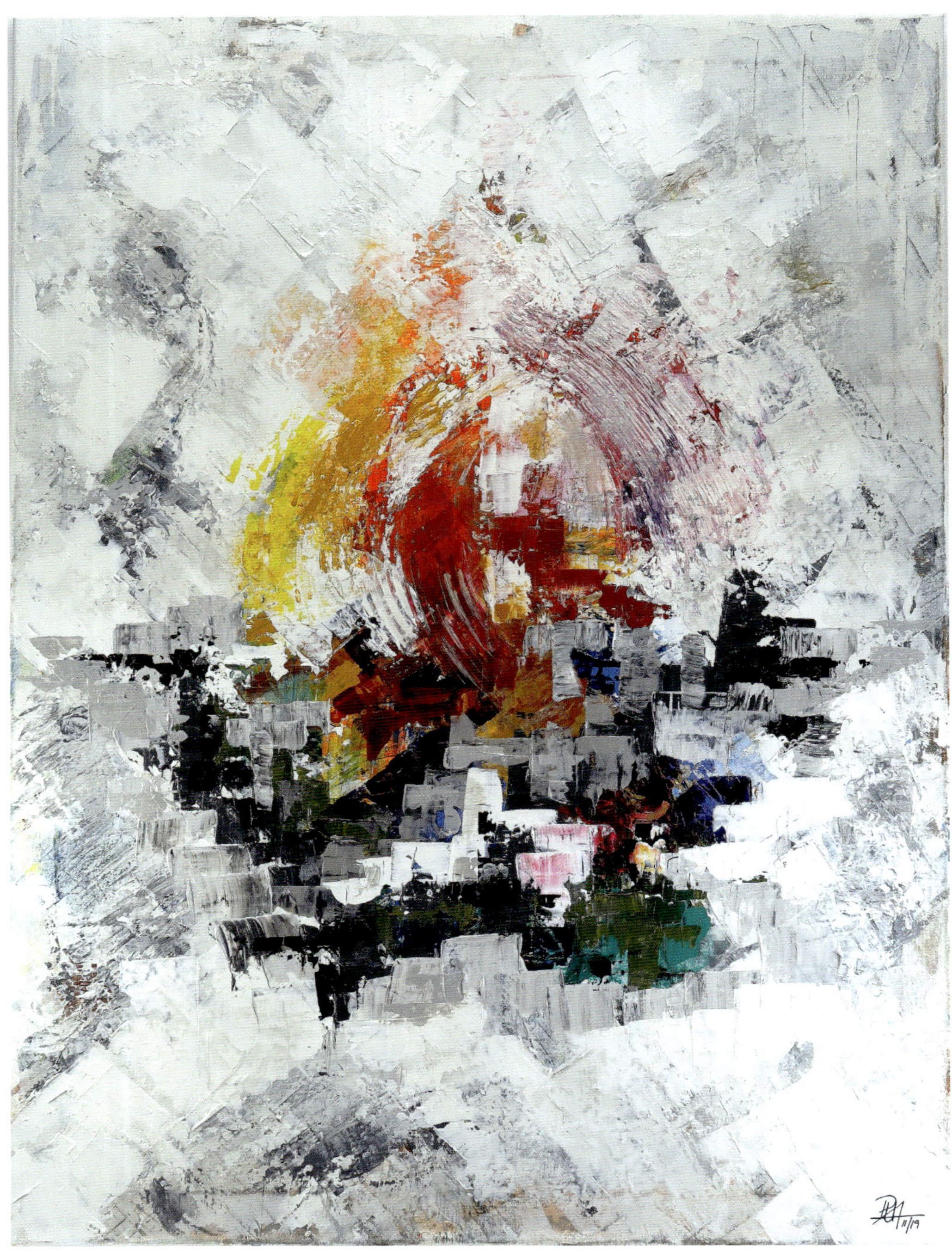

Petra Uhl

"If the language becomes too loud and without content, and you need a place where you can find your inner center again, this place is my art. The language is quiet and the energy is powerful," says Petra Ulh. Texture plays an important role in Uhl's work. When applied for the first time, the paint mixes, overlays, structures itself, remains noticeable, or disappears again under new layers of texture. It is a playful interplay between intuition, chance, space and time, happiness, and sadness. The viewer dissolves the boundaries and enters the fantasy. Ultimately, the result has to withstand the aesthetic gaze, and this provides the basis of her work.

Celebrate Life
Acrylic
31.4 x 23.6 in.

petrauhlart@gmx.de
@petra.uhl.art

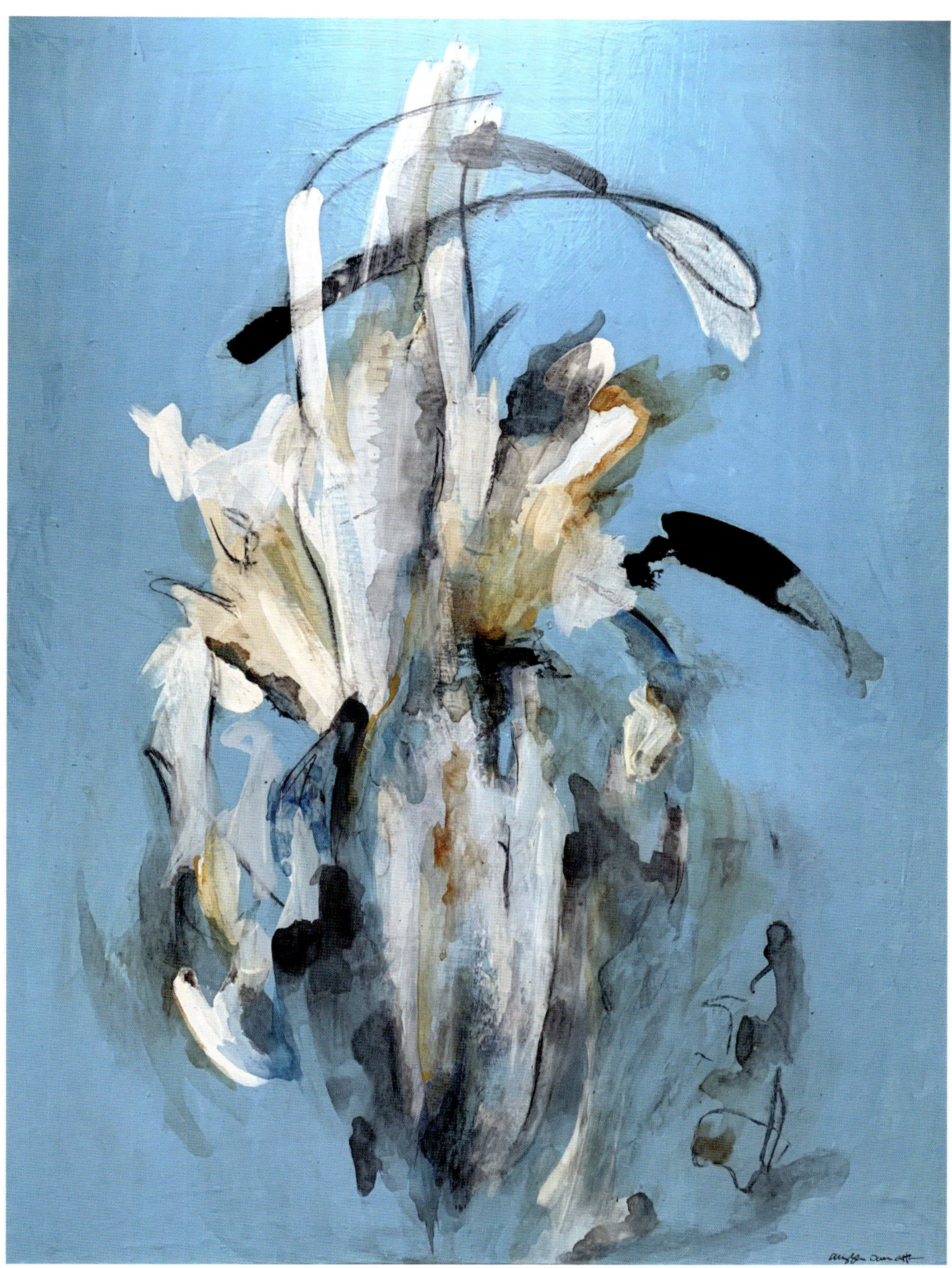

Alissa Van Atta

Alissa Van Atta would sum up her work as "skirting around ambiguity." Often classified as Abstract Expressionism, she hints toward shapes created by multiple layers, texture, and different treatments of the paint. The titles are intentionally ambiguous but encompass aspects of her thoughts and observations during the creative process.

The subjects are observations of news, events, and ideas that capture her attention as oddities. Van Atta's intention is to create an intimate connection with the piece that compels the viewer to the point where they are tempted to touch the work. She gravitates toward organic shapes and tones and has long played with texture and varying degrees of opacity and translucence in her work. Texture is often highlighted as an area of interest.

Show me the Road to Utopia
Acrylic
48 x 36 in.

alissa@avaarts.net
avaarts.net
@alissa_avaarts

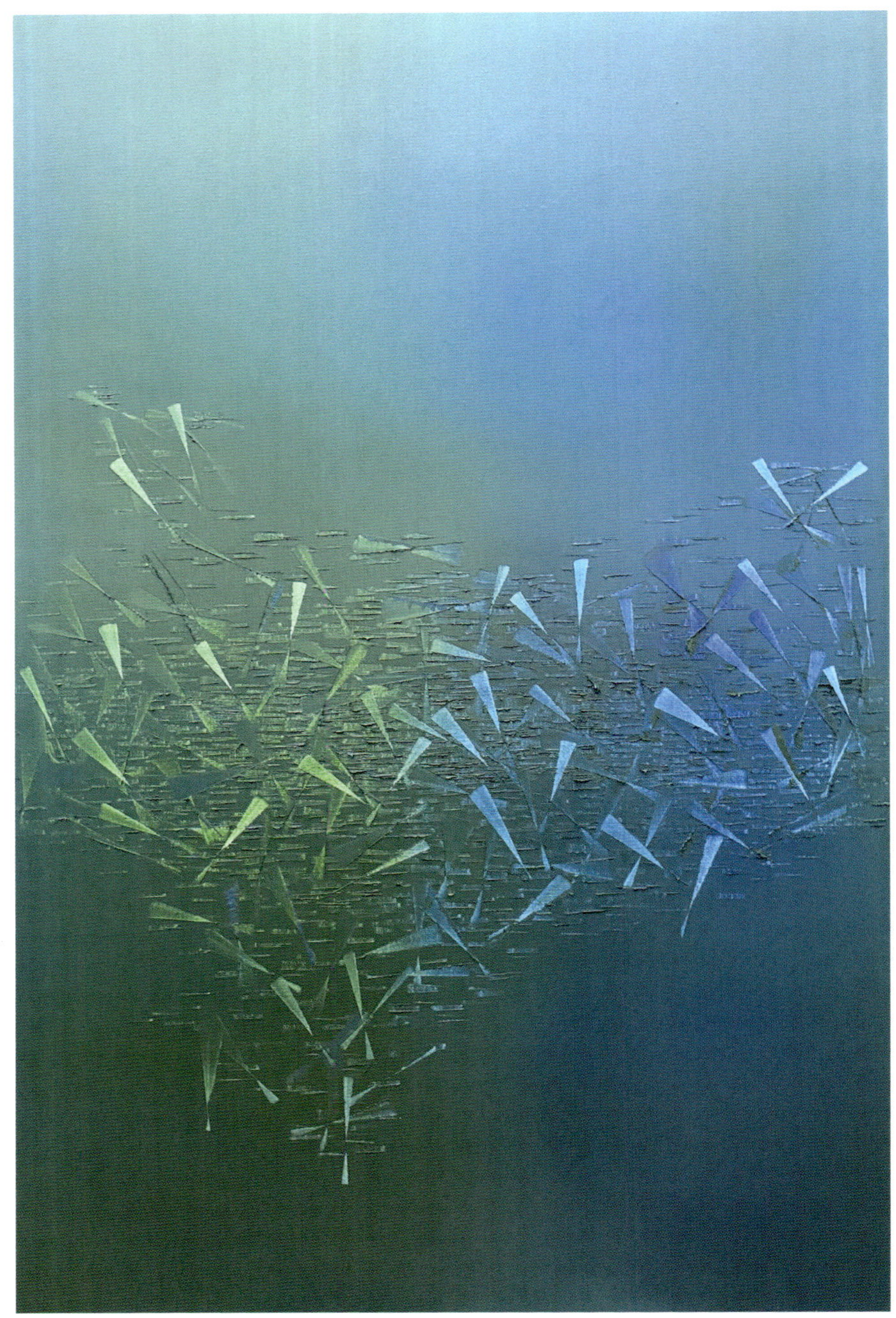

Christel Van Hemelrijck
Christel Van Hemelrijck uses oil painting to present her lyric expressionism visions. She is a self-taught artist based in Mechelen, Belgium. She gets inspired by the people who surround her and by her travel experiences. The island of Crete remains a major source of inspiration.

Van Hemelrijck's work, a vibrant collection of abstract oil paintings, stands out by the use of texture, color, and light. Her emotions are expressed through the language of bold colors, with solid composition and delicate texture. She works mainly on large canvases, overwhelming planes of monochromatic color, intrusive and captivating. In her series Stories, the backgrounds become more elaborate, more delicate, and the use of a palette knife more feminine. Van Hemelrijck paints with vibrance, expressing herself passionately.

Four Days in Lisbon
Oil
47 x 31.4 in.

christelvanhemelrijck@
telenet.be
christelvanhemelrijck
.com
@christelvanhemelrijck

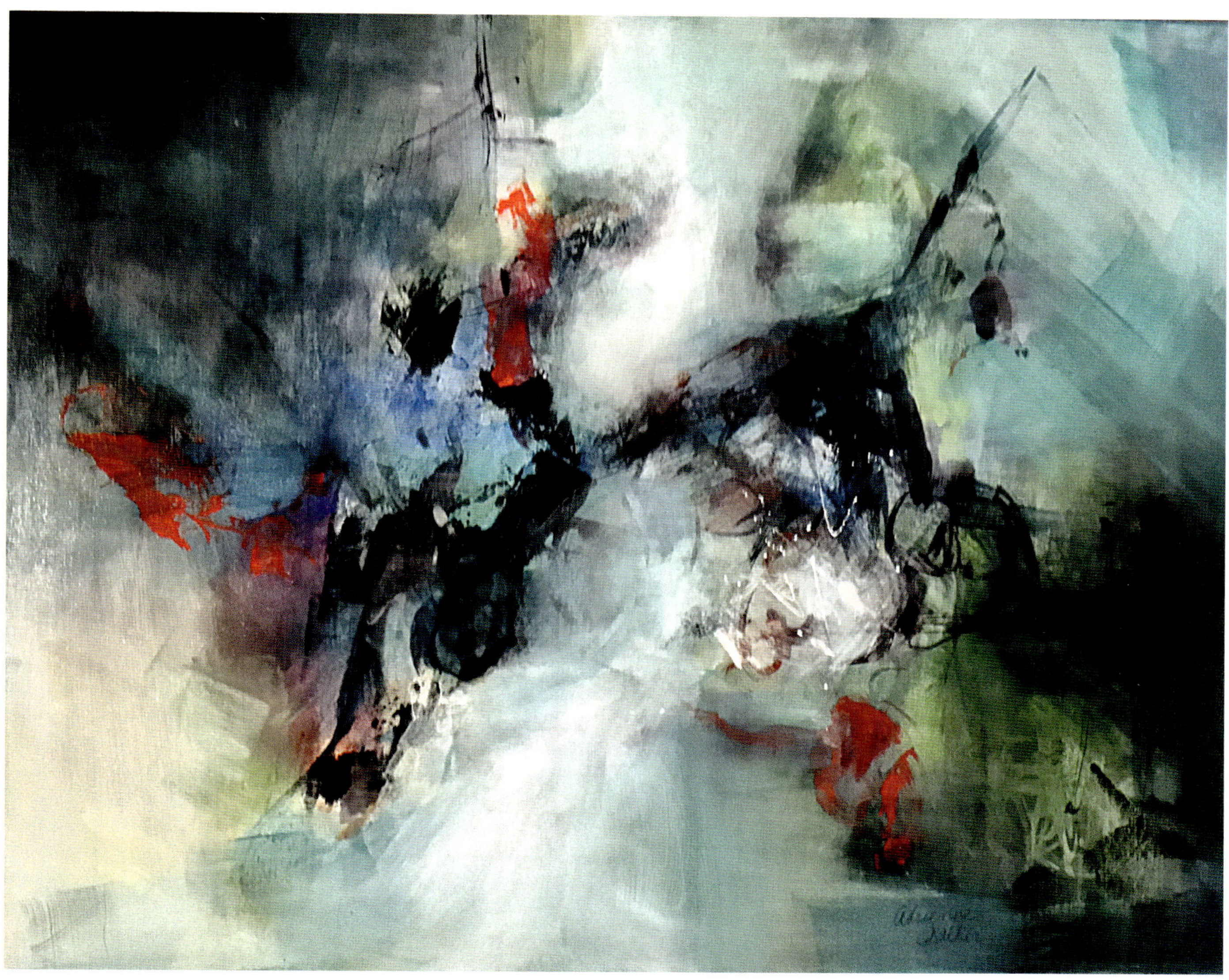

Adrienne Walker

Adrienne Walker has been passionate about art her entire life. Using watercolor and acrylics or stone, she enjoys exploring and creating worlds in many dimensions. Her work is created with passion from within her body and soul, allowing brushstrokes and sculpting to invite the viewer into her world of art. Experimenting with the flow of mixing watercolor, acrylic, and/or gouache creates stories in her mind's eye. Each painting is a journey that begins with splashes of color put onto the canvas with either a palette knife or large brush. The colors start to join in a story as they mix and mingle. As Walker layers the paint onto the canvas, shapes appear, telling her where to go and what to look for in the story that she is telling. Walker loves color, the challenge of trying something new, and creating different emotions in her work.

Into The Grotto
Acrylic
24 x 36 in.

adriennew4199@gmail.com
adriennearts.com
@adriennewalkerart

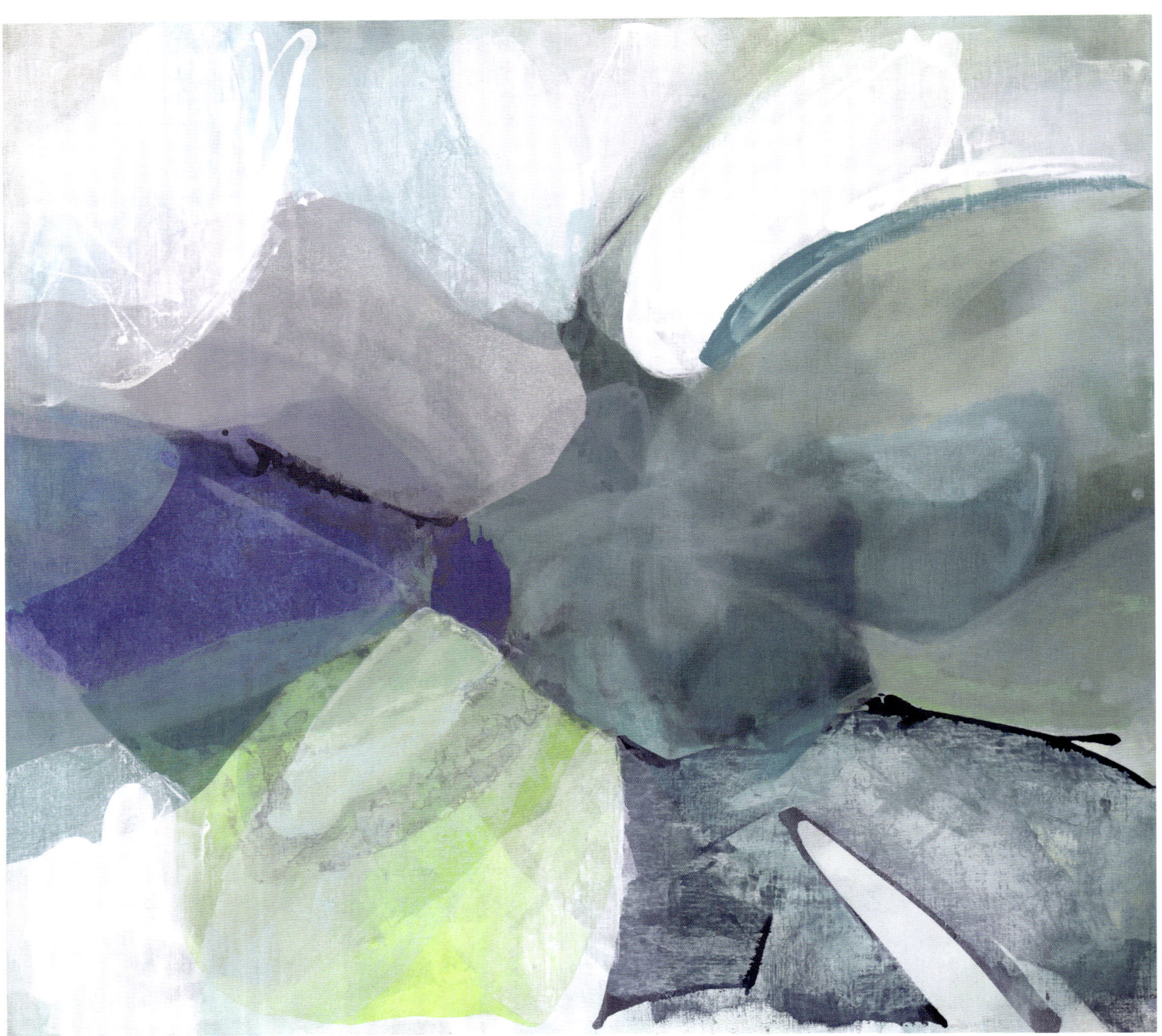

Stacey Warnix

Stacey Warnix creates large-scale, mixed-media abstract paintings using acrylics and inks on unprimed grounds. Her paintings feature layered shading and the organic, reductive shapes of natural found objects. As a gestural artist, Warnix paints to escape a world of precision, finding respite in abstract forms, textures, and tones. She approaches the creative process with fluidity. She typically begins each painting with little more than a loosely defined concept or color scheme, and she lays down the early layers with large strokes and gravitational manipulations, allowing happenstance to shape the initial composition. Warnix embraces the vague process, incorporating markings that are sometimes emotional and oftentimes inspired by natural forms— the wavy undulations of a flower petal, an insect wing, or a weathered branch. She works in abundant layers of pigment and collage to draw out tonal and textural variations that amalgamate to convey depth and visual interest.

Dreamweaver
Acrylics, inks, and collage
36 x 40 in.

stacey@staceywarnix
.com
staceywarnix.com
@staceywarnixstudio

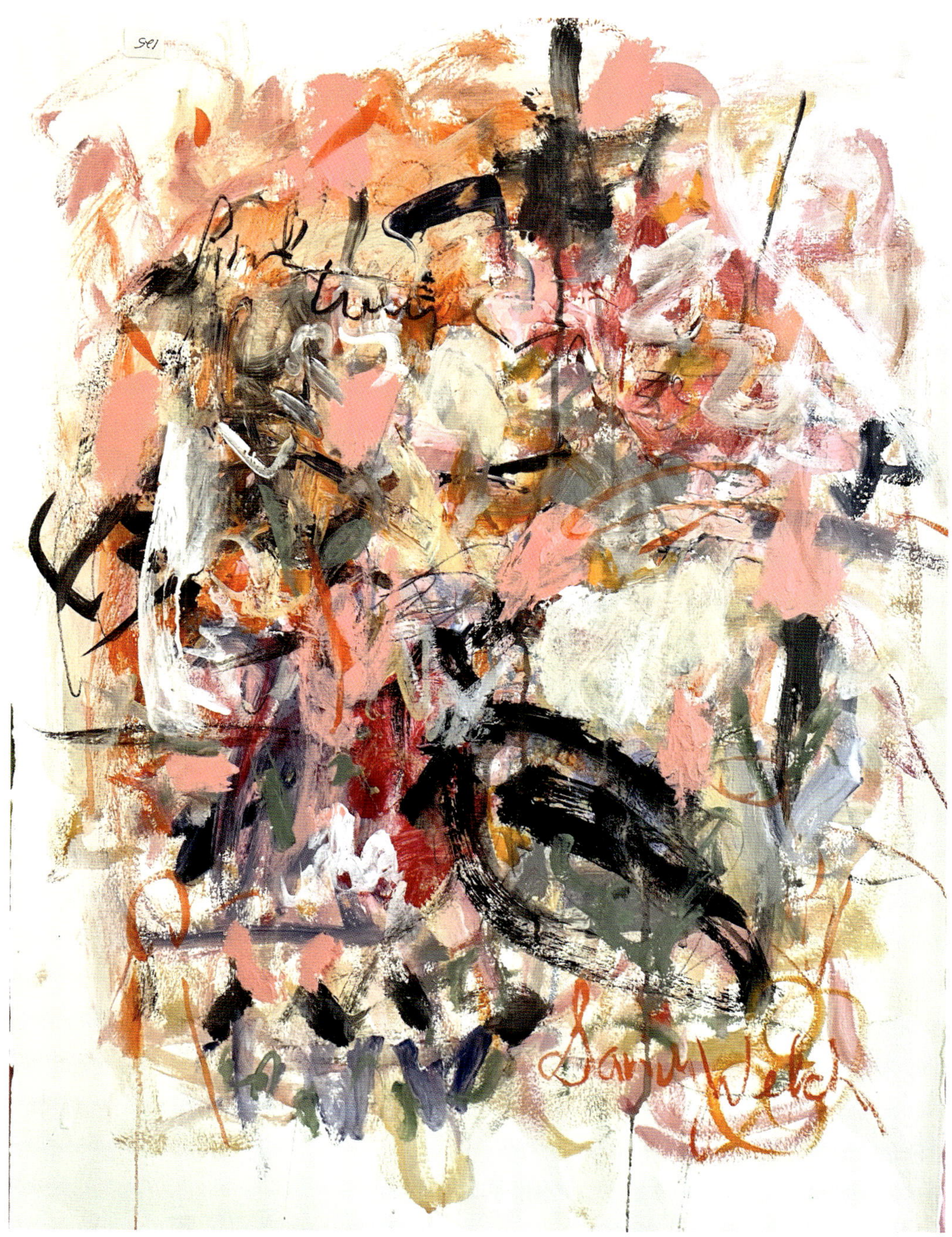

Sandy Welch

Sandy Welch is the consummate artist; she consistently endeavors to catch the essence of her subject, be it the pose of a fashionista, a luxurious sun-drenched meadow, or a coquettish shoe. Her most recent work is a turn toward abstraction. Her new direction uses the same vibrant palette, energetic mark making, and gestural flourishes of delight. Painting is her pulse, and her canvases pop with provocative color and a flirtatious style. "Painting is vital to my life," Welch says. "I paint from a youthful, fresh, feminine, and passionate perspective. Summer is my mirror, and fashion is my muse." Welch's palette is filled with the delicious colors of summer. The many faces and inner beauty of women fascinate her.

Pink Twist
Acrylic
24 x 30 in.

welcho@comcast.net
sandywelch.com.
@alwayspaint1

Sara Weldon

Sara Weldon is a graduate of NCAD and Griffith College, Dublin, Ireland. "I'm inspired by the contrast between order and chaos, and the illusion of control," Weldon says. "My work is primarily focused on those concepts. Structure contains so much internal disorder that is not inherently visible without dissection and is so much more fragile than it appears." Weldon believes that geometry and shape can describe the emotive elements of the human condition, with the same intensity as any other form of expressive art. When she begins to sketch a design, she lists the various elements that have motivated her to create the image, the message she wants to convey, and her palette is based on that psychology. She loves to hear how the viewer relates to the work, and what they see inside all those lines and forms. She finds the dialog between artist and viewer always surprising and hugely gratifying.

Modulations
Acrylic on linen
20 x 16 in.

saraeldonart@gmail
.com
@saraweldonart

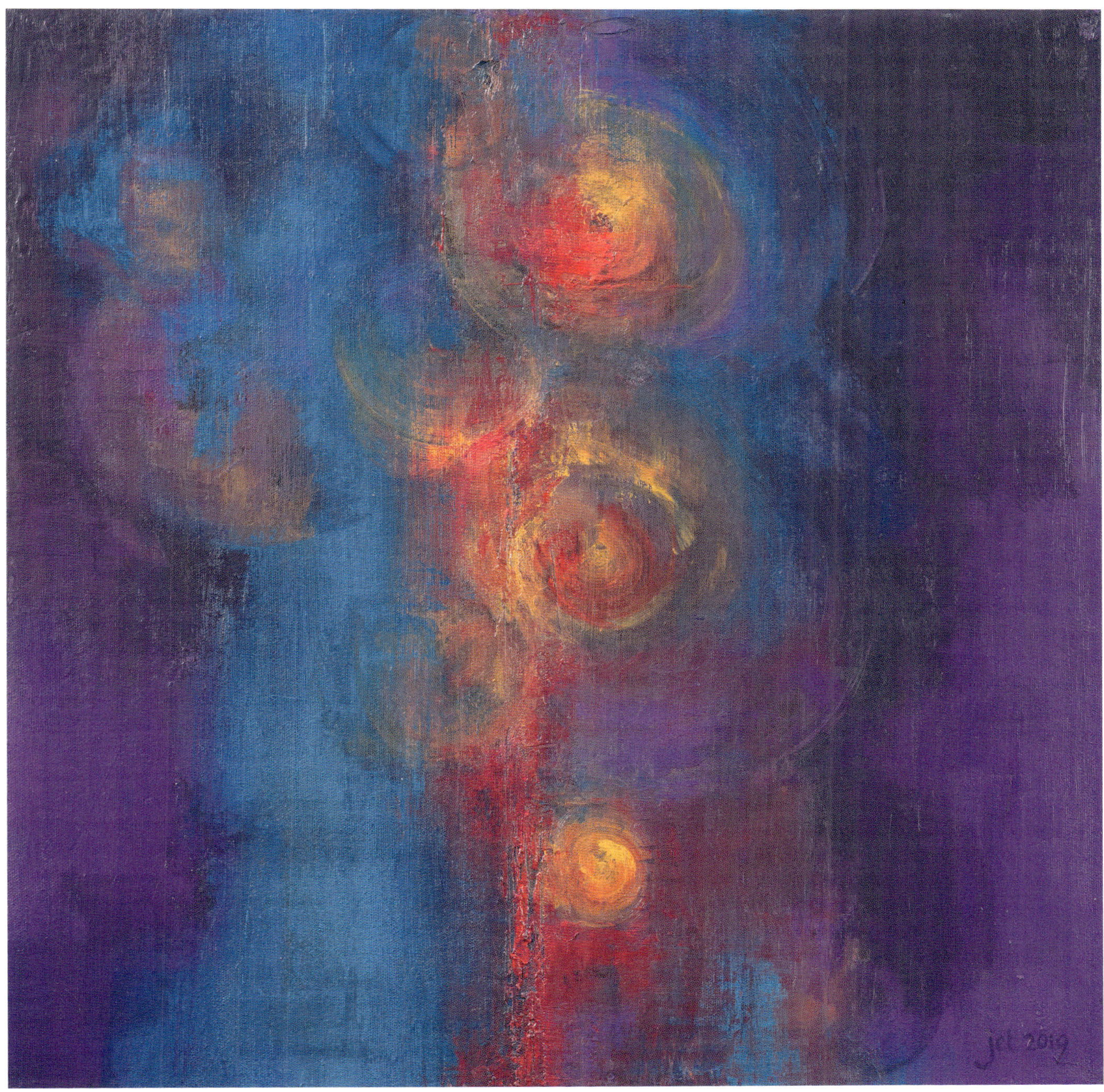

Jet Willems

The abstract and intuitive images Jet Willems creates originate from her personal mystical and spiritual experiences. The key components of her work arise from her fascination with myths, legends, the wisdom of indigenous peoples, esoteric themes, meditation, music, literature, and nature. The expression in movement, contrasts, textures, multiple layers, and the intensity of vibrant colors work together, evoking a transcendent image to the unknown, the hidden realms just beyond the veil of knowledge. Each of Willems' paintings has its own atmosphere, energy, and specific color palette. "I believe that trusting my intuition and following my heart is the best way to create my soulful art," Willems says. "I hope my works bring joy, light, peace, and healing through the experience of viewing and feeling the images."

Whisper of the Source of Life
Acrylic
50 x 50 in.

jet.willems@chello.nl
jetwillemsart.com
@jetwillemsart

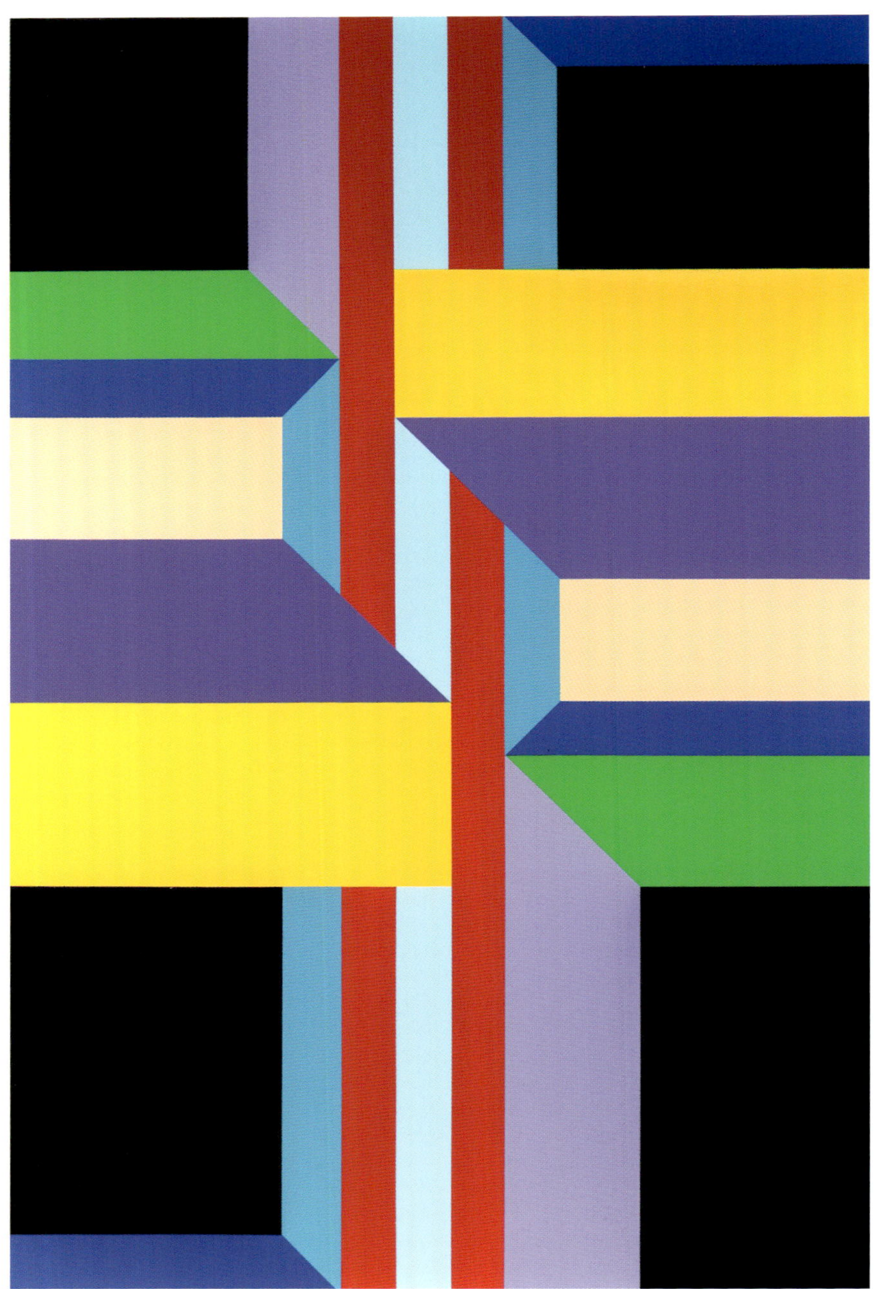

Jason Wilson
Forty-five years ago, a young boy watched his Native American grandmother design, assemble, and sew his family's quilts. This led to a lifelong artistic interest in geometric abstraction and color juxtaposition. Within Jason Wilson's style, he works hard to maintain clean lines and perfectly flat expanses of paint, without creating texture or depth, so that the viewer's focus is on the dynamic interplay of color and form. Even within a restricted set of artistic parameters, Wilson continues to experiment with new styles. His designs are about building the painting as much as painting the painting, often requiring hours of construction. Wilson wants to provoke a reaction from the viewer. It is interesting to him what people see in his work and how often one person sees something different from another person. "I have learned to let each painting stand on its own because sometimes people see in them something much better than I planned," he says.

Fortitude
Acrylic
36 x 24 in.

artbyjasonwilson@yahoo.com
artbyjasonwilson.com
@artbyjasonwilson

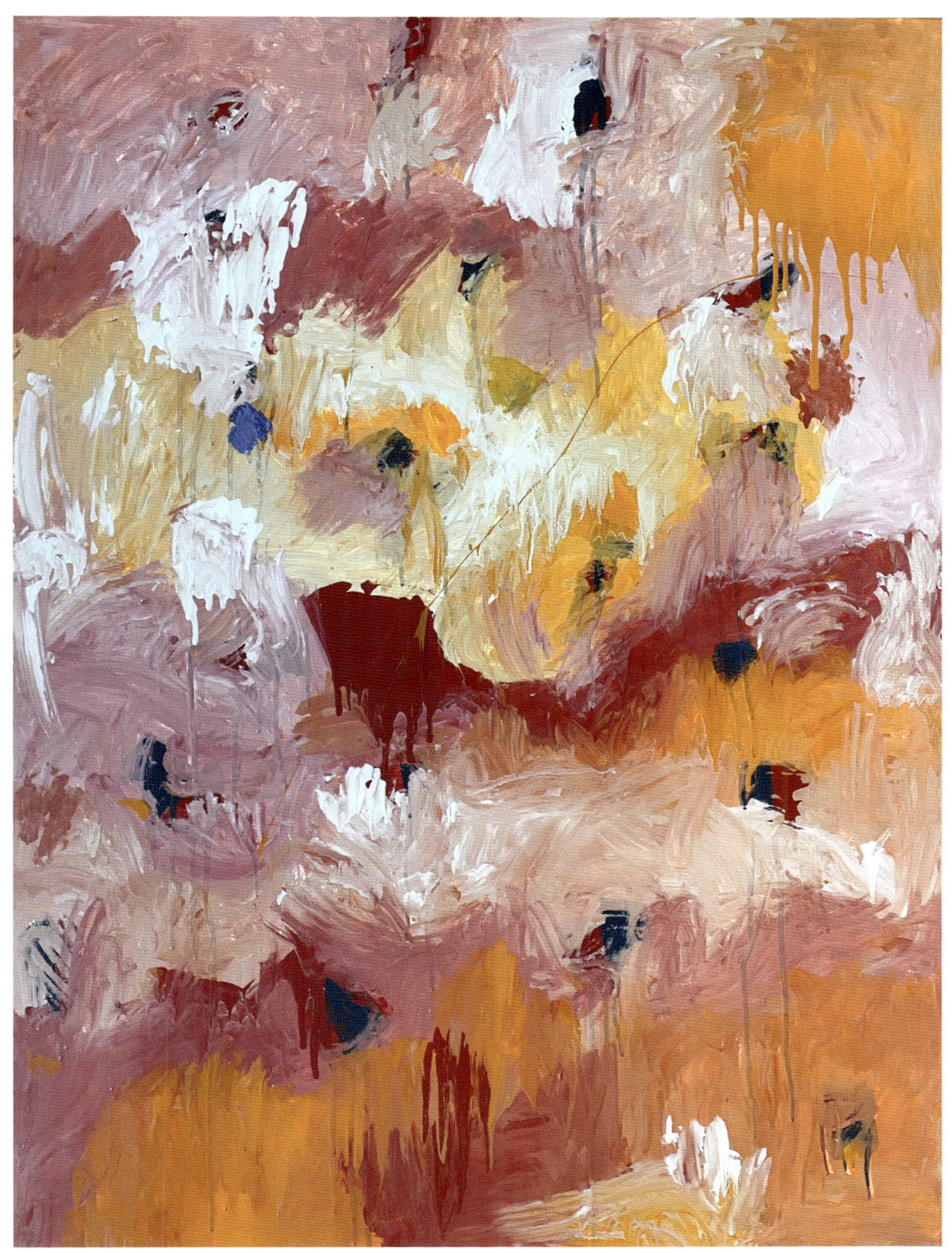

Robert G. Wilson

Robert G. Wilson's oeuvre of paintings kindles the mystery and the spiritual in abstract conceptual art making. He uses innovative color and paint layers in contrasting tones, using unique application paradigms to achieve an echo of invisible grace and beauty. Wilson's work is a spiritual statement about the time in which we live. "I am a traditionalist, painting the basic nature of humanity," he says. "Often, the title of each work provides a clue to the immense changes overriding social norms and the conflict of the soul in this ocean of unrest." Wilson explores his original concepts that are visual spiritual manifestos. His art has a solitary voice that is musical, poetic, and free. "Abstraction emancipates the more profound aesthetics necessary to document our time of new intellectual and emotional horizons," Wilson says.

Elegant Shrine
Oil
48 x 36 in.

robert@robertwilsonart
.com
robertwilsonart.com
@rrwilsonart

PAINTING: TRADITIONAL/ABSTRACT

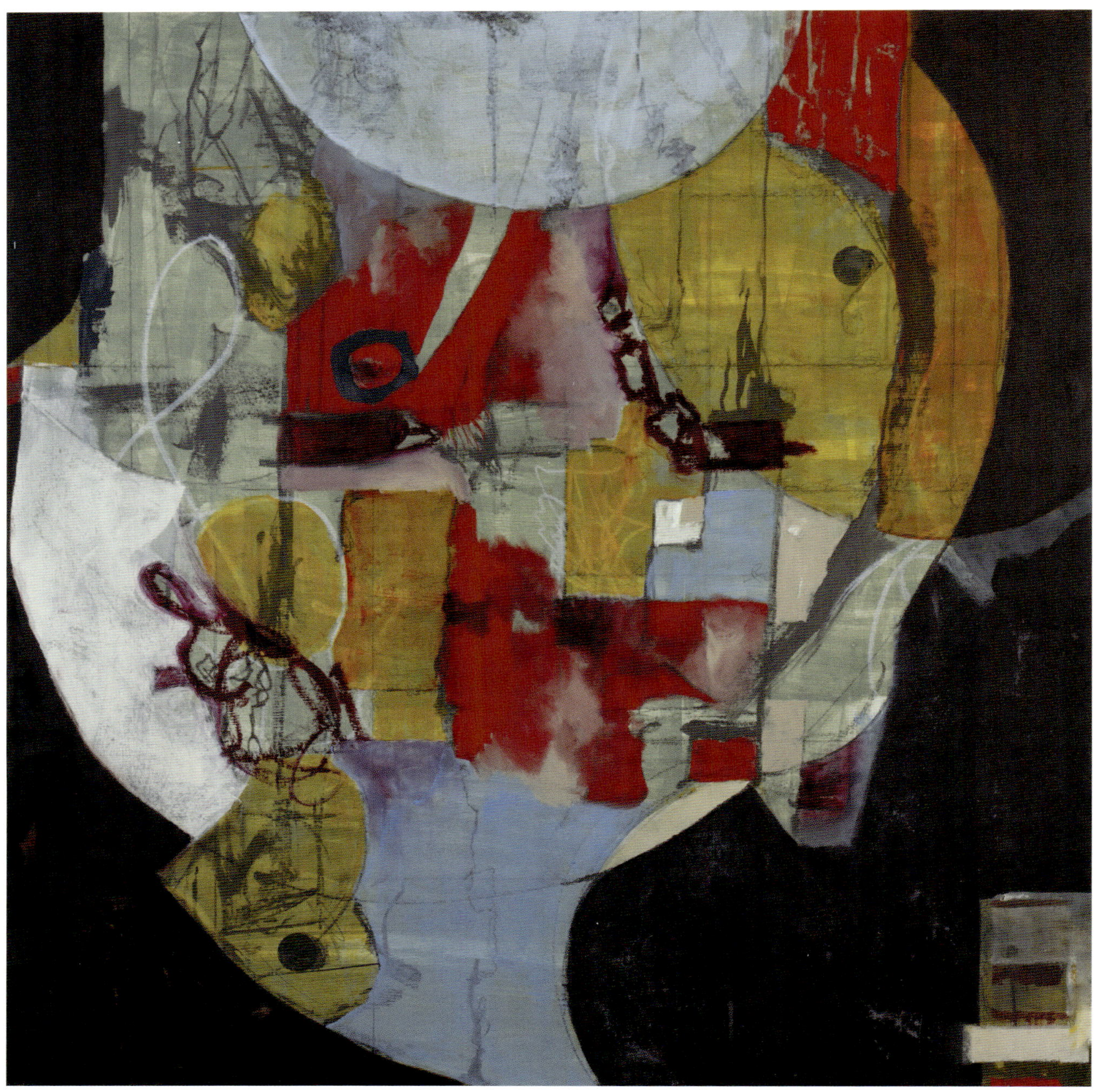

Mark Witzling

Mark Witzling creates visual experiences to bring joy into the world. The artist often challenges himself to create a painting with a technical hurdle or a new process. At the same time, he is intellectually motivated by intangible concepts, using themes to guide his approach to the painting. Recently,

Witzling has focused on the meanings of "truth" and "belonging," which have meanings on personal, group, and societal levels. These themes push the artist to work with the paint to build up layers and excavate back, repeating this push-pull process to evoke a sense of depth and understanding in each piece. While painting,

he rarely uses traditional brushes, instead working with a variety of tools like pastry scrapers, brayers, brooms, sticks, and even old credit cards to activate the surface. The result is often bold, sometimes subtle, and always optimistic, delightful, and engaging.

You Say You Want A Revolution
Oil, graphite, and cold wax on panel
42 x 42 in.

mwitzling@gmail.com
markwitzlingart.com
@witzm

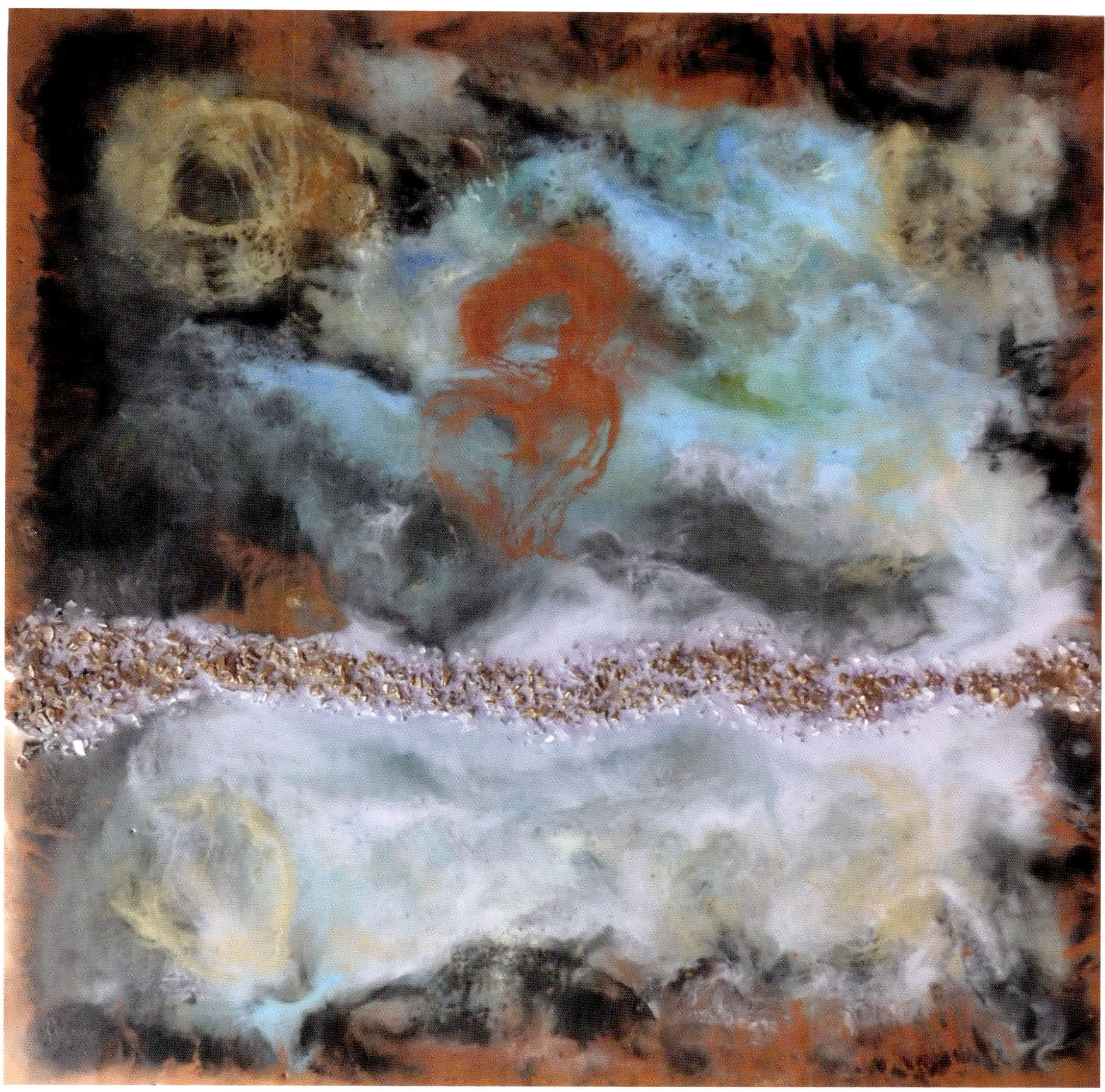

Trudie Wolking

Trudie Wolking found herself standing on a threshold, knowing that she had to do what she was meant to do and do it immediately, or it would never happen. For her, that meant creating art—taking her life experiences and feelings, placing them on a surface, and hoping their reflection touched others. Wolking works on cradled panels, repurposed wood and tin, travertine, and slate. She works in an intuitive way, and most of her work begins in a similar fashion. Her paintings are about the layers, the flow, and the strata of things substantive, imagined, physical, and implicit. Wolking works by accumulating layers of material, images, and color, then she goes back to explore, excavate, expose, and obscure. The result is a nonliteral form, a translation of that experience and process. She has gradually learned to trust the process and to be brave and confident that the intent will manifest in the finished work.

Many Faces
Encaustic and mixed media
20 x 20 in.

twolking2014@gmail.com
trudiewolking.com
@trudiewolkingart

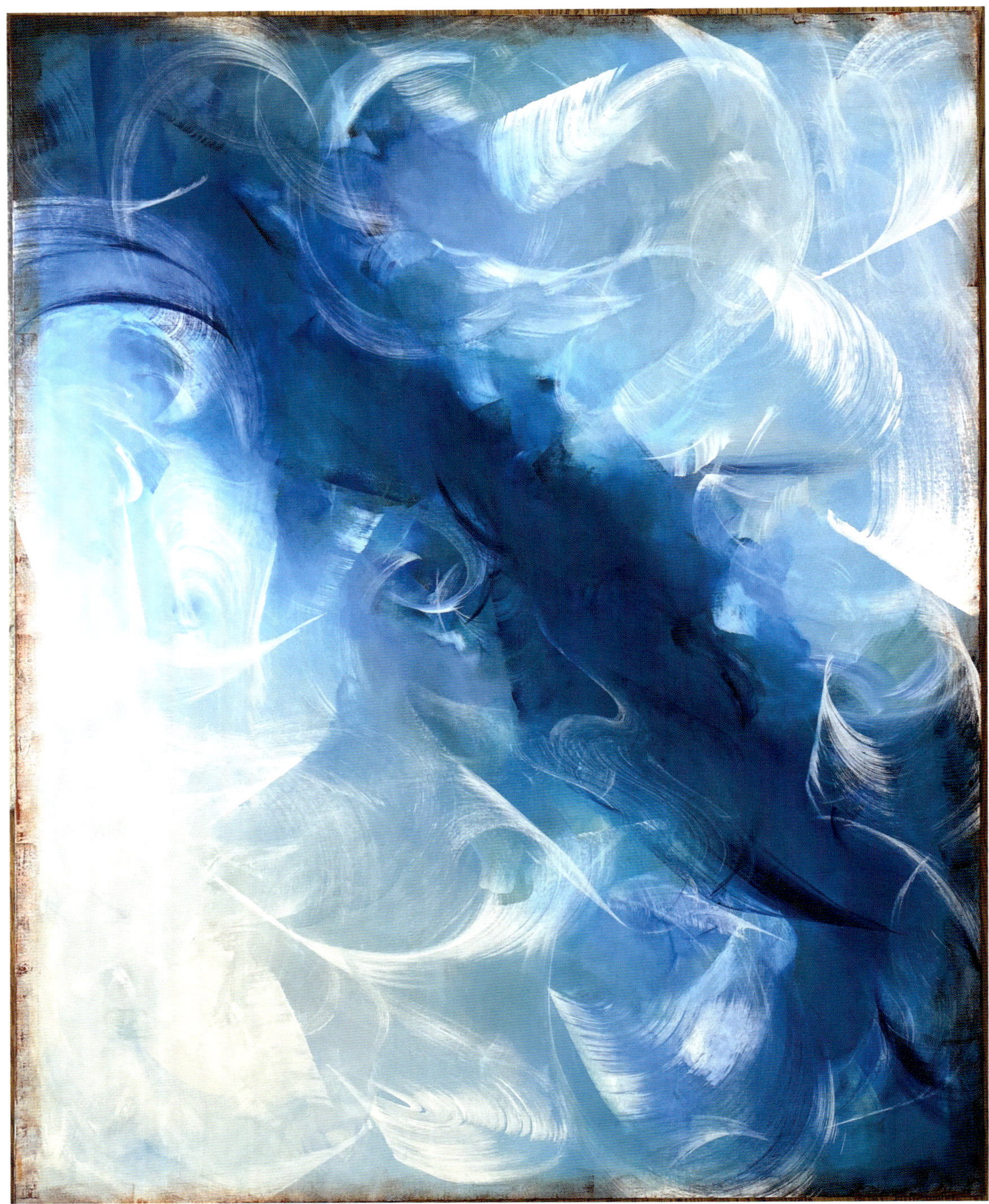

Terese Young

At the root of all Terese Young's paintings is a slight obsession with color and music, and a love of exploring how each can affect our mood. She begins with a general idea of color palette and a carefully selected playlist of songs streaming. Certain songs can take her to a meditative place that helps shut out the outside world. Young never knows what a painting will end up looking like when she begins. Even deep into the process, things can unexpectedly change directions. She does, however, always strive to balance each piece with soft stillness and bolder movement. "There's a certain flow that I look for between the two before I'll sign my name," Young says.

Ocean Dance
Acrylic
60 x 48 in.

teresemyoung@icloud.com
teresemyoung.com
@teresempaintings

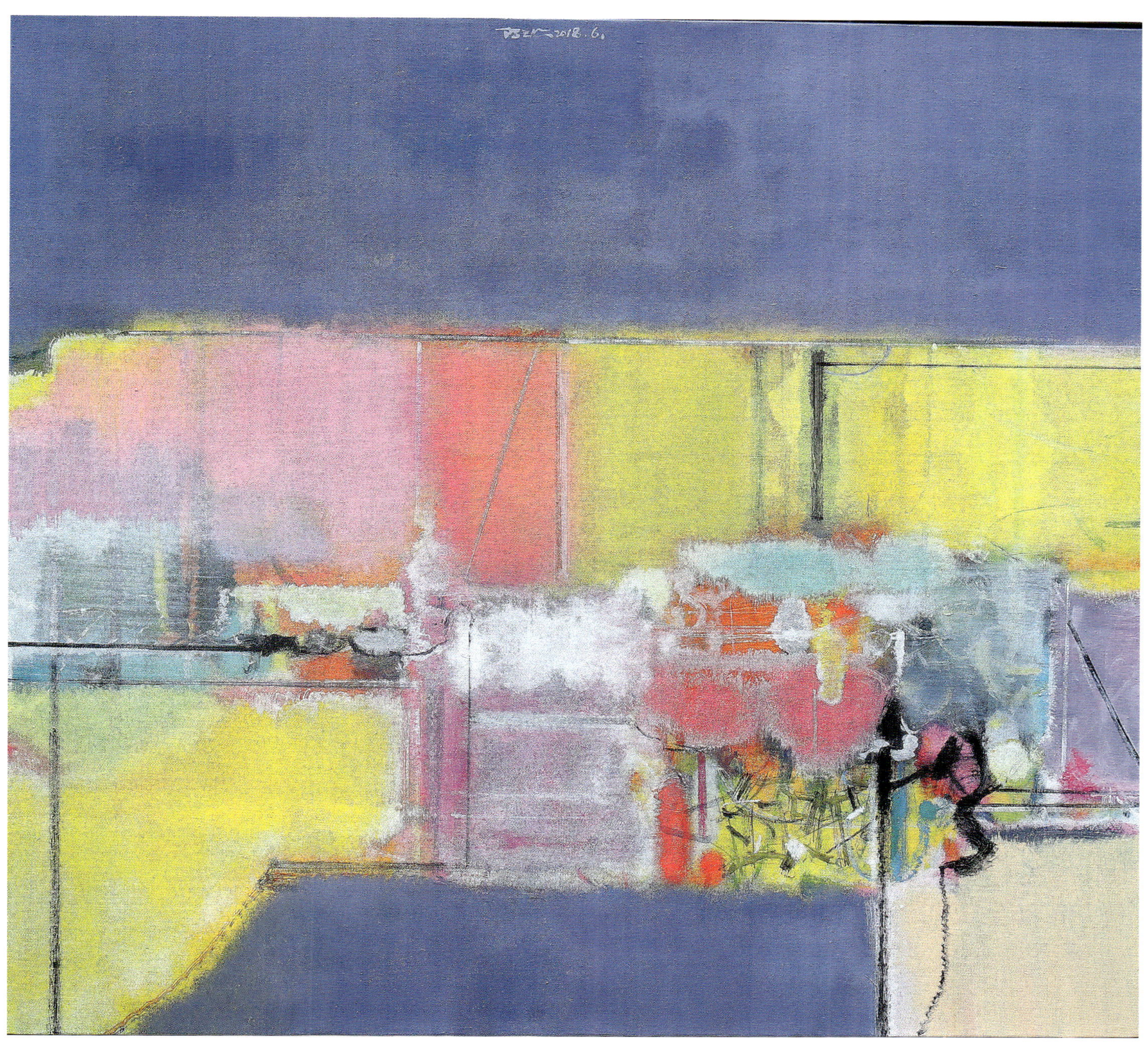

Lu Yunhua

Lu Yunhua's theme for her abstract art is the "Spiritual Garden," which is a private, idealized, and personal space. Many things can happen in this space. Yunhua's ideas revolve around this theme to express her feelings of humanity and yearning for a better life. "I strive to make my art impress more people," Yunhua says. "I like to compare colors to find the colors that match the right emotions. The emotions I want to express are as consistent as possible within the Spiritual Garden theme." Yunhua likes to connect color blocks with lines and make her paintings more artistic through texture and a variety of lines.

Spiritual Garden Series, No.9
Acrylic
37 X 39 in.

artart.6072@hotmail
.com

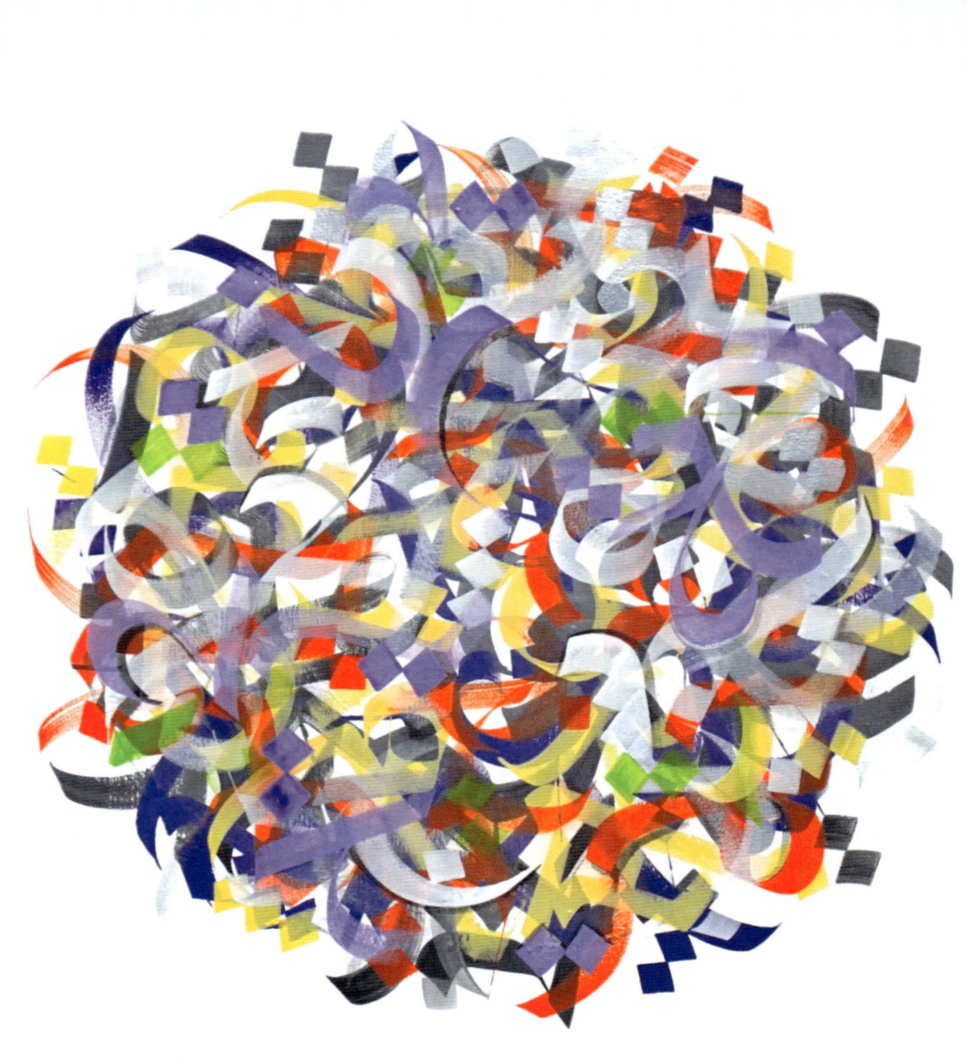

Muhammad Zaman

Muhammad Zaman is an urban artist specializing in Arabic calligraphy. Over the years, he has developed a personal style that incorporates three different languages that make up his identity: English, since he lives in the United States; Bengali, the language of his fatherland; and Arabic, which is the language of the religion he belongs to. Since childhood, Zaman was always fascinated by languages, lettering, and calligraphy from different parts of the world. His aim is to inspire people to learn from each other in harmony and mutual understanding. Although his work contains words in three different languages, there is always at least one recognizable word. This makes the audience curious to ask and decode the message, and this leads them to a deep connection with the work. "Even if I use ancient techniques and universal messages of peace, I keep going, trying new shapes and colors to present my art to the world with a modern look," Zaman says.

Hope
Acrylic
36 x 36 in.

zahin716@gmail.com
zmnart.com
@Zaman_Art

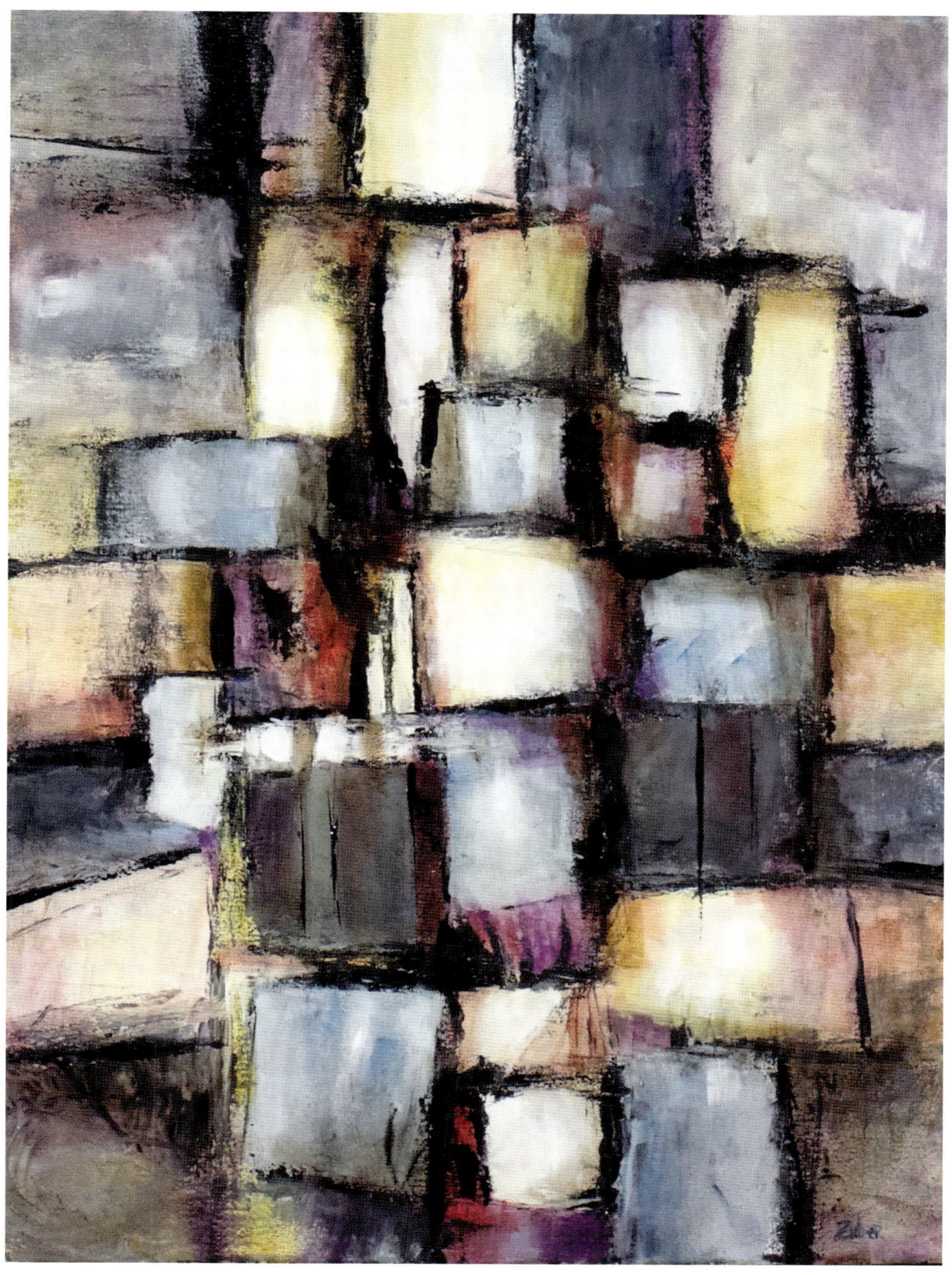

Thomas Zuber

"Working with the dichotomies of experience is what living is all about," Thomas Zuber says. "Reaching across the chasm of opposing forces or allowing myself to be at peace and live with them is what is being expressed in my current series of abstract work." Movement is opposed to structure in Zuber's art. He begins each work with gestures, as free and unconscious as possible. Forms are placed against space, complementary colors reflect off of each other, while light against dark leads the eye on a visual journey, where the viewer may find something recognizable within his paintings. "Art is a visual expression of life, and my work is mindful of that constant process," he says.

Disposition 601
Acrylic
24 x 18 in.

ubermuzz68@gmail.com
zuberart.com
@thomas_zuber_fine_art

Artist Index

Mallory Zondag
Schenectady, NY
mkzondag@gmail.com
mallorymakes.com
@badwolf124

DIGITAL GOLD
Richard Devonshire
Letchworth Garden City, Hertfordshire
Richard.Devonshire@yahoo.com
richard-devonshire.com
@richard_devonshire_art

DIGITAL SILVER
Tyler N. Horton
Charleston, SC
tnhforum@gmail.com
@tnhortonart

Guillermo Arismendi
Santa Cruz de Tenerife, Tenerife
artearismendi@gmail.com
guillermoarismendi.com
@guillermo_arismendi

Matt Evans, aka SnowSkull
London, UK
contact@snowskullart.com
snowskullart.com
@snowskull

Kat Evans
Colchester, Essex
ktheo2010@gmail.com
katevans.art
@katevansartist19

Pierre-Hugues Hetu
Québec, Canada
puguess@gmail.com
puguess.com
@puguess

Lindsay Kokoska
Alberta, Canada
linzy.kokoska@gmail.com
@infinite_mantra

John Charles Maloney
Merseyside, UK
contact@johncmaloneydigitalartist
.com
johncmaloneydigitalartist.com
@johncmaloneydigitalartist

Paul Petersen
Drums, PA
paul@paulpetersen.net
sphericalart.com
@sphericalart

Michael Pierre Price
Phoenix, AZ
michael@michaelpierreprice.com
michaelpierreprice.com
@mpp_digital_art

Ramon Rivas
Ciudad Real, Spain
ramonrivas2012@yahoo.es
rivismo.com
@ramonrivas_rivismo

Robin Roy
Playa Del Carmen, Quintana Roo
opinions@runbox.com
robinroyart.com
@robinroy1

PAINTING - TRADTIONAL/
CONTEMPORARY - GOLD
Robert Solomon
Philadelphia, PA
r.rmsolo@verizon.net
robertmsolomon.com
@rmsolomon444

PAINTING - TRADTIONAL/
CONTEMPORARY - SILVER
Carita Schmidt
Berlin, Germany
caritaschmidt@gmail.com
caritaschmidt.com
@caritaschmidt_painter

John Bacon
Bend, OR
johnwb67@gmail.com
@BaconModern

Karen Blanchet
Edmonton, Alberta
blanchet.fine.arts@gmail.com
karenblanchet.ca
@blanchetfinearts

Cindy Brewer
Dallas, TX
cabrewer58@yahoo.com
@cindybrewer1

Shelley Detton
Meridian, ID
cobalt_sm@hotmail.com
shelleydetton.com/abstractworks
@shelleydetton

Mary Lynn Engel
Yarmouth, ME
mld@engel.net
designbymle.com

Pat Fallon
Shaker Heights, OH
patfallon10@gmail.com
patfallon.com

Mylinda Farr
Wills Point, TX
farrfamilytx@gmail.com
mylindafarr.com

Leticia Herrera
McKinney, TX
leticiaherrera@leticiaherreraart.com
leticiaherreraart.com
@leticiaherreraart

Irene Hoff
Badung, Bali
irene@irenehoff.com
irenehoff.com
@art_irenehoff

Atom Hovhanesyan
Rego Park, NY
arahov63@gmail.com
artbyatom.com
@artbyatomhov

Carson Kapp
New Smyrna Beach, FL
carsonkapp@gmail.com
carsonkapp.weebly.com
@kappcarson

Christo Kasabov
Toronto, Ontario
christo.casabov@gmail.com
christokasabo.com
@ckasabo

Rebecca Katz
San Rafael, CA
rebecca@rebeccakatz.com
rebeccakatzart.com
@rebeccakatzart

Lawrence Lee
Tucson, AZ
lawrence@lawrenceleeart.com
lawrenceleeart.com
@lawrenceleeart

Erin Liljegren
Madison, WI
erinliljegren@gmail.com
erinliljegren.com
@erinliljegren

Yaroslava Liseeva
Moscow, Russia
yaroslavaliseeva@mail.ru
yarlis.org
@yaroslavaliseeva2019

Georgia Loxton Knight
Perth, Western Austraila
georgialoxtonknight@gmail.com
georgialoxtonknight.com
@georgialoxtonknight

Vince MacDermot
Staten Island, NY
vincemacdermot@gmail.com
vincemacdermot.com
@vincemacdermot

Romulo Martinez
Frisco, TX
roartma@gmail.com
romulomartinez.com
@romulomartinez

Samridh Mukhiya
Farmers Branch, TX
mukhiyas.art@gmail.com
mukhiyas.com
@mukhiyas.art

Jette Reinert
Vejle, Denmark
jette@reinert.dk
reinert.dk
@jette_reinert

Eileen Shaloum
Long Beach, NY
eileenshaloum@gmail.com
eileenshaloum.com
@eileenshaloum

Kerri Warner
Plumas Lake, CA
kerriwarnerartist@yahoo.com
kerriwarner.com
@kerri_artist

Elizabeth Wing
Sisters, OR
elizabethwingemail@gmail.com
elizabethwingart.com
@elizabethwingart

Marcia Wise
Norfolk, MA
mewise498@comcast.net
marciarwise.com
@marciafineartist

**PAINTING - TRADTIONAL/
ABSTRACT - GOLD**
Francoise Barnes
Los Ranchos, NM
franswazz@gmail.com
franswazzart.com
@franswazzart

**PAINTING - TRADTIONAL/
ABSTRACT - SILVER**
Machiel Roest
Paris, France
machiel@machielr.eu
machielr.eu
@macphi

Caren Akers
Jensen Beach, FL
carens.art@gmail.com
caren-akers.com
@carenakers

Susana Aldanondo
Astoria, NY
susanaaldanondoart@gmail.com
susanaaldanondoart.com
@susanaaldanondo

Kelly Aldridge
Dallas, TX
kellyaldridgeart@yahoo.com
kellyaldridge.com
@kelly__aldridge

Elizabeth Bernheisel
Edgewater, MD
beth.bernheisel@gmail.com
elizabethbernheisel.com
@bethbernheiselart

Cira Bhang
Salon de Provence, France
info@cirabhang.com
cirabhang.com
@cira_bhang

Johanne Brouillette
St-Jerome, Québec
johanne.brou@hotmail.com
johannebrouillette.ca
johannebrouilletteart

Julie Brown
Dallas, TX
julieshunickbrown@gmail.com
julieshunickbrown.com
@julieshunickbrown

Naomi Butler
Plano, TX
info@abstractartbynaomi.com
abstractartbynaomi.com
@naomi.butler

Patrick Canning
Clynder, Helensburgh
canningpat7@yahoo.co.uk
@canningpat7

Daniel Sánchez Casado
Madrid, Spain
danielsanchezstudio@gmail.com
@danielsanchezstudio

Kathy Cantwell
Montclair, NJ
kathy.cantwell@gmail.com
kathycantwell.com
@cantwell57

Jessica M. Chaix
Lewisville, TX
jessica_chaix@yahoo.com.mx
jessicamchaix.com
@Jesschaixart

Andrew Chalfen
Philadelphia, PA
andrewdchalfen@gmail.com
andrewchalfen.com
@i.think.like.midnight

Lavanya Challa
Plano, TX
lavanyaschalla@gmail.com
lavanyachallaart.com
@lavanyachallaart

Sally Cooper
Parkland, FL
sallycooperart@gmail.com
sally-cooper.com
@sallycooperart

Ct Cummins
Jacksonville, FL
ctcummins@gmail.com
ctcummins.com

Joy Daniels
Toronto, Ontario
joydanielsvisualartist@gmail.com
Joydanielsvisualartist.com
@joydanielsartist

Sami Davidson
Boca Raton, FL
samidavidson@gmail.com
samidavidsonart.com

Mcat Davis
Dallas, TX
davism31@gmail.com
mcatdavisart.com
@mcat.davisart

Laurie DeVault
Amherst, MA
lrdevault@icloud.com
lauriedevault.com
@lauriedevault

Terri Dilling
Atlanta, GA
terri@terridilling.com
terridilling.com
@terridilling_art

Olga Doberstein
Munich, Bavaria
olga-doberstein@gmx.de
olga-doberstein.com
@olka_daheim

Mark Dunst
Portland, OR
art@markdunst.com
markdunst.com
@markdunst.art

Melissa Ellis
Dallas, TX
melissa@melissaellisart.com
melissaellisart.com
@melissaellisart

Suedabeh Ewing
Wylie, TX
suewing2014@gmail.com
suedabehewing.blogspot.com/
@suedabeh_art

Ty Fawley
Aubrey, TX
jlfthree@gmail.com

Ben Fluno
Rowlett, TX
benfluno@gmail.com
benflunoart.com
@benfluno

Peter Foesters
Belgium
P.foesters@telenet.be
straightdimensions.com
@peter_foesters

Glen Gauthier
Dallas, TX
glen@streetfairstudios.com
streetfairstudios.com
@glengauthier

Jenna Girolamo
Rochester, NY
jgartbuzz@gmail.com
jgartbuzz.com
@jgartbuzz

Detlef Gotzens
QC, Canada
dego@degoarts.com
degoarts.com
@degoarts

NC Hagood
New Smyrna Beach, FL
hagoodnancy@gmail.com

Kathleen Hall
North Chesterfield, VA
kathy@kathleenhallart.com
KathleenHallArt.com
@KathleenHallArt

Hallie Hamilton
Austin, TX
halliehamiltonart@gmail.com
halliehamiltonart.com
@halliehamiltonart

Deborah Hartigan Viestenz
Irving, TX
dhvartworks@gmail.com
dhvartworks.com
@dhv_artworks

Kristin Herzog
Estero, FL
kherzogart@hotmail.com
kherzogart.com
@Kristin_Herzog_Art

Lee Hill
Fort Worth, TX
lee@leeahill.com
leeahill.com
@Studioleealberthill

Benjamin Hoffmann
Selm, Germany
b.b.hoffmann@gmx.de
@gangraen

Christy Hopkins
Seattle, WA
kurcreative@gmail.com
@christyhopkins_art

Tonda Howard
Dallas, TX
tondahoward59@gmail.com
tondahowardart.com
@tonda_howard_art

Newel Hunter
Port Ludlow, WA
newelh@hotmail.com
newelhunterart.com

Ewa Jaros
Magdalenka, Mazowieckie
e.jaros@onet.pl
ewajarosart.pl
@ewajarosart

Nikolina Car Jergovic
Velika Gorica, Croatia
ninanein@gmail.com
@nikolinacarjergovic

Stefanie Kamrath
Dortmund, Germany
skam.arts@gmail.com
skam-arts.de
@stefaniekamrath

Rebecca Kaushal, aka Becks
Etobicoke, ON
beckstudioart@gmail.com
beckstudio.ca
@beckstudio

Sabine Kay
Oberanven, Luxembourg
sabine.kay3@gmail.com
emergingartistplatform.com/sa-binekay
@sabine.kay3

Robbie Kaye
Santa Ynez, CA
robbie@robbiekaye.com
robbiekaye.com
@robbiekaye

Jennifer Keeney-Bleeg
Bristol, UK
jennifer@jkbleeg.com
jkbleeg.com
@jkbleeg

Viviane Laut
Châtillon, France
laut.viviane@orange.fr
@viviane_laut_17_

Taylor LeBlanc
Mobile, AL
Trleblanc88@gmail.com
trldesign.com
@trl__designs

Alise Loebelsohn
Brooklyn, NY
aliseloebelsohn@nyc.rr.com
alisemloebelsohn.com
@alise_loebelsohn

Gillian Loop
Newport Beach, CA
gillianloop@hotmail.com
gillianloop.com
@gillianloop_the_art_of

Paméla Maria
Amsterdam, Netherlands
studio@pamelamaria.nl
pamelamaria.nl
@pamela_maria_1234

Michelle Marra
Delray Beach, FL
michellemarra@comcast.net
michellemarrastudio.com
@michellemarrastudio

Lambeth Marshall
Waxhaw, NC
lambethpottery@windstream.net
lambethpottery.net
@lambeth_marshall

C.S. McIntire
Walnut Creek, CA
craigmcintire@hotmail.com
csmcintire.com
@c.s.mcintire

Lisa McLaughlin
Nashville, TN
info@lisamclaughlinart.com
lisamclaughlinart.com
@lisamclaughlinart

Kevin Megison
Anna, TX
kevinmegison@att.net
kevinmegisonart.com
@kevinmegisonart

Traci Meitzler
Gilbertsville, PA
mad7artstudio@gmail.com
mad7studio.com
@mad7studio

Christi Meril
Dallas, TX
christimerilart@gmail.com
christimerilart.com
@christimerilart

Meghan Noonan
Mississauga, ON
meghnoonan@hotmail.com
meghannoonanart.myportfolio.com/
home-1
@meghannoonanart

Bill Oakes
Kingston, NH
billo@mindleaps.com
mindleaps.com
@artofbilloakes

Florence Pages
St. Jean de Vedas, France
flo.pages@orange.fr
florencepages.net
@pages.florence

Catherine Pennington-Meyer
Augsburg, Bayern
cpm@galleriewhite.space
galleriewhite.space
@galleriewhitespace

Ludwika Pilat
Rieden, Switzerland
ludwika.pilat@gmail.com
ludwikapilat.art
@il.lu.str

Sudie Rakusin
Hillsborough, NC
info@sudierakusin.com
sudierakusin.com
@sudie.rakusin

William James Ramsay
County Durham, UK
william_ramsay@live.co.uk
espyartistry.com
@espy_artistry

Margaret Rehwinkel
Dallas, TX
shoe1955@aol.com
@margaretschumacherrehwinkel

Carole-Yvonne Richard
QC, Canada
Carole-Yvonne@CyRichard.com
cyrichard.com
@cyrichard

Lina Rincon Hoover
Tampa, FL
linarincon75@gmail.com
artitudeart.com
@artitudeartist

Fernanda Rivero
Puebla, Puebla
cherrystudio.art@gmail.com
fernandarivero.com
@fernandarivero_arte

Laura Roebuck
Sausalito, CA
studiolr@att.net
lauraroebuck.com
@roebuckstudio

Leslie Rolnick
Woodstock, NY
leslierolnick@gmail.com
@leslierolnick52

Anastacia Sadeh
Dallas, TX
anastacia_sadeh@yahoo.com
anastaciasadeh.com
@sadehstudioarts

Deborah Saks
Washington DC
d_saks@yahoo.com
deborahsaks.com
@deborahsakscollage

Antonio Salgado
Cincinnati, OH
antoniosalgadostudio@gmail.com
antoniosalgadostudio.com
@semperpictorem

Karen H. Salup
Delray Beach, FL
monet12@bellsouth.net
karenhsalup.com
@salup

Joshua Schoemaker
Plano, TX
art@carbonandcotton.com
carbonandcotton.com
@joshschoemaker

Petra Schott
Frankfurt, Germany
Petra.schott@gmx.net
petra-schott.de
@schott.petra

JL Schwartz
Coral Springs, FL
jlschwartzart@att.net
jlschwartzart.com
@jlschwartzart

Durand Seay
Fairhope, AL
durand@durandseay.com
Durandseay.com

Mafy Signo
Pioltello, Italy
artisthereason19@gmail.com
@mafy.signo

Katrina Slade
New Brunswick, Canada
hello@katrinaslade.com
katrinaslade.com
@katrina.slade.art

Roxanne Smit
Brabant Wallon, Belgium
roxsmitty@gmail.com
rxtexture.com
@Rx_texture

Martha Smith
Weston, FL
mmgsmith@gmail.com
marthasmithstudio.com
@marthasmithstudio

Christine Smith-Atkins
Fairview, TX
christinesmithtechart@gmail.com
CSAtkinsArt.com

Jen Sterling
Arnold, MD
jensterlingart@gmail.com
jensterling.com
@jensterlingart

Marine Strage
Sausalito, CA
marinestrage@gmail.com
marinestrage.com
@marinestrage

Martin Sullivan
New South Wales, Australia
martinsullivanartist@hotmail.com
sullyartist.com
@sullyartist

Hanna Supetran
Taguig, Philippines
hanna@hannaintuitiveartist.com
hannasupetranartgallery.com
@h_supetran

Nancy Teague
Lincoln, NE
nancy@nancyteague.com
nancyteague.com
@nteague_abstracts

Mark Thibeault
Telkwa, BC
mark@markthibeault.com
markthibeault.com
@markt_art

Ozlem Thompson
London, UK
ozlemsorluthompson@gmail.com
@ozlemsorluthompson

Sarah Todd
Dallas, TX
sarah@sarahtoddart.com
sarahtoddart.com
@sarahtoddart

Petra Uhl
Elchingen, Germany
petrauhlart@gmx.de
@petra.uhl.art

Alissa Van Atta
Chapel Hill, NC
alissa@avaarts.net
avaarts.net
@alissa_avaarts

Christel Van Hemelrijck
Mechelen, Antwerpen
christelvanhemelrijck@telenet.be
christelvanhemelrijck.com
@christelvanhemelrijck

Adrienne Walker
Boynton Beach, FL
adriennew4199@gmail.com
adriennearts.com
@adriennewalkerart

Stacey Warnix
Ingram, TX
stacey@staceywarnix.com
staceywarnix.com
@staceywarnixstudio

Sandy Welch
West Hartford, CT
welcho@comcast.net
sandywelch.com
@alwayspaint1

Sara Weldon
Threecastles, Kilkenny
saraweldonart@gmail.com
@saraweldonart

Jet Willems
Zwaag, Noord Holland
jet.willems@chello.nl
jetwillemsart.com
@jetwillemsart

Jason Wilson
McAlester, OK
artbyjasonwilson@yahoo.com
artbyjasonwilson.com
@artbyjasonwilson

Robert Wilson
East Wenatchee, WA
robert@robertwilsonart.com
robertwilsonart.com
@rrwilsonart

Mark Witzling
Maryland Heights, MO
mwitzling@gmail.com
markwitzlingart.com
@witzm

Trudie Wolking
Lafayette, LA
twolking2014@gmail.com
trudiewolking.com
@trudiewolkingart

Terese Young
Atlanta, GA
teresemyoung@icloud.com
teresemyoung.com
@teresempaintings

Lu Yunhua
artart.6072@hotmail.com
Frisco, TX

Muahammad Z Zaman
Buffalo, NY
zahin716@gmail.com
zmnart.com
@Zaman_Art

Thomas Zuber
Osceola, IN
ubermuzz68@gmail.com
zuberart.com
@thomas_zuber_fine_art